DEFINING DOCUMENTS IN WORLD HISTORY

Revolutions

VOLUME 1

DEFINING DOCUMENTS
IN WORLD HISTORY

Revolutions

Editor
Michael Shally-Jensen, PhD

Volume 1

SALEM PRESS
A Division of EBSCO Information Services, Inc.
Ipswich, Massachusetts

GREY HOUSE PUBLISHING

Cover: Image via iStock.com

Copyright © 2023 by EBSCO Information Services, Inc., and Grey House Publishing, Inc.

Defining Documents in World History: Revolutions, published by Grey House Publishing, Inc., Amenia, NY, under exclusive license from EBSCO Information Services, Inc.

All rights reserved. No part of this work may be used or reproduced in any manner whatsoever or transmitted in any form or by any means, electronic or mechanical, including photocopy, recording, or any information storage and retrieval system, without written permission from the copyright owner. For information, contact Grey House Publishing/Salem Press, 4919 Route 22, PO Box 56, Amenia, NY 12501.

∞ The paper used in these volumes conforms to the American National Standard for Permanence of Paper for Printed Library Materials, Z39.48 1992 (R2009).

Publisher's Cataloging-in-Publication Data
(Prepared by Parlew Associates, LLC)

Names: Shally-Jensen, Michael, editor.
Title: Revolutions / editor, Michael Shally-Jensen, PhD.
Other titles: Defining documents in world history (Salem Press)
Description: Ipswich, MA : Salem Press, a division of EBSCO Information Services, Inc. ; Amenia, NY : Grey House Publishing, 2023. | Includes bibliographic references and index. | Includes b&w photos and prints.
Identifiers: ISBN 9781637004043 (2 v. set) | ISBN 9781637004050 (v. 1) | ISBN 9781637004067 (v. 2) | ISBN 9781637004074 (ebook)
Subjects: LCSH: Revolutions. | Revolutions — History. | World politics. | World history. | BISAC: HISTORY / Military / Revolutions & Wars of Independence. | HISTORY / Modern / General. | HISTORY / World.
Classification: LCC HM876.R48 2023 (print) | LCC HM876 (ebook) | DDC 303.64 R—dc23

FIRST PRINTING
PRINTED IN THE UNITED STATES OF AMERICA

Table of Contents

Volume 1

Publisher's Note vii
Editor's Introduction ix
Contributors. xi
Full Table of Contents xiii

The Dutch Revolt 1
Dutch Declaration of Independence 3

The English Revolution 21
Resolves by the English House of Commons regarding King Charles I and the Authority of the People. . . . 23
Reflection on the Glorious Revolution of 1688. 29

The American Revolution 35
John Hancock's Boston Massacre Oration 37
Declaration of the Causes and Necessity of Taking Up Arms 51
Give Me Liberty or Give Me Death 63
The Dominion of Providence over the Passions of Men. 74
Common Sense 85
Declaration of Independence 98
From the Commissioners for Negotiating a Peace with Great Britain 111

The French Revolution 125
Declaration of the Rights of Man and of the Citizen 127
Reflections on the Revolution in France. 138
Olympe de Gouges: Declaration of the Rights of Woman and of the Female Citizen 153
Maximilien Robespierre on the Ideals of the French Revolution 164

The Wider Americas in the Nineteenth Century. 179
Haitian Declaration of Independence. 181
Cartagena Manifesto 190

Simón Bolívar: Address at Angostura 205
Treaty of Córdoba. 212
Documents relating to the Canadian Rebellions, 1837-1838. 220
Benito Juárez on *La Reforma*. 233
Montecristi Manifesto 241

The European Revolutions of 1848—Before and After 253
June Rebellion of 1832 as described in *Les Misérables* (1862) 255
The Communist Manifesto. 270
Louis Kossuth—Speech at a Dinner Given in His Honor by the U.S. Congress in Washington, D.C. 281
Manifesto of the Paris Commune. 290
King Victor Emmanuel II: Address to Parliament. 299

Japan and Korea 307
Meiji Charter Oath. 309
Korean Declaration of Independence 315

The Mexican Revolution 323
Plan de San Luis de Potosi. 325
Plan of Ayala. 332

Ireland. 341
John Morley on Irish Home Rule 343
Proclamation of the Provisional Government of the Irish Republic 361

The Russian Revolution 369
What Is to Be Done? 371
Vladimir Lenin on the Tasks of the Soviet Government. 389
Soviets in Action. 395

Publisher's Note

The *Defining Documents in World History* series, produced by Salem Press, offers a closer look at important historical documents by pairing primary source documents on a broad range of subjects with essays written especially for the series by expert writers, including historians, professors, researchers, and other authorities in the subject under examination. This established series now includes sixteen titles that present documents selected to illuminate specific themes and eras in world history—including The Renaissance & Early Modern Era, Ancient World, Women's Rights, Human Rights, Genocide & The Holocaust, and The Nuclear Age.

This set, *Defining Documents in World History: Revolutions*, offers in-depth analysis of seventy-nine documents, including addresses, cables, charters, declarations, diary excerpts, legislation, letters, manifestos, memos, negotiations, reflections, resolutions, and speeches. These selections trace the evolution of notable revolutions around the globe, from the Dutch Revolt in 1581 to recent revolutionary actions, such as the January 6, 2021, assault on the U.S. Capitol.

The first volume includes essays on the following topics:
- The Dutch Revolt;
- The English Revolution;
- The American Revolution;
- The French Revolution;
- The Wider Americas in the Nineteenth Century;
- European Revolutions of 1848—Before and After;
- Japan and Korea;
- The Mexican Revolution;
- Ireland;
- The Russian Revolution.

The second volume continues with the following:
- India;
- China;
- Mid-Century Rebels;
- Vietnam—and Cambodia;
- Mid-East Revolts and Revolutions in the Twentieth Century;
- The Revolt Against Communism in Europe;
- Other Modern Revolutionary Changes;
- Ukraine—the Orange Revolution;
- The Arab Spring—and ISIS;
- and Recent Revolutionary Disturbances.

Documents within these sections provide an overview of the history and contemporary issues surrounding revolutionary thought and action around the world.

Essay Format

Each Historical Document is supported by a critical essay, written by historians, teachers, and researchers, that includes a Summary Overview, Defining Moment, About the Author, Document Analysis, and Essential Themes. An important feature of each essay is a close reading of the primary source that develops broader themes, such as the author's rhetorical purpose, social or class position, point of view, and other relevant issues. Each essay also includes a section entitled Bibliography and Additional Reading that provides suggestions for further readings and research.

Appendixes

- Chronological List arranges all documents by year;
- Web Resources is an annotated list of websites that offer valuable supplemental resources; and
- Bibliography lists helpful articles and books for further study.

Contributors

Salem Press would like to extend its appreciation to all involved in the development and production of this work; particularly editor Michael Shally-Jensen. All essays have been written and signed by scholars of history, humanities, and other disciplines related to the essays' topics. Without these expert contributions, a project of this nature would not be possible. A full list of the contributors to this set with their affiliations appears following the Editor's Introduction.

Editor's Introduction

Revolution is a term used to designate any rapid, far-reaching or violent change in the political, social, or economic structure of society. Although there have been revolutions in areas such as industry (the Industrial Revolution), science (scientific revolutions), and the arts and culture, it is political revolutions that have garnered the most attention by historians and the public alike. In this sense, revolution entails fundamental change in the government or political constitution of a country, brought about mainly through internal forces and often achieved by violence or force of arms on the part of a sizeable mass of citizens. Examples include the American Revolution, where colonists broke free from their colonial ties and established a sovereign, independent nation; the French Revolution, where an absolute monarchy was overthrown by opposition from inside the country together with a popular uprising; and the Russian Revolution, where a repressive monarchy was overthrown by those seeking to institute widespread social and economic changes based on a socialist model.

In most great political revolutions, not only is the established government or governmental system overthrown but major changes take place in the economic system, the social structure, and sometimes in long-held cultural values. With large-scale revolutions, the ruling power of a country passes from one economic class or political group to another class or group. Moreover, revolutions are often—though not always—irreversible. In the case of the Arab Spring series of uprisings and revolutions (2010–2012), for example, numerous countries in North Africa and the Middle East experienced mass revolts and in some cases saw their governments overthrown; but in many instances the changes initially imagined by their proponents either never took hold or were eventually reversed. The old order crept back in to take its place of honor in a number of these nations.

Historical Perspective

The Greeks saw a strong cultural value system, when closely adhered to, as standing as a bulwark against revolution; it was only after societal breakdown, they believed, that a revolution could gain a toehold. Medieval thinkers generally understood revolution, like any major conflict, to be part of God's plan: just as the heavens revolved around the earth (or so it was thought), political upheavals came and went according to a universal logic known only to the supreme being. Of course, the fact that monarchs in this era (and beyond) believed themselves to be God's divine servants occasionally interrupted the flow of events. Royal decrees were taken to reflect the will of God. Thus, an incipient revolution against the monarch might be stopped in its tracks, or perhaps even sparked by the king—if in a country other than the king's own.

Some Renaissance humanists, such as Michel de Montaigne, thought that changes in government were sometimes necessary and good; in this way, revolution could serve a positive function. John Milton, witness to the overthrow of the English Anglican order by Oliver Cromwell (who Milton supported), saw revolution as the means of achieving freedom. After a brief period of rule, however, Cromwell and his Puritans were in turn tossed out by traditionalist forces. Immanuel Kant, who lived during the French Revolution and aimed to launch his own revolution in philosophical thought (largely successful), believed revolution to be a force for the advancement of humankind. Georg W. Hegel, more extravagantly, proposed that revolution was part of the fulfillment of human destiny. Hegel's philosophy in turn influenced that of Karl Marx, who saw revolution as a culminating moment in the struggle of the working masses to capture the means of economic production, which rightfully belonged to them. One of Marx's most notable later students, Vladimir I. Lenin, transformed that ideology into the October Revolution in Russia in 1917, whereby the radical Bolsheviks came to power and changed the course of global history for the next seventy years (the time of the Soviet Union). Another quasi-Marxist revolutionary, Mao Zedong, did much the same thing in China, where after decades of dictatorial rule under Mao a somewhat less ideologically correct "People's Republic" emerged under Mao's successors and, in the form of the Chinese Communist Party, continues to control the lives of 1.4 billion Chinese residents.

Subsequent communist revolutions affected countries as far afield as Cuba and Cambodia. Cuba's revolution in the 1950s, like Venezuela's less bloody political revolution in the 2000s, drew inspiration from the great nineteenth-century liberator of Latin American nations, Simón Bolívar, who fought for independence from Spain. Independence from colonial regimes, whether communist-inspired or not, has been the cause of numerous revolts and revolutions across the globe. Haiti fought for independence from France in 1804, as did both Vietnam and Algeria in 1950s. Rebels in Ireland fought for independence from Britain in the early twentieth century, as did Indians on the subcontinent through the 1940s, when they finally achieved it. Kenya, too, among many other African colonial nations, severed ties with its European hegemon after World War II. During the second half of the twentieth century, selected countries within the Soviet bloc in Eastern and Central Europe fought to end Soviet Control—and ultimately succeeded, with the dissolution of the Soviet Union beginning in 1989. This was a world-changing event in modern history, ending the Cold War and leaving many nations to their own devices as they navigated their way own in the new world order.

Revolution in Theory and Practice

While the concept of revolution encompasses the relatively peaceful actions of the overthrowing of communist regimes in Europe, as well as the more violent grand revolutions of the past, it overlaps, too, with such events as coups d'état, civil wars, revolts, and rebellions. Political scientists generally distinguish among these phenomena. In the case of the latter events, the general view is that there is less of a concerted effort to transform institutions or to justify one's political authority as an agent of change. These events are, like revolutions, actions *against* an existing regime or group, but they are arguably less comprehensive in their ideological underpinnings and less transformative in their overall effects. At the same time, there are many different kinds of revolution, and not all revolutions can be expected to follow the same pattern: one revolution may not necessarily particularly resemble another.

Given that, the present volume includes a wide variety of revolutions and revolution-adjacent events in order to allow readers to appreciate the differences and similarities among them.

The French political philosopher and historian Michel Foucault (1926–1984) argued that the notion of revolution lay at the heart of any serious struggle between opposing political forces. Revolution, for Foucault, is to be understood as a matter of a decisive reversal of the balance of forces: victory for one side, defeat for the other. Revolutionaries struggle deliberately to produce such a reversal, while "antirevolutionary" forces are opposed to it and defend the state against those who would overturn the existing order. Both sides, in effect, take the idea of political struggle to the extreme and are willing to die for their cause. And yet, when the dust settles, there is always the possibility that the successful revolutionaries will end up being merely the dominant faction, the ones who, having seized control, must now maintain their dominance through the imposition of state power. This is basically what happened in the Soviet Union, China, Iran, and other nations that were defined by revolution and adherence to an ideology.

Foucault also notes that only mass desire for revolution can bring about a revolution and sustain it in the long run; a campaign of terror designed to whip up the masses yet keep them in their place, will ultimately falter and fail.

—Michael Shally-Jensen, PhD

Bibliography and Additional Reading

DeFronzo, James. *Revolutions and Revolutionary Movements*. 6th ed. New York: Routledge, 2021.

Furtado, Peter, ed. *Revolutions: How They Changed History and What They Mean Today*. New York: Thames & Hudson, 2020.

Goldstone, Jack. *Revolutions: A Very Short Introduction*. New York: Oxford University Press, 2014.

Kelly, Mark. "Revolution." In *The Cambridge Foucault Lexicon*, edited by Leonard Lawler and John Nalem 438–42. New York: Cambridge University Press, 2014.

■ Contributors

Anna Accettola, PhD
University of California, Los Angeles

Michael P. Auerbach, MA
Marblehead, Massachusetts

James A. Baer, PhD
Northern Virginia Community College

Jakub Basista, PhD, DLitt
Jagiellonian University

Chris Bingley, PhD
Los Angeles, California

Brian Bonhomme, PhD
Youngstown State University

William E. Burns, PhD
George Washington University

Dave Corcoran, PhD
Emmanuel College

Steven L. Danver, PhD
Mesa Verde Publishing

K. P. Dawes, MA
Chicago, Illinois

Bethany Groff Dorau, MA
Historic New England

Ashleigh Fata, MA
University of California, Los Angeles

Gerald F. Goodwin, PhD
Syracuse, New York

Kevin Grimm, PhD
Regent University

Aaron John Gulyas, MA
Mott Community College

Lawrence W. Haapanen, PhD
Lewis-Clark State College

Carrie Le Glenn, MA
University of California, Los Angeles

Kay Lemay, MA
Washington, D.C.

Michael J. O'Neal, PhD
Independent Scholar

Hannah Rich, MA
Philadelphia, Pennsylvania

Peter Robinson, PhD
Independent Scholar

Michael Shally-Jensen, PhD
Amherst, Massachusetts

David Simonelli, PhD
Youngstown State University

Noëlle Sinclair, JD, MLS
Independent Scholar

Robert Surbrug, PhD
Bay Path University

Anthony Vivian, MA
University of California, Los Angeles

Donald A. Watt, PhD
Dakota Wesleyan University

Anne York, PhD
Youngstown State University

■ Full Table of Contents

Volume 1

Publisher's Note vii
Editor's Introduction ix
Contributors. xi
Full Table of Contents xiii

The Dutch Revolt 1
Dutch Declaration of Independence 3

The English Revolution 21
Resolves by the English House of Commons regarding King Charles I and the Authority of the People. . . . 23
Reflection on the Glorious Revolution of 1688. 29

The American Revolution 35
John Hancock's Boston Massacre Oration 37
Declaration of the Causes and Necessity of Taking Up Arms 51
Give Me Liberty or Give Me Death 63
The Dominion of Providence over the Passions of Men. 74
Common Sense 85
Declaration of Independence 98
From the Commissioners for Negotiating a Peace with Great Britain 111

The French Revolution 125
Declaration of the Rights of Man and of the Citizen 127
Reflections on the Revolution in France. 138
Olympe de Gouges: Declaration of the Rights of Woman and of the Female Citizen 153
Maximilien Robespierre on the Ideals of the French Revolution 164

The Wider Americas in the Nineteenth Century. 179
Haitian Declaration of Independence. 181
Cartagena Manifesto 190
Simón Bolívar: Address at Angostura 205

Treaty of Córdoba..212
Documents relating to the Canadian Rebellions, 1837-1838...............................220
Benito Juárez on *La Reforma*..233
Montecristi Manifesto...241

The European Revolutions of 1848—Before and After 253
June Rebellion of 1832 as described in *Les Misérables* (1862)..........................255
The Communist Manifesto..270
Louis Kossuth—Speech at a Dinner Given in His Honor by the U.S. Congress in Washington, D.C.....281
Manifesto of the Paris Commune..290
King Victor Emmanuel II: Address to Parliament..299

Japan and Korea 307
Meiji Charter Oath..309
Korean Declaration of Independence..315

The Mexican Revolution 323
Plan de San Luis de Potosi..325
Plan of Ayala...332

Ireland 341
John Morley on Irish Home Rule..343
Proclamation of the Provisional Government of the Irish Republic..................361

The Russian Revolution 369
What Is to Be Done?...371
Vladimir Lenin on the Tasks of the Soviet Government..................................389
Soviets in Action...395

Volume 2

Full Table of Contents ix

India 411
Karl Marx on British Rule in India 413
Government of India Act 424
Mohandas Gandhi: Statement at Trial 443
Jawaharlal Nehru's Speech on the Occasion of Indian Independence 453

China 461
Sun Yat-sen: "The Three Stages of Revolution" 463
"The Chinese People Have Stood Up!" 469
Mao Zedong on Communism and Counterrevolution 477
Letter from a Chinese "Rusticant" 491
U.S. Embassy Cables Concerning the Crackdown in Tiananmen Square 497

Mid-Century Rebels 505
¡No Pasarán! ("They Shall Not Pass!") 507
Mau Mau Warrior Oath 513
Fidel Castro's Speech at Twenty-One Nations Conference 516
Second Declaration of Havana 523

Vietnam—and Cambodia 529
Geneva Accords on Indochina 531
"The Path of Revolution in the South" 550
CIA Memo on National Liberation Front Methods 559
Message from Ho Chi Minh 566
The Paris Peace Accords 571
Story from the Khmer Rouge Killing Fields 581

Mid-East Revolts and Revolutions in the Twentieth Century 587
Proclamation of the Young Turks 589
Proclamation of the Algerian National Liberation Front 596
CIA Summary of the Overthrow of Premier Mossadeq of Iran 604
Gamal Abdel Nasser on the Nationalization of the Suez Canal 614
Ayatollah Khomeini on "The Great Satan" 623
Diary Excerpts of an American Hostage in Iran 633

The Revolt against Communism in Europe 639
Resolution of Hungarian Student Protestors 641
The "Two Thousand Words" Manifesto 648
Charter 77 655
CIA Cable on the Situation in Poland 663
Egon Krenz Letter to Mikhail Gorbachev. 670
Gorbachev's Farewell Address 675

Other Modern Revolutionary Changes 683
Corazon Aquino on Achieving Peace through Peaceful Means 685
Nelson Mandela—Nobel Peace Prize Acceptance Speech 692
Hugo Chávez Speech in Havana 700

Ukraine—the Orange Revolution. 709
Inaugural Speech by Ukrainian President Viktor Yushchenko 711
Remarks by Yulia Tymoshenko after Her Release from Prison. 717

Arab Spring—and ISIS. 723
Tawakkol Karman—Nobel Lecture 725
Egyptian President-Elect Mohamed Morsi's Acceptance Speech 736
Islamic State—Proclamation of the Caliphate 744
The Tunisian National Dialogue Quartet—Nobel Lecture 752

Recent Revolutionary Disturbances. 763
Resolution Establishing the House Select Committee to Investigate the January 6th Attack on the
    U.S. Capitol. 765
Summary of Terrorism Threat to the U.S. Homeland. 775
Remarks by President Biden One Year after the January 6 Assault on the U.S. Capitol 783
Global Leaders Condemn Assault on Brazilian Government Buildings 796

Appendixes
Chronological List 807
Web Resources. 809
Bibliography 815

Index 829

The Dutch Revolt

In the late 1500s, religious change and political unrest in the Low Countries, then part of Spain, fueled a revolt there. The Spanish monarch, Philip II, was seeking to counter the spread of Calvinism, and so directed the Spanish Inquisition against its adherents (as well as Protestants generally). Moreover, to enhance his authority, Philip suspended the traditional privileges enjoyed by citizens of the Low Country. The Dutch Revolt was the result.

It began in the southern provinces of Flanders and Brabant in 1566. The Spanish crown sent an army to quell it. However, under a compact called the Pacification of Ghent, all the provinces united to drive out the Spanish. By 1578 the Spanish governor, offering political concessions, managed to win back the southern provinces. Meanwhile, the northern provinces of Holland, Zeeland, Utrecht, and Friesland formed the Union of Utrecht and declared themselves a republic in 1581.

The Dutch Revolt gave the rebellious northern provinces of the Low Countries independence from Spanish Habsburg rule. Eventually, they became the modern kingdom of the Netherlands. The southern provinces, falling once again under Spain, later were incorporated as part of Belgium.

Dutch Declaration of Independence

Date: July 26, 1581
Authors: Jacques Tayaert; Jacob Valcke; Pieter van Dieven; Andries Hessels
Genre: act; law

Summary Overview

In July 1581 a coalition of Dutch provinces in the northern portion of the Low Countries known as the United Provinces issued a declaration to pronounce their independence from Spanish rule under King Philip II. Formally called the Act of Abjuration or, in Dutch, the Plakkaat van Verlatinghe ("Placard of Desertion"), the declaration reflected the Dutch rebels' belief that Philip had essentially deserted the Low Countries, like a shepherd might desert his flock, and the document thus outlined his abuses against the provinces.

The Dutch Declaration of Independence, regarded as the first modern declaration of independence, was forged during the Eighty Years' War, often called the Dutch War of Independence. The first phase of this war was the Dutch Revolt of 1568–1609, during which the Netherlands' northern provinces achieved independence from Spain. After Spain and the northern provinces signed the Twelve Years' Truce in 1609 at Antwerp, ending hostilities, the southern provinces continued to live under Spanish domination until the Treaty of Münster was signed in 1648. This treaty, part of the realignment brought about that year by the Treaty of Westphalia—which ended the Eighty Years' War as well as the Thirty Years' War, fought in central Europe—confirmed the existence of the Dutch provinces as an independent nation variously called the Dutch Republic, the Republic of the Seven United Netherlands, or the Republic of the Seven United Provinces.

In the twenty-first century, the names of Holland and the Netherlands tend to be used interchangeably. The terminology, though, is complex and oftentimes confusing. Netherlands literally means "Low Countries" or "Lowlands" and historically dates to the period when the Dutch Republic consisted of a loose confederation of seven provinces; the declaration refers to this confederation in the opening line as the United Provinces of the Low Countries. In 1830 two of those provinces broke off from the recently established United Kingdom of the Netherlands to form Belgium. Today, the phrase "Low Countries" is often used to refer collectively to the countries of the Netherlands, Belgium, and Luxembourg. The phrase actually has little to do with the countries' "lowness" relative to sea level; rather, it refers to the provinces' originally being the more southerly portions of earlier empires. Holland is a name commonly used to refer to the country of the Netherlands, but more accurately it reflects the names of two provinces, North Holland and South Holland, that historically were the most prominent members of the Dutch Republic. Finally, "Dutch" refers to the language spoken in the Netherlands, though the word is also used to refer to the people and the nation's institutions; it is etymologically related to "Deutsche," or German.

Defining Moment

The Dutch Declaration of Independence was signed in the midst of a complex set of events that would radically alter the balance of power in Western Europe. In the fifteenth century, the successive dukes of Burgundy held control of what were called the Seventeen Provinces, a collection of counties and fiefdoms roughly corresponding to the Dutch Republic and also including small portions of modern-day France and Germany. Accordingly, the region was often called the Burgundian Netherlands. The Burgundian Netherlands were inherited by Charles, the duke of Burgundy, in 1506. Charles was a descendant of the House of Habsburg, a branch of the Austrian royal succession that ruled a large portion of central Europe, and as such he became King Charles I of Spain in 1516; he was also the grandson of King Ferdinand II of

PLACCAERT VANDE STATEN GENERAEL VANDE

ghevnieerde Nederlanden, Bijden vvelcken, mits den redenen in't langhe in't selfde begrepen, men verclaert den Coninck van Spaegnien vervallen vande Ouerheit en heerschappije van dese voors. Nederlanden: ende verbiet sijnen naem ende zegel inde selue Landen meer te gebruycken, &c.

DE Staten generael vande ghevnieerde Nederlanden/ Allen den ghenen die dese teghenwoordige sullen sien ofte hooren lesen/ salupt. Also een yegelick kennelick is/ dat een Prince vande Lande van Godt ghestelt is hooft ouer sijne ondersaten/ om de selue te bewaren en beschermen van alle ongelijck/ ouerlast en ghewelt/ ghelijck een Herder tot bewaernisse van sijne Schapen: En dat d'ondersaten niet en zijn van Godt gheschapen tot behoef vanden Prince/ om hem in alles wat hy beveelt/ weder het goddelic oft ongoddelick/ recht oft onrecht is/ onderdanich te wesen/ en als slauen te dienen: maer den Prince om d'ondersaten wille/ sonder de welcke hy egheen Prince en is/ om de selue met recht en redene te regeeren/ ende voor te staen/ en lief te hebben als een vader sijne kinderen/ en een herder sijne schapen/ die sijn lijf en leuen sett om de selue te bewaren. En so wanneer hy sulcks niet en doet/ maer in stede van sijne ondersaten te beschermen/ de selue soect te verdrucken/ t'ouerlasten/ heure oude vrijheit/ priuilegien/ en oude herkomen te benemen/ en heur te gebieden ende gebruycken als slauen/

A ij moet

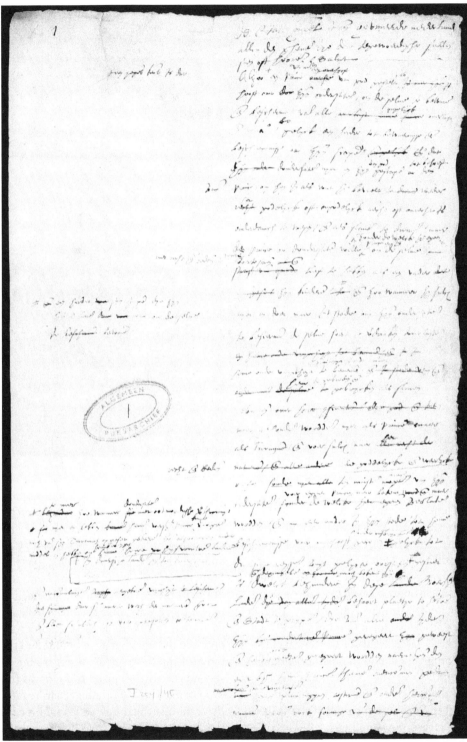

First page of the printed and written versions of the Act of Abjuration. Photos via Wikimedia Commons. [Public domain.]

19th century depiction of the signing of the Act of Abjuration, by Johannes Hinderikus Egenberger. Image via Wikimedia Commons. [Public domain.]

Aragon and Isabella I of Castile, famous for backing Christopher Columbus's voyage to the New World in 1492. Charles was Spanish, but he was born in Ghent (in Flanders, now part of Belgium), so he spoke Dutch and was sympathetic to Dutch concerns. In 1519, upon the death of his grandfather, he became the head of the House of Habsburg and was elected the monarch of the Holy Roman Empire as Charles V (though the pope did not officially crown him until 1530). He thus presided over a large swath of western, central, and southern Europe, including the Netherlands. He asserted his control over the Netherlands in 1549 when he issued the Pragmatic Sanction, which recognized the Seventeen Provinces as a unified political entity to which the Habsburgs were heirs.

During the sixteenth century, three major issues caused friction in Charles V's Dutch domains. One issue was taxation. Flanders had become a particularly wealthy province, but the other Dutch provinces were affluent as well, largely through trade and industry as spurred by an entrepreneurial ethic. Charles became embroiled in a series of wars, particularly against France as part of the Italian Wars and against the Turks in the Mediterranean. He needed funds to finance these wars, and the affluent Dutch bore more than their fair share of the tax burden, although they opposed the wars because France and the Turkish Ottoman Empire were important trading partners. The second issue that caused friction was the rise of Protestantism, which Catholic Spain regarded as heresy. Protestantism had been tolerated locally throughout the Dutch provinces, but Charles believed that it had to be suppressed and sent troops into the provinces to that end. He enacted harsh measures against Dutch

Protestants, creating numerous grievances. His attempts to suppress Dutch Protestantism took place against the backdrop of the notorious Spanish Inquisition, the oftentimes cruel effort to root out heresy, blasphemy, witchcraft, sodomy, and other departures from Catholic orthodoxy.

The third source of friction was efforts to centralize the government. The Netherlands had historically consisted of numerous principalities operating more or less autonomously under the control of local nobles. Charles wanted to increase efficiency in his empire, so he attempted to impose more centralized rule over these principalities. Charles replaced local Dutch stadtholders (heads of state) and members of the States-General, the governing body of the Seventeen Provinces, with his own appointments. He also replaced bishops and other religious authorities. Both the nobles and the increasingly influential merchants of the Netherlands resented these encroachments on their traditional prerogatives.

Thus did matters stand when Charles relinquished the throne of Spain to his son, Philip II, in 1556. While the Dutch had grown annoyed with Charles, they grudgingly tolerated his rule, for he spoke Dutch and appeared to be at least somewhat interested in Dutch welfare. Philip II, though, was more Spanish than Dutch and showed little interest in the Netherlands. The issues that had arisen during the first half of the sixteenth century became more pronounced under Philip, who governed the Dutch provinces harshly; he was at loggerheads with the Dutch nobles throughout his first decade of rule. They resisted his efforts to increase taxes. They demanded the withdrawal of Spanish troops. They resented Antoine Perrenot de Granvelle, Philip's appointed head of the States-General, and several prominent nobles resigned from the States-General in protest. Religious protests increased, as Dutch Protestants—and even Dutch Catholics—called for an end to persecution of Protestantism. In 1566 a petition to that end was submitted by some four hundred nobles to Philip's governor of the Netherlands, Margaret of Parma, who passed it along to Philip—who promptly ignored it.

As if matters were not troubled enough, they turned worse in 1566 when rioting broke out in Flanders and other provinces. These riots were led by Dutch Calvinists and were part of a so-called iconoclastic ("image breaking") movement. Calvinists in numerous cities looted churches and destroyed religious images of Catholic saints, which Calvinists thought of as idols. In response to the vandalism, in 1567 Philip sent troops to Brussels under the command of Fernando Álvarez de Toledo, the third duke of Alba. Given broad license by Philip, the duke of Alba created the Council of Troubles (in Dutch, Raad van Beroerten) to enforce harsh measures against anyone he thought to be disloyal to the king. Numerous nobles were executed, including most prominently Lamoraal, the count of Egmond, and Filips van Montmorency, the count of Hoorn, who were decapitated in Brussels in 1568. Over the next year, a thousand people were executed, prompting Netherlanders to refer to the Council of Troubles as the "Council of Blood."

Amid this turmoil, William I, the prince of Orange and an influential stadtholder, assumed leadership of the opposition to Philip, though William was politi-

Phillip II; portrait by Sofonisba Anguissola, 1565. Image via Wikimedia Commons. [Public domain.]

William I, Prince of Orange, aka William the Silent; portrait by Adriaen Thomasz, 1579. Image via Wikimedia Commons. [Public domain.]

cally savvy and did not renounce his allegiance to the king. Initially, he fled to his domains in Germany to avoid the wrath of the duke of Alba. In 1568 he returned in an effort to drive Alba out, invading the Netherlands in concert with armies led by his two brothers and a fourth army led by French Huguenots. On May 23, 1568, his forces defeated a Spanish force at the Battle of Heiligerlee, marking the first Dutch victory of the Dutch Revolt and the Eighty Years' War. Although William was victorious, the other invading armies were not. William ran out of money, his army fell apart, and the rebellion was effectively quelled until 1572.

The duke of Alba meanwhile retained his position of authority. He provoked the ire of Netherlanders anew when he instituted a tax to fund the Spanish king's war against the Ottoman Empire. The Ottoman Turks, for their part, offered direct aid to the Dutch rebels, hoping thereby to counter Habsburg hegemony over Europe. Discontent continued to grow until Dutch rebels seized the town of Brielle on April 1, 1572. This victory, entirely unexpected, emboldened the rebels, who reappointed William of Orange as their leader. William faced a difficult challenge, for he needed to find a way to unite three different factions: Calvinists who wanted to impose Dutch Protestantism, Catholics who yet remained loyal to Philip, and a large group of Catholics and Protestants who were primarily interested in ending Spanish rule over their country and restoring their privileges.

Throughout the 1570s, Philip had problems of his own. His wars were bankrupting Spain; his unpaid soldiers mutinied, and in 1576 they sacked and looted Antwerp in an event called the Spanish Fury. Again the rebels were emboldened. That same year the Seventeen Provinces signed an internal treaty called the Pacification of Ghent, an agreement to join forces against the Spanish and to enforce religious tolerance. The union, however, was still in disarray. In early 1579 the southern provinces, through the Union of Arras, withdrew from the greater union and confirmed their loyalty to the Spanish king, largely because they were uncomfortable with the fundamentalist religious fervor of the Calvinists. In response, the northern provinces of Holland, Zeeland, Utrecht, and Groningen formed the Union of Utrecht on January 23, 1579, leaving the Seventeen Provinces divided between north and south. Over the next year and a half, Gelder, Overijssel, and Friesland also joined with the northern provinces, which then declared their independence from Spain as the Republic of the Seven United Provinces in the Act of Abjuration on July 26, 1581. (Abjuration denotes a formal renunciation or repudiation, in this case, of Philip II of Spain.) One of the alliance's first tasks was to find a monarch to rule. The position was offered to Queen Elizabeth I of England, but she turned the Dutch down, unwilling to alienate the Spanish king. Accordingly, the rebel provinces turned to Hercule François, the duke of Anjou, the French king's younger brother, who agreed on the condition that the provinces renounce all allegiance to Spain.

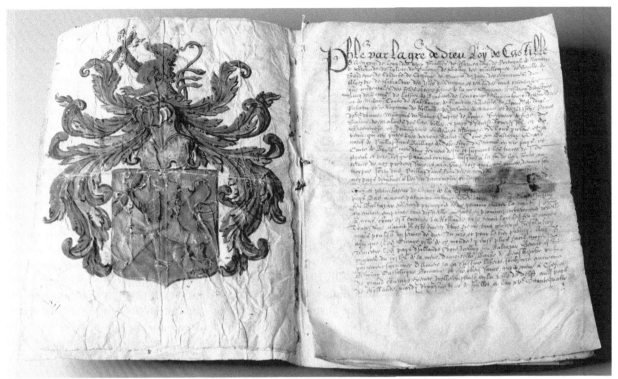

Reward letter of Philip II to the family of Balthasar Gerards, assassin of William the Silent, 1590. Photo via Wikimedia Commons. [Public domain.]

Author Biography

The Dutch Declaration of Independence was drafted by a committee of four men; details of their lives are sketchy. Andries Hessels held the position of greffier, or secretary, of Brabant. Jacques Tayaert was a pensionary, or chief functionary and legal adviser, in the city of Ghent. Jacob Valcke held the same position in the city of Ter Goes, now called Goes. Finally, Pieter van Dieven was pensionary of the city of Mechelen. A fifth name is often mentioned, that of Jan de Asseliers, the audiencer of the States-General (the official charged with drafting its declarations), who may have physically written out the declaration and may have composed the preamble. His name appears at the very end of the document as a signer.

Although he was not strictly speaking an author of the declaration, William I of Orange, often called William the Silent, reputedly for his circumspection in negotiations with the king of France, was the leader of the Dutch Revolt and thus can be considered the inspiration behind the document. (This William of Orange is not to be confused with the William of Orange who assumed the throne of England in 1689 through the Glorious Revolution; the latter was William III of Orange.) William I of Orange was born on April 24, 1533, in Germany. Upon the death of his cousin in 1544, as the family's only recognized heir, he assumed the title of prince of Orange. Later, through marriage, he gained additional royal titles. In 1555 Charles V appointed him to the Council of State; later, Philip appointed him stadtholder of Holland, Zeeland, Utrecht, and Burgundy. During the religious disturbances that followed the accession of Philip, he refused to appear before the Council of Troubles and was declared an outlaw. He then became leader of the armed resistance to Spain and won several important battles. His leadership of the Dutch was validated by the signing of the Act of Abjuration in 1581. Philip, though, had placed a bounty on his head, which proved too hard to resist on the part of one Balthasar Gérard, a Catholic Frenchman who believed that William had betrayed his king, Philip. On July 10, 1584, Gérard presented himself at William's home and shot him with a handgun—one of the earliest political assassinations by handgun in history.

Historical Document

Dutch Declaration of Independence

The States General of the United Provinces of the Low Countries, to all whom it may concern, do by these Presents send greeting:

As it is apparent to all that a prince is constituted by God to be ruler of a people, to defend them from oppression and violence as the shepherd his sheep; and whereas God did not create the people slaves to their prince, to obey his commands, whether right or wrong, but rather the prince for the sake of the subjects (without which he could be no prince), to govern them according to equity, to love and support them as a father his children or a shepherd his flock, and even at the hazard of life to defend and preserve them. And when he does not behave thus, but, on the contrary, oppresses them, seeking opportunities to infringe their ancient customs and privileges, exacting from them slavish compliance, then he is no longer a prince, but a tyrant, and the subjects are to consider him in no other view. And particularly when this is done deliberately, unauthorized by the states, they may not only disallow his authority, but legally proceed to the choice of another prince for their defense. This is the only method left for subjects whose humble petitions and remonstrances could never soften their prince or dissuade him from his tyrannical proceedings; and this is what the law of nature dictates for the defense of liberty, which we ought to transmit to posterity, even at the hazard of our lives. And this we have seen done frequently in several countries upon the like occasion, whereof there are notorious instances, and more justifiable in our land, which has been always governed according to their ancient privileges, which are expressed in the oath taken by the prince at his admission to the government; for most of the Provinces receive their prince upon certain conditions, which he swears to maintain, which, if the prince violates, he is no longer sovereign.

Now thus it was that the king of Spain after the demise of the emperor, his father, Charles the Fifth, of the glorious memory (of whom he received all these provinces), forgetting the services done by the subjects of these countries, both to his father and himself, by whose valor he got so glorious and memorable victories over his enemies that his name and power became famous and dreaded over all the world, forgetting also the advice of his said imperial majesty, made to him before to the contrary, did rather hearken to the counsel of those Spaniards about him, who had conceived a secret hatred to this land and to its liberty, because they could not enjoy posts of honor and high employments here under the states as in Naples, Sicily, Milan and the Indies, and other countries under the king's dominion. Thus allured by the riches of the said provinces, wherewith many of them were well acquainted, the said counselors, we say, or the principal of them, frequently remonstrated to the king that it was more for his Majesty's reputation and grandeur to subdue the Low Countries a second time, and to make himself absolute (by which they mean to tyrannize at pleasure), than to govern according to the restrictions he had accepted, and at his admission sworn to observe. From that time forward the king of Spain, following these evil counselors, sought by all means possible to reduce this country (stripping them of their ancient privileges) to slavery, under the government of Spaniards having first, under the mask of religion, endeavored to settle new bishops in the largest and principal cities, endowing and incorporating them with the richest abbeys, assigning to each bishop nine canons to assist him as counselors, three whereof should superintend the inquisition.

By this incorporation the said bishops (who might be strangers as well as natives) would have had the first place and vote in the assembly of the states, and always the prince's creatures at devotion; and by the addition of the said canons he would have introduced the Spanish inquisition, which has been always as dreadful and detested in these provinces as the worst of slavery, as is well known, in so much that his imperial majesty, having once before proposed it to these states, and upon whose remonstrances did desist, and entirely gave it up, hereby giving proof of the great affection he had for his subjects. But, notwithstanding the many remonstrances made to the king both by the provinces and particular towns, in writing as well as by some principal lords by word of mouth; and, namely, by the Baron of Montigny and Earl of Egmont, who with the approbation of the Duchess of Parma, then governess of the Low Countries, by the advice of the council of state were sent several times to Spain upon this affair. And, although the king had by fair words given them grounds to hope that their request should be complied with, yet by his letters he ordered the contrary, soon after expressly commanding, upon pain of his displeasure, to admit the new bishops immediately, and put them in possession of their bishoprics and incorporated abbeys, to hold the court of the inquisition in the places where it had been before, to obey and follow the decrees and ordinances of the Council of Trent, which in many articles are destructive of the privileges of the country.

This being come to the knowledge of the people gave just occasion to great uneasiness and clamor among them, and lessened that good affection they had always borne toward the king and his predecessors. And, especially, seeing that he did not only seek to tyrannize over their persons and estates, but also over their consciences, for which they believed themselves accountable to God only. Upon this occasion the chief of the nobility in compassion to the poor people, in the year 1566, exhibited a certain remonstrance in form of a petition, humbly praying, in order to appease them and prevent public disturbances, that it would please his majesty (by showing that clemency due from a good prince to his people) to soften the said points, and especially with regard to the rigorous inquisition, and capital punishments for matters of religion. And to inform the king of this affair in a more solemn manner, and to represent to him how necessary it was for the peace and prosperity of the public to remove the aforesaid innovations, and moderate the severity of his declarations published concerning divine worship, the Marquis de Berghen, and the aforesaid Baron of Montigny had been sent, at the request of the said lady regent, council of state, and of the states-general as ambassadors to Spain, where the king, instead of giving them audience, and redress the grievances they had complained of (which for want of a timely remedy did always appear in their evil consequences among the common people), did, by the advice of Spanish council, declare all those who were concerned in preparing the said remonstrance to be rebels, and guilty of high treason, and to be punished with death, and confiscation of their estates; and, what is more (thinking himself well assured of reducing these countries under absolute tyranny by the army of the Duke of Alva), did soon after imprison and put to death the said lords the ambassadors, and confiscated their estates, contrary to the law of nations, which has been always religiously observed even among the most tyrannic and barbarous princes.

And, although the said disturbances, which in the year 1566 happened on the aforementioned occasion, were now appeased by the governess and her ministers, and many friends to liberty were either banished or subdued, in so much that the king had not any show of reason to use arms and violence, and further oppress this country, yet for these causes and reasons, long time before sought by the council of Spain (as appears by intercepted letters from the Spanish ambassador, Alana, then in France, writ to the Duchess of Parma), to annul all the privileges of this country, and govern it tyrannically at pleasure as in the Indies; and in their new conquests he has, at the instigation of the council of Spain, showing the little regard he had for his people, so contrary to the duty which a good prince owes to his subjects), sent the Duke of Alva with a powerful army to oppress this land, who for his inhuman cruelties is looked upon as one of its greatest enemies, accompanied with counselors too like himself. And, although he came in without the least opposition, and was received by the poor subjects with all marks of honor and clemency, which the king had often hypocritically promised in his letters, and that himself intended to come in person to give orders to their general satisfaction, having since the departure of the Duke of Alva equipped a fleet to carry him from Spain, and another in Zealand to come to meet him at the great expense of the country, the better to deceive his subjects, and allure them into the toils, nevertheless the said duke, immediately after his arrival (though a stranger, and no way related to the royal family), declared that he had a captain-general's commission, and soon after that of governor of these provinces, contrary to all its ancient customs and privileges; and, the more to manifest his designs, he immediately garrisoned the principal towns and castles, and caused fortresses and citadels to be built in the great cities to awe them into subjection, and very courteously sent for the chief nobility in the king's name, under pretense of taking their advice, and to employ them in the service of their country. And those who believed his letters were seized and carried out of Brabant, contrary to law, where they were imprisoned and prosecuted as criminals before him who had no right, nor could be a competent judge; and at last he, without hearing their defense at large, sentenced them to death, which was publicly and ignominiously executed.

The others, better acquainted with Spanish hypocrisy, residing in foreign countries, were declared outlawed, and had their estates confiscated, so that the poor subjects could make no use of their fortresses nor be assisted by their princes in defense of their liberty against the violence of the pope; besides a great number of other gentlemen and substantial citizens, some of whom were executed, and others banished that their estates might be confiscated, plaguing the other honest inhabitants, not only by the injuries done to their wives, children and estates by the Spanish soldiers lodged in their houses, as likewise by diverse contributions, which they were forced to pay toward building citadels and new fortifications of towns even to their own ruin, besides the taxes of the hundredth, twentieth, and tenth penny, to pay both the foreign and those raised in the country, to be employed against their fellow-citizens and against those who at the hazard of their lives defended their liberties. In order to impoverish the subjects, and to incapacitate them to hinder his design, and that he might with more ease execute the instructions received in Spain, to treat these countries as new conquests, he began to alter the course of justice after the Spanish mode, directly contrary to our privileges; and, imagining at last he had nothing more to fear, he endeavored by main force to settle a tax called the tenth penny on merchandise and manufacture, to the total ruin of these countries, the prosperity of which depends upon a flourishing trade, notwithstanding frequent remonstrances, not by a single province only, but by all of them united, which he had effected, had it not been for the Prince of Orange with diverse gentlemen and other inhabitants, who had followed this prince in his exile, most of whom were in his pay, and banished by the Duke of Alva with others who between him and the states of all the provinces, on the contrary sought, by all possible promises made to the colonels already at his devotion, to gain the German troops, who were then garrisoned in the principal fortresses and the cities, that by their assistance he might master them, as he had gained many of them already, and held them attached to his interest in order, by their assistance, to force those who would not join with him in making war against the Prince of Orange, and the provinces of Holland and Zealand, more cruel and bloody than any war before. But, as no disguises can long conceal our intentions, this project was discovered before it could be executed; and he, unable to perform his promises, and instead of that peace so much boasted of at his arrival a new war kindled, not yet extinguished.

All these considerations give us more than sufficient reason to renounce the King of Spain, and seek some other powerful and more gracious prince to take us under his protection; and, more especially, as these countries have been for these twenty years abandoned to disturbance and oppression by their king, during which time the inhabitants were not treated as subjects, but enemies, enslaved forcibly by their own governors.

Having also, after the decease of Don Juan, sufficiently declared by the Baron de Selles that he would not allow the pacification of Ghent, the which Don Juan had in his majesty's name sworn to maintain, but daily proposing new terms of agreement less advantageous. Notwithstanding these discouragements we used all possible means, by petitions in writing, and the good offices of the greatest princes in Christendom, to be reconciled to our king, having lastly maintained for a long time our deputies at the Congress of Cologne, hoping that the intercession of his imperial majesty and of the electors would procure an honorable and lasting peace, and some degree of liberty, particularly relating to religion (which chiefly concerns God and our own consciences), at last we found by experience that nothing would be obtained of the king by prayers and treaties, which latter he made use of to divide and weaken the provinces, that he might the easier execute his plan rigorously, by subduing them one by one, which afterwards plainly appeared by certain proclamations and proscriptions published by the king's orders, by virtue of which we and all officers of the United Provinces with all our friends are declared rebels and as such to have forfeited our lives and estates. Thus, by rendering us odious to all, he might interrupt our commerce, likewise reducing us to despair, offering a great sum to any that would assassinate the Prince of Orange.

So, having no hope of reconciliation, and finding no other remedy, we have, agreeable to the law of nature in our own defense, and for maintaining the rights, privileges, and liberties of our countrymen, wives, and children, and latest posterity from being enslaved by the Spaniards, been constrained to renounce allegiance to the King of Spain, and pursue such methods as appear to us most likely to secure our ancient liberties and privileges. Know all men by these presents that being reduced to the last extremity, as above mentioned, we have unanimously and deliberately declared, and do by these presents declare, that the King of Spain has forfeited, ipso jure, all hereditary right to the sovereignty of those countries, and are determined from henceforward not to acknowledge his sovereignty or jurisdiction, nor any act of his relating to the domains of the Low Countries, nor make use of his name as prince, nor suffer others to do it. In consequence whereof we also declare all officers, judges, lords, gentlemen, vassals, and all other the inhabitants of this country of what condition or quality soever, to be henceforth discharged from all oaths and obligations whatsoever made to the King of Spain as sovereign of those countries. And whereas, upon the motives already mentioned, the greater part of the United Provinces have, by common consent of their members, submitted to the government and sovereignty of the illustrious Prince and Duke of Anjou, upon certain conditions stipulated with his highness, and whereas the most serene Archduke Matthias has resigned the government of these countries with our approbation, we command and order all justiciaries, officers, and all whom it may concern, not to make use of the name, titles, great or privy seal of the King of Spain from henceforward; but in lieu of them, as long as his highness the Duke of Anjou is absent upon urgent affairs relating to the welfare of these countries, having so agreed with his highness or otherwise, they shall provisionally use the name and title of the President and Council of the Province.

And, until such a president and counselors shall be nominated, assembled, and act in that capacity, they shall act in our name, except that in Holland and Zealand where they shall use the name of the Prince of Orange, and of the states of the said provinces until the aforesaid council shall legally sit, and then shall conform to the directions of that council agreeable to the contract made with his highness. And, instead of the king's seal aforesaid, they shall make use of our great seal, center-seal, and signet, in affairs relating to the public, according as the said council shall from time to time be authorized. And in affairs concerning the administration of justice, and transactions peculiar to each province, the provincial council and other councils of that country shall use respectively the name, title, and seal of the said province, where the case is to be tried, and no other, on pain of having all letters, documents, and despatches annulled. And, for the better and effectual performance hereof, we have ordered and commanded, and do hereby order and command, that all the seals of the King of Spain which are in these United Provinces shall immediately, upon the publication of these presents, be delivered to the estate of each province respectively, or to such persons as by the said estates shall be authorized and appointed, upon peril of discretionary punishment.

Moreover, we order and command that from henceforth no money coined shall be stamped with the name, title, or arms of the King of Spain in any of these United Provinces, but that all new gold and silver pieces, with their halfs and quarters, shall only bear such impressions as the states shall direct. We order likewise and command the president and other lords of the privy council, and all other chancellors, presidents, accountants-general, and to others in all the chambers of accounts respectively in these said countries, and likewise to all other judges and officers, as we hold them discharged from henceforth of their oath made to the King of Spain, pursuant to the tenor of their commission, that they shall take a new oath to the states of that country on whose jurisdiction they depend, or to commissaries appointed by them, to be true to us against the King of Spain and all his adherents, according to the formula of words prepared by the states-general for that purpose. And we shall give to the said counselors, justiciaries, and officers employed in these provinces, who have contracted in our name with his highness the Duke of Anjou, an act to continue them in their respective offices, instead of new commissions, a clause annulling the former provisionally until the arrival of his highness. Moreover, to all such counselors, accomptants, justiciaries, and officers in these Provinces, who have not contracted with his highness, aforesaid, we shall grant new commissions under our hands and seals, unless any of the said officers are accused and convicted of having acted under their former commissions against the liberties and privileges of this country or of other the like maladministration.

We farther command of the president and members of the privy council, chancellor of the Duchy of Brabant, also the chancellor of the Duchy of Guelders, and county of Zutphen, to the president and members of the council of Holland, to the receivers of great officers of Beoostersheldt and Bewestersheldt in Zealand, to the president and council of Friese, and to the Escoulet of Mechelen, to the president and members of the council of Utrecht, and to all other justiciaries and officers whom it may concern, to the lieutenants all and every of them, to cause this our ordinance to be published and proclaimed throughout their respective jurisdictions, in the usual places appointed for that purpose, that none may plead ignorance. And to cause our said ordinance to be observed inviolably, punishing the offenders impartially and without delay; for so it is found expedient for the public good. And, for better maintaining all and every article hereof, we give to all and every one of you, by express command, full power and authority. In witness whereof we have hereunto set our hands and seals, dated in our assembly at the Hague, the six and twentieth day of July, 1581, indorsed by the orders of the states-general, and signed J. De Asseliers.

Glossary

Escoulet of Mechelen: governing body of this small region of southern Holland

ipso jure: automatically (literally: by the law itself)

king of Spain: Philip II

Zealand: misspelling of Zeeland, the Dutch province comprising a strip of coastline that borders on Belgium

Document Analysis

The Dutch Declaration of Independence begins with a lengthy exposition detailing the abuses of the Spanish king, Philip II, and the historical circumstances that led to the signing of the document. This is followed by the "declaration of independence" per se, indicating that the duke of Anjou agreed to function as the Netherlands' monarch, listing specific ways in which Spanish influence was to be eliminated, and outlining provisions for the governance of the provinces.

The first seven paragraphs of the declaration effectively constitute a preamble, although the section is not specifically identified as such. In the preamble, the Dutch rebels outline in detail the historical circumstances that led to their renunciation of Spanish rule. After a very brief introduction, the document opens with harsh criticism of Spain's King Philip. Using traditional Christian imagery, the document compares the king to a shepherd and the Netherlands to his flock. Paragraph 2 argues that a king is supposed to look to the welfare of his flock. In contrast, Philip has subjected the Dutch to oppression, slavery, and tyranny and has infringed upon "their ancient customs and privileges." Accordingly, the Dutch have decided to "disallow his authority" and choose another prince to rule over them. They have been forced to take this step because their "humble petitions and remonstrances" to the king have been ignored. The paragraph asserts that the provinces accept a ruler only "upon certain conditions, which he swears to maintain"; if the prince violates these conditions, "he is no longer sovereign."

In a small gesture of political goodwill, the third paragraph casts the blame for the current circumstances less on the king and more on his "evil counselors," who, according to the document, wanted to exploit the Netherlands for their own gain, as they had in other realms. Nevertheless, the king is culpable because he listened to those counselors and took steps to subdue the Netherlands. The paragraph makes reference to the Spanish Inquisition, which locally was part of a broad effort to subjugate the Dutch by imposing church authorities on them. The fourth paragraph continues this theme, referring to the Inquisition as being "as dreadful and detested in these provinces as the worst of slavery." The document then makes reference to various petitions for religious toleration submitted by the nobles to Margaret of Parma, Philip's appointed governor of the Netherlands. Margaret, born in 1522, was Charles V's illegitimate daughter and became the duchess of Parma, in Italy, when she married Ottavio Farnese, the duke of Parma, who happened to be Pope Paul III's grandson. (The duke was just thirteen at the time, while Margaret was just sixteen—and this was her second marriage.) Philip responded to the nobles' petitions with more oppression through the Inquisition, which was charged with enforcing the doctrines enunciated at the Council of Trent—a Catholic ecumenical council that ran from 1545 to 1563 and whose primary purpose was to answer and resist Protestant heresy.

The fifth paragraph makes reference to the events that took place in 1566 and the immediate aftermath. Yet another petition for religious toleration was submitted to Margaret and, through her, to the Spanish king. Envoys were dispatched to seek relief from the king, but the king, rather than receiving them to discuss the matter and find common ground, declared that anyone who had taken part in the effort to remonstrate with him was a rebel and an outlaw, subject to punishment by death and the confiscation of his estates. It was at this point that the king empowered the duke of Alba (spelled Alva in the document), who cruelly enforced the Inquisition and later boasted that he had put to death over eighteen thousand men. Alba's rule became prominent in the so-called Black Legend, a term coined in 1914 by the Spanish writer Julián Juderías to refer to the reputation of the Spanish during the sixteenth century as cruel, oppressive, tyrannical, and intolerant. Paragraph 6 continues to outline Alba's abuses. Because so many people had been executed, there would have been little reason to send an invading army into the Netherlands, yet such an army did invade under Alba's generalship with the purpose of ruling the country as tyrannically as Spain ruled the "Indies," or its colonies in the New World. The document states that throughout all this turmoil, the people of the Netherlands yet tried to find ways to submit themselves to the king and treat his representative with courtesy. In response, they were subjected to conquest, violence, and executions.

The seventh and final paragraph of the preamble lists numerous other abuses. Dutch nobles, including William of Orange and "diverse gentlemen," were forced to flee into exile, and their lands were then confiscated by the Spanish. Spanish soldiers were quartered in people's houses. Dutch citizens were forced to pay taxes for the construction of military posts; the "tenth penny" was a 10 percent tax levied on merchandise. German mercenaries were brought into the Netherlands, again with the purpose of waging war and denying the Dutch their traditional liberties.

Having catalogued the abuses of the Spanish king, the document states in paragraph 8 that the provinces have "more than sufficient reason to renounce the King of Spain, and seek some other powerful and more gracious prince to take us under his protection." In paragraph 9, still more abuses are listed. Reference is made to Don Juan of Austria, yet another illegitimate child of Charles V. Don Juan was a military commander who was sent to the Netherlands to fulfill the role of governor-general. Like Alba, he directed a number of campaigns that led to the sacking of various Dutch cities and the execution of large numbers of rebels, until his death in 1578. His mandate in the Netherlands was to disrupt and destroy the alliance created by the Pacification of Ghent of 1576. Again, the document emphasizes that efforts were made to secure peace, particularly through the Congress of Cologne, convened in 1579. Although it was mediated by Pope Gregory XIII, the congress was unsuccessful; again, Spain refused to back down, to the extent that a price was put on William of Orange's head.

Paragraph 10 constitutes the actual declaration of independence from Spanish rule. The authors, representing "the greater part of the United Provinces," proclaim that the Dutch are renouncing their allegiance to the Spanish king, who "has forfeited, ipso jure, all hereditary right to the sovereignty of those countries." None of the members of the States-General aligned with the document would thenceforth recognize the authority of the Spanish king. All inhabitants of the Low Countries, including civil servants, the nobility, and the common people, were relieved from their oaths of allegiance to Spain. The document then indicates that the duke of Anjou—François, the youngest son of King Henry II of France—agreed to accept sovereignty over the Netherlands, replacing the authority of Archduke Matthias, a member of the House of Habsburg who had succeeded the duke of Alba but had since resigned his position as governor of the Netherlands (to later become Holy Roman Emperor). The duke of Anjou never proved popular in the Netherlands, holding but limited power; he died in 1584.

The remaining paragraphs outline the specific political steps that the rebellious provinces were taking. Paragraph 11 establishes a council that was to govern the affairs of the Netherlands until the duke of Anjou could assume his responsibilities. Paragraph 12 turns to specific issues of governance, such as the coining of money, justice, financial affairs, and the like. Paragraph 13 gives specifics relating to the establishment, membership, and powers of the president and governing council.

Essential Themes

The Dutch Declaration of Independence by no means brought peace to the United Provinces. Through the 1580s, Spain continued to send troops to the Netherlands. Yet Spanish forces were being stretched thin; they continued to fight Islam in the Mediterranean, and the Spanish Armada was defeated by the British navy in 1588—just as the northern provinces of the Netherlands were building up their own navy. Spain was virtually bankrupt, and the Spanish people, burdened with high taxes and war casualties, grew increasingly unwilling to back the war in the Netherlands. Finally, Spain capitulated and agreed to a suspension of hostilities at Antwerp in 1609, a treaty known as the Twelve Years' Truce. War erupted again, however, in 1621 over issues of religious toleration—of Protestants in the Catholic south and Catholics in the Protestant north—and sea trade routes. In 1639 the Dutch dealt the Spanish a decisive defeat in the last major campaign of the Eighty Years' War. The war officially ceased with the 1648 Treaty of Münster, which ended Spanish control over the Netherlands. This treaty was part of the larger realignment in Europe brought about by the Treaty of Westphalia, which also ended the Thirty Years' War—a complex war between Catholics and Protestants in the Holy Roman Empire that engulfed most of Europe.

Ultimately, the Dutch Revolt and the Dutch Declaration of Independence would have a far-reaching impact on Europe. The Dutch Revolt essentially challenged the divine right of kings to rule. As of 1648 the Netherlands was no longer a monarchy, a circumstance that sowed seeds of discontent with monarchial rule throughout the continent. The ultimate results of these antiroyalist sentiments were the decline of the Spanish Empire, the English Civil Wars of the mid-seventeenth century, and the French Revolution of the late eighteenth century. It has also been argued that the Dutch Declaration of Independence, read by Thomas Jefferson, had a significant effect on the crafting of the American Declaration of Independence of 1776.

The audience for the Dutch Declaration of Independence was threefold. First was the Spanish king, Philip II. The declaration represented the northern provinces' formal renunciation of the authority of the king to rule in the Netherlands. A second audience, of course, consisted of the citizens of the northern provinces, including everyone from minor nobility through the merchant class to peasants. A final audience was international. The Dutch rebels needed aid, in the forms of manpower, finances, and supplies for the ongoing Dutch Revolt as well as political or royal leadership; the need for the latter would become even more pressing upon the assassination of William of Orange three years later. Although they eventually became a republic, their initial instinct was to have the country ruled by a monarch. For these reasons, France's duke of Anjou, England's Queen Elizabeth I, the Turkish Ottoman Empire, and other international figures and states were a significant part of the audience.

—Michael J. O'Neal, PhD

Bibliography and Additional Reading

Arnade, Peter. *Beggars, Iconoclasts, and Civic Patriots: The Political Culture of the Dutch Revolt.* Ithaca, N.Y.: Cornell University Press, 2008.

Darby, Graham, ed. *The Origins and Development of the Dutch Revolt.* London: Routledge, 2001.

Geyl, Pieter. *History of the Dutch-Speaking Peoples, 1555–1648.* London: Phoenix Press, 2001.

———. *The Revolt of the Netherlands, 1555–1609.* Lanham, Md.: Rowman & Littlefield, 1980.

Israel, Jonathan I. *The Dutch Republic: Its Rise, Greatness and Fall, 1477–1806.* Oxford, U.K.: Clarendon Press, 1998.

Koenigsberger, H. G. *Monarchies, States Generals and Parliaments: The Netherlands in the Fifteenth and Sixteenth Centuries.* Cambridge, U.K.: Cambridge University Press, 2001.

Limm, Peter. *The Dutch Revolt, 1559–1648.* London: Longman, 1999.

Tracy, James D. *The Founding of the Dutch Republic: War, Finance, and Politics in Holland, 1572–1588.* Oxford, U.K.: Oxford University Press, 2008.

Van der Lem, Anton. *Revolt in the Netherlands: The Eighty Years War, 1568–1648.* Trans. Andy Brown. London: Reaktion Books, 2018.

Van Gelderen, Martin. *The Political Thought of the Dutch Revolt, 1555–1590.* Cambridge, U.K.: Cambridge University Press, 2002.

Wolff, Barbara. "Was Declaration of Independence Inspired by Dutch?" University of Wisconsin–Madison News Web site. www.news.wisc.edu/3049.

The English Revolution

The English Revolution, as it is sometimes called, is actually two distinct events in the seventeenth century separated by nearly forty years. The first is the English Civil War, which started in 1642 and itself consisted of three different, though related, wars. The second event is the Glorious Revolution of 1688, whereby Britain's King James II was deposed and replaced by his daughter Mary I and her husband William III of Orange.

The first of the English civil wars lasted until 1646. At its start, King Charles I sought to reform the Church of Scotland to align it with the Church of England, causing alarm among the Scottish Covenanters, as they were known, as well as among the Puritans in Parliament. Moreover, Charles, who had long disregarded Parliament, now aimed to raise new taxes and revive feudal debts in order to build a war chest for foreign military actions. An alliance between the Scots and Puritans in Parliament took the fight to Charles and his loyalists. In the end, the Crown's forces were defeated and Charles was taken as a prisoner.

The second civil war began after Charles escaped (November 1647) and made a separate treaty with the Covenanters to support him against his enemies in England. Several loyalist districts—Essex, Kent, and Wales—rose up on the side of the king, while the Scots invaded England. They were defeated, however, by Oliver Cromwell in 1648 and Charles I was executed. The king's son, Charles II, renewed the war with the help of royalists in Ireland and Scotland. But Cromwell defeated the Irish; he then returned to England to invade Scotland, where he crushed the Scots at Dunbar in 1650.

A second attempt was made by Charles II a year later to invade England with a Scottish army, but they were overrun at Worcester. England remained under the republican rule of Cromwell. The English Civil War is sometimes called the Puritan revolution because the victors generally belonged to or supported that religious sect, and because the king's defeat came with the abolition of the episcopacy (or bishopric). It was also a revolution that, temporarily at least, brought parliamentary democracy to the country.

The Glorious Revolution of 1688, taking place after the Restoration of the episcopy, consisted of the overthrow of the Roman Catholic James II of England. Fearing that the king might ally himself with the (Catholic) French king Louis XIV, or that his favoritism toward Catholics might provoke a civil war led by the Protestant majority, a group of English nobles invited the Dutch monarch, William III, spouse of James II's daughter Mary I, to replace the English king. When he arrived in November 1688, William saw partisans rise up on his behalf in Yorkshire and elsewhere. The Glorious Revolution was bloodless: James's forces deserted and James himself fled. When William and Mary were made joint sovereigns (1689), they accepted the idea of a bill of rights, which confirmed the authority of Parliament and opened the door to constitutional monarchy in Britain.

■ Resolves by the English House of Commons regarding King Charles I and the Authority of the People

Date: 1649
Author: English House of Commons
Genre: declaration

Summary Overview

The reign of Charles I (r. 1625–1649) was characterized by ongoing conflicts with the English Parliament. Charles was unwilling to give up his royal prerogative—governing without the advice or consent of Parliament—a stance that Parliament naturally viewed as a threat to its own authority. The resulting English Civil War (1642–1649), fought between Parliamentarians and Royalists, resulted in the trying and execution of Charles in 1649. Issued in early 1649 shortly before his execution, this Parliamentary decree gives the governing body the legal authority to dispense justice and write official laws. This decree was the first step toward putting Charles on trial, ending the monarchy, and forming a new government, the Commonwealth of England.

Defining Moment

The second son of James VI, Charles became the heir apparent after his elder brother Henry died in 1612. When James subsequently died in 1625, Charles came to power, ruling as King of England, Scotland, and Ireland. During his reign, he openly quarreled with the English Parliament, believing in his divine right to govern the country. This viewpoint, as well as Charles's intense religious devotion, was clearly inherited from his father James, who had also ruled in a ruthless manner. Charles's own increasingly agitated relationship with Parliament eventually turned public opinion against the monarch.

An early conflict between Parliament and Charles was the former's refusal to let the king levy custom taxes. Soon thereafter, Parliament attempted to impeach Charles for his handling of ongoing conflicts with Spain and France, and Charles dissolved Parliament in June 1626. Issued in 1628, the Petition of Right set out specific grievances against the king—primarily his means of collecting taxes from citizens and the imposition of martial law—and reaffirmed the Magna Carta. Further decrees and resolutions condemning the king's behavior and governance followed; as a result, from 1629 to 1640 Charles ruled without calling a Parliament.

Charles at his trial, by Edward Bower, 1649. He let his beard and hair grow long because Parliament had dismissed his barber, and he refused to let anyone else near him with a razor. Image via Wikimedia Commons. [Public domain.]

The Battle of Naseby, 14 June 1645 (artist unknown); Parliamentarian victory marked the decisive turning point in the English Civil War. Image via Wikimedia Commons. [Public domain.]

Finally, because of an ongoing conflict with the Scots, Charles convened a session of Parliament in 1640 for the purpose of raising money to fund the war. Known as the Short Parliament, this group largely condemned the conflict. And convened later that year, the so-called Long Parliament was just as critical of the king's ongoing war and erratic behavior. Charles made additional concessions during this meeting of Parliament and in the following year. For instance, Parliament's activities during this period included passing the Grand Remonstrance, which outlined grievances against the king in regard to his religious policy and appointment of councilors. Because of Parliament's efforts to impeach some of his ministers, Charles felt that his reign was threatened and reacted violently by seeking to try members of the House of Lords for treason in 1641. By this time, Parliamentary and Royalist forces had begun gathering troops as Charles fled to York in the north of England.

Fighting continued between Charles's Royalist forces, headquartered in Oxford, and Parliamentary forces centered in London over the next several years. The New Model Army in support of the Parliamentary cause began to turn the tide against Charles's forces when the king experienced a series of defeats in 1645 and 1646. Charles variously attempted to flee the country and was kept under guard by Parliamentary forces as he negotiated a settlement. But support for

Contemporary German print of Charles I's beheading outside the Banqueting House, Whitehall.

the king eventually waned, and in early 1649 Charles was brought to London to face charges of treason.

Author Biography

The English Parliament as an institution existed from at least the thirteenth century and had an ongoing complicated relationship with the reigning monarch. Early councils were comprised of knights from local shires across the country and consulted on taxation that the monarch intended. Originally a single body, Parliament was subsequently divided into a bicameral legislature composed of the House of Lords and the House of Commons. Gradually over the next two centuries, Parliament became a legislative rather than a judicial body and a parliamentary class of politicians appeared that both assented to and challenged the monarch's decisions. By the seventeenth century, divided between Tory and Whig factions, Parliament pushed for major change and revolution against the ruling monarch.

Historical Document

Resolves by the English House of Commons regarding King Charles I and the Authority of the People

4 January, 1648.

Prayers.

Court for trying the King.

MR. *Garland* reports the Amendments to the Ordinance for erecting an High Court of Justice, for Tryal of the King.

Which were this Day read the First and Second time; and, upon the Question, agreed unto: And

It is *Ordered*, That the said Ordinance be forthwith ingrossed.

Ordered, That no Copy of the Ordinance touching the King be made, or delivered forth.

[...]

Settling the Government.

Resolved, &c. That the Commons of England, in Parliament assembled, do Declare, That the People are, under God, the Original of all just Power:

And do also Declare, that the Commons of England, in Parliament assembled, being chosen by, and representing the People, have the Supreme Power in this Nation:

And do also Declare, That whatsoever is enacted, or declared for Law, by the Commons, in Parliament assembled, hath the Force of Law; and all the People of this Nation are concluded thereby, although the Consent and Concurrence of King, or House of Peers, be not had thereunto.

[...]

Document Analysis

Charles had attempted to monopolize on infighting between the New Model Army officers and the Parliament. Though the king had been unable to use these divisions for his own benefit, in late 1648 the New Model Army commander Thomas Pride dissolved the Long Parliament, Charles's main political antagonist since 1640. The remaining members were known as the Rump Parliament, and they brought charges against Charles in early 1649. Mentioned specifically in this excerpt is Augustine Garland, who was a member of Parliament from Queenborough in Kent and oversaw the committee to try and execute the king.

The decree passed in the House of Commons on January 4 gives Parliament the authority to create a high court in order to try the king. The language is specific in granting Parliament the legal authority to do so as having the binding force of law had previously only belonged to the king. In this way, the decree touches upon the nature of the relationship between a ruler and the people. According to the social contract first outlined in the Magna Carta, the latter's authority rests upon that of the other: "That the People are, under God, the Original of all just Power." Therefore, as representative of the people, the House of Commons "have the Supreme Power in this Nation." And whatever is declared by Parliament "hath the Force of Law," an authority not previously granted to the body, thus erasing the unique power of the monarch up to this point.

Essential Themes

After establishing the High Court of Justice with this document, the House of Commons conducted the trial of Charles. Yet Charles refused to recognize the authority of the High Court. And indeed, the House of Lords did not accept the Rump Parliament's actions, and only fifty-nine members of the Commons signed Charles's death warrant. Still, the king was found guilty of high treason on January 27, 1649. A scaffold was erected outside the banquet hall at the Palace of Whitehall in Westminster, the primary residence of English monarchs up to this time, and on

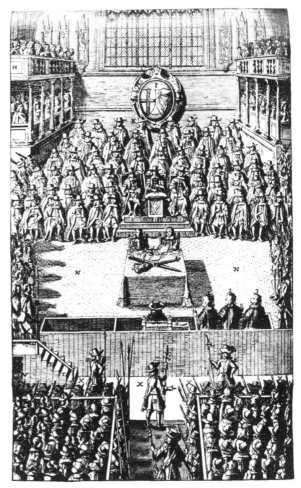

Charles (in the dock with his back to the viewer) facing the High Court of Justice, 1649. Image via Wikimedia Commons. [Public domain.]

January 30 the king was executed by beheading. Charles went to his death appealing to his affinity with his English subjects, casting himself as a "martyr" and claiming to be innocent of the charges against him.

With the monarchy abolished, a republican government was established in the country known as the Commonwealth of England (1649–1660). Though the civil war had ended, fighting continued in conflicts in Ireland and Scotland during this period. Oliver Cromwell served as Lord Protector of the country until his death in 1658. Despite his military successes, Cromwell's tenure was marked by governmental chaos and ineptitude. After a short period of rule by Cromwell's son, Parliament oversaw the restoration of the monarchy in 1660 in which Charles's son Charles II took the throne. Upon his ascension, Charles II promised many concessions to Parliament and an overall less harsh rulership than his father's, though he would have ongoing conflicts with Parliament in the 1670s.

—*Chris Bingley, PhD*

Bibliography and Additional Reading

Donagan, Barbara. *War in England 1642–1649*. Oxford: Oxford University Press, 2010.

Holmes, Clive. *Why Was Charles I Executed?* London: Hambledon Continuum, 2007.

Reeve, L. J. *Charles I and the Road to Personal Rule*. Cambridge: Cambridge University Press, 1989.

Smith, David L. *The Stuart Parliaments: 1603–1689*. London: Arnold, 1999.

Reflection on the Glorious Revolution of 1688

Date: 1740
Author: Colley Cibber
Genre: memoir

Summary Overview

This section of the memoir An Apology for the Life of Mr. Colley Cibber, *by the eponymous playwright and actor, reflects on the events of the Glorious Revolution of 1688. During this uprising, King James II of England, Ireland, and Scotland (where he was James VII) was deposed for his devout Catholicism and perceived threat to the state church of England. Considering these events, Cibber portrays James as a ruthless monarch and Catholicism as a threat to the country. According to Cibber, the united front against the king restored the British people's power, which had lain dormant since the reign of Queen Elizabeth I (r. 1558–1603). And indeed, the revolution did effect great societal change as well as the dual reign of King William III and Mary II.*

Defining Moment

After the death of his brother King Charles II, James came to power in February 1685 despite his strong devotion to Catholicism. His short reign witnessed several key moments that compounded dissatisfaction among the country's Protestant majority. First, James issued two Declarations of Indulgence that granted immunity from penal laws to those refusing to adopt Protestant practices. Second, James dissolved Parliament in England and Scotland and instead ruled by decree, giving himself immense power over the country. Third, James's wife Mary of Modena gave birth to a son in June 1688, leading to the possibility of a continuation of James's dynasty and the presence of Catholicism in the royal house for an extended period of time.

As a result, key leaders in the government, including both Whig and Tory politicians, wrote to William of Orange, the leader of the United Provinces of the Netherlands, requesting that he intervene. Deposing James was in line with the Whigs' political stance as the party was largely set against the monarchy and favored constitutional reforms with this aim. Nephew to James and married to James's daughter Mary, William sought to capitalize on James's deteriorating reputation. In addition, geopolitical events in Europe had led to growing dissatisfaction in England. French aggression and the seizure of several regions by Louis XIV encouraged William to act. He responded to the request by marching on London in November 1688,

King James II; portrait by Peter Lely. Image via Wikimedia Commons. [Public domain.]

with James soon fleeing to France as William approached.

Author Biography

Colley Cibber (1671–1757) was an English actor and playwright who wrote and acted in over twenty-five plays. Born in London, Cibber began his acting career in 1690 and quickly moved into writing. He gave himself the lead role in *Love's Last Shift; or, The Fool in Fashion* (1696), which was a sentimental comedy, a popular genre at the time. Known equally for his dramatic roles, Cibber famously adapted William Shakespeare's *Richard III* in 1700. During this period, the actor also became involved in theater management and continued into the political arena later in life, putting on plays in support of the Whigs. During his life, Cibber was largely ridiculed by his contemporaries for his bombastic personality, serving as the target of Alexander Pope's poem *The Dunciad*. Because of his role as an actor-manager, Cibber's career and life—told mainly through his autobiography, *An Apology for the Life of Mr. Colley Cibber* (1740)—serve as a source on acting and culture during this period.

William III; portrait by Godfrey Kneller, 1690. Image via Wikimedia Commons. [Public domain.]

Historical Document

Reflection on the Glorious Revolution of 1688

You must now consider me as one among those desperate Thousands, who, after a Patience sorely try'd, took Arms under the Banner of Necessity, the natural Parent of all Human Laws and Government. I question if in all the Histories of Empire there is one Instance of so bloodless a Revolution as that in *England* in 1688, wherein Whigs, Tories, Princes, Prelates, Nobles, Clergy, common People, and a Standing Army, were unanimous. To have seen all *England* of one Mind is to have liv'd at a very particular Juncture. Happy Nation! who are never divided among themselves but when they have least to complain of! Our greatest Grievance since that Time seems to have been that we cannot all govern; and 'till the Number of good Places are equal to those who think themselves qualified for them there must ever be a Cause of Contention among us. While Great Men want great Posts, the Nation will never want real or seeming Patriots; and while great Posts are fill'd with Persons whose Capacities are but Human, such Persons will never be allow'd to be without Errors; not even the Revolution, with all its Advantages, it seems, has been able to furnish us with unexceptionable Statesmen! for from that time I don't remember any one Set of Ministers that have not been heartily rail'd at; a Period long enough one would think (if all of them have been as bad as they have been call'd) to make a People despair of ever seeing a good one: But as it is possible that Envy, Prejudice, or Party may sometimes have a share in what is generally thrown upon 'em, it is not easy for a private Man to know who is absolutely in the right from what is said against them, or from what their Friends or Dependants may say in their Favour: Tho' I can hardly forbear thinking that they who have been *longest* rail'd at, must from that Circumstance shew in some sort a Proof of Capacity.——But to my History.

It were almost incredible to tell you, at the latter end of King *James's* Time (though the Rod of Arbitrary Power was always shaking over us) with what Freedom and Contempt the common People in the open Streets talk'd of his wild Measures to make a whole Protestant Nation Papists; and yet, in the height of our secure and wanton Defiance of him, we of the Vulgar had no farther Notion of any Remedy for this Evil than a satisfy'd Presumption that our Numbers were too great to be master'd by his mere Will and Pleasure; that though he might be too hard for our Laws, he would never be able to get the better of our Nature; and that to drive all *England* into Popery and Slavery he would find would be teaching an old Lion to dance.

But happy was it for the Nation that it had then wiser Heads in it, who knew how to lead a People so dispos'd into Measures for the Publick Preservation.

Here I cannot help reflecting on the very different Deliverances *England* met with at this Time and in the very same Year of the Century before: Then (in 1588) under a glorious Princess, who had at heart the Good and Happiness of her People, we scatter'd and destroy'd the most formidable Navy of Invaders that ever cover'd the Seas: And now (in 1688) under a Prince who had alienated the Hearts of his People by his absolute Measures to oppress them, a foreign Power is receiv'd with open Arms in defence of our Laws, Liberties, and Religion, which our native Prince had invaded! How widely different were these two Monarchs in their Sentiments of Glory! But, *Tantum religio potuit suadere malorum.*

When we consider in what height of the Nation's Prosperity the Successor of Queen *Elizabeth* came to this Throne, it seems amazing that such a Pile of *English* Fame and Glory, which her skilful Administration had erected, should in every following Reign down to the Revolution so unhappily moulder away in one continual Gradation of Political Errors: All which must have been avoided, if the plain Rule which that wise Princess left behind her had been observed, *viz.* That the Love of her People was the surest Support of her Throne. This was the Principle by which she so happily govern'd herself and those she had the Care of. In this she found Strength to combat and struggle thro' more Difficulties and dangerous Conspiracies than ever *English* Monarch had to cope with. At the same time that she profess'd to *desire* the People's Love, she took care that her Actions shou'd *deserve* it, without the least Abatement of her Prerogative; the Terror of which she so artfully covered that she sometimes seem'd to flatter those she was determin'd should obey. If the four following Princes had exercis'd their Regal Authority with so visible a Regard to the Publick Welfare, it were hard to know whether the People of *England* might have ever complain'd of them, or even felt the want of that Liberty they now so happily enjoy. 'Tis true that before her Time our Ancestors had many successful Contests with their Sovereigns for their *ancient Right* and *Claim* to it; yet what did those Successes amount to? little more than a Declaration that there was such a Right in being; but who ever saw it enjoy'd? Did not the Actions of almost every succeeding Reign shew there were still so many Doors of Oppression left open to the Prerogative that (whatever Value our most eloquent Legislators may have set upon those ancient Liberties) I doubt it will be difficult to fix the Period of their having a real Being before the Revolution: Or if there ever was an elder Period of our unmolested enjoying them, I own my poor Judgment is at a loss where to place it. I will boldly say then, it is to the Revolution only we owe the full Possession of what, 'till then, we never had more than a perpetually contested Right to: And, from thence, from the Revolution it is that the Protestant Successors of King *William* have found their Paternal Care and Maintenance of that Right has been the surest Basis of their Glory.

[From Colley Cibber, *An Apology for the Life of Mr. Colley Cibber,* vol. 1, chap. 3; www.gutenberg.org/files/44064/44064-h/44064-h.htm#Footnote_64]

Document Analysis

In the often irreverent and humorous memoir of his own life, Cibber writes about the revolution that had taken place early in his life. He begins by explaining the collective force of the revolution, in which "Whigs, Tories, Princes, Prelates, Nobles, Clergy, common People, and a Standing Army, were unanimous." A noted supporter of the Whigs, Cibber notes here their main antagonist group the Tories—as well as various religious officials—to show the unanimity of the revolution. The unification of such disparate groups under a common cause reflects how the revolution against James was correct and good.

This section also includes an aside about the nature of the English government in the aftermath of the revolution. Despite the positive unification of the parties involved in the revolution, the ministers put in place have been unsatisfactory. This outcome is largely due to the public reaction against the conduct of these statesmen. As Cibber explains, such is the nature of conducting oneself in the public eye: "it is not easy for a private Man to know who is absolutely in the right from what is said against them, or from what their Friends or Dependants may say in their Favour." Cibber seems to come down on neither side of the public's negative reaction, but he suggests that putting up with this sort of ridicule must speak in the politicians' favor.

Cibber equates King James's move toward Catholicism with "slavery" in this section of his memoir. But because the number of dissatisfied British citizens was so great, they were able to overcome the king's "arbitrary power," "evil," and "will and pleasure." With this imagery, King James is portrayed as ruling ruthlessly, making decisions on his own whim and without the will of the people. Cibber also uses the image of a lion, one of his favorite similes in this work, invoking the occasional national symbol of England. While the lion was often used to describe a ruthless British monarch, here Cibber co-opts the image to describe the British public refusing the will of the king.

Cibber also points back to the more distant past in order to disparage King James. Looking back exactly one hundred years, Cibber refers to the events of 1588, in which the "Princess" (Queen Elizabeth I)

Engraving of William and Mary, 1703. Image via Wikimedia Commons. [Public domain.]

fended off the invading Spanish armada. Organized by Spain's King Philip II, the fleet was to sail up the English Channel in an effort to depose Elizabeth. Instead, English vessels outmaneuvered the armada, which was mostly destroyed before it could carry out its mission. In a complete reversal, according to Cibber, James is now the one invading the country through the venue of religion, receiving the invading enemy "with open arms." The Latin quote from Lucretius is one of the most famous from this Roman poet's work, *tantum religio potuit suadere malorum*, translating as "so potent was religion in persuading to do wrong."

Cibber's characterization of Elizabeth concludes with a stark contrast to King James. Elizabeth ruled through the goodwill of the people: "At the same time that she profess'd to *desire* the People's Love, she took care that her Actions shou'd *deserve* it, without the least Abatement of her Prerogative." Her regard for the "public welfare" was not necessarily an aim of her successors over the following century. Thus, the reign of William and the aftermath of the revolution have given the people the "full Possession" of the liberty that they have only had a right to over the past century.

Essential Themes

James's flight from the country was treated as an official abdication by the government and marked the beginning of William III's reign. In early 1689, the Convention Parliament convened in order to appease William's desire to occupy the throne as quickly as possible. During this session, the Parliament drafted and ratified the Declaration of Rights, which addressed the main points of contention during James's reign, including the threats of Catholicism and expansive royal power. With this settlement, the British monarch could no longer suspend laws or have a standing army without the approval of Parliament, among other new limits.

The body that drafted this bill eventually transformed into the country's regular Parliament, and thus became its primary governing body from this point forward. William and Mary were declared king and queen together with the Declaration of Rights. But because of the Coronation Oath Act included in the Bill, they agreed to be held subject to the country's laws. In contrast to past monarchs in which laws emanated from the king or queen, here they were set apart. Thus, the Glorious Revolution and subsequent settlement is often viewed as the realization of the social contract between rulers and the people. In this case, the will of the people manifested in the power of Parliament and the limits it could impose on the monarchy.

—*Chris Bingley, PhD*

Bibliography and Additional Reading

De Krey, Gary S. *Restoration and Revolution in Britain: A Political History of the Era of Charles II and the Glorious Revolution*. London: Palgrave Macmillan, 2007.

Koon, Helene. *Colley Cibber: A Biography*. Lexington: University Press of Kentucky, 2015.

McGirr, Elaine M. *Partial Histories: A Reappraisal of Colley Cibber*. London: Palgrave Macmillan, 2016.

Miller, John. *The Glorious Revolution*. 2nd ed. London: Routledge, 1997.

The American Revolution

The American Revolution, which unfolded between 1775 and 1783, was a struggle by which the thirteen colonies that would became the United States won independence from Britain. By the time of the war's outbreak, differences in life, thought, and especially economic interests had developed between the colonies and the home country. The British government tried to regulate colonial commerce to its own advantage, and in so doing sparked colonial opposition. The Stamp Act, passed by Parliament in 1765, produced an outcry among the colonists, who labeled it an act of "taxation without representation." The Townsend Acts (1767) led to such violent incidents as the Boston Massacre (1770), the burning of the HMS *George* (1772), and the Boston Tea Party (1773). In 1774 Britain responded with the punitive Intolerable Acts. While the colonists petitioned the king for redress of their grievances, they also convened the Continental Congress to organize their efforts.

Fighting broke out on April 9, 1775, at Lexington and Concord, followed by the taking of Fort Ticonderoga from the British along with the Battle of Bunker Hill and the unsuccessful colonial campaign in Quebec. On July 4, 1776, the Continental Congress adopted the Declaration of Independence and appointed George Washington to lead the Continental Army. Many colonists, nonetheless, remained loyal to the British crown. The colonial victory in the Saratoga campaign (1777) helped forge a French-American alliance, which brought vital aid to the Americans. Following the awful ordeal of Washington's army at Valley Forge (1777–1778) and the inconclusive Battle of Monmouth (1778), the war shifted to the South during the Carolina campaign (1780–1781). At the close of the Yorktown campaign (1781), Britain's General Cornwallis surrendered. Two years later the Treaty of Paris formally recognized the United States as a nation.

Much of this story has been previously dealt with in other works in the Defining Documents series. (See, in particular, *The American Revolution* [2013].) In the present work, we provide a selection of key documents focused especially on the lead-up to war.

The American Revolution, despite its violence and its political and historical importance, was not a revolution that produced radical or total change. It was not a complete overturning of the existing political and social framework, such as later occurred with the French and Russian revolutions. Significant changes were introduced, but they were not themselves "revolutionary." What occurred was independence and political evolution rather than thoroughgoing revolution. During the conflict itself people went on working and worshiping, marrying and raising families. Many communities were not seriously disturbed by the actual fighting, and some more remote populations scarcely knew that a war was unfolding.

Even changes in the political arena were not earthshaking. In some states, notably Connecticut and Rhode Island, the war largely ratified a colonial self-rule that already existed. As British officials were ousted, they were replaced by a homegrown governing class made up exclusively of (white) male property owners of substance. The institution of slavery was permitted to continue. It would take nearly a century for that issue to cause another violent conflict, and a century after that (i.e., in the 1960s) for radical social change to occur.

John Hancock's Boston Massacre Oration

Date: March 5, 1774
Author: John Hancock
Genre: address; speech

"[H]ow dare you tread upon the earth which has drunk in the blood of slaughtered innocents, shed by your wicked hands? How dare you breathe that air which wafted to the ear of heaven the groans of those who fell a sacrifice to your accursed ambition?"

Summary Overview

As Great Britain and her American colonies moved toward revolution in the 1770s, Boston represented ground zero. Radical Bostonians, led by Samuel Adams, gradually gained influence in the city and fostered firm resistance to royal governance. With high-profile events such as the annual commemoration of the Boston Massacre (March 5, 1770), they introduced and sustained a public discourse about independence. However, it was moderates and not radicals who would eventually make an independence movement viable, and chief among the Massachusetts moderates was John Hancock. For years, the wealthy merchant had masterfully negotiated the line between loyalty and resistance to the Crown, but as tensions mounted and his commercial interests suffered, he was forced to choose a side. With his commemorative oration in 1774, Hancock asserted leadership over the rebellion in Massachusetts. Framing a practical agenda for moving forward, he called for the rejection of tyranny and the creation of political and military infrastructure—a continental congress and colonial militias—that made revolution possible.

Defining Moment

When Hancock arrived at the Old South Meeting House on Massacre Day in 1774, the building could not contain the crowds. Citizens filled every available corner and flowed out the doors into the streets. Such was the interest in hearing Hancock speak that the venue had been changed at the last minute from the stately Faneuil Hall, which proved too small to accommodate the audience. Dressed in velvet and wearing a powdered wig that marked him as an aristocrat, Hancock stepped down from his elaborate car-

John Hancock; portrait by John Singleton Copley, c. 1770-72. Image via Wikimedia Commons. [Public domain.]

The Bloody Massacre, *Paul Revere's engraving of The Boston Massacre, 1770, hand-colored by artist Christian Remick. Image via Wikimedia Commons. [Public domain.]*

riage and made his way to pulpit at the front of the church.

Four years had passed since five colonists had died at the hands of British troops in what came to be called the Boston Massacre. Through this annual address, radicals had kept the memory of the bloody day alive. After the shootings, a trial had acquitted the commanding officer and all but two of his soldiers, and tensions in the city slowly declined. The busiest port in British America, Boston, went back to business. Yet radicals refused to forget the day when soldiers had turned guns on citizens; thus were commemorative orations annually scheduled. On March 5, 1774, the political atmosphere was more heavily charged than in previous years. Only three months before, on December 16, 1773, the Boston Tea Party had set the city on a collision course with the British Parliament and Crown. Refusing to allow tea to be unloaded on the city's docks, merchants joined radicals in resisting an import tax on what was a staple of all colonial homes. When residents, masquerading as American Indians, dumped more than three hundred chests of tea into the harbor, a line had been crossed. Anticipating retribution from Parliament and the Crown, the annual Massacre Day oration took on heightened significance. As the city awaited punishment, the citizenry debated their next move.

In the wake of the Tea Party, Hancock and other selectmen on Boston's town council would be formally charged with treason. Warrants for their arrests preceded a series of coercive measures, called the Intolerable Acts, which were designed to force the city into submission. On Massacre Day 1774, as the wealthy merchant entered the meeting house and took his place at the rostrum, his future and that of his city had never been so uncertain. The crowd looked to Hancock for direction; through the commemorative oration, he unequivocally set a new course.

Author Biography

John Hancock was born on January 23, 1737, south of Boston at Quincy, Massachusetts, where his father served as a Congregational minister. When his father died suddenly, his mother moved her children to the home of their paternal grandfather, an aging but influential minister in Lexington. Hancock did not remain in his grandfather's home for very long. At the age of seven, he went to Boston to live with his uncle and aunt, Thomas and Lydia Hancock. Childless, they raised the boy as their own. Thomas Hancock had amassed a fortune through ship building, trans-Atlantic trade, retail, and real estate, and he provided his nephew with a luxurious life. Educated at the Boston Latin School before attending Harvard University, Hancock emerged from formal education to begin his business training. Over a dozen years, Thomas Hancock groomed his nephew to run the business he would eventually inherit—the House of Hancock, Boston's most successful commercial operation. With mentoring, Hancock learned every aspect of the family business. He worked in offices at the docks in Boston and spent a year abroad building commercial relationships in London.

At his uncle's death, Hancock continued to expand the operations and investments of the House of Hancock. The business had historically earned huge profits by outfitting British soldiers and sailors who waged battles with the French on both sides of the Atlantic. Yet perpetual British-French conflict was costly, and by the 1760s, parliament instituted a series of tax-based revenue schemes to reduce imperial debt. In the American colonies, new taxes on British imports produced public resentment toward the royal government and the local merchant class.

As Massachusetts moved toward open rebellion, Hancock was regularly elected to the colony's legislature and Boston's town council. In the aftermath of the Tea Party, parliament enacted the Coercive Acts, or Intolerable Acts, and issued arrest warrants for Hancock and other city leaders. Though resolution of the conflict was in Hancock's best interest as a merchant, he acted on behalf of the broader community. Offering leadership and financial support to the emerging revolution, he became president of the Massachusetts Provincial Congress, a rebel body that illegally operated in opposition to the colony's royal government. By 1775, after the first shots of the war were fired at Lexington and Concord on April 19, Hancock assumed the presidency of the Second Continental Congress at Philadelphia. There in 1776, he boldly affixed his now famous signature to the Declaration of Independence. A national hero, Hancock remained president of the Second Continental Congress until November 1777, and spent much of his personal fortune on the war effort. Elected governor of the State of Massachusetts in 1780, he served in that office twice, for a combined ten years, until his death in 1793.

Historical Document

John Hancock's Boston Massacre Oration

Men, Brethren, Fathers, and Fellow-Countrymen:

The attentive gravity; the venerable appearance of this crowded audience; the dignity which I behold in the countenances of so many in this great assembly; the solemnity of the occasion upon which we have met together, joined to a consideration of the part I am to take in the important business of this day, fill me with an awe hitherto unknown, and heighten the sense which I have ever had of my unworthiness to fill this sacred desk. But, allured by the call of some of my respected fellow-citizens, with whose request it is always my greatest pleasure to comply, I almost forgot my want of ability to perform what they required. In this situation I find my only support in assuring myself that a generous people will not severely censure what they know was well intended, though its want of merit should prevent their being able to applaud it. And I pray that my sincere attachment to the interest of my country, and the hearty detestation of every design formed against her liberties, may be admitted as some apology for my appearance in this place....

But I forbear, and come reluctantly to the transactions of that dismal night, when in such quick succession we felt the extremes of grief, astonishment, and rage; when heaven in anger, for a dreadful moment, suffered hell to take the reins; when Satan, with his chosen band, opened the sluices of New England's blood, and sacrilegiously polluted our land with the dead bodies of her guiltless sons! Let this sad tale of death never be told without a tear; let not the heaving bosom cease to burn with a manly indignation at the barbarous story, through the long tracts of future time; let every parent tell the shameful story to his listening children until tears of pity glisten in their eyes, and boiling passions shake their tender frames; and whilst the anniversary of that ill-fated night is kept a jubilee in the grim court of pandemonium, let all America join in one common prayer to heaven that the inhuman, unprovoked murders of the fifth of March, 1770, planned by Hillsborough, and a knot of treacherous knaves in Boston, and executed by the cruel hand of Preston and his sanguinary coadjutors, may ever stand in history without a parallel. But what, my countrymen, withheld the ready arm of vengeance from executing instant justice on the vile assassins? Perhaps you feared promiscuous carnage might ensue, and that the innocent might share the fate of those who had performed the infernal deed. But were not all guilty? Were you not too tender of the lives of those who came to fix a yoke on your necks? But I must not too severely blame a fault, which great souls only can commit. May that magnificence of spirit which scorns the low pursuits of malice, may that generous compassion which often preserves from ruin, even a guilty villain, forever actuate the noble bosoms of Americans! But let not the miscreant host vainly imagine that we feared their arms. No; them we despised; we dread nothing but slavery. Death is the creature of a poltroon's brains; 'tis immortality to sacrifice ourselves for the salvation of our country. We fear not death. That gloomy night, the pale-faced moon, and the affrighted stars that hurried through the sky, can witness that we fear not death. Our hearts which, at the recollection, glow with rage that four revolving years have scarcely taught us to restrain, can witness that we fear not death; and happy it is for those who dared to insult us, that their naked bones are not now piled up an everlasting lasting monument of Massachusetts' bravery. But they retired, they fled, and in that flight they found their only safety. We then expected that the hand of public justice would soon inflict that punishment upon the murderers, which, by the laws of God and man, they had incurred. But let the unbiased pen of a Robertson, or perhaps of some equally famed American, conduct this trial before the great tribunal of succeeding generations. And though the murderers may escape the just resentment of an enraged people; though drowsy justice, intoxicated by the poisonous draught prepared for her cup, still nods upon her rotten seat, yet be assured such complicated crimes will meet their due reward....

Ye dark designing knaves, ye murderers, parricides! how dare you tread upon the earth which has drunk in the blood of slaughtered innocents, shed by your wicked hands? How dare you breathe that air which wafted to the ear of heaven the groans of those who fell a sacrifice to your accursed ambition? But if the laboring earth cloth not expand her jaws; if the air you breathe is not commissioned to be the minister of death; yet, hear it and tremble! The eye of heaven penetrates the darkest chambers of the soul, traces the leading clue through all the labyrinths which your industrious folly has devised; and you, however you may have screened yourselves from human eyes, must be arraigned, must lift your hands, red with the blood of those whose death you have procured, at the tremendous bar of God!

But I gladly quit the gloomy theme of death, and leave you to improve the thought of that important day when our naked souls must stand before that Being from whom nothing can be hid....

But since standing armies are so hurtful to a State, perhaps my countrymen may demand some substitute, some other means of rendering us secure against the incursions of a foreign enemy. But can you be one moment at a loss? Will not a well-disciplined militia afford you ample security against foreign foes? We want not courage; it is discipline alone in which we are exceeded by the most formidable troops that ever trod the earth. Surely our hearts flutter no more at the sound of war than did those of the immortal band of Persia, the Macedonian phalanx, the invincible Roman legions, the Turkish janissaries, the gens d'armes of France, or the well-known grenadiers of Britain. A well-disciplined militia is a safe, an honorable guard to a community like this, whose inhabitants are by nature brave, and are laudably tenacious of that freedom in which they were born. From a well-regulated militia we have nothing to fear; their interest is the same with that of the State. When a country is invaded, the militia are ready to appear in its defense; they march into the field with that fortitude which a consciousness of the justice of their cause inspires; they do not jeopard their lives for a master who considers them only as the instruments of his ambition, and whom they regard only as the daily dispenser of the scanty pittance of bread and water. No; they fight for their houses, their lands, for their wives, their children; for all who claim the tenderest names, and are held dearest in their hearts; they fight pro aris et focis, for their liberty, and for themselves, and for their God. And let it not offend if I say that no militia ever appeared in more flourishing condition than that of this province now cloth; and pardon me if I say, of this town in particular. I mean not to boast; I would not excite envy, but manly emulation. We have all one common cause; let it, therefore, be our only contest, who shall most contribute to the security of the liberties of America. And may the same kind Providence which has watched over this country from her infant state still enable us to defeat our enemies! I cannot here forbear noticing the signal manner in which the designs of those who wish not well to us have been discovered. The dark deeds of a treacherous cabal have been brought to public view. You now know the serpents who, whilst cherished in your bosoms, were darting the envenomed stings into the vitals of the constitution. But the representatives of the people have fixed a mark on these ungrateful monsters, which, though it may not make them so secure as Cain of old, yet renders them, at least, as infamous. Indeed, it would be effrontive to the tutelar deity of this country even to despair of saving it from all the snares which human policy can lay....

Surely you never will tamely suffer this country to be a den of thieves. Remember, my friends, from whom you sprang. Let not a meanness of spirit, unknown to those whom you boast of as your fathers, excite a thought to the dishonor of your mothers I conjure you, by all that is dear, by all that is honorable, by all that is sacred, not only that ye pray, but that ye act; that, if necessary, ye fight, and even die, for the prosperity of our Jerusalem. Break in sunder, with noble disdain, the bonds with which the Philistines have bound you. Suffer not yourselves to be betrayed, by the soft arts of luxury and effeminacy, into the pit digged for your destruction. Despise the glare of wealth. That people who pay greater respect to a wealthy villain than to an honest, upright man in poverty, almost deserve to be enslaved; they plainly show that wealth, however it may be acquired, is, in their esteem, to be preferred to virtue.

But I thank God that America abounds in men who are superior to all temptation, whom nothing can divert from a steady pursuit of the interest of their country, who are at once its ornament and safeguard. And sure I am, I should not incur your displeasure, if I paid a respect, so justly due to their much-honored characters, in this place. But when I name an Adams, such a numerous host of fellow-patriots rush upon my mind, that I fear it would take up too much of your time, should I attempt to call over the illustrious roll. But your grateful hearts will point you to the men; and their revered names, in all succeeding times, shall grace the annals of America. From them let us, my friends, take example; from them let us catch the divine enthusiasm; and feel, each for himself, the godlike pleasure of diffusing happiness on all around us; of delivering the oppressed from the iron grasp of tyranny; of changing the hoarse complaints and bitter moans of wretched slaves into those cheerful songs, which freedom and contentment must inspire. There is a heartfelt satisfaction in reflecting on our exertions for the public weal, which all the sufferings an enraged tyrant can inflict will never take away; which the ingratitude and reproaches of those whom we have saved from ruin cannot rob us of. The virtuous asserter of the rights of mankind merits a reward, which even a want of success in his endeavors to save his country, the heaviest misfortune which can befall a genuine patriot, cannot entirely prevent him from receiving.

I have the most animating confidence that the present noble struggle for liberty will terminate gloriously for America. And let us play the man for our God, and for the cities of our God; while we are using the means in our power, let us humbly commit our righteous cause to the great Lord of the Universe, who loveth righteousness and hateth iniquity. And having secured the approbation of our hearts, by a faithful and unwearied discharge of our duty to our country, let us joyfully leave our concerns in the hands of him who raiseth up and pulleth down the empires and kingdoms of the world as he pleases; and with cheerful submission to his sovereign will, devoutly say: "Although the fig tree shall not blossom, neither shall fruit be in the vines; the labor of the olive shall fail, and the field shall yield no meat; the flock shall be cut off from the fold, and there shall be no herd in the stalls; yet we will rejoice in the Lord, we will joy in the God of our salvation."

Glossary

coadjutors: assistants, collaborators

effrontive: offensive

gens d'armes: French cavalry

grenadiers: an elite infantry regiment in the British army

Hillsborough: Lord Hillsborough, Marquess of Downshire (1718–1793), British secretary of state for the colonies

iniquity: injustice

knaves: dishonest people

miscreant: a villain

parricide: one who kills his own father

Philistine: seen as a natural enemy; lacking in cultural values

poltroon: a coward

Preston: Captain Thomas Preston (c. 1722–98), a British officer present at the Boston Massacre

pro aris et focis: Latin phrase meaning "for god and country"; literal translation is "for altars and hearth"

public weal: the wellbeing of the community

sluices: channels that carry liquid

Turkish janissaries: soldiers of the Ottoman Empire

Document Analysis

John Hancock's commemoration of the Boston Massacre came exactly four years after five Bostonians died at the hands of British soldiers. Joining a tradition established on the one year anniversary of that event, Hancock took his turn standing before a large crowd to condemn the captain, soldiers, and parliamentary policies that had produced bloodshed in the streets of the city. Yet while the explicit focus of the oration was the tragedy of 1770, the implicit message responded to a more recent event. Only three months separated the 1774 observation of Massacre Day from a December 1773 evening when frustrated Bostonians had dumped a boatload of tea into the city's harbor. Although parliament's response to the Tea Party was not yet known—at the time, trans-Atlantic communication took months—rumors of impending arrests and brutal retribution were widely circulating in Boston. With nervous speculation thick in the air, Hancock used the opportunity to outline a new course of action. As much as a commemorative reflection on the past, his address was a provocative assessment of the present and a proactive agenda for the future.

A Call for Organized Resistance

While condemning British Parliament in his speech, Hancock focuses much of his anger on the troops sent to enforce its policies. He recounts the massacre but makes clear references to the troops still occupying the city center—a force that would certainly increase in the wake of the Tea Party. Questioning the use of a standing army during peacetime, he catalogs soldiers' "barbarous" acts in the city. British troops in Boston had arrived not to protect the public against a foreign enemy, he rails, but to act against citizens. As they were not from Massachusetts, they did not understand the social, economic, and political climate in the colony. In the eyes of Hancock, such men were nothing more than paid mercenaries who followed orders for a "scanty pittance of bread and water." Led by a commander who manipulated "them only as the instruments of his ambition," they knew nothing of local grievances. Fighting not for God and country—"pro aris et focis"—but for a salary, they were prone to committing abuse against the public. Hancock collectively equates officers, soldiers, and the politicians who sent them to Boston, with Satan.

Recounting the massacre and the ongoing "shameful" crimes committed by the troops, Hancock makes the case for coordinated defensive action by the colonists. More than a year before the first shots of the American Revolution were fired, he calls for the establishment and expansion of colonial militias for the protection of local communities. Previewing a near future, when the region's militias would band together to fight a powerful standing army, he tells locals to be on guard. Anticipating harsh retribution for the Tea Party, the colonists had to be strong and courageous. They should not fear death, Hancock asserts, but the slavery of tyranny. Instilling confidence for what was to come, he articulates the strengths of the citizen militia over the professional army they would face. Local troops had the courage of the most celebrated armies of history—the Persians, Macedonians, Romans, Ottomans, French, and British—because justice was on their side. In defense of family, property, and community, colonial militias were not "instruments" of someone else's ambition but defenders of liberty.

In rallying support for an impending fight, Hancock recognizes the need for leadership to coordinate resistance. Militias would stand ready to protect local communities, but in preparing to face a standing army, communication and coordination could not be left to chance. Under the influence of radicals like Samuel Adams, mob violence had become commonplace in Boston, but Hancock hoped to avoid it; it could do more harm than good. Advocating a more moderate course than what radicals were advocating, Hancock celebrates the benefits of restraint. Reviewing Bostonians' immediate reaction to the massacre, he emphasizes that the restraint they had shown gave them moral superiority over the soldiers. Such superiority was a powerful psychological weapon that should not be forfeited by the vengeful acts of a reactionary mob. Though the temptations were great to unleash the "hand of public justice," rage over abuses by soldiers and parliament had to be directed effectively. If the colonists acted in the moment without building consensus among them, the advantage of moral superiority would be lost. If, on the other hand, they coordinated their response and restrained angry mobs, "the great tribunal of succeeding generations" would validate their actions. Complementing his endorsement of local militias, Hancock also suggests the organization of a continental congress to coordinate the broader American response to the looming crisis. In doing so, he provides a blueprint for building the military and political infrastructure that would make a revolutionary movement viable.

Ultimately, the success of that revolution would not have been possible without the military and political infrastructure that Hancock encourages in his oration. Soon, community militias and the Continental Congress coordinated their efforts, and in doing so, they brought down one of the world's most powerful standing armies. Also crucial to the victory, however, was the emergence of an American identity among individuals in each of the thirteen British colonies. Once a majority began to view themselves as distinctly American, cultural bonds to Britain and loyalty to the Crown weakened. As citizens of the colonies recognized their common "American" interests, a declaration of political independence became possible. Hancock's oration grounds a common American identity in commitment to freedom, justice, and the common good. Repeated references to American geography, character, and history punctuate the address, demonstrating how American identity was emerging in public discourse. For example, Hancock tells his audience: "let all America join in one common prayer." Though not a nation, America was the land they loved and the "country" that united them. A "noble" people, Americans were born into freedom; "the liberties of America" were their common cause and they were willing to sacrifice "and even die, for the prosperity" of it.

Reacting to British Taxation

Tensions between British Parliament and the colonies had been mounting since the mid-1760s, and they gradually fostered American identity. In the wake of the Seven Years' War (1756–63) in Europe and its counterpart, the French and Indian War, in North America, Britain's economy suffered. Typical of wartime, economic production in key areas had increased dramatically as troops on both sides of the Atlantic were outfitted and provisioned for battle. Merchants who held contracts to gather and transport supplies to battle zones profited handsomely during the war, and Boston's House of Hancock was among the greatest beneficiaries of the conflict. Yet economic downturn came with the war's end as production orders slowed and businesses attempted to adapt to changing markets. Temporarily at least, many producers and shippers faced high economic uncertainty. Significantly, as postwar commerce dropped, so too, did collections of tax revenues by the British government. With the national treasury heavily in debt after years of warfare and with tax revenues declining, Parliament looked in desperation for new revenue streams from the American colonies.

The Sugar Act of 1764 targeted the smuggling of molasses from which colonists made rum. The legislation actually lowered the existing tax on molasses in an attempt to increase compliance, but it simultaneously banned importation of the sugary syrup from anywhere but British colonies. For merchants like Hancock, who bought molasses from Spanish and French colonies in the Caribbean and were remarkably successful in avoiding payment of import taxes, the measure constituted a serious restriction on trade and a limitation on profits. For the consuming public, decreased smuggling and more effective tax collection drove the price of the liquor upward and created tremendous resentment. Subsequently, the Stamp Act of 1765 created taxes on a variety of legal documents that the average citizen required. Individuals, families, businesses, and estates now had to pay a royal agent to fix a stamp to their wills, bills of sale, insurance policies, and other formal papers. Like the Sugar Act, this revenue raising measure fueled anger among the colonists. That the stamps constituted a direct tax paid by individuals—as opposed to an indirect tax on imports paid by merchants—made the newer act particularly unpopular.

Opposition to the stamp tax was fierce, and mob violence was common. Creating more problems than the royal governments in Massachusetts and other colonies could handle, parliament relented and passed the Declaratory Act of 1766 to repeal the stamp taxes. In conceding defeat, however, the new act clarified that parliamentary authority over the colonies was absolute. Still searching for a revenue stream and anxious to reassert that authority, Parliament passed the Townshend Act the following year. Not surprisingly, new import taxes on paper, lead, glass, paint, and tea all met with intense opposition in Boston. Adams and the Sons of Liberty organized boycotts of targeted products and pressured merchants to sign nonimportation agreements. Merchants who continued to import these products faced boycotts and angry mobs prone to vandalism.

A few years later, as boycotts continued, the Boston Massacre resulted from growing conflict between British soldiers stationed in Boston and a general public that resented their presence. Sent to the colonies to enforce royal authority and suppress resistance to the new tax measures, the troops were treated as foreigners. They were openly harassed by the citizens, and on March 5, 1770, soldiers faced a particularly intimidating mob. Overreacting, they opened fire. After five colonists were killed—whom Hancock mentions by name in his oration—and another was severely wounded, the deaths of innocents became a rallying cry for radicals who had then grown comfortable speaking in bold words against Parliament, the king, and the injustice of the colonial relationship more generally.

In the years leading up to the outbreak of the American Revolution, customs officers and merchants in Boston were frequent targets of vandals and angry mobs. Before "taxation without representation" became the rallying cry for revolution, most colonists were simply concerned with rising prices, and they despised any agent who complied with new tax laws. As imported merchandise became the focus of parliamentary revenue schemes, merchants were caught in the middle. They had much to lose by signing nonimportation agreements, but if they did not, they faced boycotts, vandals, and decreased sales. At the same time, with new efforts by Parliament to control smuggling and with soldiers and sailors deployed to collect taxes on imports, a merchants' vessel might be seized. Livelihoods were placed in jeopardy. When one of Hancock's ships, Liberty, was seized in 1768 under charges of smuggling, his public defiance earned him the respect of many in the city. Hancock was wealthy enough to suffer occasional losses, but many fellow merchants were not. Those who paid their import taxes, stocked their shelves with boycotted goods, and grudgingly accepted Parliament's authority to levy taxes were branded traitors to the local community.

From the mid-1760s through Massacre Day 1774, both radical Bostonians and the royal governors vied for Hancock's support. Radicals courted him for his influence among the general public. Though an aristocrat, his reputation in the city was strong. Generous to the poor and philanthropic toward the community, he was embraced by the city he endowed. Radical opponents of royal rule made tremendous efforts to win Hancock to their position. Simultaneously, as conflict was increasing, the royal government also recognized Hancock's influence among merchants, radicals, and the general public; though they had been suspicious of his leanings and knew him to be a smuggler who evaded taxes, it was better to have him on their side. Repeatedly elected to the Massachusetts legislature and Boston town council, Hancock had great influence among the public. Though royal governors had more than once used their authority to reject Hancock's appointment to leadership positions in the legislature, as revolution approached his more moderate views made him more acceptable to the local representatives of the Crown.

For any who doubted it, Hancock's Massacre Day oration makes clear that his loyalties rested with the colonists of Massachusetts. He was proud to be a British subject, but his submission to the Crown was not without limits. The rights extended to subjects of the Crown were clear, and all violations had to be resisted. Regardless of how their actions might be framed by royal governors, parliamentarians or the Crown, Hancock assures the crowd of their righteousness in resisting new taxes, rejecting restrictions on commerce, and condemning repression at the hands of British soldiers. Framing contemporary British rule over Boston as tyrannical, he challenges the public to remain steadfast in opposition. Doing so constituted the "discharge of our duty to our country."

Four years after the massacre, moderate Hancock, who had earlier sought justice within and not outside British dominion, adopted the language of the radicals; though he rejected many of their tactics, his oration engages their rhetoric: "how dare you tread upon the earth which has drunk in the blood of slaughtered innocents." While stopping short of invoking independence directly, his words suggest his growing comfort with American autonomy. Following the Boston Massacre, a formal trial acquitted the commanding officer and six of the soldiers implicated in the shootings. Two others were convicted of manslaughter, but they legally escaped imprisonment and were allowed to leave the colony. Had the end of the trial not coincided with Parliament's decision to repeal much of the Townshend Act, frustrations with the judicial outcomes might have flamed continuing mob violence in the colony. But the repeal was interpreted as a victory by most Bostonians, and the city was calmed.

Though the repeal of the Townshend Act was a clear win for the colonists, one element of the original law remained: a tea tax. Colonists continuing their boycotts and nonimportation campaigns took a toll on the British economy. In reaction, parliament devised a new strategy with the Tea Act of 1773. Offering discounted prices on the product, the measure also circumvented colonial merchants like Hancock by allowing the East India Company to sell directly to colonists. Yet after years of successfully fighting new taxes, the colonists were not so easily manipulated. In refusing to allow the unloading of tea on the city's docks, they prevented the collection of the import taxes. When a standoff developed in early winter and the royal governor ordered the tea unloaded, radicals fired up crowds; they boarded a ship and dumped more than three hundred crates into the harbor. Tea was carried by currents for miles. As a merchant, Hancock was not unhappy to see the monopoly of the East India Company resisted by the consuming public or nor did he mind that their product was carried away with the tides.

Retribution for destruction of the tea, the most recent in a series of bold challenges to English authority, would come in the form of the Intolerable Acts of 1774. As Hancock began his oration on March 5, the provisions of the acts were not yet known, but all expected them to be severe. And they were. Soon, the port of Boston was closed pending reimbursement to the East India Company. The colony's legislature was officially disbanded. In addition, trials of any accused royal official or soldier could now be removed from the colony, and increased burdens were placed on the public for the quartering of troops. While these coercive measures were meant to punish Boston and Massachusetts into submission, they had the opposite effect; they solidified the resistance movement. In joining radicals like Adams and moderates like Hancock in common cause, the Intolerable Acts fueled a revolution.

Essential Themes

More than two centuries after his death, Hancock is most remembered for his elegant signature on the Declaration of Independence. The presiding officer at the Philadelphia congress that adopted the document, Hancock signed his name in large, clear script. By July 1776, he had lived under threat of arrest for years, but as his bold signature demonstrates, he had courage that matched his conviction. Later, as the Declaration of Independence assumed a revered position in American history, the name John Hancock became a synonym for the word signature.

While the efforts of Samuel Adams, John Adams, Thomas Jefferson, Patrick Henry, George Washington, and others are the subject of countless books and articles, Hancock and his revolutionary activities are less celebrated. That Hancock was not a prolific writer and that his public addresses were few helps to explain his relative absence from the historical record. Still, his leadership was crucial to the independence movement.

Boston's most successful merchant, Hancock spent much of his personal wealth financing the American Revolution, but his contribution was much more than monetary. In the aftermath of the Tea Party and with the implementation of the Intolerable Acts, the independence movement achieved critical mass as moderates embraced the radical philosophy of those such as the Sons of Liberty. To the movement, Hancock offered the skills he had developed over decades leading a massive, trans-Atlantic commercial operation. More than the radicals who had inspired resistance through agitation and mob tactics, he understood the logistics of moving people and supplies over great distances, the necessity of establishing communication lines and chains of command, and the value of establishing consensus. Reactionary violence had worked for the radicals in the narrow streets of Boston, but it would not sustain a broader war. More moderate and realistic strategies were needed.

Hancock used his Massacre Day oration to redirect rebellion in Massachusetts and beyond. Stoking colonists' anger but advocating restraint, he began to build consensus around an agenda for moving forward. Fostering American identity and articulating the infrastructure which would make victory possible, he masterfully asserted new leadership just as the rebellion moved into a more serious phase. In the weeks following his address, as the Intolerable Acts became the catalyst for the first battles of the war, fellow citizens acted on his recommendations regarding militias and a continental congress. Over the course of America's independence struggle, the experienced hand of Hancock would continue to guide the movement.

—Dave Corcoran, PhD

Bibliography and Additional Reading

Boston Massacre Historical Society. Boston Massacre Historical Society, 2008.

"The Boston Massacre." *The Coming of the American Revolution, 1764–1776*. Massachusetts Historical Society, 2008.

Boston Tea Party Ships & Museum. Historic Tours of America, n.d.

Fowler, William M. Jr. *The Baron of Beacon Hill: A Biography of John Hancock.* Boston: Houghton, 1980.

Heller, Louie R. *Early American Orations, 1760–1824.* New York: Macmillan, 1902.

Thomas, Peter D. *Tea Party to Independence: The Third Phase of the American Revolution, 1773–1776.* Oxford: Clarendon, 1991.

Unger, Harlow G. *John Hancock: Merchant King and American Patriot.* New York: Wiley, 2000.

Zobel, Hiller B. *The Boston Massacre.* W. W. Norton & Co., 1996.

Declaration of the Causes and Necessity of Taking Up Arms

Date: July 6, 1775
Author: Thomas Jefferson; John Dickinson
Genre: political tract

"Our cause is just. Our union is perfect. Our internal resources are great, and, if necessary, foreign assistance is undoubtedly attainable."

Summary Overview

During the Second Continental Congress in the American colonies in July 1775, Thomas Jefferson and John Dickinson issued their Declaration of the Causes and Necessity of Taking Up Arms. *In it, the authors took note of the deterioration of the relationship between Great Britain and the American colonies, citing what they saw as examples of British efforts to subjugate and enslave the colonists. Jefferson and Dickinson identified Parliament as the primary instigators of the conflict and appealed to King George III to intervene and help bring about peace. While they sought reconciliation with the king, they also approved the use of armed force in the pursuit of ceasing all British hostilities against the colonies.*

Defining Moment

By the 1770s, tensions between the British Empire and the American colonies had reached a fever pitch, hastened by the violent incident known as the Boston Massacre. Parliament had already approved a wide range of tax increases on colonial goods, including paper goods, tea, and sugar. Parliament also enacted a series of laws that impinged upon the liberties of colonial residents, including laws that permitted English soldiers to take up quarters in colonists' homes. Furthermore, strict measures were put into place restricting colonial trade with countries other than Great Britain. The conflict spilled onto the battlefield on April 19, 1775, when American minutemen and British troops clashed in Lexington and Concord, Massachusetts. Two months later, the two sides met again at the Battle of Bunker Hill.

Although the tensions had devolved into violent confrontations, the colonies had not yet raised a formalized military force to fight the British. In fact, no official pursuit of independence been launched by the colonists. On May 10, 1775, the Second Continental Congress met in Philadelphia to address these issues. Despite the presence of pro-independence fig-

Thomas Jefferson; portrait by Rembrandt Peele, 1801. Image via Wikimedia Commons. [Public domain.]

ures such as John Adams, Benjamin Franklin, and Thomas Jefferson, not all of the delegates were in favor of complete dissolution of the Anglo–colonial relationship. In order to appease these moderate voices, the Continental Congress opted to send a final appeal to King George III, asking him to intervene on their behalf with Parliament, whom it identified as the primary source of the tensions. That document—known as the Olive Branch Petition—was sent to the King on July 14, 1775.

As the Olive Branch Petition was being finalized, however, the Congress worked on another document. The Declaration of the Causes and Necessity of Taking Up Arms, like the Olive Branch Petition, identifies Parliament as the main instigator of the violence and bitterness between the two parties. Written by Jefferson and John Dickinson, the declaration excludes King George III from the debate in the hope that he would order Parliament to halt its anticolonial policies as requested in the Olive Branch Petition.

Meanwhile, however, the declaration states that the Continental Congress was prepared to raise weapons and forces in defense of the colonists should England continue its policies. According to the declaration, the colonists were prepared to fight for their liberties, laying down their arms only when the English government ceased its offensive policies and operations in America.

Author Biography

John Dickinson

John Dickinson was born on November 13, 1732, in Talbot County, Maryland, to a moderately wealthy family. While still a newborn, his family moved to Delaware. He was educated in Pennsylvania, where he was trained as an attorney before receiving his formal training in this field at the prestigious Temple in London. Upon his return to the colonies in 1757, he established a law practice before entering public office.

Dickinson began his political career as a member of the Delaware Assembly in 1759. In 1762, he moved over to the Pennsylvania Assembly. There, he wrote a number of articles and essays, including "Resolutions of the Stamp Act Congress" in 1765. In 1767, Dickinson wrote "Letters from a Farmer in Pennsylvania," a pivotal essay and a bold statement against what he saw as increasingly oppressive governance by England. Although he was outspoken on the English treatment of the colonists, Dickinson was also opposed to launching any sort of military offensive to resist British rule, a policy that ran counter to his devout Quaker beliefs. Instead, he advocated peaceful demonstration and civil disobedience.

In 1774 and 1775, Dickinson attended the First and Second Continental Congresses. He remained a dissenter to many of the proactive policies adopted by the pro-independence camp, refusing to sign the Declaration of Independence in 1776 (although he absented himself from the proceedings to avoid making it seem as if the declaration's adoption was not unanimous). Later, Dickinson himself joined the Del-

Portait of John Dickinson, *by Charles Wilson Peale, 1780. Image via Wikimedia Commons. [Public domain.]*

aware militia. He was elected to be President of Delaware in 1781 and would later play a major role in the writing of the Constitution of the United States. He died on February 14, 1808.

Thomas Jefferson

Born in 1743 near Charlottesville, Virginia, Thomas Jefferson came from a well-established family. He was formally educated near his home before he enrolled at the College of William and Mary, where he studied classical languages and mathematics. After graduating, he built a successful early career as an attorney.

In addition to his tenures as a magistrate and county lieutenant, Jefferson was elected to the Virginia House of Burgesses. There, he became connected with Patrick Henry and George Washington. In 1774, he wrote "A Summary View of the Rights of British America," which cemented his reputation as an individual who could eloquently present colonials issues and agendas.

In 1775, Jefferson attended the Second Continental Congress, which appointed Jefferson's colleague, Washington, as the commander in chief of the newly established Continental Army. A year later—in light of the reception of "A Summary View of the Rights of British America"—Jefferson (working with John Adams, Roger Sherman, Benjamin Franklin, and Robert Livingston) drafted the Declaration of Independence.

From 1776 until 1779, Jefferson served as a member of Virginia's House of Delegates. From 1779 to 1781, Jefferson served as Virginia's governor. He returned to the Congress in 1783 and was made the American Minister to France in 1785. Upon his 1789 return to the United States he was appointed George Washington's Secretary of State, a post he held until 1794. He was defeated by John Adams to succeed Washington as president, but was eventually elected as the nation's third president in 1800. In 1819, Jefferson founded the University of Virginia. He died in 1826.

Historical Document

Declaration of the Causes and Necessity of Taking Up Arms

A declaration by the representatives of the united colonies of North America, now met in Congress at Philadelphia, setting forth the causes and necessity of their taking up arms.

If it was possible for men, who exercise their reason to believe, that the divine Author of our existence intended a part of the human race to hold an absolute property in, and an unbounded power over others, marked out by his infinite goodness and wisdom, as the objects of a legal domination never rightfully resistible, however severe and oppressive, the inhabitants of these colonies might at least require from the parliament of Great-Britain some evidence, that this dreadful authority over them, has been granted to that body. But a reverance for our Creator, principles of humanity, and the dictates of common sense, must convince all those who reflect upon the subject, that government was instituted to promote the welfare of mankind, and ought to be administered for the attainment of that end. The legislature of Great-Britain, however, stimulated by an inordinate passion for a power not only unjustifiable, but which they know to be peculiarly reprobated by the very constitution of that kingdom, and desparate of success in any mode of contest, where regard should be had to truth, law, or right, have at length, deserting those, attempted to effect their cruel and impolitic purpose of enslaving these colonies by violence, and have thereby rendered it necessary for us to close with their last appeal from reason to arms. Yet, however blinded that assembly may be, by their intemperate rage for unlimited domination, so to sight justice and the opinion of mankind, we esteem ourselves bound by obligations of respect to the rest of the world, to make known the justice of our cause. Our forefathers, inhabitants of the island of Great-Britain, left their native land, to seek on these shores a residence for civil and religious freedom. At the expense of their blood, at the hazard of their fortunes, without the least charge to the country from which they removed, by unceasing labour, and an unconquerable spirit, they effected settlements in the distant and unhospitable wilds of America, then filled with numerous and warlike barbarians.—Societies or governments, vested with perfect legislatures, were formed under charters from the crown, and an harmonious intercourse was established between the colonies and the kingdom from which they derived their origin. The mutual benefits of this union became in a short time so extraordinary, as to excite astonishment. It is universally confessed, that the amazing increase of the wealth, strength, and navigation of the realm, arose from this source; and the minister, who so wisely and successfully directed the measures of Great-Britain in the late war, publicly declared, that these colonies enabled her to triumph over her enemies.—Towards the conclusion of that war, it pleased our sovereign to make a change in his counsels.—From that fatal movement, the affairs of the British empire began to fall into confusion, and gradually sliding from the summit of glorious prosperity, to which they had been advanced by the virtues and abilities of one man, are at length distracted by the convulsions, that now shake it to its deepest foundations.—The new ministry finding the brave foes of Britain, though frequently defeated, yet still contending, took up the unfortunate idea of granting them a hasty peace, and then subduing her faithful friends.

These colonies were judged to be in such a state, as to present victories without bloodshed, and all the easy emoluments of statuteable plunder.—The uninterrupted tenor of their peaceable and respectful behaviour from the beginning of colonization, their dutiful, zealous, and useful services during the war, though so recently and amply acknowledged in the most honourable manner by his majesty, by the late king, and by parliament, could not save them from the meditated innovations.—Parliament was influenced to adopt the pernicious project, and assuming a new power over them, have in the course of eleven years, given such decisive specimens of the spirit and consequences attending this power, as to leave no doubt concerning the effects of acquiescence under it. They have undertaken to give and grant our money without our consent, though we have ever exercised an exclusive right to dispose of our own property; statutes have been passed for extending the jurisdiction of courts of admiralty and vice-admiralty beyond their ancient limits; for depriving us of the accustomed and inestimable privilege of trial by jury, in cases affecting both life and property; for suspending the legislature of one of the colonies; for interdicting all commerce to the capital of another; and for altering fundamentally the form of government established by charter, and secured by acts of its own legislature solemnly confirmed by the crown; for exempting the "murderers" of colonists from legal trial, and in effect, from punishment; for erecting in a neighbouring province, acquired by the joint arms of Great-Britain and America, a despotism dangerous to our very existence; and for quartering soldiers upon the colonists in time of profound peace. It has also been resolved in parliament, that colonists charged with committing certain offences, shall be transported to England to be tried. But why should we enumerate our injuries in detail? By one statute it is declared, that parliament can "of right make laws to bind us in all cases whatsoever." What is to defend us against so enormous, so unlimited a power? Not a single man of those who assume it, is chosen by us; or is subject to our control or influence; but, on the contrary, they are all of them exempt from the operation of such laws, and an American revenue, if not diverted from the ostensible purposes for which it is raised, would actually lighten their own burdens in proportion, as they increase ours. We saw the misery to which such despotism would reduce us. We for ten years incessantly and ineffectually besieged the throne as supplicants; we reasoned, we remonstrated with parliament, in the most mild and decent language.

Administration sensible that we should regard these oppressive measures as freemen ought to do, sent over fleets and armies to enforce them. The indignation of the Americans was roused, it is true; but it was the indignation of a virtuous, loyal, and affectionate people. A Congress of delegates from the United Colonies was assembled at Philadelphia, on the fifth day of last September. We resolved again to offer an humble and dutiful petition to the King, and also addressed our fellow-subjects of Great-Britain. We have pursued every temperate, every respectful measure; we have even proceeded to break off our commercial intercourse with our fellow-subjects, as the last peaceable admonition, that our attachment to no nation upon earth should supplant our attachment to liberty.—This, we flattered ourselves, was the ultimate step of the controversy: but subsequent events have shewn, how vain was this hope of finding moderation in our enemies.

Several threatening expressions against the colonies were inserted in his majesty's speech; our petition, tho' we were told it was a decent one, and that his majesty had been pleased to receive it graciously, and to promise laying it before his parliament, was huddled into both houses among a bundle of American papers, and there neglected. The lords and commons in their address, in the month of February, said, that "a rebellion at that time actually existed within the province of Massachusetts-Bay; and that those concerned with it, had been countenanced and encouraged by unlawful combinations and engagements, entered into by his majesty's subjects in several of the other colonies; and therefore they besought his majesty, that he would take the most effectual measures to inforce due obediance to the laws and authority of the supreme legislature."—Soon after, the commercial intercourse of whole colonies, with foreign countries, and with each other, was cut off by an act of parliament; by another several of them were intirely prohibited from the fisheries in the seas near their coasts, on which they always depended for their sustenance; and large reinforcements of ships and troops were immediately sent over to general Gage.

Fruitless were all the entreaties, arguments, and eloquence of an illustrious band of the most distinguished peers, and commoners, who nobly and strenuously asserted the justice of our cause, to stay, or even to mitigate the heedless fury with which these accumulated and unexampled outrages were hurried on.—equally fruitless was the interference of the city of London, of Bristol, and many other respectable towns in our favor. Parliament adopted an insidious manoeuvre calculated to divide us, to establish a perpetual auction of taxations where colony should bid against colony, all of them uninformed what ransom would redeem their lives; and thus to extort from us, at the point of the bayonet, the unknown sums that should be sufficient to gratify, if possible to gratify, ministerial rapacity, with the miserable indulgence left to us of raising, in our own mode, the prescribed tribute. What terms more rigid and humiliating could have been dictated by remorseless victors to conquered enemies? in our circumstances to accept them, would be to deserve them.

Soon after the intelligence of these proceedings arrived on this continent, general Gage, who in the course of the last year had taken possession of the town of Boston, in the province of Massachusetts-Bay, and still occupied it a garrison, on the 19th day of April, sent out from that place a large detachment of his army, who made an unprovoked assault on the inhabitants of the said province, at the town of Lexington, as appears by the affidavits of a great number of persons, some of whom were officers and soldiers of that detachment, murdered eight of the inhabitants, and wounded many others....

The general, further emulating his ministerial masters, by a proclamation bearing date on the 12th day of June, after venting the grossest falsehoods and calumnies against the good people of these colonies, proceeds to "declare them all, either by name or description, to be rebels and traitors, to supercede the course of the common law, and instead thereof to publish and order the use and exercise of the law martial."—His troops have butchered our countrymen, have wantonly burnt Charlestown, besides a considerable number of houses in other places; our ships and vessels are seized; the necessary supplies of provisions are intercepted, and he is exerting his utmost power to spread destruction and devastation around him.

We have received certain intelligence, that general Carleton, the governor of Canada, is instigating the people of that province and the Indians to fall upon us....

Our cause is just. Our union is perfect. Our internal resources are great, and, if necessary, foreign assistance is undoubtedly attainable.—We gratefully acknowledge, as signal instances of the Divine favour towards us, that his Providence would not permit us to be called into this severe controversy, until we were grown up to our present strength, had been previously exercised in warlike operation, and possessed of the means of defending ourselves. With hearts fortified with these animating reflections, we most solemnly, before God and the world, declare, that, exerting the utmost energy of those powers, which our beneficent Creator hath graciously bestowed upon us, the arms we have been compelled by our enemies to assume, we will, in defiance of every hazard, with unabating firmness and perseverance, employ for the preservation of our liberties; being with one mind resolved to die freemen rather than to live slaves.

Lest this declaration should disquiet the minds of our friends and fellow-subjects in any part of the empire, we assure them that we mean not to dissolve that union which has so long and so happily subsisted between us, and which we sincerely wish to see restored.—Necessity has not yet driven us into that desperate measure, or induced us to excite any other nation to war against them.—We have not raised armies with ambitious designs of separating from Great-Britain, and establishing independent states. We fight not for glory or for conquest. We exhibit to mankind the remarkable spectacle of a people attacked by unprovoked enemies, without any imputation or even suspicion of offence. They boast of their privileges and civilization, and yet proffer no milder conditions than servitude or death.

In our own native land, in defence of the freedom that is our birthright, and which we ever enjoyed till the late violation of it—for the protection of our property, acquired solely by the honest industry of our fore-fathers and ourselves, against violence actually offered, we have taken up arms. We shall lay them down when hostilities shall cease on the part of the aggressors, and all danger of their being renewed shall be removed, and not before.

With a humble confidence in the mercies of the supreme and impartial Judge and Ruler of the Universe, we most devoutly implore his divine goodness to protect us happily through this great conflict, to dispose our adversaries to reconciliation on reasonable terms, and thereby to relieve the empire from the calamities of civil war.

Glossary

despotism: absolute political power, tyranny

garrison: body of troops located in a fort or single location

indignation: anger generated by unfair treatment

Providence: acts of God on Earth

statuteable: lawful, legal

Document Analysis

Jefferson and Dickinson begin the Declaration of the Causes and Necessity of Taking Up Arms by suggesting that, even if God had allowed for certain parties to have irresistible and total power over others, the colonies would still need validation from Great Britain's Parliament. After all, such a power is supposed to be used out of wisdom and goodness, and it had become clear in the minds of the colonists that Parliament was not acting with either concept in mind.

Instead of proceeding with benevolence, Jefferson and Dickinson say, the Parliament seems to be driven by a pursuit of power. Indeed, their declaration accuses Parliament of demonstrating an "inordinate passion" for a type of power that was not only unjustified but, according to Jefferson and Dickinson, illegal. The declaration makes this statement to demonstrate that the actions taken by Great Britain were against the tenets of the British Constitution itself. It amplifies this tone, saying that any reasonable leader within the Parliament should remain dedicated to making policy that was right, legal, and truthful, regardless of the conditions at hand.

These conditions were the grumblings of civil war between the colonies and Britain. The relationship between the two parties had clearly devolved into distrust and open conflict. Jefferson and Dickinson's declaration comments that Parliament has an obligation as the legislators of England, to pursue policies that would work to improve relations. However, the authors accuse Parliament of struggling to wrest control from the colonies instead. As the "contest" between Parliament and the colonies grew more intense and closer to a stalemate, the declaration says that Parliament is becoming desperate to end the conflict. In light of this desperation, Parliament was turning to the imposition of cruel and oppressive measures.

The declaration specifically cites Parliament, not King George III, for instigating and exacerbating the conflict. In fact, there was no mention of the king in this document. By purposely leaving the king out of the focus of the colonists' grievances, the authors leave open the door for the king to intervene and perhaps direct Parliament away from its hostile stance. In its censure of Parliament, the declaration accuses the British government of being so blinded by its "intemperate rage" for domination over the colonies that it had become willing to launch a campaign of brutality and hostility against the colonies. In spite of this campaign, the document says, the colonies had remained morally upright and respectful.

Jefferson and Dickinson remind the king of the colonies' history. More than a century earlier, the Puritans had left their native England in search of civil and religious freedom. They experienced hardships in their new home in New England, not the least of which were harsh weather and occasionally violent encounters with American Indians. They spent their personal fortunes in order to come to the New World and worked tirelessly once there in order to build a new society. They were successful, the authors say, building governmental institutions that support the colonists and, at the same time, remaining loyal to the British government.

England benefited greatly from the colonists' success. Dickinson and Jefferson state that, once the colonies were established, the British Empire had a new base from which it could launch exploration and trade missions. Also, the goods produced in the colonies added considerably to the wealth of Great Britain's economy. Furthermore, the contributions of the colonies (which included military personnel and supplies) greatly aided the British army in its efforts against the French in Canada during the French and Indian War.

However, the conclusion of the French and Indian War led the Parliament to refocus on subduing England's "faithful friends"—the colonies. Jefferson and Dickinson theorize that Parliament, which enjoyed increased power over the colonies through King George III, saw the need for this subjugation based on two facts. First, the colonies had long been willing and loyal subjects of the Crown—they would not, Parliament assumed, object to further management by the British government. Second, there was a wealth of resources in New England that could be accessed by Great Britain by increasing pressure on the colonists legally. The authors dub such a policy "statuteable plunder."

Parliament's inflammatory policies were myriad, according to Jefferson and Dickinson. For example, the British military had been given increased liberties and protections in the colonies. Under the 1765 Quartering Act, for example, British Army soldiers were allowed to stay at colonists' private residences. In 1774, the colonists' faith in the acceptable behavior of British soldiers was further shaken by a law that stated that British soldiers and officials who were accused of murder in the colonies would not be tried by the colonial judiciary—rather, they would be taken back to Britain and given what the colonists saw as mock trials with minimal punishments, if any.

Additionally, Dickinson and Jefferson accuse Parliament of collecting and spending colonial money without the consent of the New England governments. This comment refers to the number of occurrences during the 1760s and 1770s in which new taxes on tea, paper, molasses, and other products were applied. The revenues from these taxes were spent at the discretion of Parliament for the benefit of the entire Empire.

Furthermore, Parliament made a number of changes to the colonial legal structure, placing officials in key positions within the judicial system, which gave Parliament enhanced oversight over the colonial legal system. These officials' power was useful in implementing many new legal policies, such as the 1769 law that allowed colonists who were accused of treason to be extradited to Britain for prosecution and those colonists accused of smuggling and other trade-related crimes to be prosecuted in court without a jury of their peers present.

Other grievances include the accusation of political and economic manipulation, citing the 1767 suspension of the New York Assembly for refusing to comply with the Quartering Act; the extreme restrictions on the colonists' trade relationships with other nations; and the 1774 Quebec Act, which moved the border between that colony and the Ohio River, placing one of Britain's greatest rivals at the doorstep of its colonies.

Jefferson and Dickinson state that the Second Continental Congress chose to list these grievances because Parliament had effectively stripped away the colonial governments' areas of authority. The 1766 Declaratory Act was the most egregious example of this fact—this law said that the royal government retained the authority to make any and all laws for the colonies. Through this act, Parliament had been able to enact the wide range of laws and policies that rendered colonial legislatures nearly powerless. For the better part of a decade, the colonists had attempted to communicate their concerns to Parliament and the king, using respectful and "decent" language, with no positive response or changes emanating from Britain.

The response the colonists did receive was one of further heavy-handedness. Parliament sent more ships and troops to New England to address what was seen as growing indignation among the colonists. Colonial delegates met twice, at the First Continental Congress in New York and again at the Second Congress in Philadelphia, in order to create a reasonable, peaceful response to Parliament's actions. The product of the Second Congress was the Olive Branch Petition, which had been sent while the Declaration of the Causes and Necessity of Taking Up Arms was being drafted. The declaration states that the colonists took every reasonable step to appeal to Great Britain.

The British response to these "reasonable" steps was, according to Jefferson and Dickinson, a combination of neglect and hostile rhetoric. First, the colonists expected the Olive Branch Petition and other appeals to be received graciously by the king and read into Parliament. Instead, the documents were lost in the bureaucracy. Meanwhile, Parliament spoke of the fact that the colonies—particularly Massachusetts Bay—were in a state of full rebellion against the king. When the legislative body relayed this charge to the king, he acted immediately, calling upon Parliament to enact and enforce any measure to halt this rebellion. Trade was restricted and more troops and ships were sent to enforce the law and maintain order in the colonies.

Britain also attempted to undermine the increasingly united front of colonies. One example of this effort was the "auctioning" of tax rates to potential supporters in colonial governments; by rewarding colonies that supported the king's policies with lower taxes, Parliament sought to create divisions, pitting colony against colony. Jefferson and Dickinson's declaration says that this tax policy maneuver led the colonies to closely examine the social and moral costs of accepting such proposals. The colonies, according to the document, refused to comply with such extortive

In late 1774, General Thomas Gage, the British-installed Governor of the Massachusetts Bay colony, took notice of the growing pro-liberty movement the confrontations and incidents it incited. Gage declared Massachusetts to be in a state of martial law and began a search for any weapons and supplies the rebellion might be gathering. In April of 1775, British intelligence revealed that such a depot could be found in Concord. Gage deployed his military forces to secure the supplies and arrest John Hancock and Samuel Adams (two of the most outspoken critics of England). Colonial minutemen were alerted to the British force's imminent arrival and engaged them in two major skirmishes (which would become known as the Battle of Lexington and Concord).

The declaration says that Gage's attack was unprovoked and an "assault on the inhabitants" of that region, suggesting that not all of the targets of Gage's campaign were military. Gage would take this approach to pursuing civilians farther two months later, declaring all colonists to be rebels and traitors. This policy, according to Jefferson and Dickinson, would further allow Gage to crack down on the colonists with martial law. The military launched attacks on Breed's Hill in Charlestown (a battle known as the Battle of Bunker Hill) and other targets. American ships were seized and their crews forced to take up arms against the colonists, while troops also stopped inbound supply ships in order to choke the rebellion. It is at this point that Jefferson and Dickinson state the justification for formally raising arms against the British. In light of the inability of the colonies to gain the King's favor and halt Parliament's ongoing effort to clamp down on the colonists, the authors say that the colonies have no other recourse. Their cause, according to the document, was just. Additionally, the union that was being forged in the face of this poor treatment was strong and becoming stronger.

Furthermore, the resources that the colonists had to defend themselves were many. The Americans could obtain weapons and supplies and could even call upon the assistance of Britain's rivals if necessary. Finally, the colonies had the benefit of divine Providence—it was the view of Jefferson and Dickinson that God would not have placed the colonists in this situation if they could not call upon their experience and tap into the resources at hand in order to defend themselves and achieve their freedom from British tyranny.

The Declaration of the Causes and Necessity of Taking Up Arms states a clear case for independence. The colonists, the victims of two decades of increased oppression, had reached out repeatedly to Parliament, the king, and anyone else within the British Empire who might intervene. According to the declaration, the colonists felt that they were entirely justified to respond to the Crown's actions by taking up arms against Britain; they believed that the pursuit of independence was a reasonable pursuit under such circumstances.

However, the declaration left open the possibility for reconciliation. Jefferson and Dickinson state that the colonies do not wish to dissolve their union with Great Britain and their fellow subjects. The colonists' situation was not irreversible—they had not yet reached so desperate a point at which open war was the only option, nor had they raised an army whose sole purpose was to achieve independence. Nevertheless, the colonists were, in the minds of Jefferson and Dickinson, a group endangered by British policies. They had every right to defend themselves and act in a spirit of self-preservation against such unprovoked attacks. Now, the document says, the colonists would need to take up arms against such oppressive actions, laying them down again when British hostilities came to an end.

The declaration comes to a conclusion by offering a prayer. The authors pray to God to protect them from the coming conflict, which despite their hopes of a lasting peace, seems to be moving closer to reality. They add that it was the hope of the colonists that God would steer the British toward reconciliation (with reasonable terms) in order to avoid sending the colonies and Great Britain into deeper into civil war.

Essential Themes

The Declaration of the Causes and Necessity of Taking Up Arms served a number of important purposes during the pivotal years between 1774 and 1776 in colonial America. To serve these purposes, Thomas Jefferson and John Dickinson deliberately used respectful, peaceful language, although they also showed indignation at the ongoing events and issues between the colonies and Great Britain. This dual tone was reflective of the moderate, non-contentious approach preferred by Dickinson and Jefferson's more vehement pro-independence attitude.

The first purpose of this document was to issue one last appeal to the king to intervene with Parliament and move the country from the brink of civil war with its colonies. To be sure, according to the declaration, Parliament had done its part to instigate conflict with the colonies. The growing sense of anger among the colonies that was generated by these actions could have elicited a positive response from Parliament, said Jefferson and Dickinson, but instead the colonies' anger was only met with more oppressive measures. Only the king, who had previously shown appreciation for the colonies—at least in terms of the strategic and economic benefits they gave to the British Empire—could intervene and reverse Parliament's actions.

The declaration therefore served another important purpose—justifying the eventual raising of arms in self-defense against the British. It served as a sort of low-key rallying cry for the colonists and provided a clear outline of the despotic and unfair governance that Parliament demonstrated in the colonies. This document did not call for independence, but it did make a clear case for standing up against the tyranny of British government and its disruptive impact on the colonial way of life. It left open the hope that moderation and reconciliation would be offered by the British, but also made clear that the colonies would no longer be passive if reconciliation did not occur.

—*Michael Auerbach, MA*

Bibliography and Additional Reading

"American Political Writing, 1760–1769: A Declaration of the Causes and Necessity of Taking Up Arms". *Cambridge History of English and American Literature in 18 Volumes.* Bartleby.com, 2000.

"Brief Biography of Thomas Jefferson". *The Jefferson Monticello.* Thomas Jefferson Foundation, 2012.

Calvert, Jane E. "John Dickinson Biography." *John Dickinson Writings Project.* University of Kentucky, 2011.

———. *Quaker Constitutionalism and the Political Thought.* Cambridge: Cambridge UP, 2008.

"The Declaration of Arms". *Archiving Early America.* Archiving Early America, 2012.

Ferling, John. *A Leap in the Dark: The Struggle to Create the American Republic.* Oxford: Oxford UP, 2003.

Middlekauff, Robert. *The Glorious Cause: The American Revolution, 1763–1789.* Oxford: Oxford UP, 2007.

Mintz, S. "Was the Revolution Justified?" *Digital History.*

Wood, Gordon S. *The Radicalism of the American Revolution.* New York: Vintage, 1993.

Give Me Liberty or Give Me Death

Date: March 23, 1775
Author: Patrick Henry
Genre: speech

"I know not what course others may take; but as for me, give me liberty or give me death!"

Summary Overview

Patrick Henry's fiery "Give Me Liberty or Give Me Death" oratory was presented to the Second Virginia Convention on March 23, 1775. This speech was part of a debate over whether the colony of Virginia should arm itself against potential British attacks or whether it should, like the other colonies, continue to seek a diplomatic resolution to the British colonial crisis. Henry's words turned the focus of this debate toward the topic of whether Virginia wanted its freedom or wanted to continue being subservient to Great Britain. The speech was seen by many as one of the most famous cries for freedom in world history.

Defining Moment

In the mid-eighteenth century, the long-standing relationship between the American colonies and Britain began to experience great strains. Many colonists embraced the philosophical notions of a government run by the people rather than a sovereign. This idealism might have been isolated if not for a number of key incidents and trends that fanned the flames of the pro-independence movement.

One of the first of these events was the passage of the Stamp Act in 1765. Britain, which needed to repay its debts from the French and Indian War, sought to generate revenues from the colonies by requiring that all official documents (such as legal papers, almanacs, diplomas, and books) be printed on stamped paper, to which a special tax was attached.

The Stamp Act was received with great negativity in the colonies, inciting riots and other protests. It also helped bring together a number of key figures in the American Revolution, such as James Otis, John Adams, and Patrick Henry, all of whom railed against the measure. The Stamp Act would not be the only such measure, however—Parliament levied more taxes and onerous policies on the colonies, prompting even stronger protests and confrontations, including the Boston Massacre in 1770 and the Boston Tea Party in 1773.

As Britain proceeded to crack down on the colonies, Adams and others formed the First Continental Congress in the fall of 1774, organizing boycotts on British goods and raising local militias in response to the increasingly oppressive British activity. In February 1775, Parliament—responding to these colonial actions—declared the colonies to be in a state of open rebellion.

On March 1775, a convention was called at St. John's Church in Richmond, Virginia, drawing the colony's leaders away from the capital in Williamsburg. The purpose of the convention was to discuss a series of proposals to raise a colonial militia to defend the colony from British attack. Although coordinated attacks had not yet taken place, delegate Patrick Henry spoke in support of raising an army, stating that the war with the British had already begun. According to Henry, the time had come for Virginia to engage the British and fight for independence. His words, fiery and eloquent, called for the delegates to consider fighting for freedom or remain in submission to the Crown. The final words of this speech—"Give me liberty or give me

Patrick Henry's "Give me liberty, or give me death!" speech, depicted in an 1876 lithograph by Currier and Ives and now housed in the Library of Congress in Washington, D.C. Image via Wikimedia Commons. [Public domain.]

death!"—were received by the audience first with shock and then with enthusiastic support.

Author Biography

Patrick Henry was born on May 29, 1736, in Studley, a Virginia community located in Hanover County near Richmond. Although he was the son of a successful planter, Henry did not receive much formal education, with most of his early education coming from his father. Although he did launch some business ventures in his early career (most notably a small store), he did not prove successful as an entrepreneur. After marrying Sarah Shelton in 1754, Henry started a brief career as a farmer. When a fire destroyed their home, Henry and his wife moved into an apartment above the tavern owned by his father-in-law. As he worked in the tavern, Henry also educated himself, studying law on his own for over a year. In 1760, he proved successful in his pursuits, receiving admittance to the bar and launching another career as a defense attorney.

As an attorney, Patrick Henry was particularly interested in defending the common people. The most famous of Henry's defense cases was part of the Parsons' Cause. In response to poor crop yields that inflated the value of tobacco (the colony's primary form of payment) in the late 1750s, colonial leaders issued the Two Penny Acts of 1755 and 1758. These measures allowed the use of paper money for payment, prevented taxes from skyrocketing, and stabilized public salaries, including those for Anglican clergy, who protested the de facto salary cut after the acts were vetoed in 1759 by the Crown. In 1763, Henry vigorously defended a parish against Reverend James Maury's lawsuit, railing against the Church of England and the king for interfering in the natural rights of his clients. Ultimately, the case was decided in favor of the defendant, and Henry was hailed for his pro-colonial stance.

In 1765, Henry's legal success as well as his oratory skills helped him gain a seat at the Virginia House of Burgesses. After the Stamp Act was introduced, Henry used his position to publicly compare King George III to other tyrants of the past. These charges were branded as treasonous by conservatives in the House. Henry responded famously by stating, "If this be treason, make the most of it." A day after he made these comments, the House passed most of Patrick's resolutions criticizing taxation without representation.

In the fall of 1774, Henry became a delegate to the First Continental Congress before returning to Virginia, where he gave his famous "Give Me Liberty or Give Me Death" speech in March 1775. That May, Henry again represented Virginia at the Second Continental Congress. During the Revolutionary War, he briefly commanded a group of militia while continuing his service to Virginia. He was elected governor five times during and after the war. Although he opposed ratification of the US Constitution, he contributed significantly to the formulation of the Bill of Rights. Henry continued to serve in the Virginia state government until he died of cancer on June 6, 1799.

Historical Document

Give Me Liberty or Give Me Death

No man thinks more highly than I do of the patriotism, as well as abilities, of the very worthy gentlemen who have just addressed the house. But different men often see the same subject in different lights; and, therefore, I hope it will not be thought disrespectful to those gentlemen if, entertaining as I do opinions of a character very opposite to theirs, I shall speak forth my sentiments freely and without reserve. This is no time for ceremony. The question before the house is one of awful moment to this country. For my own part, I consider it as nothing less than a question of freedom or slavery; and in proportion to the magnitude of the subject ought to be the freedom of the debate. It is only in this way that we can hope to arrive at the truth, and fulfill the great responsibility which we hold to God and our country. Should I keep back my opinions at such a time, through fear of giving offense, I should consider myself as guilty of treason towards my country, and of an act of disloyalty toward the Majesty of Heaven, which I revere above all earthly kings.

Mr. President, it is natural to man to indulge in the illusions of hope. We are apt to shut our eyes against a painful truth, and listen to the song of that siren till she transforms us into beasts. Is this the part of wise men, engaged in a great and arduous struggle for liberty? Are we disposed to be of the numbers of those who, having eyes, see not, and, having ears, hear not, the things which so nearly concern their temporal salvation? For my part, whatever anguish of spirit it may cost, I am willing to know the whole truth, to know the worst, and to provide for it.

I have but one lamp by which my feet are guided, and that is the lamp of experience. I know of no way of judging of the future but by the past. And judging by the past, I wish to know what there has been in the conduct of the British ministry for the last ten years to justify those hopes with which gentlemen have been pleased to solace themselves and the House. Is it that insidious smile with which our petition has been lately received?

Trust it not, sir; it will prove a snare to your feet. Suffer not yourselves to be betrayed with a kiss. Ask yourselves how this gracious reception of our petition comports with those warlike preparations which cover our waters and darken our land. Are fleets and armies necessary to a work of love and reconciliation? Have we shown ourselves so unwilling to be reconciled that force must be called in to win back our love? Let us not deceive ourselves, sir. These are the implements of war and subjugation; the last arguments to which kings resort. I ask gentlemen, sir, what means this martial array, if its purpose be not to force us to submission? Can gentlemen assign any other possible motive for it? Has Great Britain any enemy, in this quarter of the world, to call for all this accumulation of navies and armies? No, sir, she has none. They are meant for us: they can be meant for no other. They are sent over to bind and rivet upon us those chains which the British ministry have been so long forging. And what have we to oppose to them? Shall we try argument? Sir, we have been trying that for the last ten years. Have we anything new to offer upon the subject? Nothing. We have held the subject up in every light of which it is capable; but it has been all in vain. Shall we resort to entreaty and humble supplication? What terms shall we find which have not been already exhausted? Let us not, I beseech you, sir, deceive ourselves. Sir, we have done everything that could be done to avert the storm which is now coming on. We have petitioned; we have remonstrated; we have supplicated; we have prostrated ourselves before the throne, and have implored its interposition to arrest the tyrannical hands of the ministry and Parliament. Our petitions have been slighted; our remonstrances have produced additional violence and insult; our supplications have been disregarded; and we have been spurned, with contempt, from the foot of the throne! In vain, after these things, may we indulge the fond hope of peace and reconciliation.

There is no longer any room for hope. If we wish to be free—if we mean to preserve inviolate those inestimable privileges for which we have been so long contending—if we mean not basely to abandon the noble struggle in which we have been so long engaged, and which we have pledged ourselves never to abandon until the glorious object of our contest shall be obtained—we must fight! I repeat it, sir, we must fight! An appeal to arms and to the God of hosts is all that is left us! They tell us, sir, that we are weak; unable to cope with so formidable an adversary. But when shall we be stronger? Will it be the next week, or the next year? Will it be when we are totally disarmed, and when a British guard shall be stationed in every house? Shall we gather strength by irresolution and inaction? Shall we acquire the means of effectual resistance by lying supinely on our backs and hugging the delusive phantom of hope, until our enemies shall have bound us hand and foot? Sir, we are not weak if we make a proper use of those means which the God of nature hath placed in our power. The millions of people, armed in the holy cause of liberty, and in such a country as that which we possess, are invincible by any force which our enemy can send against us. Besides, sir, we shall not fight our battles alone. There is a just God who presides over the destinies of nations, and who will raise up friends to fight our battles for us. The battle, sir, is not to the strong alone; it is to the vigilant, the active, the brave. Besides, sir, we have no election. If we were base enough to desire it, it is now too late to retire from the contest. There is no retreat but in submission and slavery! Our chains are forged! Their clanking may be heard on the plains of Boston! The war is inevitable—and let it come! I repeat it, sir, let it come.

It is in vain, sir, to extentuate the matter. Gentlemen may cry, Peace, Peace—but there is no peace. The war is actually begun! The next gale that sweeps from the north will bring to our ears the clash of resounding arms! Our brethren are already in the field! Why stand we here idle? What is it that gentlemen wish? What would they have? Is life so dear, or peace so sweet, as to be purchased at the price of chains and slavery? Forbid it, Almighty God! I know not what course others may take; but as for me, give me liberty or give me death!

Glossary

arduous: difficult, strenuous

extentuate (extenuate): diminish the importance of, excuse

insidious: treacherous, traitorous

ministry: in this context, representatives of a monarchy

reconciliation: restoration of friendly relations

remonstrances: forceful protests

supplication: a humble or earnest request or prayer

Document Analysis

In 1774, Patrick Henry took part in the First Continental Congress in Philadelphia. He made apparent his views that America was on the brink of war. Although not all of the delegates to the Continental Congress concurred, Henry gained the attention of John Adams. Adams later recalled that only Henry seemed to appreciate the severity of the situation and that the colonies were on the precipice of war against Britain. Figures like Adams, Jefferson and others eventually generated support as Henry returned to Virginia.

In early 1775, the American colonies were declared by Parliament to be in a state of rebellion. The Second Virginia Convention would have taken place in the colonial capital of Williamsburg were it not for the careful eye and wrathful nature of the royal governor, Lord Dunmore. Without a capitol building in which to hold the proceedings, the participants therefore found a venue large enough in St. John's Church in Richmond. The atypical venue made for a long series of debates and presentations by the delegates. The church setting also gave Henry an opportunity to speak more freely than he might have under the charge of the governor, a venue not dissimilar from Philadelphia, where he shared his thoughts a year earlier.

Like the First Continental Congress, the delegates to the Second Virginia Convention were split on the course of action necessary to address the British policies regarding the colonies. Although few doubted that Virginia needed to be defended from Britain's continuing encroachment, many hoped that the crisis could be averted through continued appeals to the king and Parliament. As was the case in Philadelphia, Henry was among the minority with his views. His comments to the convention would therefore need to be emphatic and stirring.

Any formal actions, such as the raising of a militia and other anti-British policies, might have been tabled during the Second Virginia Convention if not for Henry's speech. Loyalists (conservatives who sided with Britain as the pro-independence movement grew) were among the many delegates on hand, representing a large Loyalist base in the general population of Virginia. These delegates were joined by others who were wary of passing any sort of resolution that openly defied the king and fostered war and were in favor of seeking conciliation. Before Henry took the floor, historians believe that the vote to arm Virginia and enter war with Britain was split. It was therefore incumbent upon him to argue that war was already upon the colonies and the time had come to defend Virginia.

When Henry took the floor, he immediately distinguished his views on the conflict from those of his Loyalist peers. He begins his speech by stating his respect for the delegates who have spoken before him, commending their patriotism as well as their knowledge and abilities as legislators. However, Henry holds a different point of view from his fellow delegates, as well as a different approach to expressing his ideals. Because of the location of the convention—a church instead of a capitol building—there was less pressure to remain decorous and completely respectful of the king and Parliament. Additionally, Henry acknowledges his reputation for breaking such careful rules in order to speak his mind freely without fear of reprisal. Indeed, Henry asserts that the proceedings of the Second Virginia Convention should not be mired in ceremony or hampered by tempered language. Rather, the task before the convention was pivotal—to answer the question of whether Virginia should remain in "slavery" under the British government or if the colony, along with the rest of the colonies, should fight for its freedom. Henry adds that an issue of this magnitude warrants a frank and open debate and that such an approach is the only way the truth could be established and the issue addressed responsibly.

With this demand for free speech, Henry also proclaims that he must not hold back his tongue for fear of insulting or offending anyone—to do so, would make him guilty of treason against America and God. He therefore presents his proposals and resolutions to the convention in an unapologetic and unflinching manner.

Henry states that it is a natural response for men, when faced with painful truths, to shut their eyes and hold out hope that the hard issues at hand will be rectified. He equates such an action to the men of

Homer's Odyssey—such men would be lured, entranced, by the intoxicating call of the siren, who led the men's ships to crash in shallow, rocky waters. In colonial America, Henry argues, a similar siren's call was being sounded, leading the colonies' leaders to shut their eyes to British hostilities until the colonies were defeated and crushed.

Henry calls upon his fellow leaders to remove their hands from their eyes as he did. Although the truths that would become evident were painful ones, Henry had prepared himself for such harsh truths, but many in colonial governments were not choosing this course of action. He therefore implores his colleagues to behave wisely, engage in the struggle for liberty, and fearlessly open their eyes to the truth.

Henry next states that his experience has led him to seek independence. Over the decade leading up to the Second Virginia Convention, Henry says, the British government seemed to be focused on increasing its oppressive rule over the colonies. Neither Parliament nor the king, in light of these events, had demonstrated a desire for open government that would justify the hope in the eyes of the colonists.

Henry cautions his fellow delegates not to be swayed by hopes that the situation would change. In his view, though the British claimed to seek a resolution to these issues, they had done nothing to validate that promise. Instead, every petition and appeal offered by the colonists was either ignored or given a response in the form of more oppressive measures and troop buildups. The British had embraced the pursuit of continued oppression and subjugation of their subjects in America, and despite several good-faith attempts at reconciliation offered by the colonists, Britain proceeded along its warlike path.

Henry adds that there was no evidence to support the notion that Britain was a nation with which the colonists could reconcile their differences. He advises his colleagues not to trust the false hope that war could be avoided, reminding them that the colonists had sent petitions to the king and Parliament, only to see the king respond by sending more troops and ships. He cautions his fellow delegates not to deceive themselves with the possibility that Britain might seek a peaceful resolution—the increased presence of British troops and ships amounted to nothing more than "the implements of war and subjugation."

Furthermore, such deployments were typically a king's last resort when faced with an unyielding enemy. There was no other reason for an increased troop buildup—by then, Great Britain had no other enemy in the region that would warrant such a force. The heightened presence of military forces had but one unmistakable focus: to secure and render submissive the colonies.

Henry's repeated references to the intentions of the British were meant to clear what he saw as the clouded minds of those who did not want to engage Britain militarily. Henry felt that too many within the convention would rather seek peace at any cost, when it was painfully clear to him and other pro-independence advocates that peace simply was not going to be offered by the main instigator of this conflict, Britain.

Henry next asks his colleagues how they would prefer to deal with the situation. He discounts the viability of further negotiation, which had been attempted for more than ten years. He suggests that no further ideas had been offered because no other viable avenue was available. The only other option was complete submission, which he implies the colonists simply could not do. Henry concludes that even this course of action had inadvertently been followed while the colonists appealed to the king and Parliament.

Put simply, Henry argues, the colonists could do nothing more to halt the oppressive actions of the tyrannical British government. They had petitioned, protested, pled, and even "prostrated" themselves before the king in order to "arrest the tyrannical hands" of Parliament and the king. Each of these efforts was ignored, dismissed, or reciprocated with further sanctions. To embrace the hope that Britain might change its policies and instead embrace peace and reconciliation, Henry claims, was pure vanity.

Henry next acknowledges what was at stake with regard to lifting the yoke of British tyranny. The basic rights of all the colonists had been suppressed under these policies, he says, despite the colonists' efforts to preserve them over many years. Henry spoke from experience, having been a central figure in the fight over the Stamp Act and having witnessed other key events leading up to the First Continental Congress.

Given the stakes, the colonists' many attempts to have their interests represented and issues addressed, and the negative responses these petitions garnered, Henry proclaims it is time to embrace reality rather than hope. For a long time, Henry reminds his listeners, the colonists worked toward the goals of fair treatment and representation in government as well as the basic rights due to all men. Unless the colonists wished to abandon this effort, there was but one course of action left for the America to take: "We must fight!" Henry urges repeatedly, adding that the only avenue toward peace is through the strength of arms and the support of God.

Henry further asserts that the pursuit of military action must occur quickly. Britain believed the colonists to be weak and unable to withstand the formidable force of the British military. The British continued to build their strength in the colonies, sending more and more troops and weapons into the colonies while the colonists stood idly. Henry implores his fellow delegates to show resolve and decisiveness, for the British troops would do so.

In Henry's estimation, no success would be found in inaction. As the colonists continued to talk and negotiate, he predicts, the British would disarm and bind them as they clung to a delusion of a peaceful resolution. The British idea of colonial weakness and submissiveness would be validated if Americans continued to cling to "the phantom of hope."

America, Henry argues, was not inherently weak, however—the American colonists had the potential to be so strong and formidable that even the great powers of Britain could not defeat them. After all, Henry states, God had presented the colonists with a number of great assets. First, they had strength in numbers—over two million people were living in the American colonies by that time, and most of them could take up arms and/or contribute to the cause. Second, the battle would be fought in their own country, which meant that the colonists could draw their own supplies and resources to support the effort, while the British would need to bring in supplies on ships.

Above all, Henry reminds his colleagues, they would not be fighting alone. In fact, the pursuit of liberty, he maintains, is a holy cause, and therefore God, who presides over the destiny of all nations, would raise other nations to come to the aid of the colonists as they fought the British. These nations would even fight Britain on behalf of the colonies, disrupting and undermining the British campaign in America.

Although military might is important in war, Henry acknowledges, the colonies had a number of great traits that would make them seemingly invincible in the face of the British. He notes that to win the war, the colonists must be vigilant, ever ready and watchful. Second, they must be active, rather than passive—Henry repeatedly warns his colleagues of the dangers of complacency. Furthermore, Henry urges the colonists to be brave—desire would lead them to the battlefield but fearlessness would lead the Americans to victory.

Henry next repeats his warning that, whether the colonists were prepared or not, war with Britain had already begun. The colonists rightly desired a change from the oppressive nature of British rule, and the king and Parliament had responded with brute force. They could not "retire" from this battle, unless the colonists wished to remain in a state of submission and "slavery." Henry says that his fellow delegates could hear the colonists' metaphorical chains rattling in Boston, which suggested that their will to be free would not be undone. The British would therefore be coming to silence them and bring America once again into submission. War with Britain, Henry claims, is inevitable, and he welcomes it, saying emphatically, "Let it come!"

Henry nears the end of his remarks by again reminding his colleagues that attempting to maintain peaceful conditions during the ongoing conflict between the colonies and Britain is an exercise in futility. Besides, he states, there is no peace. The next sound Patrick Henry and his fellow Virginians would hear from New England would be the sounds of war, as guns, cannons, and swords rattled on the battlefield. Their fellow colonists were already engaged in combat, and this fighting was spreading rapidly throughout the colonies.

Henry concludes his remarks by questioning why the convention's delegates remained idle as war raged in the north. He asks them what they sought that prevented them from immediately joining the war. Only through war would they gain the liberty they sought and protect the life and peace so dear to them. With no compunction, Henry defiantly proclaims his own preference: "I know not what course others may take; but as for me, give me liberty or give me death!"

As described earlier, the Second Virginia Convention entered this session divided on the subject of arming the Virginia colony and joining with the other colonies in war against the British. Henry's impassioned, blunt words swayed a number of key swing votes, and his proposals were accepted. The speech resonated beyond the walls of St. John's Church, reaching the ears of Governor Dunmore in Williamsburg. Dunmore soon dispatched troops to the public magazine in Williamsburg to remove all munitions. Henry and the local militia were vocal in their protests, marching on Williamsburg and demanding compensation for the theft. Dunmore proclaimed that Henry had steered Virginia into war with Britain, lending credence to the notion that the American War of Independence had already begun.

Essential Themes

Patrick Henry's iconic "Give Me Liberty or Give Me Death" speech was presented during a pivotal period for the eighteenth-century American colonies. The colonies had been subjected to increased sanctions and heavy-handed policies, including the Stamp Act of 1765. These policies helped fan the flames of such pro-liberty figures as John Adams, Thomas Jefferson, and James Otis (as well as Deputy Postmaster General Benjamin Franklin, who initially agreed to the Stamp Act but later became outwardly critical of British policy). Coupled with incidents like the Boston Massacre, these policies added to tensions and confrontations that left the colonies teetering on the edge of war.

For many of the delegates to the First Continental Congress and the Second Virginia Convention, however, there was a glimmer of hope that war could be averted and reconciliation with the Crown could be accomplished. Some elements remained loyal to Britain, while others simply sought an amicable solution that avoided violence. Patrick Henry was not among either of these camps—he, like John Adams and other so-called radicals, believed that there was no hope of reconciliation, and that war was inevitable.

As he had done on previous occasions, Henry here offers blunt, unapologetic language about the state of British-American relations. He states clearly to his colleagues in Richmond that any further humble, forceful appeals sent to Parliament and the king would be almost certainly rebuffed and returned with additional sanctions. Whether the delegates embraced it or not, he adds, the only way to defend America's way of life is by taking up arms against the oncoming British forces. Henry also gives the delegates reason to believe that they could, through strength of arms, bravery, and faith in God, wrest freedom from Britain. Henry therefore encourages his fellow leaders to face reality and enthusiastically prepare for the coming war.

To foster this attitude and energy, Henry reminds his colleagues of what was at stake. Life, liberty, and peace were qualities far too important to the colonists to be exchanged for submission to the king's continued pursuit of colonial subjugation. Henry further argues that for the colonists to remain hopeful for a reconciliation that would never come only hastened the shackling of the colonies into utter submission. Now, he says, is the time for fight for their liberty.

Shortly after Henry gave this speech, it became clear that the British were indeed seeking to disarm the colonies and put down the growing rebellion. Less than a month after the convention, colonial minutemen engaged the British army in the battles of Lexington and Concord. Two months later, the two sides fought on another battlefield, this time at the Battle of Bunker Hill. Branded a traitor after his "Give Me Liberty or Give Me Death" speech, Patrick Henry came to be viewed among the colonists less as a radical and more as a critical leader in the American Revolution.

—*Michael Auerbach, MA*

Bibliography and Additional Reading

Elson, James M., ed. *Patrick Henry in His Speeches and Writings and in the Words of His Contemporaries.* Lynchburg, VA: Warwick House, 2007.

"Give Me Liberty or Give Me Death!" *The Colonial Williamsburg Foundation.* The Colonial Williamsburg Foundation, 2012.

Harkins, Susan Sales. *The Life and Times of Patrick Henry.* Hockessin: Lane, 2007.

Hayes, Kevin J. *The Mind of a Patriot: Patrick Henry and the World of Ideas.* Charlottesville: U of Virginia P, 2008.

Kidd, Thomas S. *Patrick Henry: First among Patriots.* New York: Basic, 2011.

Kurla, Jon. "Patrick Henry (1736–1799)." *Encyclopedia Virginia.* Virginia Foundation for the Humanities, 30 Jan. 2012.

Sutton, Robert P. *Revolution to Succession: Constitution Making in the Old Dominion.* Charlottesville: U of Virginia P, 1989.

Unger, Harlow Giles. *Lion of Liberty: Patrick Henry and the Call to a New Nation.* Cambridge: Da Capo, 2010.

■ The Dominion of Providence over the Passions of Men

Date: May 17, 1776
Author: John Witherspoon
Genre: sermon

> *"There is not a single instance in history, in which civil liberty was lost, and religious liberty preserved entire. If therefore we yield up our temporal property, we at the same time deliver the conscience into bondage."*

Summary Overview

As 1776 progressed, the Continental Congress understood that momentous events lay ahead. In line with common practice at the time, they called for a day of fasting to help people focus on the decisions that needed to be made and on the likelihood that the conflict in New England would expand to other areas. In response to the call for religious preparation, John Witherspoon, president of what is now Princeton University, delivered a sermon to the gathered community in which he proclaimed the need for repentance, based on his understanding of the Christian faith, and presented his views on the political situation. In Witherspoon's mind, political freedom and religious freedom were intricately linked, so that one could not truly exist without the other. Given the recent tightening of British control over colonial affairs, Witherspoon regarded revolution as inevitable.

Defining Moment

The Revolutionary War began with the Battles of Lexington and Concord in April 1775. It was in that year that the colonies began to organize an army to confront the British; by March 1776, enough American military forces had amassed in the area of Boston that commander in chief George Washington was able to begin an attack. At the same time, the Continental Congress was trying in a variety of ways to prepare for the uncertainty and strife that lay ahead. A resolution was passed in early April to proclaim May 17, 1776, a day of fasting, prayer, and humility in hopes of unifying Americans in the various colonies. It was clear to everyone that the fighting in New England was just a prelude to a much larger conflict. Even though the British had withdrawn from Boston by May 17, raising the hopes and morale of the colonists, preparations remained under way to defend New York. In this dramatic moment, John Witherspoon wrote and delivered a sermon calling all Americans to unite in the cause of civil and religious liberty.

John Witherspoon; portrait by Charles Willson Peale, c. 1790. Image via Wikimedia Commons. [Public domain.]

Those who gathered in Princeton, New Jersey, to hear Witherspoon speak were not yet American leaders, although some went on to leadership positions. He spoke to college students, faculty, and members of the community so forcefully that requests were made, and granted, that his sermon be published for mass distribution. Copies were also printed in Britain, adding to the British certainty that American religious leaders played an important role in causing the unrest.

The American people were facing an important point in their history. Although fighting had started, it had been thus far been confined to the radical area of New England; as it was poised to spread to the south, collectively the colonies had to ask whether the people really wanted to split from Great Britain and if they were prepared for the war that was looming. Witherspoon's words were chosen not only to honestly convey his understanding of the situation but also to add to the fervor for freedom from Britain. As an ordained minister, Witherspoon called for faith in God; as a political leader, he called for faith in the emerging America. While the response to his first point is not well documented, the response to the second was strongly in the affirmative for a new and free nation of united colonies.

Author Biography

John Witherspoon was born in Gifford, Scotland, on February 15, 1723, the first child of Anne Walker and ordained minister James Alexander Witherspoon. After earning a master of arts degree from the University of Edinburgh, Witherspoon remained there to study divinity. He became politically active in opposition to the Jacobite rebellion against the English; although Witherspoon supported Scottish nationalism, he did not support the Stuart family. He was ordained as a Presbyterian minister in the Church of Scotland and, in 1745, began serving the parish in Beith, Ayrshire, Scotland. During his thirteen years in Beith, he married Elizabeth Montgomery, with whom he had ten children. In 1758, he moved to Laigh Kirk, Paisley, Scotland, where he continued as a local church pastor. During this time, he continued to write and study, earning additional degrees from the University of Saint Andrews.

In 1768, Witherspoon accepted the invitation to become the president of the College of New Jersey (later Princeton University), which was founded by members of the Presbyterian Church. He would hold this post until his death in 1794. When he arrived, the college was in desperate straits. In addition to teaching, Witherspoon excelled at the central tasks of a college president, namely raising money and assisting the school in moving toward a more optimal structure. He transformed the college by strengthening the course of study, basing it more on that of Scottish schools, and introducing a new philosophy and purpose. His work on the curriculum and with the library allowed the college to move toward parity with the top New England colleges. Just when Witherspoon's goals were being reached, the Revolutionary War caused the closure of the school and the destruction of some of its, and his, resources; after the war, however, he successfully rebuilt the college into a top-tier academic institution.

Although Witherspoon had been in the colonies for only a few years when the revolution started, he was a strong supporter of the effort. By 1774, he was taking an active role in Somerset County, New Jersey's committee of correspondence, which worked to replace the British government. He was a member of the Second Continental Congress and voted for and signed the Declaration of Independence. He helped develop the Articles of Confederation and later advocated for the Federalist cause in the adoption of the Constitution.

Historical Document

The Dominion of Providence over the Passions of Men

In the first place, I would take the opportunity on this occasion, and from this subject, to press every hearer to a sincere concern for his own soul's salvation. There are times when the mind may be expected to be more awake to divine truth, and the conscience more open to the arrows of conviction than at others. A season of public judgment is of this kind. Can you have a clearer view of the sinfulness of your nature, than when the rod of the oppressor is lifted up, and when you see men putting on the habit of the warrior, and collecting on every hand the weapons of hostility and instruments of death? I do not blame your ardour in preparing for the resolute defense of your temporal rights; but consider, I beseech you, the truly infinite importance of the salvation of your souls. Is it of much moment whether you and your children shall be rich or poor, at liberty or in bonds? Is it of much moment whether this beautiful country shall increase in fruitfulness from year to year, being cultivated by active industry, and possessed by independent freemen, or the scanty produce of the neglected fields shall be eaten up by hungry publicans, while the timid owner trembles at the tax-gatherer's approach? And is it of less moment, my brethren, whether you shall be the heirs of glory, or the heirs of hell? Is your state on earth for a few fleeting years, of so much moment? And is it of less moment what shall be your state through endless ages? Have you assembled together willingly to hear what shall be said on public affairs, and to join in imploring the blessing of God on the counsels and arms of the United Colonies, and can you be unconcerned what shall become of you for ever, when all the monuments of human greatness shall be laid in ashes, for "the earth itself, and all the works that are therein shall be burnt up."

Wherefore, my beloved hearers, as the ministry of reconciliation is committed to me, I beseech you in the most earnest manner, to attend to "the things that belong to your peace, before they are hid from your eyes." How soon, and in what manner a seal shall be set upon the character and state of every person here present, it is impossible to know. But you may rest assured, that there is no time more suitable, and there is none so safe as that which is present, since it is wholly uncertain whether any other shall be yours. Those who shall first fall in battle, have not many more warnings to receive. There are some few daring and hardened sinners, who despise eternity itself, and set their Maker at defiance; but the far greater number, by staving off their convictions to a more convenient season, have been taken unprepared, and thus eternally lost. I would therefore earnestly press the apostle's exhortation, 2 Cor. vi. 1, 2. "We then, as workers together with him, beseech you also, that ye receive not the grace of God in vain: For he faith, I have heard thee in a time accepted, and in the day of salvation have I succoured thee. Behold, now is the accepted time; behold, now is the day of salvation."

Suffer me to beseech you, or rather to give you warning, not to rest satisfied with a form of godliness, denying the power thereof. There can be no true religion, till there be a discovery of your lost state by nature and practice, and an unfeigned acceptance of Christ Jesus, as he is offered in the gospel. Unhappy are they who either despise his mercy, or are ashamed of his cross. Believe it, "There is no salvation in any other." "There is no other name under heaven given amongst men by which we must be saved." Unless you are united to him by a lively faith, not the resentment of a haughty monarch, the sword of divine justice hangs over you, and the fulness of divine vengeance shall speedily overtake you. I do not speak this only to the heaven-daring profligate or grovelling sensualist, but to every insensible, secure sinner; to all those, however decent and orderly in their civil deportment, who live to themselves, and have their part and portion in this life; in fine, to all who are yet in a state of nature, for "except a man be born again, he cannot see the kingdom of God." The fear of man may make you hide your profanity; prudence and experience may make you abhor intemperance and riot; as you advance in life one vice may supplant another and hold its place; but nothing less than the sovereign grace of God can produce a saving change of heart and temper, or fit you for his immediate presence.

From what has been said upon this subject, you may see what ground there is to give praise to God for his favours already bestowed on us, respecting the public cause. It would be a criminal inattention not to observe the singular interposition of Providence hitherto, in behalf of the American colonies. It is however impossible for me, in a single discourse, as well as improper at this time, to go through every step of our past transactions; I must therefore content myself with a few remarks. How many discoveries have been made of the designs of enemies in Britain, and among ourselves, in a manner as unexpected to us as to them, and in such season as to prevent their effect! What surprising success has attended our encounters in almost every instance! Has not the boasted discipline of regular and veteran soldiers been turned into confusion and dismay, before the new and maiden courage of freemen, in defence of their property and right? In what great mercy has blood been spared on the side of this injured country! Some important victories in the south have been gained with so little loss, that enemies will probably think it has been dissembled, as many even of ourselves thought, till time rendered it undeniable. But these were comparatively of small moment. The signal advantage we have gained by the evacuation of Boston, and the shameful flight of the army and navy of Britain, was brought about without the loss of a man. To all this we may add, that the counsels of our enemies have been visibly confounded, so that I believe I may say with truth, that there is hardly any step which they have taken, but it has operated strongly against themselves, and been more in our favour than if they had followed a contrary course.

While we give praise to God, the supreme Disposer of all events, for his interposition in our behalf, let us guard against the dangerous error of trusting in, or boasting of an arm of flesh. I could earnestly wish, that while our arms are crowned with success, we might content ourselves with a modest ascription of it to the power of the Highest. It has given me great uneasiness to read some ostentatious, vaunting expressions in our newspapers, though happily, I think, much restrained of late. Let us not return to them again. If I am not mistaken, not only the Holy Scriptures in general, and the truths of the glorious gospel in particular, but the whole course of providence, seem intended to abase the pride of man, and lay the vain-glorious in the dust. How many instances does history furnish us with of those who, after exulting over and despising their enemies, were signally and shamefully defeated. The truth is, I believe, the remark may be applied universally, and we may say, that through the whole frame of nature, and the whole system of human life, that which promises most, performs the least. The flowers of finest colour seldom have the sweetest fragrance. The trees of quickest growth or fairest form, are seldom of the greatest value or duration. Deep waters move with least noise. Men who think most are seldom talkative. And I think it holds as much in war as in any thing, that every boaster is a coward.

Pardon me, my brethren, for insisting so much upon this, which may seem but an immaterial circumstance. It is in my opinion of very great moment. I look upon ostentation and confidence to be a sort of outrage upon Providence, and when it becomes general, and infuses itself into the spirit of a people, it is a forerunner of destruction. How does Goliath the champion, armed in a most formidable manner, express his disdain of David the stripling, with his sling and his stone: 1 Sam. xvii. 42, 43, 44, 45. "And when the Philistine looked about and saw David, he disdained him; for he was but a youth, and ruddy, and of a fair countenance. And the Philistine said unto David, Am I a dog that thou comest to me with staves? And the Philistine cursed David by his gods; and the Philistine said to David, Come to me, and I will give thy flesh unto the fowls of the air, and to the beasts of the field." But how just and modest the reply! "Then said David to the Philistine, Thou comest to me with a sword, and with a spear, and with a shield, but I come to thee in the name of the Lord of hosts, the God of the armies of Israel, whom thou hast defied." I was well pleased with a remark of this kind thirty years ago in a pamphlet, in which it was observed, that there was a great deal of profane ostentation in the names given to ships of war, as the Victory, the Valiant, the Thunderer, the Dreadnought, the Terrible, the Firebrand, the Furnace, the Lightning, the Infernal, and many more of the same kind. This the author considered as a symptom of the national character and manners very unfavourable, and not likely to obtain the blessing of the God of heaven.

From what has been said you may learn what encouragement you have to put your trust in God, and hope for his assistance in the present important conflict. He is the Lord of hosts, great in might, and strong in battle. Whoever hath his countenance and approbation, shall have the best at last. I do not mean to speak prophetically, but agreeably to the analogy of faith, and the principles of God's moral government. I leave this as a matter rather of conjecture than certainty, but observe, that if your conduct is prudent, you need not fear the multitude of opposing hosts.

If your cause is just, you may look with confidence to the Lord, and intreat him to plead it as his own. You are all my witnesses, that this is the first time of my introducing any political subject into the pulpit. At this season, however, it is not only lawful but necessary, and I willingly embrace the opportunity of declaring my opinion without any hesitation, that the cause in which America is now in arms, is the cause of justice, of liberty, and of human nature. So far as we have hitherto proceeded, I am satisfied that the confederacy of the colonies has not been the effect of pride, resentment, or sedition, but of a deep and general conviction that our civil and religious liberties, and consequently in a great measure the temporal and eternal happiness of us and our posterity, depended on the issue. The knowledge of God and his truths have from the beginning of the world been chiefly, if not entirely confined to those parts of the earth where some degree of liberty and political justice were to be seen, and great were the difficulties with which they had to struggle, from the imperfection of human society, and the unjust decisions of usurped authority. There is not a single instance in history, in which civil liberty was lost, and religious liberty preserved entire. If therefore we yield up our temporal property, we at the same time deliver the conscience into bondage.

Glossary

abhor: strongly dislike; hate

approbation: approval

countenance: face; also approval

moment: importance

passions: emotions

publicans: tax collectors

Document Analysis

John Witherspoon came to the understanding that the British government was attempting to stifle freedom in all its forms in the colonies, which led him to call for a separation between Great Britain and America. He did not do this as a political radical or as one seeking the glory of the battlefield. Witherspoon's Christian faith gave him direction for his life, and this included a social dimension; for him, public morality was not possible without personal morality. Recognizing that war was unfolding in front of him, Witherspoon called for his listeners to seek salvation by developing a strong personal faith in God. In addition, he asked that they seek God's guidance and blessing to achieve the true freedom of a democracy, which would ensure not only civil liberty but religious liberty as well.

Sermons in the eighteenth century tended to be long, and Witherspoon's is no exception. The full text of "The Dominion of Providence over the Passions of Men" is about eight times the length of the extract printed in this text. In the opening section, he identifies two related points that will be the essence of the sermon. The first proposes that people's anger can actually be used to serve God; the second applies this theological proposition to current events. This second point is where the excerpted text begins.

In order to understand the application of this theological proposition, it needs to be briefly described. The progression of thought, according to Witherspoon, begins with the human passion of wrath. Witherspoon states that this emotion illustrates the fact that human nature is corrupt, or sinful. In his theology, the anger people have with each other leads to the problems of society, and these social problems, in conjunction with individual greed, create the conditions for social destruction, including war. Witherspoon continues that these destructive results should cause people to consider the love and grace offered by God. Human anger, and the physical manifestations of it, can bring people to repent because of the suffering it causes. Witherspoon believed that in the face of great suffering, people cannot be indifferent to God or to faith. Thus he asserts that human passion (anger), resulting from the sinful nature of all people, causes suffering, which in turn creates the conditions for salvation by doing away with people's ability to be indifferent to articles of faith. Witherspoon also cites historical examples of persecution to illustrate how human anger can lead to salvation, referring to ways in which religious persecution has strengthened the church, up to and including the settling of New England. Thus, for Witherspoon, God can use human passions in such a way that good can arise from evil intent.

Applying this to the situation in which he found himself, Witherspoon sought to discover what course of action Americans could take that seemed to be most in line with this theological thesis. As might be expected of an evangelical preacher, he first turned to personal salvation. In line with his theological beliefs, Witherspoon reminds those hearing or reading his sermon that there are opportune times for salvation, saying that "there are times when the mind may be expected to be more awake to divine truth." He considers uncertainty or adversity to be central to these times of spiritual wakefulness; what is happening in the colonies, according to him, is a "season of public judgment." Witherspoon asserts that everyone should have "a clearer view of the sinfulness of [their] nature" because of the calamity facing them. Using biblical language, he describes the current events as "the rod of the oppressor." Because for Witherspoon this is not just a secular endeavor, he describes preparations for war in terms of religious garb, as "putting on the habit of the warrior." The seriousness of the situation is emphasized by the graphic depiction of weapons as "instruments of death." He saw the massive preparations for the war, in the process of unfolding as he spoke, as the primary task before the colonists.

As a Patriot (one who opposed the British policy regarding the colonies), Witherspoon understood the obsession many colonists had with stockpiling the things that would be necessary during a war, whether they be provisions with which to sustain oneself or the "weapons of hostility." As a Christian minister, however, he called upon the people to think beyond the physical aspect of life and turn more to the spiritual. Temporal things are important, he argues, but of "truly infinite importance" is the "salvation of your souls." Witherspoon urges the people to put God first in their lives and to seek salvation—a priority very much in line with mainstream Christian thought down through the ages. A skilled preacher, he questions the things people thought were important in the 1770s, asking whether it is "of much moment" for those gathered that day that their families be "rich or poor, at liberty or in bonds"; the economic state of one's family had always been a consideration for most people, while the emphasis on freedom or servitude was seen as a vital issue of the day by the colonists. Witherspoon asks rhetorically if it is important that the country prosper in both rural and urban areas. He asks if it is important whether free and strong Americans be sustained in this manner or whether the colonies become virtual serfs of the British government, neglected and declining in productivity. These issues were on people's minds because of the perceived threat posed by the British government to the colonial way of life. When Witherspoon asked these questions, he would have expected his congregation to agree that such things were important and they should take steps to make certain a positive future comes to pass. Anticipating this, he then changes direction; if these things are important, he asks, is it not at least as important to plan for what will happen throughout eternity as it is to plan for what will happen in this temporary place of residence? He wants his audience to consider "what shall be [their] state through endless ages."

In his sermon, Witherspoon raises an issue that is not uncommon in what might be called civil religious ceremonies. It is important to remember that, at the time this sermon was preached, similar services were being held throughout the thirteen colonies, the object of which was to seek "the blessing of God on the counsels and arms of the United Colonies." If this is the case, Witherspoon asks, how can people expect this to happen if they are "unconcerned" about their personal relationship with God? In accordance with traditional Christian thought that this universe is not eternal, Witherspoon raises the issue of the relative value of transient things of this world versus those things that are eternal. The manner in which he asks these questions, in the opening paragraph of the document excerpt above, makes it clear that while physical preparation is important, spiritual preparation is even more so.

Like many evangelistic preachers, Witherspoon continues the sermon with a plea for people to respond immediately. He states that no one knows when death will come and urges his audience to find salvation now, reminding them "that there is no time more suitable." He has no doubt that the war will soon be upon them, and many will soon fall in battle. Witherspoon expresses his conviction that most people who have not yet found salvation have simply never gotten around to it, and he entreats them not to wait for a "more convenient season" but to accept salvation "now."

If one were inclined to accept what Witherspoon says about salvation, this might lead to the question of how to achieve it. The third paragraph of the excerpted text deals solely with this issue. Witherspoon is adamant that salvation is only possible by "an unfeigned acceptance of Christ Jesus." As an educated individual, he was aware of many of the other religions that existed throughout the world, but for him there was only one "true religion." The faith of salvation, for Witherspoon, was more than just an affirmation of the goodness of Jesus or the general need for a moral system such as he found in the Bible. He argues that only a faith that changes lives can be the true faith. As noted earlier in regard to the section of the sermon not in this text, Witherspoon states that only when people discover their true nature (that is, weak and sinful) can the process of salvation begin; those who discovered the true nature of humanity without accepting Christ, he believed, would live a wretched life. He says that some willfully reject God's grace, while others are uncertain of truthfulness of the message of Christ crucified, but for most, as in the preceding paragraph, it is just laziness that keeps them separated from God. Witherspoon argues that "the sword of divine justice hangs over you" and that the members of the congregation must accept salvation through Christ. He understands that fear of things of this world does affect how some act, because they do not want to face earthly consequences; however, Witherspoon proclaims that a real change can occur and true morality can come about only when a person accepts the "grace of God."

In the fourth paragraph, Witherspoon begins to address current events, recounting recent military successes, especially those in the area of Boston. While the British did withdraw from Boston because of the American control of the surrounding highlands, Witherspoon seems to be exaggerating a little when he asserts that British military discipline had turned into "confusion and dismay" when confronted by the American troops. All that had happened prior to May 1776 was seen by Witherspoon as coming from God's blessings.

The fifth paragraph of the text sees Witherspoon repeat his thanksgiving to God. In line with many American theologians and preachers of his day, he saw the positive results of the first few engagements of the war as blessings directly from God. While as a Presbyterian, Witherspoon was not directly a part of the Puritan tradition, his view of the United Colonies was very much in line with that tradition, in which the colonists had become God's chosen people. Because of this, Witherspoon advocates trusting in and giving thanks to God, rather than attributing any military success solely to the soldiers' or the generals' prowess. He speaks about his displeasure with the "ostentatious, vaunting expressions in our newspapers" regarding the power and success of the American forces. While Witherspoon desires for the Americans' "arms [to be] crowned with success," he urges that even though much is due to the physical preparations of the military and its leaders, they should not allow pride to overwhelm the need to thank God, saying that pride and vanity will lead to destruction.

In the following passage, Witherspoon continues to discuss national pride. He uses the image of Goliath to represent Britain, citing the pride Goliath had just prior to his death when facing David in individual combat, and considers the "unfavourable" "national character and manners" demonstrated by the names given to British naval ships. Then, in the last two paragraphs of the printed text, Witherspoon reaffirms his understanding of God's relationship with the faithful. According to his theology, those who are believers, who have God's "countenance and approbation," will ultimately do well. He tries to deny that he is "speak[ing] prophetically," and yet here he is projecting into the future his beliefs regarding God's promises.

Witherspoon's reference to "the principles of God's moral government" is a slight against the British; philosophically, he was a strong advocate of public morality for government officials. His understanding of public morality came from a combination of sources: biblical, personal, and spiritual morality and the philosophy of the Enlightenment. From both perspectives, he believed that the British were trying to infringe upon the civil and religious rights of the colonists, and it is on this basis that he states the colonists "need not fear the multitude of opposing hosts." In this context, Witherspoon again rhetorically claims not to speak with "certainty," but what he says leaves no doubt that he is in fact certain.

The last paragraph of the text moves into the heart of the matter for those in Princeton. While Witherspoon claims that this sermon is his "first time...introducing any political subject into the pulpit," he continually, throughout the revolution, incorporated politics into his preaching. It was at this time and place that he clearly moved beyond a theoretical application of his theology to current political and military events, stating that "the cause in which America is now in arms, is the cause of justice, of liberty, and of human nature." Witherspoon's belief and proclamation that the revolution was "not only lawful but necessary" was a major step in gaining more support for the effort. With many other Scottish emigrants having settled in America, the Presbyterian Church was very influential among what might be seen as average citizens; thus, as Witherspoon was a leader among Presbyterians in America, his assertion of the need to rebel against British rule had an effect well beyond Princeton.

Witherspoon's analysis of what had recently occurred gave strong support to colonial leaders. The revolution was not based upon "pride, resentment, or sedition"; these aspects of sinful human nature, against which Witherspoon speaks during the first half of this sermon, were not the foundation of the American cause. Rather, it was the fact that "civil and religious liberties" would be at risk if there were no rebellion. The revolution, according to Witherspoon, would have ramifications not only in terms of earthly kingdoms but also with regard to people's relationship with God. For him, the facts were simple: if religious liberty were not preserved, then personal salvation would not be possible. Because, as he asserts, "civil liberty" has never been lost without a corresponding corruption of "religious liberty," then in Witherspoon's view, to give up colonial freedoms to the British would result not only in political subjugation but also in the loss of the possibility of salvation.

Following the excerpted section, there remains another third of the sermon, in which Witherspoon continues to speak forcefully against the British leaders, political and military. He asserts that he would never say from the pulpit what he would not say in private conversation, thus assuring that his congregation will take to heart his statements regarding British leaders. He then goes on to discuss the strong consensus in the colonies, the need to be faithful to the cause, and his belief in the American church as the purest form of Christianity. Witherspoon concludes his sermon with an exhortation to serve God and the emerging nation. He was certain that if the colonists did so, the American soldiers would be invincible in their struggle against the British.

Essential Themes

Of all the sermons preached on the day of fasting proclaimed by the Continental Congress, the most significant one was John Witherspoon's. Shortly after it was delivered, it was printed for wider distribution. When it was reprinted in Great Britain the following year, the publisher felt it necessary to add numerous footnotes, through which he tried to demonstrate the errors of Witherspoon's theological and political positions. The confidence with which Witherspoon addressed the prospects for the revolution was extraordinary; he was utterly certain that God wanted the revolution to succeed in order to preserve religious freedom and would guarantee the Americans' victory. One of the consequences of this sermon, and similar ones, has been the persistent belief that the United States is a Christian nation, and Witherspoon's certainty regarding God's position on the Revolutionary War, in combination with the Puritan vision of the colonies as the new Israel, has been used to support this belief. Thus the impact of the sermon has gone well beyond the events Witherspoon discussed.

After moving to America in 1768, John Witherspoon quickly became active in colonial affairs. He became convinced of the need for a new path for the colonies, one that would lead to separation from Great Britain. To Witherspoon, the basis for the revolution was the sinful nature of humanity; more specifically, he saw it as the result of the corrupt nature of those leading the British government, with the image of the "haughty monarch" in the sermon being an indirect reference to King George III. If the Americans do not revolt, Witherspoon argues, then his imagined future of "scanty produce" from "neglected fields," tended by the "timid owner" who has to give everything to the "publicans," will come to pass. In the context of urging people to seek salvation, Witherspoon was able to use theological concepts as barbs against the British. The "analogy of faith" and "moral government" he mentions were not only a positive for America but also, in his view, lacking in the British government.

It is clear that Witherspoon's preaching, as well as his other work, did assist in boosting morale and creating broader support for the war. If people are truly certain that God supports their position or efforts, most of them will work more diligently to bring such things to pass. While one sermon did not transform the war effort any more than Witherspoon's plea for everyone to seek personal salvation resulted in widespread mass conversion, it did play an important role in convincing many to persevere against the British.

—Donald A. Watt, PhD

Bibliography and Additional Reading

Barthelmas, Della Gray. *The Signers of the Declaration of Independence.* Jefferson: McFarland, 1997.

Berkovitch, Sacvan. *The Puritan Origins of the American Self.* New Haven: Yale University Press, 2011.

Eustace, Nicole. *Passion Is the Gale: Emotion, Power, and the Coming of the American Revolution.* Chapel Hill: University of North Carolina Press, 2008.

Fea, John. *Was America Founded as a Christian Nation? A Historical Introduction.* Louisville: Westminster, 2011.

Mailer, Gideon. *John Witherspoon's American Revolution.* Williamsburg, VA, and Chapel Hill, NC: Omohundro Institute/University of North Carolina Press, 2016.

Tait, L. Gordon. *The Piety of John Witherspoon.* Louisville: Geneva, 2001.

Witherspoon, John. *The Dominion of Providence over the Passions of Men.* 1777 Glasgow ed. Google Books, 2009.

■ *Common Sense*

Date: January 9, 1776
Author: Thomas Paine
Genre: political tract

"Society in every state is a blessing, but Government, even in its best state, is but a necessary evil... The cause of America is in a great measure the cause of all mankind."

Summary Overview

A seminal document in the cause of American independence, the pamphlet Common Sense *was radical and original in both message and writing style. Its author, Thomas Paine, was a newcomer to America who took full advantage of two opportunities: pursuing a career as a writer and joining in creating a new nation free of the imperfections that he felt he had left behind in England. Among the latter were excessive taxation, rigid class distinctions, and, especially, a hereditary monarchy.* Common Sense *made its appearance at what was arguably the ideal moment for a call for American independence, when blood had already been spilled in battle and hopes for reconciliation between America and Britain were rapidly dimming; also, it made the case for independence with both reason and passion. The pamphlet attracted a huge audience and did much to set the stage for the congressional deliberations that led to the signing of the Declaration of Independence in July 1776.*

Defining Moment

When the first edition of *Common Sense* was published, anonymously, in Philadelphia on January 9, 1776, the American Revolution was already in its ninth month. The battles at Lexington and Bunker Hill had taken their toll on both sides, the Continental Army had been formed under the command of George Washington, and the Second Continental Congress had convened in Philadelphia on July 8, 1775, signing the Olive Branch Petition affirming American loyalty to the British Crown and asking King George III to take steps toward effecting a reconciliation between the two warring sides. When envoys arrived in London with the petition, not only were they rebuffed, they also found that the king had just issued his Proclamation for Suppressing Rebellion and Sedition, which promised the harshest measures against the rebelling colonists.

Thomas Paine; portrait by Laurent Dabos, c. 1792. Image via Wikimedia Commons. [Public domain.]

News of the proclamation reached Philadelphia on November 9, 1775, and was a setback to the cause of those seeking reconciliation, as was the word that arrived from England, almost simultaneously with the publication of Common Sense, that King George had delivered a speech to Parliament in late October 1775 that denounced the American revolutionaries as a "desperate conspiracy" that he would suppress with armed force. At this critical moment, Paine's was not the only voice calling for independence, but his vigorous style and reasoning in Common Sense captivated the American people. At least 100,000 copies were sold in the colonies in three months, making it the most successful political tract in history to that time, and the pamphlet was printed in several other cities as well as in revised editions with added material. Once it gripped the minds of so many readers, it occupied a position from which it could not be easily dislodged, and it put the opponents of independence on the defensive.

Following the publication of Common Sense, events proved sufficiently favorable to the revolutionary cause that nearly six months could comfortably elapse before Paine's recommendations became a reality. British forces were driven out of Boston and had yet to arrive in New York City as the Continental Congress deliberated behind closed doors in Philadelphia. In early June 1776 the Congress appointed a five-man committee to draft the Declaration of Independence. This declaration embodied Paine's idea that the tribulations that the colonies had suffered should be laid before the entire world, along with the record of futility they had experienced in soliciting justice from the king. Paine's ability to seize the moment and write a document that had so strong an impact on the course of events secured his place in American history.

Author Biography

Thomas Paine was born January 29, 1737, at Thetford, England. His father, Joseph Pain, was a Quaker and a maker of corset stays, and his mother, Frances, was the daughter of a local attorney. In keeping with his grandfather's status, Paine (who added the "e" to his surname when he migrated to America) attended the local grammar school but left at age

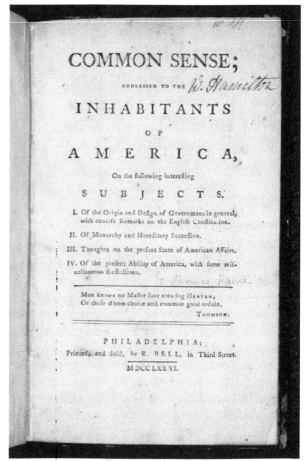

Front cover of the original pamphlet, Common Sense. *Photo via Wikimedia Commons. [Public domain.]*

twelve and pursued a living as a corset maker, schoolteacher, and excise officer (a kind of tax collector). He also served aboard a privateer during the Seven Years' War. From 1768 to 1774, he was an excise man at Lewes, England, where he joined the Headstrong Club, a forum for discussing politics. During this time, he wrote his first political tract, *The Case of the Officers of Excise* (1772).

While in London lobbying for higher pay, Paine was introduced by a member of the Excise Board to the representative of the American colonies, Benjamin Franklin, who in 1774 gave Paine a letter of introduction he could use in America. Fired from his government post, Paine legally separated from his second wife (the first had died in childbearing) and, with high hopes, set out for a fresh start in America.

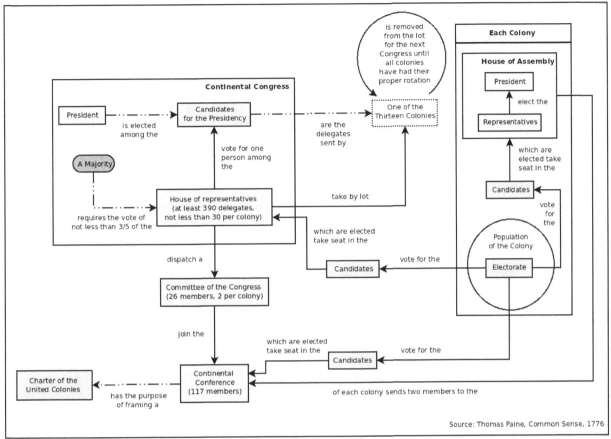

Constitution of the United States as proposed by Thomas Paine in Common Sense. *Image by Mathieu Gauthier-Pilote, via Wikimedia Commons.*

Arriving in Philadelphia in late 1774, he was employed as editor of the *Pennsylvania Magazine,* and, showing himself to be of an independent mind, wrote articles in favor of women's rights and against slavery. His reputation as a revolutionary writer was secured when his pamphlet "Common Sense" was printed in Philadelphia in early January 1776. An avid supporter of General George Washington, he joined the army in the field, writing stories for Philadelphia newspapers. Between 1776 and 1783, he wrote thirteen political pamphlets in defense of the revolution, published as a series titled *The American Crisis,* and his wartime posts included secretary to the Continental Congress Committee of Foreign Affairs and clerk of the Pennsylvania Assembly.

In 1780, he traveled to Europe, receiving on his return to America a government position, awards of money and land, and election to the American Philosophical Society. Returning to Europe in 1790 to promote a bridge design, he was made an honorary citizen of France, which had begun its own revolution the year before. As he believed the principles he stood for in the American Revolution were the cause of people everywhere, in 1791 he produced a tract entitled *Rights of Man* that called on the British to rid themselves of the evils of monarchy and institute a government along the lines of that in the United States. Called to Paris in 1792 to help write a constitution for France, he was caught up in that country's revolutionary power struggle and spent almost a year in prison. Upon his release in 1794, he broke with Washington (by this time the first US president), accusing him of laxity in trying to secure Paine's release from prison, and saw to the publication of his antireligion tract, *The Age of Reason.* He settled again in the United States in 1802 and died in New York City on June 8, 1809.

Historical Document

Common Sense

Thoughts on the Present State of American Affairs

In the following pages I offer nothing more than simple facts, plain arguments, and common sense: and have no other preliminaries to settle with the reader, than that he will divest himself of prejudice and prepossession, and suffer his reason and his feelings to determine for themselves that he will put on, or rather that he will not put off, the true character of a man, and generously enlarge his views beyond the present day.

Volumes have been written on the subject of the struggle between England and America. Men of all ranks have embarked in the controversy, from different motives, and with various designs; but all have been ineffectual, and the period of debate is closed. Arms as the last resource decide the contest; the appeal was the choice of the King, and the Continent has accepted the challenge...

But admitting that matters were now made up, what would be the event? I answer, the ruin of the continent. And that for several reasons.

First. The powers of governing still remaining in the hands of the king, he will have a negative over the whole legislation of this continent. And as he hath shewn himself such an inveterate enemy to liberty, and discovered such a thirst for arbitrary power; is he, or is he not, a proper man to say to these colonies, *"You shall make no laws but what I please."* And is there any inhabitant in America so ignorant, as not to know, that according to what is called the *present constitution,* that this continent can make no laws but what the king gives it leave to; and is there any man so unwise, as not to see, that (considering what has happened) he will suffer no law to be made here, but such as suit *his* purpose. We may be as effectually enslaved by the want of laws in America, as by submitting to laws made for us in England. After matters are made up (as it is called) can there be any doubt, but the whole power of the crown will be exerted, to keep this continent as low and humble as possible? Instead of going forward we shall go backward, or be perpetually quarrelling or ridiculously petitioning.—We are already greater than the king wishes us to be, and will he not hereafter endeavour to make us less? To bring the matter to one point. Is the power who is jealous of our prosperity, a proper power to govern us? Whoever says *No* to this question is an *independent,* for independency means no more, than, whether we shall make our own laws, or, whether the king, the greatest enemy this continent hath, or can have, shall tell us, *"there shall be no laws but such as I like."*

But the king you will say has a negative in England; the people there can make no laws without his consent. In point of right and good order, there is something very ridiculous, that a youth of twenty-one (which hath often happened) shall say to several millions of people, older and wiser than himself, I forbid this or that act of yours to be law. But in this place I decline this sort of reply, though I will never cease to expose the absurdity of it, and only answer, that England being the King's residence, and America not so, make quite another case. The king's negative here is ten times more dangerous and fatal than it can be in England, for *there* he will scarcely refuse his consent to a bill for putting England into as strong a state of defence as possible, and in America he would never suffer such a bill to be passed.

America is only a secondary object in the system of British politics, England consults the good of *this* country, no farther than it answers her *own* purpose. Wherefore, her own interest leads her to suppress the growth of *ours* in every case which doth not promote her advantage, or in the least interferes with it. A pretty state we should soon be in under such a second-hand government, considering what has happened! Men do not change from enemies to friends by the alteration of a name: And in order to shew that reconciliation now is a dangerous doctrine, I affirm, *that it would be policy in the king at this time, to repeal the acts for the sake of reinstating himself in the government of the provinces*; in order that HE MAY ACCOMPLISH BY CRAFT AND SUBTILITY, IN THE LONG RUN, WHAT HE CANNOT DO BY FORCE AND VIOLENCE IN THE SHORT ONE. Reconciliation and ruin are nearly related.

Secondly. That as even the best terms, which we can expect to obtain, can amount to no more than a temporary expedient, or a kind of government by guardianship, which can last no longer than till the colonies come of age, so the general face and state of things, in the interim, will be unsettled and unpromising. Emigrants of property will not choose to come to a country whose form of government hangs but by a thread, and who is every day tottering on the brink of commotion and disturbance; and numbers of the present inhabitants would lay hold of the interval, to dispose of their effects, and quit the continent.

But the most powerful of all arguments, is, that nothing but independence, i.e. a continental form of government, can keep the peace of the continent and preserve it inviolate from civil wars. I dread the event of a reconciliation with Britain now, as it is more than probable, that it will be followed by a revolt somewhere or other, the consequences of which may be far more fatal than all the malice of Britain.

Thousands are already ruined by British barbarity; (thousands more will probably suffer the same fate.) Those men have other feelings than us who have nothing suffered. All they *now* possess is liberty, what they before enjoyed is sacrificed to its service, and having nothing more to lose, they disdain submission. Besides, the general temper of the colonies, towards a British government, will be like that of a youth, who is nearly out of his time; they will care very little about her. And a government which cannot preserve the peace, is no government at all, and in that case we pay our money for nothing; and pray what is it that Britain can do, whose power will be wholly on paper, should a civil tumult break out the very day after reconciliation?...

The colonies have manifested such a spirit of good order and obedience to continental government, as is sufficient to make every reasonable person easy and happy on that head. No man can assign the least pretence for his fears, on any other grounds, that such as are truly childish and ridiculous, viz. that one colony will be striving for superiority over another....

If there is any true cause of fear respecting independence, it is because no plan is yet laid down. Men do not see their way out—Wherefore, as an opening into that business, I offer the following hints; at the same time modestly affirming, that I have no other opinion of them myself, than that they may be the means of giving rise to something better. Could the straggling thoughts of individuals be collected, they would frequently form materials for wise and able men to improve into useful matter.

Let the assemblies be annual, with a President only. The representation more equal. Their business wholly domestic, and subject to the authority of a Continental Congress.

Let each colony be divided into six, eight, or ten, convenient districts, each district to send a proper number of delegates to Congress, so that each colony send at least thirty. The whole number in Congress will be least 390. Each Congress to sit and to choose a president by the following method. When the delegates are met, let a colony be taken from the whole thirteen colonies by lot, after which, let the whole Congress choose (by ballot) a president from out of the delegates of *that* province...

But as there is a peculiar delicacy, from whom, or in what manner, this business must first arise, and as it seems most agreeable and consistent that it should come from some intermediate body between the governed and the governors, that is, between the Congress and the people, let a CONTINENTAL CONFERENCE be held, in the following manner, and for the following purpose.

A committee of twenty-six members of Congress, viz. two for each colony. Two members for each House of Assembly, or Provincial Convention; and five representatives of the people at large, to be chosen in the capital city or town of each province...

The conferring members being met, let their business be to frame a CONTINENTAL CHARTER, or Charter of the United Colonies; (answering to what is called the Magna Charta of England) fixing the number and manner of choosing members of Congress, members of Assembly, with their date of sitting, and drawing the line of business and jurisdiction between them: (Always remembering, that our strength is continental, not provincial:) Securing freedom and property to all men, and above all things, the free exercise of religion...

Should any body of men be hereafter delegated for this or some similar purpose, I offer them the following extracts from that wise observer on governments *Dragonetti*. "The science" says he "of the politician consists in fixing the true point of happiness and freedom. Those men would deserve the gratitude of ages, who should discover a mode of government that contained the greatest sum of individual happiness, with the least national expense."—*Dragonetti on virtue and rewards*.

But where says some is the King of America? I'll tell you Friend, he reigns above, and doth not make havoc of mankind like the Royal Brute of Britain. Yet that we may not appear to be defective even in earthly honors, let a day be solemnly set apart for proclaiming the charter; let it be brought forth placed on the divine law, the word of God; let a crown be placed thereon, by which the world may know, that so far as we approve as monarchy, that in America THE LAW IS KING. For as in absolute governments the King is law, so in free countries the law *ought* to be King; and there ought to be no other. But lest any ill use should afterwards arise, let the crown at the conclusion of the ceremony be demolished, and scattered among the people whose right it is.

A government of our own is our natural right: And when a man seriously reflects on the precariousness of human affairs, he will become convinced, that it is infinitely wiser and safer, to form a constitution of our own in a cool deliberate manner, while we have it in our power, than to trust such an interesting event to time and chance. If we omit it now, some, Massanello may hereafter arise, who laying hold of popular disquietudes, may collect together the desperate and discontented, and by assuming to themselves the powers of government, may sweep away the liberties of the continent like a deluge...

To talk of friendship with those in whom our reason forbids us to have faith, and our affections wounded through a thousand pores instruct us to detest, is madness and folly. Every day wears out the little remains of kindred between us and them, and can there be any reason to hope, that as the relationship expires, the affection will increase, or that we shall agree better, when we have ten times more and greater concerns to quarrel over than ever?

Ye that tell us of harmony and reconciliation, can ye restore to us the time that is past? Can ye give to prostitution its former innocence? Neither can ye reconcile Britain and America. The last cord now is broken, the people of England are presenting addresses against us. There are injuries which nature cannot forgive; she would cease to be nature if she did. As well can the lover forgive the ravisher of his mistress, as the continent forgive the murders of Britain. The Almighty hath implanted in us these unextinguishable feelings for good and wise purposes. They are the guardians of his image in our hearts. They distinguish us from the herd of common animals. The social compact would dissolve, and justice be extirpated from the earth, or have only a casual existence were we callous to the touches of affection. The robber, and the murderer, would often escape unpunished, did not the injuries which our tempers sustain, provoke us into justice.

O ye that love mankind! Ye that dare oppose, not only the tyranny, but the tyrant, stand forth! Every spot of the old world is overrun with oppression. Freedom hath been hunted round the globe. Asia, and Africa, have long expelled her.—Europe regards her like a stranger, and England hath given her warning to depart. O! receive the fugitive, and prepare in time an asylum for mankind.

Glossary

Dragonetti: Giacinto Dragonetti, an Italian reformer whose book A Treatise on Rewards and Virtues was published in England in 1769 Extirpated: eradicated

English constitution: not a single written document but a series of documents, laws, and accepted practices forming the basis of English government

extirpated: eradicated

Magna Charta: (Magna Carta) document signed by King John of England in 1215 pledging himself to be bound by law

Massanello: (Masaniello) Tommaso Aniello, a fisherman of Naples, Italy, who led a revolt against Spanish rule in 1647

Document Analysis

Far from being chosen arbitrarily, the title of *Common Sense* has to be recognized as a useful rhetorical commonplace that sets the tone for the entire document. Recommended as a fitting title by Paine's fellow revolutionary Benjamin Rush of Philadelphia, the term "common sense" had already picked up in English political discourse a connotation of simple, practical reasoning, often by an anonymous writer, offered to make clear the wisest course of action in a given situation. Paine's readers can see the reasoning thread its way through the pamphlet as Paine speaks of his subject seemingly as a practical man who wants nothing more than to promote the best possible government for the American people. Appeal to authority, which might be thought of as an alternative to common sense as a way of establishing truth, is used sparingly, as only a handful of authors and one book (the Bible) are mentioned, and Paine offers neither his own name nor his credentials as a means of bolstering his arguments.

It is the historical anecdote, the factual observation (not always strictly accurate), and the apt metaphor (occasionally offering an insidious comparison) on which Paine chiefly relies to support his reasoning. Apparently he sees his target audience as those who are as yet undecided on independence, or even skeptical of it, as he does not make an explicit call for independence until the end, and he precedes that call with a set of arguments designed to bring the reader to embrace the thesis step-by-step once the inductive pattern is complete. However, Paine also signals that he has on his mind inhabitants of every land when he writes in the introduction, "The cause of America is in a great measure the cause of all mankind."

"On the Origin and Design of Government in General, with Concise Remarks on the English Constitution"

The body of the pamphlet is divided into four major sections, the first of which is "On the Origin and Design of Government in General, with Concise Remarks on the English Constitution." In this first section, Paine asserts that "society in every state is a blessing, but Government, even in its best state, is but a necessary evil." He elaborates on this by describing how people in some remote place presumably will unite in society to pool their labor, but when the worse side of human nature threatens to disrupt that society, government becomes necessary "to supply the defect of moral virtue." As a society advances, a parliament will form, consisting of every man with his own vote; later a representative assembly will assume this role but maintain the democratic nature of the earlier system. This picture of government emerging out of necessity is obviously one that Paine's readers can apply, if they wish, to the development of colonial America, and its natural simplicity lays the ground for Paine to attack the English constitution as bloated, overly complicated, and given to divided government, with a king checked not so much by the defective constitution as by the nature of the English people.

"On Heredity and Hereditary Succession"

The second major section of the pamphlet is entitled "On Heredity and Hereditary Succession," in which Paine attacks the very institution of monarchy. Asserting that monarchies originated among heathens, he draws on the Book of Judges and the Book of Samuel in the Old Testament to present his own version of "Hebraic Republicanism," a doctrine that had emerged in the seventeenth century in England as a means of discrediting the English monarchy and that was based on the belief that ancient Israel provided a model for a kingless nation-state. As Paine recounts the historical record set down in the Old Testament sources, the ancient Hebrews did without kings for thousands of years, ruled instead by judges and elders, and only out of delusion and sinfulness did they eventually ask God to give them a king. In developing this argument, Paine quotes at length from scripture, constituting the most extensive use of quotation from authority in any part of Common Sense. As Paine still adhered to Quakerism at this point in his life (he later became a deist), he presumably accepted the authority of the Bible and assumed here that his largely Protestant audience would do so as well (the fact that he aims his message at a Protestant audience and spurns Catholic readers is shown at another point by his equating the monarchy to "Popery," an example of his use of insidious comparison).

Switching his attention to the future, Paine goes on to attack hereditary monarchy as posterity threat to the future health of the nation. He points out the folly of giving any king the right to impose the rule of his heirs upon the governed, as such a practice could easily lead to rule by an incompetent successor. Further, Paine argues that any hereditary line of kingly succession likely began with a usurper who took power by force. Usurpation, Paine says, is but one way of gaining a throne, the other two being by election or by lot; he asserts that if by lot or election, it should have continued so, but if by usurpation, as he believes is the case in England, then no one can reasonably defend the monarchy.

Paine continues to attack hereditary monarchy by further examining the history of the English Crown. Rule by kings, he argues, is no method of avoiding civil strife, as thirty English kings and two minors had ruled since the Norman Conquest, with a consequent eight civil wars and nineteen rebellions. Paine can find no useful purpose in having a king, especially in England. In sum, Paine finds nothing good and much bad about monarchy as a form of government (in later years, Paine claimed to have been influenced in these opinions by two tracts written by the seventeenth-century writer John Milton. However, Milton's grievance was chiefly against King Charles I, and he wrote in justification of the king's execution, whereas Paine's grievance is clearly against the hereditary monarchy as an institution).

"Thoughts on the Present State of American Affairs"
The third major section of *Common Sense*—from which the above excerpt is taken—is devoted to "Thoughts on the Present State of American Affairs." Paine first dismisses all plans and proposals regarding the colonies and England before the Battle of Lexington in April 1775 as "superseded and useless now." With this statement, his need for narrative is greatly lessened, and, indeed, he is freed from expounding on much that, as a recent immigrant to America, he would know of only secondhand. Being well aware that many colonists still hold hopes of reconciliation, however, he sets out to refute the arguments for that option, which he enumerates as follows: America has thrived under British rule; British military might has protected America; Britain is the parent country and the colonies her children; Americans are of English descent and should therefore maintain allegiance to Britain; and united, the colonies and Britain can defy the world. To the first argument, Paine replies that America would have thrived as much under no European power. To the argument about military protection, he replies that Britain's protection was always pursued in the self-interest of Britain and not of America. Regarding the next point, he replies that if Britain is the parent country, so greater is its shame for the way it has treated the colonies. To the argument about family connections, he asserts that such bonds are too tenuous to apply to occupants of another continent, and, even if all Americans were of English descent, which they are not, it would signify little, as Britain has become America's enemy. To the final argument, that Britain and the colonies are stronger together, he argues that the supposed advantage is mere presumption, and that, furthermore, America's future is not one of defiance but of "peace and friendship with all Europe." In sum, Paine writes, "I challenge the warmest advocate for reconciliation to show a single advantage that this continent can reap by being connected with Great Britain."

After his rebuttals to the arguments in favor of reconciliation, Paine offers additional arguments for separation from England. The first argument is that beyond the bloodshed already inflicted, in the future, America will be dragged by England into European wars: "The blood of the slain, the weeping voice of nature cries, 'TIS TIME TO PART.'" A second argument is geographical, but (again with an eye to his readers' religiosity) imbued with divine meaning, as Paine argues that the sheer distance between England and America shows that the former's authority over the latter was "never the design of heaven." A third argument is that a split between America and England is inevitable, that it would be best accomplished immediately, and that among Americans it is only from the self-interested, the weak, the prejudiced, and the delusional that opposition is made to independence, thus stigmatizing those who will not yield to his arguments.

Paine argues that even if the pre-Revolution relations were somehow restored between America and

Britain, they would eventually relapse with even worse results. Indeed, he writes, some men take too lightly the injuries already inflicted on America, and these men only deceive themselves and invite ruin on their posterity. Noting the death and destitution that had been visited on many, he asks his readers if they have so suffered, and brands those who answer yes but who are still for reconciliation as having "the heart of a coward, and the spirit of a sycophant." Paine knows that here he is evoking emotions of shame and horror, but he excuses himself on the grounds that he only wants to awaken his audience and make it understand that America, not Britain, is the stumbling block to freedom: "'Tis not in the power of Britain or of Europe to conquer America, if she do not conquer herself by *delay* and *timidity*."

After arguing that things cannot be left to the next generation to settle, and that anything short of independence would be an insufficient solution to the colonists' predicament, and by asserting that it is the king, and not merely his ministries, that must be defeated, Paine tackles the question of what will transpire if the king is left with power over America. First, Paine writes, there will be no laws over America except what the king allows, and, thus, the welfare of England will always be given top priority. Second, things will be in an unsettled state that over time will dissuade immigration to and encourage emigration from America.

On the other hand, to allay fears over the unknown consequences independence might bring, Paine paints an agreeable picture of America's ability for self-governance, the colonies having so far handled their affairs in an orderly fashion. He proposes that the new government might be best organized along the lines of a president and an assembly of at least 390 men representing districts in their respective colonies; that a continental conference be convened for the purpose of establishing a continental charter; and that in the absence of a human king, it will be that "in America the LAW IS KING." Paine closes this third section of Common Sense with a recapitulation that the time to act is now, that no good will come of delay, and that true reconciliation is impossible, invoking an insidious comparison by asking, "Can ye give to prostitution its former innocence? Neither can you reconcile England and America."

"Of the Present Ability of America with Some Miscellaneous Reflections"

The fourth and last major section of *Common Sense* is entitled "Of the Present Ability of America with Some Miscellaneous Reflections." Here, Paine addresses the practical questions that arise from a consideration of independence. He cites the lack of American debt as a good sign that an adequate army and navy can be established; in a later edition of the pamphlet, he appears to fall back on his knowledge of naval affairs from his voyage on a privateer by adding an explanation of how practical and affordable an American navy would be, while at the same time denigrating the British Navy as being much more formidable on paper than in reality. To play up America's ability to field an army, he asserts that a small population and modest trade is more conducive to raising a large army than a large population consumed by matters of trade, and that it is typically the new nation that displays the greatest achievements.

Paine also speaks in favor of religious freedom, which he says independence would protect (he does not claim that it is in danger, but again it may sit well with the religious in his audience to be assured that whatever sect they may embrace, it will be more secure in a country without an official church). Finally, after repeating his earlier arguments in favor of a large and equal representation, he comes to his conclusion by spelling out the need for a "declaration of independence" and its advantages; specifically, he says that without such a declaration, no foreign power will mediate the American quarrel with Britain (although nowhere earlier does he claim any need for mediation), that neither France nor Spain will assist the American cause (this despite his earlier argument that America can raise a sufficient army and navy by itself), and that Americans will appear as rebels in the eyes of foreign nations (and that it would be injurious to their own peace if they were to support America). On the other hand, Paine asserts, by declaring to foreign powers all the injustices heaped on America by Britain and the unsuccessful steps taken to gain redress for these injustices, the result will be far better than that gained by further petitions to Britain. The steps to be taken, Paine promises, will soon seem agreeable, and Americans will no longer be like a man who keeps putting off unpleasant business.

The fact that *Common Sense* was a political tract has a great deal to do with the uses Paine made of it. He wished to present his arguments anonymously, for they are bold. Being likely to excite public sentiment, he wanted to avoid making himself the focus of controversy or seeming to seek personal glory through his discourse. This anonymity would not be possible through a sermon or other form of public speaking. Furthermore, from a strictly practical standpoint, Paine was a writer and not an orator. Paine undoubtedly recognized the value of communicating in enough detail to adequately explain and support his claims, which would argue against not only a brief article or letter but also an overly lengthy format that would tire the reader's attention or create too high a purchase price for the average person; in these respects a pamphlet was clearly superior to a book. Many of the figures of speech that might be useful in a spoken message could be dispensed with, and Paine was free to write in an accessible style that still had force and occasionally gave rise to truly memorable and artful phrases that have stood the test of time and mark Paine as a great political writer.

Essential Themes

The idea of American independence was not Paine's alone, but of the many writers that appeared in print following the outbreak of the American Revolution, none expressed his arguments with such vigor and clarity. Not only did Paine espouse the ideas in *Common Sense* itself, but also he was eager to defend them against the attacks that inevitably came from the opposing side. The Reverend William Smith, provost of what became the University of Philadelphia and a leading Loyalist, wrote a series of articles under the pen name of "Cato" that called for continued efforts to reach reconciliation with England, stressed the advantages that the connection with England afforded the colonies, and warned of the unforeseeable risks of independence. Writing under the pseudonym of "Forester," Paine shot back with a series of letters published in April and May 1776 that not only offered a detailed rebuttal to Smith's arguments but also served to keep the public's attention fixed on the subject of independence. While the Declaration of Independence that emerged in July 1776 was the work of other men, notably Thomas Jefferson, it was a document that clearly took inspiration from, among other sources, Paine and *Common Sense*.

If independence was a theme that was of particular concern to Americans, the cause of freedom and democratic rule was one with wider appeal that could find adherents among those in other countries who took their inspiration from Enlightenment thinkers such as John Locke. Paine claimed late in life that he had never read Locke, but he was sufficiently immersed in the world of ideas of his day to develop a practical philosophy adequate to his task. Coming on the heels of success in America, his efforts to stimulate democracy in Britain and France and to oppose the monarchies of both were natural extensions of his belief that the cause of freedom knew no national boundaries. In America, his vision of a national government was in its basic design not unlike the framework adopted by the Constitutional Convention in 1787, but there were those (including John Adams, who later dubbed the period of the Revolutionary War the "Age of Paine," in a derisive rather than complimentary sense) who tended to equate democracy with mob rule and thus felt no admiration for Paine's democratic tendencies. In England, any thought of abandoning the hereditary monarchy was doomed by tradition, and thus the arguments against it in Paine's *Rights of Man* were offered in vain. In France, mob rule did indeed seem to take hold after the overthrow of Louis XVI led to the Reign of Terror; Paine's efforts to point revolutionary France in a positive direction almost cost him his life and did nothing to impede the eventual rise of dictatorship.

—Lawrence W. Haapanen, PhD

Bibliography and Additional Reading

Ellis, Joseph J. *American Creation: Triumphs and Tragedies of the Founders of the Republic.* New York: Knopf, 2007.

Ferling, John. *Setting the World Ablaze: Washington, Adams, Jefferson, and the American Revolution.* New York: Oxford UP, 2000.

Larkin, Edward. *Thomas Paine and the Literature of Revolution.* New York: Cambridge UP, 2005.

Nelson, Craig. *Thomas Paine: Enlightenment, Revolution, and the Birth of Modern Nations.* New York: Viking, 2006.

Paine, Thomas. *Common Sense and Other Writings.* Ed. J. M. Opal. New York: Norton, 2012.

Rosenfeld, Sophia. *Common Sense: A Political History.* Cambridge, MA: Harvard UP, 2011.

Smith, Barbara Clark. *The Freedoms We Lost: Consent and Resistance in Revolutionary America.* New York: New, 2010.

Wilson, David A. *Paine and Cobbett: The Transatlantic Connection.* Kingston, ON: McGill-Queen's UP 1988.

Wood, Gordon S. *The Radicalism of the American Revolution.* New York: Knopf, 1992.

———. *Revolutionary Characters: What Made the Founders Different.* New York: Penguin, 2006.

Declaration of Independence

Date: July 4, 1776
Author: Thomas Jefferson
Genre: political tract

"Whenever any form of government becomes destructive of these ends, it is the right of the people to alter or to abolish it."

Summary Overview

An iconic document the world over, the Declaration of Independence represented the first formal statement by the American colonists of their intention to become independent from British rule. In the decades that preceded the American Revolution, anti-British fervor had been growing, catalyzed by such laws passed by Parliament as the Stamp Act and the Intolerable Acts. The document was published and distributed as the British military stepped up its efforts to quell growing anti-British activity in the colonies. The Declaration took issue specifically with King George III and stated that the colonies had a right to declare independence if their rights to life, liberty, and the pursuit of happiness were to be denied by the British government. The Declaration served as a landmark document, accelerating the American Revolution, fostering the notion of democratic government, and inspiring other revolutions around the world, most notably the French Revolution.

Defining Moment

In many ways, the Declaration of Independence may be seen as a mere formality after decades of growing secessionist sentiment in the American colonies. This anti-British fervor had roots in the Enlightenment that took shape in Europe during the eighteenth century. The philosophical notions proffered by philosophers Jean-Jacques Rousseau, François-Marie Arouet Voltaire, the Baron de Montesquieu, and John Locke heavily influenced the political convictions of colonial leaders such as John and Samuel Adams, Benjamin Franklin, and Thomas Jefferson. The "revolutionary" idea that circulated during this era was that government should derive its power from the people it rules and that only through the will of the people can a government make decisions. Further, all citizens of a nation have the right to life to life, liberty, and property, and should any government try to suppress these rights, it is the right of the people to throw off that government for a new one.

Although the American Revolution could look to the Enlightenment for its inspiration, a number of incidents pushed the colonists to revolt. During the middle of the eighteenth century, for example, in order to help finance a burdensome, seven-year war with France, the English increased taxes on the colonies, most notably on products such as molasses and sugar. Relations became even more strained in the years that followed. The British imposed even stronger sanctions on the colonies, passing laws that included increased taxes on a wide range of products, allowances for British soldiers to be housed in private residences, and restrictions on imports to Boston.

The colonial responses to these measures were increasingly overt. In 1770, a confrontation between colonists and British soldiers in Boston resulted in the soldiers firing upon the crowd, killing five and wounding six others. The Boston Massacre, as it became known, was used as a trigger event to foster more widespread support for the revolutionary cause. Five years later, the violence between the two sides had escalated, culminating in such notable battles between the colonial Minutemen and the British army at Lexington and Concord and at Bunker Hill.

In 1776, Thomas Paine's pamphlet *Common Sense* was distributed among the colonists, using plain, simple language to widen its appeal to even the most uneducated of people. That document called upon all Americans to rise up in opposition to British rule. Later that year, the newly formed Continental Congress called for a formal declaration of the colonists' intention to seek independence. Thomas Jefferson, who was noted for his eloquent writing style, was chosen for the task. After a few revisions, the Declaration of Independence was adopted by the congress on July 4, 1776, and read aloud four days later. On August 2, fifty-six delegates from all thirteen colonies signed the document.

Author Biography

Thomas Jefferson was born in Shadwell, Virginia, on April 13, 1743. His parents were well established; his mother came from a prominent Virginia family, the Randolphs, while his father was a successful planter and surveyor. Jefferson received a formal education in the classical languages and mathematics at a prestigious private school near his home before enrolling in the College of William and Mary in 1760.

Jefferson attended the College of William and Mary and studied law with established lawyer George Wythe. After his graduation, Jefferson became a successful attorney from 1764 to 1774. During this period, Jefferson met his future wife, Martha Skelton, with whom he would have six children (only two of whom survived to adulthood). He also spent a great deal of his time working on his prized plantation, Monticello. He inherited two hundred slaves from both his father and father-in-law; he freed two of them during his lifetime and allowed for the freedom of five more in accordance with his will.

Thomas Jefferson's political career coincided with the slowly building revolutionary fervor. In addition to his tenures as a magistrate and county lieutenant, Jefferson was elected to the Virginia House of Burgesses, the representative body in the colonial government. There, he connected with a group of so-called radicals, including fellow representatives Patrick Henry and George Washington. In 1774, he wrote his first major political document, "A Summary View of the Rights of British America," which cemented his reputation as an individual who could eloquently present the colonials' issues and agenda.

In 1775, Jefferson attended the Second Continental Congress, which assigned Jefferson's colleague George Washington to be the commander in chief of the newly established Continental Army. A year later, in light of the reception of "A Summary View," Jefferson was asked by the congress to work with delegates John Adams, Roger Sherman, Benjamin Franklin, and Robert Livingston to draft the Declaration of Independence.

After his work with the congress, Thomas Jefferson returned to Virginia as a member of its House of Delegates, a position he held from 1776 to 1779. From 1779 until 1781, Jefferson served as Virginia's governor, although his tenure ended when, with the British advancing on the American South, he failed (in the public eye) to show resolve and defiance against the British army. Although he desired to return to Monticello for good, his wife's death in 1782 drew him back into public service. In 1783, he returned to the congress, which in 1785 named him the American minister to France. Upon returning to America in 1789, he was appointed George Washington's secretary of state, a post he held until 1794. He was defeated by John Adams to succeed Washington, but in 1800, he succeeded in becoming the nation's third president. In 1809, Jefferson returned to Monticello and founded the University of Virginia. He died in 1826, fifty years to the day after his Declaration of Independence was adopted by the Continental Congress.

Historical Document

Declaration of Independence

When in the course of human events, it becomes necessary for one people to dissolve the political bands which have connected them with another, and to assume among the powers of the earth, the separate and equal station to which the laws of nature and of nature's God entitle them, a decent respect to the opinions of mankind requires that they should declare the causes which impel them to the separation.

We hold these truths to be self-evident:

That all men are created equal; that they are endowed by their Creator with certain unalienable rights; that among these are life, liberty, and the pursuit of happiness; that, to secure these rights, governments are instituted among men, deriving their just powers from the consent of the governed; that whenever any form of government becomes destructive of these ends, it is the right of the people to alter or to abolish it, and to institute new government, laying its foundation on such principles, and organizing its powers in such form, as to them shall seem most likely to effect their safety and happiness. Prudence, indeed, will dictate that governments long established should not be changed for light and transient causes; and accordingly all experience hath shown that mankind are more disposed to suffer, while evils are sufferable than to right themselves by abolishing the forms to which they are accustomed. But when a long train of abuses and usurpations, pursuing invariably the same object, evinces a design to reduce them under absolute despotism, it is their right, it is their duty, to throw off such government, and to provide new guards for their future security. Such has been the patient sufferance of these colonies; and such is now the necessity which constrains them to alter their former systems of government. The history of the present King of Great Britain is a history of repeated injuries and usurpations, all having in direct object the establishment of an absolute tyranny over these states. To prove this, let facts be submitted to a candid world.

He has refused his assent to laws, the most wholesome and necessary for the public good.

He has forbidden his governors to pass laws of immediate and pressing importance, unless suspended in their operation till his assent should be obtained; and, when so suspended, he has utterly neglected to attend to them.

He has refused to pass other laws for the accommodation of large districts of people, unless those people would relinquish the right of representation in the legislature, a right inestimable to them, and formidable to tyrants only.

He has called together legislative bodies at places unusual uncomfortable, and distant from the depository of their public records, for the sole purpose of fatiguing them into compliance with his measures.

He has dissolved representative houses repeatedly, for opposing, with manly firmness, his invasions on the rights of the people.

He has refused for a long time, after such dissolutions, to cause others to be elected; whereby the legislative powers, incapable of annihilation, have returned to the people at large for their exercise; the state remaining, in the mean time, exposed to all the dangers of invasions from without and convulsions within.

He has endeavored to prevent the population of these states; for that purpose obstructing the laws for naturalization of foreigners; refusing to pass others to encourage their migration hither, and raising the conditions of new appropriations of lands.

He has obstructed the administration of justice, by refusing his assent to laws for establishing judiciary powers.

He has made judges dependent on his will alone, for the tenure of their offices, and the amount and payment of their salaries.

He has erected a multitude of new offices, and sent hither swarms of officers to harass our people and eat out their substance.

He has kept among us, in times of peace, standing armies, without the consent of our legislatures.

He has affected to render the military independent of, and superior to, the civil power.

He has combined with others to subject us to a jurisdiction foreign to our Constitution and unacknowledged by our laws, giving his assent to their acts of pretended legislation:

For quartering large bodies of armed troops among us;

For protecting them, by a mock trial, from punishment for any murders which they should commit on the inhabitants of these states;

For cutting off our trade with all parts of the world;

For imposing taxes on us without our consent;

For depriving us, in many cases, of the benefits of trial by jury;

For transporting us beyond seas, to be tried for pretended offenses;

For abolishing the free system of English laws in a neighboring province, establishing therein an arbitrary government, and enlarging its boundaries, so as to render it at once an example and fit instrument for introducing the same absolute rule into these colonies;

For taking away our charters, abolishing our most valuable laws, and altering fundamentally the forms of our governments;

For suspending our own legislatures and declaring themselves invested with power to legislate for us in all cases whatsoever.

He has abdicated government here, by declaring us out of his protection and waging war against us.

He has plundered our seas, ravaged our coasts, burned our towns, and destroyed the lives of our people.

He is at this time transporting large armies of foreign mercenaries to complete the works of death, desolation, and tyranny already begun with circumstances of cruelty and perfidy scarcely paralleled in the most barbarous ages, and totally unworthy the head of a civilized nation.

He has constrained our fellow-citizens, taken captive on the high seas, to bear arms against their country, to become the executioners of their friends and brethren, or to fall themselves by their hands.

He has excited domestic insurrection among us, and has endeavored to bring on the inhabitants of our frontiers the merciless Indian savages, whose known rule of warfare is an undistinguished destruction of all ages, sexes, and conditions.

In every stage of these oppressions we have petitioned for redress in the most humble terms; our repeated petitions have been answered only by repeated injury. A prince, whose character is thus marked by every act which may define a tyrant, is unfit to be the ruler of a free people.

Nor have we been wanting in our attentions to our British brethren. We have warned them, from time to time, of attempts by their legislature to extend an unwarrantable jurisdiction over us. We have reminded them of the circumstances of our emigration and settlement here. We have appealed to their native justice and magnanimity; and we have conjured them, by the ties of our common kindred, to disavow these usurpations which would inevitably interrupt our connections and correspondence. They too, have been deaf to the voice of justice and of consanguinity. We must, therefore, acquiesce in the necessity which denounces our separation, and hold them as we hold the rest of mankind, enemies in war, in peace friends.

We, therefore, the representatives of the United States of America, in General Congress assembled, appealing to the Supreme Judge of the world for the rectitude of our intentions, do, in the name and by the authority of the good people of these colonies solemnly publish and declare, That these United Colonies are, and of right ought to be, FREE AND INDEPENDENT STATES; that they are absolved from all allegiance to the British crown and that all political connection between them and the state of Great Britain is, and ought to be, totally dissolved; and that, as free and independent states, they have full power to levy war, conclude peace, contract alliances, establish commerce, and do all other acts and things which independent states may of right do. And for the support of this declaration, with a firm reliance on the protection of Divine Providence, we mutually pledge to each other our lives, our fortunes, and our sacred honor.

[Signed by]

John Hancock [President]

New Hampshire
Josiah Bartlett, Wm. Whipple, Matthew Thornton.

Massachusetts Bay
Saml. Adams, John Adams, Robt. Treat Pain, Elbridge Gerry

Rhode Island
Step. Hopkin, William Ellery.

Connecticut
Roger Sherman, Sam'el Huntington, Wm. Williams, Oliver Wolcott.

New York
Wm. Floyd, Phil. Livingston, Frans. Lewis, Lewis Morris.

New Jersey
Richd. Stockton, Jno. Witherspoon, Fras. Hopkinson, John Hart, Abra. Clark.

Pennsylvania
Robt. Morris, Benjamin Rush, Benja. Franklin, John Morton, Geo. Clymer, Jas. Smith, Geo. Taylor, James Wilson, Geo. Ross.

Delaware
Caesar Rodney, Geo. Reade, Tho. M'Kean.

Maryland
Samuel Chase, Wm. Paca, Thos. Stone, Charles Carroll of Carrollton.

Virginia
George Wythe, Richard Henry Lee, Th. Jefferson, Benja. Harrison, Ths. Nelson, Jr., Francis Lightfoot Lee, Carter Braxton.

North Carolina
Wm. Hooper, Joseph Hewes, John Penn.

South Carolina
Edward Rutledge, Thos. Hayward, Junr., Thomas Lynch, Junr., Arthur Middleton.

Georgia
Button Gwinnett, Lyman Hall, Geo. Walton.

Glossary

mercenaries: professional soldiers hired to serve in the army of another country

perfidy: treachery, deceit, or betrayal

tyranny: a political system ruled by an oppressive government

unalienable: not to be separated or taken away

usurpations: wrongful seizures and exercises of authority

Document Analysis

On June 7, 1776, Richard Henry Lee of Virginia, as ordered by the convention of the colony of Virginia, offered a resolution to the Continental Congress that the congress declare the thirteen American colonies to be free and independent from Great Britain. After some delay and discussion, the congress agreed to form a committee (dubbed the Committee of Five) to draft such a statement. The committee consisted of John Adams of Massachusetts, Roger Sherman of Connecticut, Benjamin Franklin of Pennsylvania, Robert Livingston of New York, and Thomas Jefferson of Virginia. The Committee of Five turned to Jefferson to write the statement, and although he later claimed that his initial draft was edited in some parts by Adams and Franklin, the final draft was clearly Jefferson's verbiage.

The Declaration of Independence was written in several parts. The first, the introduction, summarizes the colonists' position: As a result of the oppression exhibited by the British government, the colonies were left with no choice but to separate from Great Britain. The second part, the preamble, outlines the principles on which the colonies' independence was declared. The third part, the body, was presented in two sections: first, the specific issues that existed between Great Britain and the colonies, and second, the efforts made by the colonists to address those issues prior to secession. The last part is the conclusion, stating that the colonies are no longer to be considered a part of the British Empire and that all previous relationships between these two parties were no longer valid.

Enlightenment Influence

The introduction and preamble to the Declaration of Independence echo a number of themes that were introduced during the Enlightenment. For example, Jefferson comments that men (all of whom stood on equal footing) were endowed by God with the basic rights of life, liberty, and the pursuit of happiness. These rights, according to Jefferson, were therefore inalienable (impossible to surrender). It is the role of government, according the Declaration, to develop a system in which those tenets would be vigorously upheld and defended.

The notion of life, liberty, and the pursuit of happiness as basic human rights stems from the ideals of John Locke nearly a century earlier. Locke argued that life, liberty, and property should all be considered "natural rights." In fact, Locke criticized the British monarch's authority to protect the interests of the people, suggesting that the monarchy was constantly at odds with its people. Meanwhile, the legislature (in the case of Great Britain, the Parliament) was a far more effective representative for the people. Meanwhile, Charles de Montesquieu made a similar assertion in France, although he saw the monarchy as an executive, serving as a check and balance to the legislature's activity.

Jefferson built on the ideals of Montesquieu, Locke, and other Enlightenment-era philosophers, making an argument that, if government did not uphold its responsibility to structure itself in a manner suited for the protection of those human rights, it should be replaced. According to the Declaration, the new government would replace the former regime's intransigent elements with institutions that speak to the needs of the people. To be sure, the Declaration argued, many governments had existed and operated in their repressive ways for a long time. The decision to change long-standing political regimes and institutions should not be made lightly or in mercurial fashion, but rather based on prudent, careful consideration. After all, Jefferson acknowledged, many societies continued to experience "sufferable" hardships—to these people, simply adapting to one or two oppressive policies was more desirable than working to completely undermine the government. For those nations in which government oppression was far too egregious, however, Jefferson argued, it is the duty of the people to "throw off" those governments and replace them with new institutions that ensure the future health and well-being of the citizens.

Grievances without Redress

In the first section of the body of the Declaration of Independence, Thomas Jefferson makes clear that the colonies had been subjected to such long-term oppression. The king of Great Britain, the Declaration charged, had a long history of usurpation and injurious treatment of the American colonies. The body of the Declaration next provides a long list of examples of this treatment.

Some of the allegations the Declaration makes to generate pro-revolutionary sentiment concern the political and public policy process. The king, for example, refused to agree to the introduction of laws (as approved by the colonial governments) that served the public good. If new colonies or similar entities formed, the king would refuse to provide any political protection unless these new parties relinquished authority to British rule. Furthermore, the document alleged, the king deliberately forbade his governors to pass important and pressing legislation without his consent—a pace and process that were convenient only for the king.

In addition to the Declaration's accusations of the king's apparent indifference, Jefferson's document claimed that the king was in many ways deliberately stifling the growth and success of the colonies. In fact, this conscious undermining of the colonies was meant to render the colonial leaders exhausted and frustrated to the point at which they would capitulate to the king's authority. The Declaration cites incidents in which the king called for colonial legislators to meet in locations and at times that were completely inconvenient to them. In other examples, the king was alleged to have refused to allow the election of qualified people to colonial government, thus slowing the public policy process. Furthermore, any colonial governing body that opposed the decisions of the king was quickly dissolved by the royal governors and replaced with leadership more amenable to the king's agenda. In the meantime, the royal government in Britain frequently appointed tax commissioners and other senior officials whose tasks interfered with the efforts of colonial officials.

While the king's sophomoric attempts to slow the colonies' public policy process made life difficult, the Declaration of Independence stated that there were many more egregious and oppressive measures and actions undertaken by the king. For example, the judiciary, which was expected to protect the people's rights through strict interpretation of the law, was manned by people handpicked by the king, despite any colonial laws to the contrary. In fact, the king interjected himself into the legal process, applying his own legal decisions and interpretations on a number of cases.

Some of the most confrontational decisions made by the king with regard to the colonies involved his allowance for military personnel to live among the colonists, even during peacetime. This issue was particularly evident in the years following the French and Indian War—although the campaign came to a close, British soldiers called up to take part in the effort were stationed over the long term in the colonies. These soldiers were largely protected from prosecution by the colonial judicial system as well. According to a 1774 law passed by Parliament, if a crime such as murder was committed by a British loyalist in the army or by a British official, he was sent back to Britain, given what amounted to a sham trial, and released without punishment. The presence of such personnel caused undue stress for the people of the colonies, resulting in cases of harassment and other issues. In fact, under the Quartering Act of 1765, the king allowed British troops to enter, without warning, and take up temporary residence in colonists' private homes.

As the Declaration of Independence continued to present its list of grievances against the king, the accusations became more severe. Jefferson accuses the British government of increasing taxes on products such as sugar, molasses, paper, and tea without the input of the colonists. Additionally, the document takes issue with a 1769 law passed by Parliament that allowed for the extradition to Britain of colonists accused of treason. The Declaration accuses the king of unlawfully arresting and prosecuting colonists for fabricated crimes. Furthermore, colonists who were arrested for smuggling and other trade-related crimes would likely be tried in America, but British law permitted them to be tried without a jury of their peers present.

In another complaint, the Declaration took King George III to task for the Quebec Act of 1774. The British government had allowed for the extension of Quebec's borders to the Ohio River, thereby allowing French law to apply in those regions. In doing so, the British could impose more severe controls over their own provinces.

By the 1760s and 1770s, it became clear to the colonists that the British government was directly pursuing total domination over the colonies. For example, Jefferson's document cited the Declaratory Act of 1766, which declared that the royal government had the authority to make any and all laws for the colonies, rendering moot the colonial governments' lawmaking activities. Additionally, Parliament passed a number of laws that restricted the colonies' ability to negotiate and conduct trade with nations other than Great Britain, moves that the Declaration states are akin to cutting off the colonies' international trade policies.

As the Revolution continued to build, the British government consistently clamped down on the institutions that fomented the liberty movement. In 1774, Parliament ordered that all town meetings in Massachusetts be restricted and that its local officials be appointed directly by the king rather than elected by the general public. Parliament did not stop at removing the charters of local communities, either; in 1767, Parliament suspended the New York Assembly (that colony's legislative body) altogether, as that institution refused to comply with the Quartering Act.

The king's efforts to squelch the pro-independence movement, documented in the Declaration of Independence, became more overt and confrontational as violent confrontations between the colonists and British army increased. Thomas Jefferson's document describes how the king "abdicated government here," an accusation that the Declaration states gave the king an opening to wage war against the colonies. This warfare was carried out on a number of fronts. For example, the Declaration accuses the British government of attempting to incite anti-independence violence from within the colonial population, thereby creating divisions and competing factions. Such factions would threaten to undermine the united front driving the Revolution.

In addition to his subversive activities, the king was accused of kidnapping American sailors while at sea and forcing them to take up arms against their fellow colonists or else face execution. The power to do so had been given to British ships by the Restraining Act of 1775. Furthermore, the British were accused of attempting to gain favor with the American Indians residing in the colonies, convincing them to take up arms against the colonists. The Declaration commented on the brutality employed by the Indians in previous colonial conflicts (as reported from King Philip's War of 1675–76 and the aforementioned French-Indian War), citing the fact that the Indians did not respect the rules of war and demonstrated a willingness to kill women and children during such conflicts.

Furthermore, Jefferson commented on the fact that the king hired and delivered mercenaries to America to add their armies as they continued their assault on the colonists. This section spoke directly Great Britain's hiring of entire units of Hessian soldiers from its principalities in what is now Germany. Although the British expected to defeat the colonists quickly, the battles of Bunker Hill, Lexington, and Concord gave Great Britain cause to believe that the colonists would not yield easily. The cost of raising troops in Great Britain was high, particularly in comparison to the costs of hiring Hessians, many of whom had already been relocated to New England and Canada to fight on Great Britain's behalf during the French and Indian War. Jefferson and his contemporaries considered Hessians brutish and uncivilized barbarians brought to America by a government bent on unleashing torture and cruelty upon the colonists. Furthermore, the colonists were outraged that the British would introduce another foreign combatant into what they believed should be an internal matter between the Crown and its colonies.

Finally, the Declaration cites the fact that the British were actively engaged in the destruction of the colonies' interests, plundering colonial ships, burning villages, and killing many citizens. This line spoke to a number of incidents, such as the capture of American vessels suspected of breaking the new trade laws. It also recalled the destruction of Falmouth, Maine; Bristol, Rhode Island; and Norfolk, Virginia, that occurred as the conflict raged.

According to the Declaration, the colonists had exhausted every resource to address these complaints in a peaceful manner. It claims that the colonists first attempted to file petitions of complaint with the king, seeking relief from such actions and policies. The response they received came in the form of "repeated injury." In light of this oppressive policy, it became

In 1820, the Declaration of Independence was already showing signs of age. Secretary of State John Quincy Adams commissioned printer William J. Stone to make a full-size copperplate engraving. This plate was used to print copies of the Declaration. The 1823 Stone engraving is the most frequently reproduced version of the Declaration. National Archives.

clear to the colonists that they were not serving under a benevolent monarch but a tyrant who was "unfit to be the ruler of a free people."

Having seen no improvement in the British attitude toward the colonies, the leaders of the independence movement deemed it appropriate to warn the king of the consequences of his actions. They reminded the king of their common heritage—the colonists may have immigrated to America but remained "brethren." This comment appealed to what the colonists hoped would be a more respectful response, one that never came. In the absence of a response, the colonists next made clear their position that increased restrictions, surreptitious activities, and direct belligerence would ultimately be met with colonial resistance. According to the Declaration, this approach generated no response other than continued conflict.

With the British government showing no intention of halting their attacks and oppressive rule over the colonies, Jefferson and his colleagues declared that they had no choice but to secede. They asserted that this policy was the only option available to the leaders who sought a better life for the colonists. Therefore, the Declaration was as a "necessity" in the decision to consider Great Britain an enemy.

In light of the colonies' plight, according to the conclusion of the Declaration of Independence, it was the right of the colonies to declare—not just to the king but to the entire world—that they would become "free and independent states." In light of this status, the colonies would no longer be subject to British law or allegiance to the Crown. Additionally, any political connections between these new states and Great Britain would be immediately dissolved.

Finally, Jefferson's document made clear to the king that, as a result of the Declaration, the independent states formed thereafter would have the full power to form their own governments and economies. The states would have the ability to enter into contracts with other states and nations, establish trade and commerce institutions, and form alliances. Furthermore, the states would have the power to wage war on their enemies (namely Great Britain) and enter into peace treaties.

The Declaration of Independence was officially adopted by the congress on July 4, 1776, although the New York Convention did not sign until July 9. Thereafter, it was distributed throughout the colonies and their respective conventions as well as to officers of the Continental Army. Fifty-six delegates would sign the document by August 2, 1776.

Essential Themes

The Declaration of Independence marked a significant change in the relationship between the American colonies and the British government. To be sure, the royal government had already acknowledged that the colonies were in a state of revolt a year before the Declaration was completed. However, the revolutionaries were, until the Declaration's completion, fighting for their rights under the Crown. After the Declaration's ratification, the colonies were fighting a war against a foreign power.

Like the revolutionaries who wrote and supported it, the Declaration of Independence was heavily influenced by the philosophical notions introduced during the Enlightenment. Chief among these beliefs was the notion that if the subjects of a government become oppressed or their basic rights otherwise denied, those subjects had a responsibility to change that government. The language utilized in the Declaration's preamble, describing the basic and inalienable rights of all citizens, echoes the themes of government powered by and representative of the people as espoused by a number of philosophers from the Enlightenment era.

The Declaration made a clear case for this imperative. The document provided a long list of examples of the increasingly oppressive policies of the king and the royal government. These examples included political manipulation through laws that rendered colonial legislation ineffectual, the installation of political leaders loyal to the Crown without the vote of the colonists, the delay of the passage of useful colonial laws, and even the altering of borders to facilitate the imposition of martial law.

The Declaration also cited the Crown's application of new taxes without colonial input—the purpose for these increased taxes was to pay for the British war effort against France—none of the new revenues were spent in the colonies. Furthermore, the British passed laws and directives for military personnel to take up residence among the colonists, including in their homes, but not be subject to many of the colonial laws. The accusations even included violence against innocent colonists, the disruption of trade, the destruction of property, and the use of Hessian troops to squelch the revolutionaries.

The Declaration claims that the colonies did everything they could to find a political solution to these issues but were either rebuffed by Great Britain or simply ignored. Lacking an amicable resolution, the document states, the colonists had no choice but to leave the British Empire. The Declaration states that this decision was not entered into lightly, as the new states would have to implement new political and economic systems for themselves while engaging their new foreign enemy, the British Empire. Nevertheless, prudence dictated that the colonies take action or else remain mired in an oppressive political system.

—Michael Auerbach, MA

Bibliography and Additional Reading

Bailyn, Bernard. *The Ideological Origins of the American Revolution*. Cambridge: Harvard UP, 1992.

"Brief Biography of Thomas Jefferson." *Jefferson Monticello*. Montecello.org, 2012.

"Declaration of Independence." *Charters of Freedom*. US National Archives and Records Administration, 2012.

Freedman, Russell. *Give Me Liberty! The Story of the Declaration of Independence*. New York: Holiday, 2000.

"Hobbes, Locke, Montesquieu, and Rousseau on Government." *Bill of Rights in Action* 20.2 (Spring 2004): n. pag.

Lanning, Michael Lee. *The American Revolution 100: The People, Battles, and Events of the American War for Independence, Ranked by the Their Significance*. Naperville: Sourcebooks, 2008.

Maier, Pauline. *American Scripture: Making the Declaration of Independence*. New York: Vintage, 1998.

Middlekauff, Robert. *The Glorious Cause: The American Revolution, 1763–1789*. Rev. ed. New York: Oxford UP, 2005.

Wills, Garry. *Inventing America: Jefferson's Declaration of Independence*. New York: Vintage 2018 (reprint).

Wood, Gordon S. *The Radicalism of the American Revolution*. New York: Vintage, 1993.

From the Commissioners for Negotiating a Peace with Great Britain

Date: 1783
Author: Adams, John; Franklin, Benjamin; Jay, John
Genre: letters; political correspondence

> *"Since we have assumed a place in the political system of the world, let us move like a primary and not secondary planet."*

Summary Overview

The end of wars of revolution can be just as significant as their beginnings. In this set of letters, from John Adams, Benjamin Franklin, and John Jay to Chancellor Robert Livingston (a fellow member of the former Continental Congress), the authors explain several components of the ongoing peace negotiations between Great Britain and America. Topics of discussion include postwar land boundaries, treatment of British loyalists—or Tories—still residing within American territory, commerce agreements, and deference to the king of France. More importantly, the authors articulate an image of the new nation that not only underscores its autonomy but also its readiness to position itself as an equal among the European powers, Britain, France, and Spain. Despite a reciprocity agreement signed with Louis XVI of France in 1788 that forbade a separate peace with Britain, Americans maneuvered around the terms of that treaty to work directly with British ministers. In doing so, Americans asserted their political prerogatives and shielded their new country from subservience to France.

Defining Moment

When fighting for the War for Independence commenced in 1775, American colonists faced the world's strongest army and navy. In 1774, the First Continental Congress created the Committees of Observation and Safety for each colony. The committees organized autonomous legislative bodies throughout the colonies and helped establish militias as well. Moreover, the committees established a degree of continuity and unity among the colonies. In June 1775, the Second Continental Congress elected George Washington as the commander-in-chief of the Continental Army. Initially, each colonial government was charged with providing funding for the army and war effort, but this proved insufficient. Americans quickly found an ally in King Louis XVI of France, whose ongoing feud with Great Britain fueled his interest in helping the colonies gain independence. Beginning in 1776, the Committee of Secret Correspondence sent emissaries to France to secure supplies and funding. One of the authors of the letter, Benjamin Franklin, proved instrumental in winning over the French public to the American cause.

Five years prior to the commissioners' letter, in February 1778, Congress and the king of France signed the Treaty of Alliance. It forbade each party from negotiating a peace with Great Britain independently and without the other's explicit acquiescence. Over the course of the war, France provided troops, supplies, naval support, and money to the colonial cause. Furthermore, the extent to which French military forces, including the Comte de Rochambeau's troop maneuvers at Yorktown, ensured a British surrender increasingly suggested that America would be saddled in an obeisant position regarding the French monarch. The commissioners' letters to Robert Livingston, a fervent proponent of Franco-American relations, underscore this tension between the allied parties. Although reaffirming their affection for Louis

XVI and gratitude for French assistance, the commissioners' actions reflect a shift in diplomatic relations and an endeavor to assert American autonomy.

The French Revolution of 1789 initially pleased Americans, who took joy in the shared political and ideological principles of the Enlightenment. Enthusiasm began to wane, however, during the early 1790s as the revolution entered a radical phase known as the Terror. The Treaty of Alliance with France from 1778 had no expiration, leaving the United States vulnerable to European politics. When France declared war against Austria in 1792, America was left wondering if their treaty, nearly fifteen years old, still applied. President George Washington firmly decided on a policy of neutrality. The United States, still in its infancy, did not yet have the necessary funds or military at their disposal to aid France. In 1793, Washington declared that America would remain neutral. They remained so even after Britain entered the engagement against France in 1794.

Private peace discussions with Great Britain allowed the American commissioners more flexibility in negotiating the terms of the agreement, but also fostered an atmosphere of suspicion among the belligerent powers. In the early 1780s, several European powers, Spain included, desired a quick end to the war and for Britain to retain a large portion of her colonies. France even had ambiguous motives in 1781 and sent missives to the other European powers outlining a potential cease-fire. Had not the combined forces of the French and American armies defeated Cornwallis at Yorktown in the same year, an alternative history may have been written. That the American commissioners instigated secret talks with Britain to ensure that their political aims were met reflects their impressive skill at maneuvering in the game of diplomacy. At the close of the war, Americans adopted a cautious stance toward defensive treaties, being wary of "entangling alliances."

Author Biography

John Adams

John Adams was born on October 30, 1735, in Braintree, Massachusetts, to Susanna Boylston Ad-

John Adams; portrait by Gilbert Stuart, c. 1800. Image via Wikimedia Commons. [Public domain.]

ams and Deacon John Adams. Adams had a modest childhood, his father being a farmer and religious figure in the community. Adams descended from the first generation of Puritans that fled England from religious persecution and settled in America during the 1630s. He enjoyed an affectionate relationship with both his father and mother, praising their virtues and modeling his own character after theirs. His marriage to Abigail Adams on October 25, 1764, produced six children, one of them being future president John Quincy Adams.

As an adult, Adams quickly emerged as a respected and adept lawyer. He had received a Harvard education beginning at age fifteen and developed a fondness for reading. His erudition and honesty aided him throughout his career as a lawyer. In 1770, Adams successfully defended the British soldiers who fired on a Boston crowd, an event that became known as the Boston Massacre. Adams became a leading figure in the War for Independence and was a Massachusetts delegate to the First and Second Continental

Congresses. At the closing of the war, he helped Benjamin Franklin and John Jay draw up peace negotiations with Great Britain.

Adams served as vice president during George Washington's presidency from 1789 to 1797. He became a federalist in the 1790s, and in 1796 he ran for the presidency. He served one term, which lasted from 1797 to 1801. John Adams died on July 4, 1826, in Quincy, Massachusetts.

Benjamin Franklin

Benjamin Franklin was born on January 17, 1706, in Boston, Massachusetts, to Josiah and Abiah Franklin. Despite his parents' urging to pursue a career in the clergy, Franklin pursued a different path. For a brief time, he worked at his brother's print shop. During the 1720s, Franklin mastered the printing trade and published secretly in his brother's paper under the pseudonym, "Mrs. Silence Dogood." Franklin left his brother's shop on bad terms and moved to Philadelphia. By the end of the decade, he had established his own paper, the *Pennsylvania Gazette*. On September 1, 1730, Franklin entered into a common-law marriage with Deborah Read, a woman with whom he had two children.

Franklin published under various pseudonyms and enjoyed great popularity, especially with *Poor Richard's Almanac,* a project that lasted from 1733 to 1758. In addition to being an accomplished writer, Franklin developed an interest for scientific and philanthropic projects. Known in France as the "man who tamed lightning," Franklin also helped fund public works, including the University of Pennsylvania and a public library in Philadelphia.

During the War for Independence, Franklin most notably served as ambassador to France and helped negotiate the 1778 treaty between America and King Louis XVI. As the war reached its conclusion, Franklin retained a central role in diplomatic affairs and, with the help of Adams and Jay, ensured Americans received recognition from Britain as an autonomous nation. Benjamin Franklin died on April 17, 1790.

Benjamin Franklin; portrait by Joseph-Siffred Duplessis, c. 1785. Image via Wikimedia Commons. [Public domain.]

John Jay; portrait by Gilbert Stuart, c. 1800. Image via Wikimedia Commons. [Public domain.]

His death was mourned by both Americans and the French, with whom he had spent several years.

John Jay

John Jay, son of Peter and Mary Jay, was born in New York City on December 12, 1745, to a prosperous merchant family. He descended from French Huguenots who fled France after Louis XIV rescinded the Edict of Nantes, a law which stipulated limited tolerance for French Protestants. As the son of a prominent member of New York, Jay received an extensive education, his parents having hired private tutors. When Jay was fifteen, he went to King's College (now Columbia University), entering the legal profession after graduating. In April 1774, Jay married Sarah Livingston, a member of the New Jersey elite. They had six children.

Jay was a conservative who served on both the First and Second Continental Congresses. During the revolution, he went to Spain to try and secure funding and Spanish recognition of America's independence. Though Spain eventually entered the war against Britain, Jay never obtained their recognition. In mid-1782, Jay traveled to Paris where he aided John Adams and Benjamin Franklin in negotiating the Treaty of Paris. After the revolution, Jay served his country in a variety of ways. He first became Secretary of Foreign Affairs, advocated a strong central government in the *Federalist Papers*, became the Chief Justice on the United States Supreme Court, negotiated a treaty with Britain in 1795, and later served as governor of New York. He died on May 17, 1829, in Bedford, New York.

Historical Document

From the Commissioners for Negotiating a Peace with Great Britain

TO ROBERT R. LIVINGSTON.

Passy, July 18th, 1783.

Sir,

We have had the honor of receiving by Captain Barney your two letters of the 25th of March and 21st of April, with the papers referred to in them.

We are happy to find, that the Provisional Articles have been approved and ratified by Congress, and we regret, that the manner in which that business was conducted, does not coincide with your ideas of propriety. We are persuaded, however, that this is principally owing to your being necessarily unacquainted with a number of circumstances, known to us, who were on the spot, and which will be particularly explained to you hereafter, and, we trust, to your satisfaction, and that of the Congress.

Your doubts respecting the Separate Article, we think, are capable of being removed; but as a full state of the reasons and circumstances, which prompted that measure, would be very prolix, we shall content ourselves with giving you the general outlines.

Mr Oswald was desirous to cover as much of the eastern shores of the Mississippi with British claims as possible; and, for this purpose, we were told a great deal about the ancient bounds of Canada, Louisiana, &c. &c. The British Court, who had, probably, not yet adopted the idea of relinquishing the Floridas, seemed desirous of annexing as much territory to them as possible, even up to the mouth of the Ohio. Mr Oswald adhered strongly to that object, as well to render the British countries there of sufficient extent to be (as he expressed it) worth keeping and protecting, as to afford a convenient retreat to the tories, for whom it would be difficult otherwise to provide; and, among other arguments, he finally urged his being willing to yield to our demands to the east, north, and west, as a further reason for our gratifying him on the point in question. He also produced the commission of Governor Johnson, extending the bounds of his government of West Florida, up to the river Yazoo; and contended for that extent as a matter of right, upon various principles, which, however, we did not admit, the King not being authorised, in our opinion to extend or contract the bounds of the colonies at pleasure.

We were of opinion, that the country in contest was of great value, both on account of its natural fertility and of its position, it being, in our opinion, the interest of America to extend as far down towards the mouth of the Mississippi as we possibly could. We also thought it advisable to impress Britain with a strong sense of the importance of the navigation of that river to their future commerce on the interior waters, from the mouth of the St Lawrence to that of the Mississippi, and thereby render that Court averse to any stipulations with Spain to relinquish it. These two objects militated against each other, because to enhance the value of the navigation, was also to enhance the value of the countries contiguous to it, and thereby disincline Britain to the dereliction of them. We thought, therefore, that the surest way to reconcile and obtain both objects would be by a composition beneficial to both parties. We therefore proposed, that Britain should withdraw her pretensions to all the country above the Yazoo, and that we would cede all below it to her, in case she should have the Floridas at the end of the war; and, at all events, that she should have a right to navigate the river throughout its whole extent. This proposition was accepted, and we agreed to insert the contingent fact of it in a separate Article, for the express purpose of keeping it secret for the present. That Article ought not, therefore, to be considered as a mere matter of favor to Britain, but as the result of a bargain, in which that Article was a quid pro quo.

It was in our opinion, both necessary and justifiable, to keep this Article secret. The negotiations between Spain, France, and Britain were then in full vigor, and embarrassed by a variety of clashing demands. The publication of this Article would have irritated Spain, and retarded, if not have prevented her coming to an agreement with Britain.

Had we mentioned it to the French Minister, he must have not only informed Spain of it, but also been obliged to act a part respecting it, that would probably have been disagreeable to America; and he certainly has reason to rejoice that our silence saved him that delicate and disagreeable task.

This was an Article, in which France had not the smallest interest, nor is there anything in her treaty with us, that restrains us from making what bargain we please with Britain about those or any other lands, without rendering account of such transaction to her or any other power whatever. The same observation applies with still greater force to Spain; and, neither justice nor honor forbid us to dispose as we pleased of our own lands without her knowledge or consent. Spain at that very time extended her pretensions and claims of dominion, not only over the tract in question but over the vast region lying between the Floridas and Lake Superior; and this Court was also, at that very time, soothing and nursing those pretensions by a proposed conciliatory line for splitting the difference. Suppose, therefore, we had offered this tract to Spain, in case she retained the Floridas, should we even have had thanks for it? or would it have abated the chagrin she experienced from being disappointed in her extravagant and improper designs on that whole country! We think not.

We perfectly concur with you in sentiment, Sir, that "honesty is the best policy." But, until it be shown that we have trespassed on the rights of any man, or body of men, you must excuse our thinking that this remark as applied to our proceedings was unnecessary.

Should any explanations, either with France or Spain become necessary on this subject, we hope and expect to meet with no embarrassment. We shall neither amuse them nor perplex ourselves with flimsy excuses, but tell them plainly, that it was not our duty to give them the information; we considered ourselves at liberty to withhold it. And we shall remind the French Minister that he has more reason to be pleased than displeased with our silence. Since we have assumed a place in the political system of the world, let us move like a primary and not like a secondary planet.

We are persuaded, Sir, that your remarks on these subjects resulted from real opinion and were made with candor and sincerity. The best men will view objects of this kind in different lights even when standing on the same ground; and it is not to be wondered at, that we, who are on the spot and have the whole transaction under our eyes, should see many parts of it in a stronger point of light, than persons at a distance, who can only view it through the dull medium of representation.

It would give us great pain if anything we have written or now write respecting this Court should be construed to impeach the friendship of the King and nation for us. We also believe that the Minister is so far our friend, and is disposed so far to do us good offices, as may correspond with, and be dictated by his system of policy for promoting the power, riches, and glory of France. God forbid that we should ever sacrifice our faith, our gratitude, or our honor, to any considerations of convenience; and may He also forbid that we should ever be unmindful of the dignity and independent spirit, which should always characterize a free and generous people.

We shall immediately propose an Article to be inserted in the definitive treaty for postponing the payment of British debts for the time mentioned by Congress.

There are, no doubt, certain ambiguities in our Articles, but it is not to be wondered at, when it is considered how exceedingly averse Britain was to any expressions, which explicitly wounded the tories; and how disinclined we were to use any, that should amount to absolute stipulations in their favor.

The words for returning the property of real British subjects were well understood and explained between us, not to mean or comprehend American refugees. Mr Oswald and Mr Fitzherbert know this to have been the case, and will readily confess and admit it. This mode of expression was preferred by them, as a more delicate mode of excluding those refugees, and of making a proper distinction between them and the subjects of Britain, whose only particular interest in America consisted in holding lands or property there.

The 6th Article, viz. where it declares, that no future confiscations shall be made, &c. ought to have fixed the time with greater accuracy. We think the most fair and true construction is, that it relates to the date of the cessation of hostilities. That is the time when peace in fact took place, in consequence of prior informal, though binding, contracts to terminate the war. We consider the definitive treaties, as only giving the dress of form to those contracts, and not as constituting the obligation of them. Had the cessation of hostilities been the effect of truce, and consequently nothing more than a temporary suspension of war, another construction would have been the true one.

We are officially assured by Mr Hartley, that positive orders for the evacuation of New York have been despatched, and that no avoidable delay will retard that event. Had we proposed to fix a time for it, the British Commissioner would have contended, that it should be a time posterior to the date of the definitive treaty, and that would have been probably more disadvantageous to us, than as that Article now stands.

We are surprised to hear, that any doubts have arisen in America, respecting the time when the cessation of hostilities took place there. It most certainly took place at the expiration of one month after the date of that declaration, in all parts of the world, whether by land or sea, that lay north of the latitude of the Canaries.

The ships afterwards taken from us, in the more northerly latitudes, ought to be reclaimed and given up. We shall apply to Mr Hartley on this subject, and also on that of the transportation of negroes from New York, contrary to the words and intention of the provisional articles.

We have the honor to be, &c.

JOHN ADAMS,

B. FRANKLIN,

JOHN JAY.

TO ROBERT R. LIVINGSTON.

Paris, July 27th, 1783.

Sir,

The definitive treaties between the late belligerent powers are none of them yet completed. Ours has gone on slowly, owing partly to the necessity Mr Hartley, successor of Mr Oswald, thinks himself under of sending every proposition, either his own or ours, to his Court for their approbation, and their delay in answering, through negligence perhaps, since they have heard our ports are open, or through indecision, occasioned by ignorance of the subject, or through want of union among the Ministers. We send you herewith copies of several papers, that have passed between us. He has for some time assured us, that he is in hourly expectation of answers, but they do not arrive. The British Proclamation, respecting the commerce, appears to vex him a good deal. We enclose a copy. And we are of opinion, that finally we shall find it best to drop all commercial articles in our definitive treaty, and leave everything of that kind to a future special treaty, to be made either in America or in Europe, as Congress shall think fit to order. Perhaps it may be best to give powers for that purpose to the Minister, that probably will be sent to London. The opinion here is, that it will be becoming in us to take the first step towards the mutual exchange of Ministers, and we have been assured by the English Minister, who treats with us here, that ours will be well received.

Glossary

approbation: permission; support

candor: honesty; frankness

cessation: the end of an event or action

dereliction: abandonment

posterior: succeeding; afterward

prolix: wordy; verbose

quid pro quo: an exchange of something for something else of comparable value

Document Analysis

The commissioners' letters to Robert Livingston illustrate the difficulties that American diplomats faced when negotiating a treaty with Great Britain as a result of their alliance with France. Letters during the eighteenth century were not always meant for private consumption. Although the letter, written from Passy, a residence in Paris, France, was directed to Livingston, the authors intended for its message to be delivered to Congress as well.

The treaty with France stipulated that both parties should provide full exposure of the peace discussions with Great Britain. Despite their feelings of amity toward Louis XVI and the financial and material support granted by the French, the commissioners recognized the danger in becoming too reliant on their ally. Moreover, John Adams, Benjamin Franklin, and John Jay expressed overt suspicion concerning Spanish territorial goals in North America. As a result, the commissioners carried out secret negotiations with Great Britain in 1782 to settle the geographical boundaries of America, make arrangements for loyalists still residing in America, and stipulate terms for repayment of debts owed to British lenders. These "quid pro quo" settlements, as the commissioners euphemistically called them in their missive to Livingston, would allow Americans to navigate toward friendlier and economically advantageous relations with Great Britain in the following years. More importantly, the secret negotiations reflected a sense of urgency by the diplomats to assert American sovereignty in determining the terms of independence and recognition.

As the document demonstrates, Robert Livingston, the US Secretary of Foreign Affairs from 1781 to 1783, addressed two letters to the commissioners, one on March 25 and one on April 21. In the letters, Livingston expressed his displeasure at having learned of the secret negotiations undertaken by the three men. He alluded to America's 1778 Treaty of Alliance with France. Article VIII indicated that "Neither of the two parties shall conclude either truce or peace, with Great Britain, without the formal consent of the other first obtained." Instructions sent by Congress reaffirmed this article and charged the commissioners to make all negotiations with the British diplomats known to the French king. Livingston recognized America's indebtedness to France's generosity. Moreover, he and members in Congress faced daily pressure from the French ambassador. Explaining that "honesty was the best policy," Livingston asked for a recapitulation of the commissioners' actions.

The commissioners' response to Livingston is somewhat problematic. It reflects the germination of obstacles to the Franco-American alliance. Yet, it was with uneasiness that the diplomats negotiated separately from their allies. From 1776 to 1785, Benjamin Franklin served as ambassador to France and integrated himself thoroughly into several elite circles. Initially, Franklin opposed secret negotiations, but later yielded to Adams and Jay on the matter. Writing back to Livingston, they remarked that if their actions had insulted France, it would "give us great pain."

The defensive strategies used by Adams, Franklin, and Jay in their missive reveal some nuances of eighteenth-century diplomacy. Despite being charged with undermining the defensive alliance with France, the diplomats countered by depicting the secret negotiations as advantageous to the French. Although not conforming to Livingston's rules of diplomatic "propriety," they assured him that the Compte de Vergennes, the French minister, had "more reason to be pleased than displeased with [their] silence." Put simply, they asserted that their separate discussions and subsequent reticence helped France avoid delay in forming her own treaty with Britain. More importantly, the American diplomats underscored another vital theme—the notion that national interests and needs trumped alliances. Although the diplomats wanted to keep the "separate Article" about the Floridas "secret for the present," they maintained that "France had not the smallest interest" in the matter. The negotiations, they argued, were inconsequential and benign to France's interests. The commissioners' strong attitudes toward the Spanish underscore another layer of tension that occurred during the peace negotiations. Spain had entered the war under the Family Compact with France. The Treaty of Aranjuez (1801) outlined Spain's role in the conflict against Britain, which made no reference to America's independence. Rather, their aims involved controlling the Mississippi River, ceding Gibraltar, and gaining Minorca and the Floridas. More covertly, they wished to limit the geographic expanse of America. For the duration of the war, Spain—itself a monarchy and not wanting to fan enthusiasm for republicanism—refused to recognize the independence of Americans. The commissioners writing to Livingston witnessed these animosities, according to their letter, and argued that Spain "extended her pretensions and claims of dominion, not only over the tract in question but over the vast region lying between the Floridas and Lake Superior." They explained that "[t]he negotiations between Spain, France, and Britain were then in full vigor, and embarrassed by a variety of clashing demands." Put simply, the diplomats explained to Congress that in order for America's demands to be met, it was necessary to prevent Spain from learning of their work. That France was tied to Spain in a separate treaty muddled Franco-American relations even further. Had France known of the American acquiescence to Britain over the Floridas, they asserted, they would have felt it necessary to share the information with Spain and even further complicate negotiations.

Adams, Franklin, and Jay also recognized and accepted that the individual interests of nations could undermine treaties. Prior to Yorktown, each "belligerent" party in 1781 looked to settle the dispute diplomatically. The cost to each nation in men and money had dampened morale and their respective economies. France, a party in two treaties, was especially vulnerable to a protracted war. They had agreed to remain in the conflict until America received recognition from Britain as a separate nation and until Spain obtained Gibraltar. The diplomats observed that while the French Minister appeared as "our friend," his primary objective remained to "promot[e] the power, riches, and glory of France." Adams and the others sought to do the same, naturally. Against the interests of Spain, they advised Britain against relinquishing areas surrounding the Mississippi River to the Spanish, as it would impact their trade. Despite America's urging, Britain eventually did abandon the mouth of the Mississippi and the Floridas to Spain.

Land comprised a large portion of the secret negotiations with Britain. American commissioners did not seek access to the entire North American continent. Much of what is America today was purchased in 1803 as part of the Louisiana Purchase. The Mexican-American War from 1846 to 1848 extended America's boundaries further. Comparatively, in 1783, delegates sought to "extend as far down towards the mouth of the Mississippi" because of the "natural fertility and position" of the land. They denied Britain's claims to "extend the bounds...of West Florida, up to the Yazoo River." Moreover, they successfully renegotiated the ownership of the eastern shores of the Mississippi River despite the British delegate's verbose explanation about "the ancient bounds of Canada, Louisiana, &c." To Livingston, they explained that "the surest way to reconcile and obtain both objects would be a composition beneficial to both parties." The map of America at the end of the war reflects the successful maneuvering of the American delegates in refusing British geographic claims. By 1783, Georgia extended to the eastern shore of the Mississippi River and south toward the Gulf of Mexico. However, Spain and Georgia claimed some of the same territory.

The letter to Livingston also alludes to some of the strategies for dealing with colonists who had remained loyal to Britain during the war. Large pockets of loyalists resided in areas of New York, including the borough of Queens in New York City, which was under British control for much of the war. Southern loyalists, for instance, adhered to strong political maxims that situated the monarch at the forefront of the social and religious hierarchy. During the revolution, states articulated treason laws. Essentially, treason was defined as assisting the enemy, in this case, Great Britain. Treason was punishable by property confiscation, exile, or death. In the 1770s and 1780s, revolutionaries used the term "tories" to allude to loyalists. The moniker was replete with negative connotations. Great Britain had depended heavily on loyalist factions in New York and colonies in the south to fight the revolutionaries. At the closure of the war, loyalists were left without property and branded as traitors. The commissioners worked with Britain to develop a plan for allowing loyalists to leave America. Mr. Hartley, a British commissioner, assured the diplomats that "positive orders for the evacuation of New

York have been dispatched, and that no avoidable delay will retard that event." The British delegate also desired portions of southern land to remain under British control to facilitate a "convenient retreat to the tories." The sixth article articulated that America should cease confiscating property of loyal British subjects. Yet, Britain enunciated a deference to and preference for British subjects and refugees, hoping to preserve the property of absentee landowners.

Another central component to the negotiations for the Treaty of Paris involved debt owed to British lenders. Naturally, Britain was eager to recoup these funds. In the eighteenth century, Britain followed a mercantilist policy which emphasized trade regulations both internally and externally. American debts represented a long-established economic relationship whereby Britain controlled the distribution of American goods. Though Americans disliked Article Four of the treaty, as represented by the delegates' offer to Livingston to "propose an Article...postponing the payment of British debts for the time," it was nevertheless imperative in order to make room for future trade agreements between the two countries. In 1776, Adam Smith published a tract, abbreviated as *The Wealth of Nations,* which instigated a break from traditional mercantilism by calling for free trade. British merchant Richard Oswald (who was an emissary for the signing of the Treaty of Paris), mentioned in the letter by Adams, Franklin, and Jay, recognized the economic opportunities in trading with Americans. In his journal, he recounted these sentiments, rationalizing that because of the vast amount of open land, Americans would focus on production, leaving opportunities for British manufacturing. Seeing that future commercial exchanges were inevitable, the delegates proposed a "future special treaty, to be made either in America or Europe."

Collectively, the concerns set out by Adams, Franklin, and Jay culminated in a desire to assert American autonomy from both their allies and former king. Although the revolutionaries depended on French assistance, their letter reflects uneasiness at acquiescing control over the peace proceedings to France. Put simply, they did not want to trade obeisance from a constitutional monarchy to an absolute monarchy. By initiating and constructing a provisional treaty with Great Britain, the delegates positioned themselves on equal footing with Vergennes and Oswald. They demonstrated to Great Britain that the newly formed nation would not be a puppet to France, subservient to their needs. Instead, they articulated that "Since we have assumed a place in the political system of the world, let us move like a primary and not a secondary planet." In addition to this show of American nationalism, the delegates countered Livingston's admonitions of dishonesty, exclaiming that, unlike France who clamored for "riches," they had not "sacrifice[ed] our faith, our gratitude, or our honor, to any considerations of convenience." Rather, they worked according to "the dignity and independent spirit, which should always characterize a free and generous people." The delegates drew an invisible line between what benefited America and their obligations under the Treaty of Alliance. They contended that it was not their "duty" to be forthright or offer "flimsy excuses" to France regarding their discussions with Britain. Though indebted to France for her assistance, the delegates skillfully acknowledged the diplomatic need to assert autonomy from all parties involved in negotiations.

Essential Themes

Taken together, the themes represented in these two letters illustrate the complex nature of treaty negotiations. American diplomats walked a tightrope in Paris, hoping to negotiate terms favorable to their wishes. Most importantly, the delegates needed Britain to relinquish all authority over the states and recognize American independence. That the commissioners achieved this and other gains in spite of Britain's continuing war with France and Spain into 1783 reflects their skill but also their willingness to put their nation's needs over the interests of their allies. Each ally entered the conflict with specific goals in mind. As the delegates explained to Livingston, these aims often conflicted with American designs. For instance, although Spain entered the war against Britain, the monarchy never recognized America's independence. Rather, they viewed the revolution as dangerous to their colonial possessions. Though the delegates agreed to allow Britain to retain the Floridas for other land concessions, a capitulation they defined as quid pro quo, they successfully achieved most of their objectives.

Although France had come to America's aid in 1778, the provisional treaty outlined in November 1792 by John Adams, Benjamin Franklin, and John Jay reflected a growing rift between the two allies and a growing sentiment of suspicion over entangling or protective alliances. The goals of each party, as the diplomats observed, conflicted with one another, causing confusion and delays in the settlement process. While Congress enjoyed French assistance during the war, they moved increasingly closer to neutralism as the 1780s progressed.

—*Carrie Le Glenn, MA*

Bibliography and Additional Reading

Franklin, Benjamin. *Autobiography of Benjamin Franklin.* ed. Charles W. Eliot. New York: SoHo, 2012.

Hoffman, Ronald and Peter J. Albert eds. *Diplomacy and Revolution: The Franco-American Alliance of 1778.* Charlottesville: UP of Virginia, 1981.

___. *Peace and the Peacemakers: The Treaty of 1783.* Charlottesville: University Press of Virginia, 1986.

Kerber, Linda K. "The Paradox of Women's Citizenship in the Early Republic: The Case of Martin vs. Massachusetts, 1805." *American Historical Review* 97.2 (1992): 349–78.

McCullough, David. *John Adams.* New York: Simon and Schuster, 2001.

Meier, Pauline. *American Scripture: Making the Declaration of Independence.* New York: First Vintage, 1997.

Stinchcombe, William C. *The American Revolution and the French Alliance.* Syracuse: Syracuse University Press, 1969.

Wood, Gordon. *The Radicalism of the American Revolution.* New York: First Vintage, 1991.

The French Revolution

The French Revolution was a revolutionary movement that shook France between 1787 and 1799 and ended the old French system (the *ancien régime*). Through a series of radical social and political changes, the country was transformed from a monarchy to a democratic republic. The events and ideas that made up the revolution had an important influence on European history.

The causes behind the revolution are many and varied. They include the waning of popular support for the feudal system; general agreement with the reformist writings of the French *philosophes*, or public intellectuals; an emerging bourgeoisie that felt excluded from the body politic; and an economic crisis partly linked to French participation in the American Revolution, exacerbated by crop failures. The attempt by the monarchy in 1787 to raise taxes on the privileged classes—nobles and clergy—created an uproar. In response, in 1789 Louis XVI convened the Estates-General, made up of clergy, nobility, and commoners (the Third Estate). Seeking to quell the crisis by passing reforms, it swore to establish a new constitution. The king accepted the formation of the National Assembly. Worries about a rising "aristocratic conspiracy" led to the Great Fear of July 1789, as Parisians seized the Bastille on July 14. This event is generally regarded as the symbol of the collapse of the old regime.

The National Assembly drafted a new constitution, the preamble of which was the famous Declaration of the Rights of Man and of the Citizen. That document, influenced by the American experience of democracy, proclaimed liberty, equality (for all "Men"), and fraternity as the basis for popular sovereignty. The Constitution of 1791 also established a short-lived constitutional monarchy. Church lands were nationalized to pay off the public debt, and the church was reorganized and made subordinate to the state. In an expression of nationalist fervor, the assembly declared war on Austria and Prussia in 1792, partly to maintain popular support for the revolution. Revolutionaries imprisoned the royal family and massacred nobles and clergy at the Tuileries in 1792. A new assembly called the National Convention, split between the moderate Girondins and the more extremist Montagnards, abolished the monarchy and established the First Republic in September 1792. Louis XVI was brought before the National Convention and executed for treason in January 1793. When the Montagnards seized power and enacted radical economic and social policies, a violent reaction took place, including a conservative insurrection in western France and various citizens' revolts elsewhere. The resistance was largely quashed by the Reign of Terror, led by Maximilien Robespierre and the Committee of Safety. Enemies of both the right and the left were eliminated or dealt with harshly.

In 1794 a set of military victories bolstered public resolve, and Robespierre was overthrown and executed. The next year royalists tried to seize power in Paris but were crushed by Napoleon Bonaparte. A new constitution was written placing executive power in a five-member Directory; but the war and disagreements within the Directory caused schisms that in turn led to coups d'état, notably those of 9 Thermidor (July 27, 1794) and 18 Brumaire (November 9–10, 1799). The latter was led by Napoleon, who abolished the Directory and declared himself leader of France.

The French Revolution, together with the ensuing Napoleonic Wars, brought down the old political structures of medieval Europe, opened the way to nineteenth-century liberal thought, and, for better or worse, ushered in the modern notion of nationalism.

■ Declaration of the Rights of Man and of the Citizen

Date: August 26, 1789
Author: National Assembly of France
Genre: law

Summary Overview

Near the start of the French Revolution, the new the National Assembly approved the Declaration of the Rights of Man and of the Citizen, a document that ended the ancien régime (old political system) in France. That system had been characterized by an absolute monarch as ruler, a hierarchical social structure with each social class having a set of privileges, and a restrictive labor system controlled by the guilds (associations of tradesmen). In composing the Declaration of the Rights of Man and of the Citizen, the representatives in the National Assembly borrowed heavily on the writings of Marie-Joseph du Motier, marquis de Lafayette. In July 1789 Lafayette wrote a preamble to a future constitution of France, proclaiming that the principle of all sovereignty resided in the nation. This preamble provided a model for the version of the preamble written by the liberal Emmanuel Joseph Sieyès, also known as Abbé Sieyès. The latter preamble, expanded in August 1789, was based on the motto of the French Revolution—"liberty, equality, and fraternity"—and was inspired by the U.S. Declaration of Independence (1776). Strongly influenced by Enlightenment ideas, the Declaration of the Rights of Man and of the Citizen was accepted by the French king Louis XVI on October 5, 1789, and was promulgated on November 3, 1789.

Defining Moment

At the beginning of the eighteenth century, France experienced a period of expansion, population growth, and increased urbanization, and the newer colonial empires of France began to pay off. By the end of the century, the population surge had begun to press against the food supply. Land hunger and food shortages went hand in hand with increasing social dissatisfactions in the country. France was experiencing growing pains. Although France was changing, the structure of French society, a system of privilege, was not. The social structure was more than one hundred years old. The population was divided into three "estates," each with its own set of privileges, although the privileges were not equal. The First Estate was the clergy, the Second Estate consisted of the nobility, and the Third Estate included everyone else. The economic crises of 1787, 1788, and 1789 showed the weakness of the social order. This situation stimulated suspicions between the lower and the upper classes and between all classes and the government; it gave rise to an indefinite fear of complacency. Moreover, there was a general lack of confidence in the established social and political order.

The response of King Louis XVI was to call an Assembly of Notables, a meeting of select members of the nobility. In 1788 he invited them to come to his palace, Versailles, in the hope that the nobility would agree to gifts to the crown and to a new taxation structure. Thus the nobility, by acting in concert with the crown, would relieve the fiscal crisis faced by Louis XVI and the government. The assembly failed to produce the desired results, however, and Louis was forced to call a meeting of the Estates-General of France in 1789. This medieval representative institution in France had not met for 175 years before Louis XVI reconvened it on May 5, 1789, to deal with the looming financial crisis. France was on the verge of bankruptcy.

The meeting of the Estates-General provided those elected to it with the opportunity to present their grievances. On June 20, 1789, the members of the newly formed National Assembly took the Tennis Court Oath, pledging to remain together until they had drafted and passed a new constitution. The Na-

Declaration of the Rights of Man and of the Citizen, *painted by Jean-Jacques-François Le Barbier. Photo via Wikimedia Commons. [Public domain.]*

tional Assembly, also called the Constituent Assembly, is what the Third Estate's delegation to the Estates-General decided to call itself when, on June 16, 1789, it proclaimed itself the sole legitimate representative of the French nation. The name stuck when, after a failed attempt to undo this clear usurpation of royal authority, Louis XVI ordered the noble and clerical delegations to join the National Assembly on June 27, 1789. (The National Assembly differed greatly from the Estates-General. The latter organization, which dated to the fourteenth century, was primarily a consultative assembly, convoked at the pleasure of the king.) These events marked the birth of the Patriot Party, resulting in part from the success of a small pamphlet published by Emmanuel-Joseph Sieyès in January 1789 titled "What Is the Third Estate?" It contains these stirring lines: "What is the Third Estate? *Everything*. What has it been until now in the political order? *Nothing*. What does it want to be? *Something*" (qtd. in Baker, p. 154). Sieyès's argument was based on the concepts of utility and nationalism. The Third Estate was the most useful class to the nation. The nobles constituted an *imperium in imperio*, or empire within an empire. The Third Estate's demands for equality were moderate. It was by itself the National Assembly and therefore should create a system that eliminated class privilege.

To put all of these events in context, a thumbnail summary of the key events of the French Revolution is necessary. The French Revolution actually began in the spring and summer of 1789, when food riots erupted throughout France. However, the traditional date marking the start of the Revolution is July 14, 1789, when revolutionaries stormed and seized the royal prison, the Bastille, in Paris. The next month, the National Assembly issued the Decrees Abolishing the Feudal System and the Declaration of the Rights of Man and of the Citizen. In October of that year, Parisian women marched on the king's palace at Versailles and forced him to return to Paris. But in June 1791 the royal family, fearing for their lives, attempted to flee France and were arrested at Varennes, France (the so-called "flight to Varennes"). Later, in October, the new Legislative Assembly met for the first time. By 1792 counterrevolutionary movements were forming, though in August of that year the king was imprisoned; that same month, the National Convention replaced the Legislative Assembly. The Revolution began to turn violent when prisoners, most of them aristocrats, were killed during the so-called September Massacres of 1792. In 1792 the monarchy was abolished, and the First French Republic was proclaimed. Louis XVI was executed on January 21, 1793, and in March the Revolutionary Tribunal was created, leading to the Reign of Terror under Maximilien de Robespierre and the radical Jacobins. Then, on October 16, 1793, Marie-Antoinette was executed. Further violence took place when Robespierre and other radicals were executed by moderates. By 1794 the Reign of Terror had come to an end.

The storming of the Bastille had few practical consequences, but symbolically it was of enormous significance. It represented the Revolution-inspired attack on the ancien régime. Today it is celebrated as Bastille Day, or French Independence Day. Shortly after the fall of the Bastille, in a series of disturbances in the countryside of France, rural peasants revolted against their feudal overlords during July and August 1789, a period known as the Great Fear. These revolts were occasioned by rumors of an aristocratic plot to hoard grain and drive up prices while sending gangs of bandits to ruin the peasants' crops in the countryside. France's economic crisis reached a peak in 1788 and 1789. The harvest of 1788 was terrible, leading to food shortages, high prices, and famine in 1789. Fearful that the peasants would next begin to attack the property of the bourgeois, or middle class, the National Assembly in August issued a series of decrees that, in effect, destroyed the ancien régime. Once they had agreed on the importance of drafting a declaration of rights, the deputies in the National Assembly faced the more difficult task of crafting a declaration that a majority could accept. They agreed on seventeen articles that laid out a new vision of government; the protection of natural rights replaced the will of the king as the justification for authority. The National Assembly deliberated carefully and on August 4, 1789, granted France the equality demanded by the bourgeois as Armand II, duke of Aiguillon, a liberal nobleman, renounced his rights, prerogatives, and dues in order to satisfy the peasants and restore order to the countryside. Effectively, this act ended the feudal system in France. On August 26, 1789, the assembly approved the Declaration of the Rights of Man and of the Citizen.

The declaration expresses the liberal and universal goal of the philosophes, the general term for those academics and intellectuals who became the leading voices of the French Enlightenment during the eighteenth century. The most important of these men were Voltaire, Jean-Jacques Rousseau, Denis Diderot, and Charles-Louis de Secondat, baron of Montesquieu. The two fundamental ideas of the Enlightenment were rationalism and relativism. Rationalism was the belief that through the power of reason, humans could arrive at truth and improve human society. The philosophes were eager to demonstrate that human reason was the best guide for organizing society and government. Relativism, a philosophy that different ideas, cultures, and beliefs had equal worth, gripped the European mind as the impact of the Age of Exploration demonstrated that adherence to this philosophy had practical and intellectual value in any societal program for reform. Europeans were exposed to a variety of cultures and peoples worldwide. The Declaration of the Rights of Man and of the Citizen also addressed the interests of the bourgeois, including their demands for government by the people and the idea that the aim of the government is to preserve the natural rights of the individual. The political ideas of John Locke and Montesquieu and Rousseau's work *The Social Contract*, along with Voltaire's thoughts on equality and an end to government censorship, spring from the pages of the document. In addition, the National Assembly helped businesses stop tariffs, ended the guild system, and decreed that French colonies trade only with France.

Following August 26, 1789, the National Assembly got the breathing space it needed and proceeded to rebuild France from the ground up. The Great Reforms of 1789–1791, all rooted in the ideological foundations of the declaration and the writings of the philosophes, fall roughly into three categories. First, the Patriots wanted to limit the government by decentralizing the administration and the judiciary. On December 14, 1789, the National Assembly established a structure for municipal governments throughout France. For this purpose it created a distinction between active citizens (men who paid yearly taxes equal to three days' wages) who could vote and passive citizens who could not vote. On December 22, 1789, the assembly established a structure for new departmental administration. The number of departments throughout France was reduced. The departments were subdivided into districts and cantons. In the cantons only active citizens could vote and then only for electors who would choose deputies to the National Assembly and district officials who had to pay yearly taxes equal to ten days' wages. Deputies to the National Assembly had to pay yearly taxes equal to a silver mark. On August 16, 1790, cantons, districts, and departments were given courts staffed by elected judges.

Second, to deal further with the bankruptcy problem, the National Assembly on December 19, 1789, authorized the issuance of paper money (assignats) to be backed by church lands and to be redeemable when they were sold. On February 13, 1790, the National Assembly suppressed the monastic orders, thus creating a supply of salable land. Members of the National Assembly did not wish to destroy the church, which they considered to be a useful source of popular moral inspiration. On July 12, 1790, they issued the Civil Constitution of the Clergy, making departments and dioceses coterminous. Bishops and priests were to be elected in the same fashion as other departmental and district officials; they were paid by the state. Moreover, they were required to pledge allegiance to the constitution of the nation. Only a few members of the clergy did so; most clergy became refractory, or nonaccepting, clergy. Many left France or went into hiding.

Finally, in more general financial and economic reforms, the National Assembly was strongly influenced by physiocratic doctrines (doctrines of utility or usefulness). In October 1790 it established a unified tariff for France. In November 1790 it set up two basic taxes—a contribution on land and a contribution on personal property. Also, on June 14, 1791, the National Assembly passed the Le Chapelier Law, which prohibited industrial and labor strikes. On May 21, 1791, the assembly established the met-

Author Biography

The Declaration of the Rights of Man and of the Citizen sought to define natural and civil rights for the citizens of France. Much of the document was taken from a draft done by General Lafayette, a liberal and a heroic participant in the American Revolution, at the request of the National Assembly during the summer of 1789.

Born to the Motier family in the Auvergne on September 6, 1757, Lafayette studied at the prestigious Collège du Plessis in Paris before joining the French army in 1771. Leaving France for America, he participated in the American War of Independence. He then fought in the French Revolutionary Wars, a series of conflicts (1792–1802) fought between the French Revolutionary government and several European states. Thus he became a hero on both sides of the Atlantic. Politically liberal, Lafayette rose to leadership as early as 1788, favoring a parliamentary monarchy like England's but one based on a formal written constitution like that of the United States. Increasingly, Lafayette's efforts to hold the Revolution to a more moderate course grew difficult. Given the position of commander of the National Guard, Lafayette unwisely ordered the guard to fire on a crowd gathered in the Champs de Mars in 1791. The general refused to support Napoléon's Imperial France and returned to political life in France only after Napoléon's final abdication in 1815. Strongly opposing Louis XVIII and Charles X, Lafayette sat in the Chamber of Deputies as a member of the opposition party from 1818 to 1824. He died on May 20, 1834, in Paris.

The modifications of the Declaration of the Rights of Man and of the Citizen took place through a series of debates held from August 1 through August 4, 1789. The principal proponent of a declaration was Mathieu de Montmorency, duke of Montmorency-Laval. Montmorency was born in 1767 and, as an adolescent, had served along with his father in the American Revolution. He returned from that war imbued with democratic ideals. In 1789 he was elected deputy to the Estates-General, becoming closely allied with Lafayette and the reforming faction of nobles.

Historical Document

Declaration of the Rights of Man and of the Citizen

The representatives of the French people, organized as a National Assembly, believing that the ignorance, neglect, or contempt of the rights of man are the sole cause of public calamities and of the corruption of governments, have determined to set forth in a solemn declaration the natural, unalienable, and sacred rights of man, in order that this declaration, being constantly before all the members of the Social body, shall remind them continually of their rights and duties; in order that the acts of the legislative power, as well as those of the executive power, may be compared at any moment with the objects and purposes of all political institutions and may thus be more respected, and, lastly, in order that the grievances of the citizens, based hereafter upon simple and incontestable principles, shall tend to the maintenance of the constitution and redound to the happiness of all. Therefore the National Assembly recognizes and proclaims, in the presence and under the auspices of the Supreme Being, the following rights of man and of the citizen:

Articles:

Men are born and remain free and equal in rights. Social distinctions may be founded only upon the general good.

The aim of all political association is the preservation of the natural and imprescriptible rights of man. These rights are liberty, property, security, and resistance to oppression.

The principle of all sovereignty resides essentially in the nation. No body nor individual may exercise any authority which does not proceed directly from the nation.

Liberty consists in the freedom to do everything which injures no one else; hence the exercise of the natural rights of each man has no limits except those which assure to the other members of the society the enjoyment of the same rights. These limits can only be determined by law.

Law can only prohibit such actions as are hurtful to society. Nothing may be prevented which is not forbidden by law, and no one may be forced to do anything not provided for by law.

Law is the expression of the general will. Every citizen has a right to participate personally, or through his representative, in its foundation. It must be the same for all, whether it protects or punishes. All citizens, being equal in the eyes of the law, are equally eligible to all dignities and to all public positions and occupations, according to their abilities, and without distinction except that of their virtues and talents.

No person shall be accused, arrested, or imprisoned except in the cases and according to the forms prescribed by law. Any one soliciting, transmitting, executing, or causing to be executed, any arbitrary order, shall be punished. But any citizen summoned or arrested in virtue of the law shall submit without delay, as resistance constitutes an offense.

The law shall provide for such punishments only as are strictly and obviously necessary, and no one shall suffer punishment except it be legally inflicted in virtue of a law passed and promulgated before the commission of the offense.

As all persons are held innocent until they shall have been declared guilty, if arrest shall be deemed indispensable, all harshness not essential to the securing of the prisoner's person shall be severely repressed by law.

No one shall be disquieted on account of his opinions, including his religious views, provided their manifestation does not disturb the public order established by law.

The free communication of ideas and opinions is one of the most precious of the rights of man. Every citizen may, accordingly, speak, write, and print with freedom, but shall be responsible for such abuses of this freedom as shall be defined by law.

The security of the rights of man and of the citizen requires public military forces. These forces are, therefore, established for the good of all and not for the personal advantage of those to whom they shall be intrusted.

A common contribution is essential for the maintenance of the public forces and for the cost of administration. This should be equitably distributed among all the citizens in proportion to their means.

All the citizens have a right to decide, either personally or by their representatives, as to the necessity of the public contribution; to grant this freely; to know to what uses it is put; and to fix the proportion, the mode of assessment and of collection and the duration of the taxes.

Society has the right to require of every public agent an account of his administration.

A society in which the observance of the law is not assured, nor the separation of powers defined, has no constitution at all.

Since property is an inviolable and sacred right, no one shall be deprived thereof except where public necessity, legally determined, shall clearly demand it, and then only on condition that the owner shall have been previously and equitably indemnified.

֎֍

Glossary

imprescriptible: not subject to loss or diminution for any reason

Document Analysis

On the August 4, 1789, Armand II, the duke of Aiguillon, a liberal nobleman, renounced rights, prerogatives, and dues in order to satisfy the peasants and restore order to the countryside. Effectively, this action ended the feudal system in France. On August 26, 1789, the National Assembly deputies faced the difficult task of composing a bill of rights that a majority of the deputies could accept. A lengthy debate ensued, with the following questions raised: Should the declaration be short and limited to general principles, or should it include a long explanation of the significance of each article? Should the declaration include a list of duties or only rights? What precisely were "the natural, inalienable, and sacred rights of man"? After several days of debate and voting, the deputies suspended their deliberations on the declaration, having agreed on seventeen articles that laid out a new vision of government. The basis of authority was no longer the king but the will of the people. The duty of the government was to protect the natural rights of its citizens.

The document embodies the political ideas of Locke and Rousseau with regard to the idea of the social contract and the general will, as well as Montesquieu's work *The Spirit of the Laws*, which calls for a separation of powers. Montesquieu argues that the power of the government should be divided into separate branches, usually legislative, judicial, and executive, so that no one branch of government could gain too much authority. The ideas expressed in the Declaration of the Rights of Man and of the Citizen were influenced by the preamble to the U.S. Constitution. In his preamble to the French Constitution, Sieyès wrote in August 1789 that after having set forth the natural and civil rights of citizens, political rights would follow. He believed that all inhabitants of France were entitled to the right of protection of their person, their property, and their liberty; however, all did not have the right to take an active part in the formation of the public authorities—including women, children, foreigners, and those who contributed nothing to maintaining the public establishment. All could enjoy the benefits of society, but only those who contributed to the public establishment could declare themselves to be true active citizens, true members of the association.

Paragraph 1

"The representatives of the French people constituted as a National Assembly ... have resolved to set forth in a solemn declaration the natural, inalienable, and sacred rights of Man." Rather than ending debate about rights, the vote on the declaration opened it up in new ways. The people of France now possessed an official document based on universal principles; this document encouraged further discussion of human rights and, in fact, demanded clarification concerning who was included in the definition of "man and citizen." Should the definition include the poor, those without property, the religious minority, blacks, mulattoes (people of mixed race), or even women? Where should the lines defining citizenship be drawn? The question of citizenship helped drive the Revolution into increasingly radical directions after 1789. Each group excluded in 1789 began to assert its claims to the right to be citizens of France. French legislators approached the question of citizenship step by step over a period of five years after 1789. France was in flux, the Patriot Party walked a tightrope, and the Revolution was never on solid ground.

Articles 1–4

In proclaiming the Declaration of the Rights of Man and of the Citizen, the National Assembly defined liberty in broad terms in order to provide essential freedoms and liberties with few restrictions. This is evident in Article 1, which states that men are born and remain free and equal in rights. Article 2 provides a definition of the social contract theory's idea of natural rights: These rights are liberty, property, security, and resistance to oppression. Article 3 states the radical notions that the sovereignty of the nation resides in the nation; the nation is defined as the only source from which authority is delivered. This statement constituted an attack on the ancien régime concept of absolute monarchs ruling by divine right; the power of royalty was to be taken by the National Assembly, "the nation assembled." Article 4 offers an explanation of the limits of freedom and liberty and clearly puts all freedoms and protections under the written law.

Articles 5–9

Articles 5–8 of the declaration deal with the establishment of new laws of the nation. These laws protect citizens from arbitrary arrest and imprisonment and grant equality to all citizens, especially in the eyes of the law. Article 5 is closely tied to the principles asserted in the previous article. Article 6 provides a direct statement of an important element in Jean-Jacques Rousseau's work *The Social Contract.* Here the idea that the general will expresses the law of the land provides for citizen political participation, whether directly or through elected representatives. Being equal before the law, every citizen is likewise entitled to all dignities and public positions—a strong statement that suggests the revolutionary principle that careers should be open only to those with talent. Articles 7–9 address the legal system. Under the ancien régime, each order had its own law courts, and certain provinces had their own courts. With enough influence one could have one's case transferred to the king's court. No member of the clergy could be tried in any court other than an ecclesiastical court. Taken together, these articles establish equality under the law and a more humane penal code. The importance of the written law as the foundation of these rights is evident.

Articles 10 and 11

Article 10 addresses the ancien régime's practice of censorship and the lack of "free speech." The written law is held up as the determinant of limits—citizens are free to communicate ideas and opinions, including speech related to religious beliefs, "provided their manifestation [speech] does not disturb the public order established by law." Article 11 makes clear that the right of free speech is "one of the most precious rights of man."

Articles 12–14

Article 12 addresses the need for public military forces—a national army, not the private army of the monarch—to be gathered by conscription, or the *levee en masse*. Article 13 redresses the ancien régime's secrecy in accounts—that is, how public funds are spent—and proposes an equitable distribution for the costs of administering the government, stating that citizens must be told exactly what their share of this cost would be. Article 14 takes the power of taxation out of the hands of the king and the Estates-General, reserving these decisions to either direct action by the individual or action through elected representatives. Included in this article is the right to determine not only the mode of assessment but the duration of the taxation.

Articles 15–17

Article 16 makes every civil servant, administrator, and public agent accountable for his administration. This article redresses the practice of venality under the ancien régime, where government offices were bought and accountability was owed only to the king. Article 16 demands that the written law be placed above everything in creating a new society, for the written law legitimizes society. Clearly, this article makes the legislative separation of powers—the idea of the philosophe Montesquieu—and a written law governing all elements of this society the necessary foundation for a constitutional society. Finally, Article 17 establishes the right to own property, as described by John Locke. The article also sets forth the principle of eminent domain, or the right of the state to seize property in cases of necessity.

Essential Themes

The reforms of the National Assembly dismantled the ancien régime in France. The instrument by which this was done was the Declaration of the Rights of Man and of the Citizen. With the National Assembly's decrees of August 4, 1789, the equality demanded by the bourgeois was achieved. The declaration expressed the liberal and universal goal of Enlightenment philosophers and the middle class—government by the people—with the aim of ensuring that government would exist to preserve the natural rights of the individual. The declaration struck at the Roman Catholic Church in France by ending tithes, taking church lands, and resulting in passage of the Civil Constitution of the Clergy in 1790, making the clergy civil servants elected by the people and paid by the state. This issue divided the French people.

The 1791 constitution upheld the principles of the Declaration of the Rights of Man and of the Citizen by limiting the power of the king and guaranteeing equal taxation under the law. The provincial units in France were replaced with eighty-three departments, bishoprics were reduced to the same number, a standardized system of courts and a uniform law code were introduced, and the sale of judicial offices was ended. The declaration also introduced a more humane penal code. The National Assembly aided businesses by ending tariffs and the guild system, instituting a uniform system of weights and measures, decreeing that French colonies trade only with France, and implementing an external tariff to protect French manufacturers. In effect, the Declaration of the Rights of Man and of the Citizen ended the ancien régime in France. People had entered a stage in human history characterized by emancipation from superstition, prejudice, cruelty, and enthusiasm. Liberty had triumphed over tyranny.

—*Anne York, PhD*

Bibliography and Additional Reading

Baker, Keith Michael. *The Old Regime and the French Revolution*. Chicago: University of Chicago Press, 1987.

Best, Geoffrey, ed. *The Permanent Revolution: The French Revolution and Its Legacy, 1789–1989*. London: Fontana Press, 1988.

Doyle, William. *The French Revolution: A Very Short Introduction,* 2nd ed. Oxford, U.K.: Oxford UP, 2020.

Hunt, Lynn. *The French Revolution and Human Rights: A Brief Documentary History*. New York: Bedford Books, 1996.

"Liberty, Equality, Fraternity: Exploring the French Revolution." George Mason University Web site. chnm.gmu.edu/revolution.

Mason, Laura, and Tracey Rizzo. *The French Revolution: A Document Collection*. Boston: Houghton Mifflin, 1999.

Popkin, Jeremy. *A Short History of the French Revolution,* 7th ed. New York: Routledge, 2019.

Roberts, J. M. *The French Revolution,* 2nd ed. Oxford, U.K.: Oxford UP, 1997.

Reflections on the Revolution in France

Date: 1790
Author: Edmund Burke
Genre: essay

Summary Overview

Edmund Burke's Reflections on the Revolution in France *(1790) represents a controversial and impassioned plea in support of the hereditary principle of monarchial succession in England. Published against the advice of close friends, who feared it would open a Pandora's box to political reformers, its publication spawned a wave of pamphlet replies in the early 1790s, most notably by Thomas Paine, Mary Wollstonecraft, and James Mackintosh, who challenged Burke's interpretation of the constitutional implications of the English Revolution of 1688. While Burke's rhetorical tour de force focused on events in France, they were interpreted with an eye to their implications for the English political system.*

In Reflections on the Revolution in France, *the Irish-born politician Burke comprehensively rebutted the political doctrines advanced by the Revolution Society, a society founded to celebrate the centenary of the "Glorious Revolution" of 1688. Against the assertions of its founding member Richard Price, outlined in his Discourse on the Love of Our Country (1789)—that the English people have the right to elect their own governors, to cashier (rebuke) them for misconduct, and to select the system by which they are governed—Burke drew a seductive picture of a stable and legally sanctioned hereditary monarchy.*

Defining Moment

Burke, a onetime member of the British Parliament, had followed events in France for many years by the time he published *Reflection on the Revolution in France* in November 1790. He was aware of the weaknesses of the *ancien régime* (old monarchy), but believed that its problems could be addressed through reform rather than revolution. Having monitored the unfolding revolution during its first year, Burke found the revolutionaries at fault for trying to found a new political system on abstract principles based on reason. As Burke saw it, society was too complex to be refashioned in such a manner, and human reason was too unsteady to serve as the sole basis of political decisions. Although he supported the ideals of the American Revolution, in the case of France Burke held that the conventional deference shown the monarchy had been built on longstanding beliefs and rituals that honored France and paid tribute to its culture and history. The British essayist predicted that, if things continued down their current path, the French would execute their king, the French economy would collapse, and a military dictatorship would be installed —all things that later came to pass.

In many respects, Burke's chief audience was readers in Britain—as is evident in the excerpt reprinted here. He presented the revolution in France as a model which hotheaded reformers in Britain absolutely should *not* try to imitate. In making his case for caution, Burke was at the same time becoming a founding figure in what would eventually become conservative political philosophy. Yet his essay struck many at the time as being at odds with his own reputation as a defender of freedom and an enemy of the corruption that commonly affected monarchical (and non-monarchical) regimes. Most reactions to Burke's *Reflections* were negative, even though the essay would be pointed to by later generations as a defining statement in the development of modern conservatism.

Author Biography

Edmund Burke was born in 1729 in Dublin, Ireland. Raised as an Anglican, he attended Trinity College be-

The Storming of the Bastille, *14 July 1789. Oil on canvas, unknown artist. Image via Wikimedia Commons. [Public domain.]*

fore relocating to London to become a writer in the circle of Samuel Johnson. His early writings on aesthetics attracted the attention of Denis Diderot and Immanuel Kant. After being hired to edit an annual survey of world affairs, he became secretary to the Whig prime minister the Marquess of Rockingham. In a controversy over the limits of executive authority as held by the British monarch, Burke argued in favor of royal power generally but also found that George III had, in spirit at least, overstepped this authority. In addition, Burke advocated for the development of strong political parties, and stated that members of Parliament should rely on their own judgment rather than merely echo the wishes of their constituents. Burke was himself elected to Parliament in 1774, where he called for conciliation with the American colonists and claimed that they were poorly governed (by Britain) and unfairly taxed. Burke also supported the end of the slave trade. In an effort to reform the East India Company, he launched impeachment proceedings against its head (and governor general of India), Warren Hastings. In his best-known publication, *Reflections on the Revolution in France* (1790), written after having left Parliament, Burke expressed his disapproval of the French Revolution—particularly its leaders and their violent actions against the aristocracy. Burke's writings are considered central to the emergence of conservative political thought. He died in 1797.

Historical Document

Whatever may be the success of evasion in explaining away the gross error of *fact*, which supposes that his Majesty (though he holds it in concurrence with the wishes) owes his crown to the choice of his people, yet nothing can evade their full explicit declaration concerning the principle of a right in the people to choose; which right is directly maintained, and tenaciously adhered to. All the oblique insinuations concerning election bottom in this proposition, and are referable to it. Lest the foundation of the king's exclusive legal title should pass for a mere rant of adulatory freedom, the political divine proceeds dogmatically to assert, that, by the principles of the Revolution, the people of England have acquired three fundamental rights, all which, with him, compose one system, and lie together in one short sentence; namely, that we have acquired a right

"To choose our own governors."

"To cashier them for misconduct."

"To frame a government for ourselves."

This new, and hitherto unheard-of, bill of rights, though made in the name of the whole people, belongs to those gentlemen and their faction only. The body of the people of England have no share in it. They utterly disclaim it. They will resist the practical assertion of it with their lives and fortunes. They are bound to do so by the laws of their country, made at the time of that very Revolution which is appealed to in favour of the fictitious rights claimed by the Society which abuses its name.

These gentlemen of the Old Jewry, in all their reasonings on the Revolution of 1688, have a Revolution which happened in England about forty years before, and the late French Revolution, so much before their eyes, and in their hearts, that they are constantly confounding all the three together. It is necessary that we should separate what they confound. We must recall their erring fancies to the acts of the Revolution which we revere, for the discovery of its true principles. If the principles of the Revolution of 1688 are anywhere to be found, it is in the statute called the *Declaration of Right*. In that most wise, sober, and considerate declaration, drawn up by great lawyers and great statesmen, and not by warm and inexperienced enthusiasts, not one word is said, nor one suggestion made, of a general right "to choose our own governors; to cashier them for misconduct; and to form a government for ourselves."

This Declaration of Right (the act of the 1st of William and Mary, sess. 2, ch. 2) is the corner-stone of our constitution, as reinforced, explained, improved, and in its fundamental principles for ever settled. It is called "An Act for declaring the rights and liberties of the subject, and for settling the succession of the crown." You will observe, that these rights and this succession are declared in one body, and bound indissolubly together.

A few years after this period, a second opportunity offered for asserting a right of election to the crown. On the prospect of a total failure of issue from King William, and from the Princess, afterwards Queen Anne, the consideration of the settlement of the crown, and of a further security for the liberties of the people, again came before the legislature. Did they this second time make any provision for legalizing the crown on the spurious revolution principles of the Old Jewry? No. They followed the principles which prevailed in the Declaration of Right; indicating with more precision the persons who were to inherit in the Protestant line. This act also incorporated, by the same policy, our liberties, and an hereditary succession in the same act. Instead of a right to choose our own governors, they declared that the succession in that line (the Protestant line drawn from James the First) was absolutely necessary "for the peace, quiet, and security of the realm," and that it was equally urgent on them "to maintain a certainty in the succession thereof, to which the subjects may safely have recourse for their protection." Both these acts, in which are heard the unerring, unambiguous oracles of revolution policy, instead of countenancing the delusive, gipsy predictions of a "right to choose our governors," prove to a demonstration how totally adverse the wisdom of the nation was from turning a case of necessity into a rule of law.

Unquestionably there was at the Revolution, in the person of King William, a small and a temporary deviation from the strict order of a regular hereditary succession; but it is against all genuine principles of jurisprudence to draw a principle from a law made in a special case, and regarding an individual person. *Privilegium non transit in exemplum*. If ever there was a time favourable for establishing the principle, that a king of popular choice was the only legal king, without all doubt it was at the Revolution. Its not being done at that time is a proof that the nation was of opinion it ought not to be done at any time. There is no person so completely ignorant of our history as not to know, that the majority in parliament of both parties were so little disposed to anything resembling that principle, that at first they were determined to place the vacant crown, not on the head of the Prince of Orange, but on that of his wife Mary, daughter of King James, the eldest born of the issue of that king, which they acknowledged as undoubtedly his. It would be to repeat a very trite story, to recall to your memory all those circumstances which demonstrated that their accepting King William was not properly a choice; but to all those who did not wish, in effect, to recall King James, or to deluge their country in blood, and again to bring their religion, laws, and liberties into the peril they had just escaped, it was an act of *necessity*, in the strictest moral sense in which necessity can be taken.

In the very act, in which for a time, and in a single case, parliament departed from the strict order of inheritance, in favour of a prince, who, though not next, was however very near, in the line of succession, it is curious to observe how Lord Somers, who drew the bill called the Declaration of Right, has comported himself on that delicate occasion. It is curious to observe with what address this temporary solution of continuity is kept from the eye; whilst all that could be found in this act of necessity to countenance the idea of an hereditary succession is brought forward, and fostered, and made the most of, by this great man, and by the legislature who followed him. Quitting the dry, imperative style of an act of parliament, he makes the Lords and Commons fall to a pious, legislative ejaculation, and declare, that they consider it "as a marvellous providence, and merciful goodness of God to this nation, to preserve their said Majesties' royal persons, most happily to reign over us on the throne of their ancestors, for which, from the bottom of their hearts, they return their humblest thanks and praises."—The legislature plainly had in view the act of recognition of the first of Queen Elizabeth, chap. 3rd, and of that of James the First, chap. 1st, both acts strongly declaratory of the inheritable nature of the crown, and in many parts they follow, with a nearly literal precision, the words and even the form of thanksgiving which is found in these old declaratory statutes.

The two Houses, in the act of King William, did not thank God that they had found a fair opportunity to assert a right to choose their own governors, much less to make an election the only lawful title to the crown. Their having been in a condition to avoid the very appearance of it, as much as possible, was by them considered as a providential escape. They threw a politic, well-wrought veil over every circumstance tending to weaken the rights, which in the meliorated order of succession they meant to perpetuate; or which might furnish a precedent for any future departure from what they had then settled for ever. Accordingly, that they might not relax the nerves of their monarchy, and that they might preserve a close conformity to the practice of their ancestors, as it appeared in the declaratory statutes of Queen Mary and Queen Elizabeth, in the next clause they vest, by recognition, in their Majesties, all the legal prerogatives of the crown, declaring, "that in them they are most fully, rightfully, and entirely invested, incorporated, united, and annexed." In the clause which follows, for preventing questions, by reason of any pretended titles to the crown, they declare, (observing also in this the traditionary language, along with the traditionary policy of the nation, and repeating as from a rubric the language of the preceding acts of Elizabeth and James,) that on the preserving "a certainty in the SUCCESSION thereof, the unity, peace, and tranquillity of this nation doth, under God, wholly depend."

They knew that a doubtful title of succession would but too much resemble an election; and that an election would be utterly destructive of the "unity, peace, and tranquillity of this nation," which they thought to be considerations of some moment. To provide for these objects, and therefore to exclude for ever the Old Jewry doctrine of "a right to choose our own governors," they follow with a clause containing a most solemn pledge, taken from the preceding act of Queen Elizabeth, as solemn a pledge as ever was or can be given in favour of an hereditary succession, and as solemn a renunciation as could be made of the principles by this Society imputed to them. "The Lords spiritual and temporal, and Commons, do, in the name of all the people aforesaid, most humbly and faithfully submit themselves, their heirs and posterities for ever; and do faithfully promise that they will stand to maintain, and defend their said Majesties, and also the limitation of the crown, herein specified and contained, to the utmost of their powers," &c. &c.

So far is it from being true, that we acquired a right by the Revolution to elect our kings, that if we had possessed it before, the English nation did at that time most solemnly renounce and abdicate it, for themselves, and for all their posterity for ever. These gentlemen may value themselves as much as they please on their Whig principles; but I never desire to be thought a better Whig than Lord Somers; or to understand the principles of the Revolution better than those by whom it was brought about; or to read in the Declaration of Right any mysteries unknown to those whose penetrating style has engraved in our ordinances, and in our hearts, the words and spirit of that immortal law.

It is true, that, aided with the powers derived from force and opportunity, the nation was at that time, in some sense, free to take what course it pleased for filling the throne; but only free to do so upon the same grounds on which they might have wholly abolished their monarchy, and every other part of their constitution. However, they did not think such bold changes within their commission. It is indeed difficult, perhaps impossible, to give limits to the mere abstract competence of the supreme power, such as was exercised by parliament at that time; but the limits of a moral competence, subjecting, even in powers more indisputably sovereign, occasional will to permanent reason, and to the steady maxims of faith, justice, and fixed fundamental policy, are perfectly intelligible, and perfectly binding upon those who exercise any authority, under any name, or under any title, in the state. The House of Lords, for instance, is not morally competent to dissolve the House of Commons; no, nor even to dissolve itself, nor to abdicate, if it would, its portion in the legislature of the kingdom. Though a king may abdicate for his own person, he cannot abdicate for the monarchy. By as strong, or by a stronger reason, the House of Commons cannot renounce its share of authority. The engagement and pact of society, which generally goes by the name of the constitution, forbids such invasion and such surrender. The constituent parts of a state are obliged to hold their public faith with each other, and with all those who derive any serious interest under their engagements, as much as the whole state is bound to keep its faith with separate communities. Otherwise competence and power would soon be confounded, and no law be left but the will of a prevailing force. On this principle the succession of the crown has always been what it now is, an hereditary succession by law: in the old line it was a succession by the common law; in the new by the statute law, operating on the principles of the common law, not changing the substance, but regulating the mode, and describing the persons. Both these descriptions of law are of the same force, and are derived from an equal authority, emanating from the common agreement and original compact of the state, *communi sponsione reipublicae*, and as such are equally binding on king and people too, as long as the terms are observed, and they continue the same body politic.

It is far from impossible to reconcile, if we do not suffer ourselves to be entangled in the mazes of metaphysic sophistry, the use both of a fixed rule and an occasional deviation; the sacredness of an hereditary principle of succession in our government, with a power of change in its application in cases of extreme emergency. Even in that extremity, (if we take the measure of our rights by our exercise of them at the Revolution,) the change is to be confined to the peccant part only; to the part which produced the necessary deviation; and even then it is to be effected without a decomposition of the whole civil and political mass, for the purpose of originating a new civil order out of the first elements of society.

A state without the means of some change is without the means of its conservation. Without such means it might even risk the loss of that part of the constitution which it wished the most religiously to preserve. The two principles of conservation and correction operated strongly at the two critical periods of the Restoration and Revolution, when England found itself without a king. At both those periods the nation had lost the bond of union in their ancient edifice; they did not, however, dissolve the whole fabric. On the contrary, in both cases they regenerated the deficient part of the old constitution through the parts which were not impaired. They kept these old parts exactly as they were, that the part recovered might be suited to them. They acted by the ancient organized states in the shape of their old organization, and not by the organic moleculae of a disbanded people. At no time, perhaps, did the sovereign legislature manifest a more tender regard to that fundamental principle of British constitutional policy, than at the time of the Revolution, when it deviated from the direct line of hereditary succession. The crown was carried somewhat out of the line in which it had before moved; but the new line was derived from the same stock. It was still a line of hereditary descent; still an hereditary descent in the same blood, though an hereditary descent qualified with Protestantism. When the legislature altered the direction, but kept the principle, they showed that they held it inviolable.

On this principle, the law of inheritance had admitted some amendment in the old time, and long before the era of the Revolution. Some time after the conquest, great questions arose upon the legal principles of hereditary descent. It became a matter of doubt, whether the heir per capita or the heir per stirpes was to succeed; but whether the heir per capita gave way when the heirdom per stirpes took place, or the Catholic heir when the Protestants was preferred, the inheritable principle survived with a sort of immortality through all transmigrations—*multosque per annos stat fortuna domus, et avi numerantur avorum*. This is the spirit of our constitution, not only in its settled course, but in all its revolutions. Whoever came in, or, however he came in, whether he obtained the crown by law, or by force, the hereditary succession was either continued or adopted. The gentlemen of the Society for Revolutions see nothing in that of 1688 but the deviation from the constitution; and they take the deviation from the principle for the principle. They have little regard to the obvious consequences of their doctrine, though they must see, that it leaves positive authority in very few of the positive institutions of this country. When such an unwarrantable maxim is once established, that no throne is lawful but the elective, no one act of the princes who preceded this era of fictitious election can be valid. Do these theorists mean to imitate some of their predecessors, who dragged the bodies of our ancient sovereigns out of the quiet of their tombs? Do they mean to attaint and disable backwards all the kings that have reigned before the Revolution, and consequently to stain the throne of England with the blot of a continual usurpation? Do they mean to invalidate, annul, or to call into question, together with the titles of the whole line of our kings, that great body of our statute law which passed under those whom they treat as usurpers? to annul laws of inestimable value to our liberties—of as great value at least as any which have passed at or since the period of the Revolution? If kings, who did not owe their crown to the choice of their people, had no title to make laws, what will become of the *statute de tallagio non concedendo?*—of the petition of right?—of the act of habeas corpus? Do these new doctors of the rights of men presume to assert, that King James the Second, who came to the crown as next of blood, according to the rules of a then unqualified succession, was not to all intents and purposes a lawful king of England, before he had done any of those acts which were justly construed into an abdication of his crown? If he was not, much trouble in parliament might have been saved at the period these gentlemen commemorate. But King James was a bad king with a good title, and not an usurper. The princes who succeeded according to the act of parliament which settled the crown on the Electress Sophia and on her descendants, being Protestants, came in as much by a title of inheritance as King James did. He came in according to the law, as it stood at his accession to the crown; and the princes of the House of Brunswick came to the inheritance of the crown, not by election, but by the law as it stood at their several accessions of Protestant descent and inheritance, as I hope I have shown sufficiently.

The law, by which this royal family is specifically destined to the succession, is the act of the 12th and 13th of King William. The terms of this act bind "us and our heirs, and our posterity, to them, their heirs, and their posterity," being

Protestants, to the end of time, in the same words as the Declaration of Right had bound us to the heirs of King William and Queen Mary. It therefore secures both an hereditary crown and an hereditary allegiance. On what ground, except the constitutional policy of forming an establishment to secure that kind of succession which is to preclude a choice of the people for ever, could the legislature have fastidiously rejected the fair and abundant choice which our country presented to them, and searched in strange lands for a foreign princess, from whose womb the line of our future rulers were to derive their title to govern millions of men through a series of ages?

The Princess Sophia was named in the act of settlement of the 12th and 13th of King William, for a stock and root of inheritance to our kings, and not for her merits as a temporary administratrix of a power, which she might not, and in fact did not, herself ever exercise. She was adopted for one reason, and for one only, because, says the act, "the most excellent Princess Sophia, Electress and Duchess Dowager of Hanover, is daughter of the most excellent Princess Elizabeth, late Queen of Bohemia, daughter of our late sovereign lord King James the First, of happy memory, and is hereby declared to be the next in succession in the Protestant line," &c., &c.; "and the crown shall continue to the heirs of her body, being Protestants." This limitation was made by parliament, that through the Princess Sophia an inheritable line not only was to be continued in future, but (what they thought very material) that through her it was to be connected with the old stock of inheritance in King James the First; in order that the monarchy might preserve an unbroken unity through all ages, and might be preserved (with safety to our religion) in the old approved mode by descent, in which, if our liberties had been once endangered, they had often, through all storms and struggles of prerogative and privilege, been preserved. They did well. No experience has taught us, that in any other course or method than that of an hereditary crown our liberties can be regularly perpetuated and preserved sacred as our hereditary right. An irregular, convulsive movement may be necessary to throw off an irregular, convulsive disease. But the course of succession is the healthy habit of the British constitution. Was it that the legislature wanted, at the act for the limitation of the crown in the Hanoverian line, drawn through the female descendants of James the First, a due sense of the inconveniences of having two or three, or possibly more, foreigners in succession to the British throne? No!—they had a due sense of the evils which might happen from such foreign rule, and more than a due sense of them. But a more decisive proof cannot be given of the full conviction of the British nation, that the principles of the Revolution did not authorize them to elect kings at their pleasure, and without any attention to the ancient fundamental principles of our government, than their continuing to adopt a plan of hereditary Protestant succession in the old line, with all the dangers and all the inconveniences of its being a foreign line full before their eyes, and operating with the utmost force upon their minds.

A few years ago I should be ashamed to overload a matter, so capable of supporting itself, by the then unnecessary support of any argument; but this seditious, unconstitutional doctrine is now publicly taught, avowed, and printed. The dislike I feel to revolutions, the signals for which have so often been given from pulpits; the spirit of change that is gone abroad; the total contempt which prevails with you, and may come to prevail with us, of all ancient institutions, when set in opposition to a present sense of convenience, or to the bent of a present inclination: all these considerations make it not unadvisable, in my opinion, to call back our attention to the true principles of our own domestic laws; that, you, my French friend, should begin to know, and that we should continue to cherish them. We ought not, on either side of the water, to suffer ourselves to be imposed upon by the counterfeit wares which some persons, by a double fraud, export to you in illicit bottoms, as raw commodities of British growth, though wholly alien to our soil, in order afterwards to smuggle them back again into this country, manufactured after the newest Paris fashion of an improved liberty.

The people of England will not ape the fashions they have never tried, nor go back to those which they have found mischievous on trial. They look upon the legal hereditary succession of their crown as among their rights, not as among their wrongs; as a benefit, not as a grievance; as a security for their liberty, not as a badge of servitude. They look on the frame of their commonwealth, such as it stands, to be of inestimable value; and they conceive the undisturbed succession of the crown to be a pledge of the stability and perpetuity of all the other members of our constitution.

I shall beg leave, before I go any further, to take notice of some paltry artifices, which the abettors of election, as the only lawful title to the crown, are ready to employ, in order to render the support of the just principles of our constitution a task somewhat invidious. These sophisters substitute a fictitious cause, and feigned personages, in whose favour they suppose you engaged, whenever you defend the inheritable nature of the crown. It is common with them to dispute as if they were in a conflict with some of those exploded fanatics of slavery, who formerly maintained, what I believe no creature now maintains, "that the crown is held by divine hereditary and indefeasible right."—These old fanatics of single arbitrary power dogmatized as if hereditary royalty was the only lawful government in the world, just as our new fanatics of popular arbitrary power maintain that a popular election is the sole lawful source of authority. The old prerogative enthusiasts, it is true, did speculate foolishly, and perhaps impiously too, as if monarchy had more of a divine sanction that any other mode of government; and as if a right to govern by inheritance were in strictness indefeasible in every person, who should be found in the succession to a throne, and under every circumstance, which no civil or political right can be. But an absurd opinion concerning the king's hereditary right to the crown does not prejudice one that is rational, and bottomed upon solid principles of law and policy. If all the absurd theories of lawyers and divines were to vitiate the objects in which they are conversant, we should have no law and no religion left in the world. But an absurd theory on one side of a question forms no justification for alleging a false fact, or promulgating mischievous maxims, on the other.

The second claim of the Revolution Society is "a right of cashiering their governors for misconduct." Perhaps the apprehensions our ancestors entertained of forming such a precedent as that "of cashiering for misconduct," was the cause that the declaration of the act, which implied the abdication of King James, was, if it had any fault, rather too guarded, and too circumstantial. But all this guard, and all this accumulation of circumstances, serves to show the spirit of caution which predominated in the national councils in a situation in which men irritated by oppression, and elevated by a triumph over it, are art to abandon themselves to violent and extreme courses: it shows the anxiety of the great men who influenced the conduct of affairs at that great event to make the Revolution a parent of settlement, and not a nursery of future revolutions.

No government could stand a moment, if it could be blown down with anything so loose and indefinite as an opinion of "misconduct." They who led at the Revolution grounded the virtual abdication of King James upon no such light and uncertain principle. They charged him with nothing less than a design, confirmed by a multitude of illegal overt acts, to subvert the Protestant church and state, and their fundamental, unquestionable laws and liberties: they charged him with having broken the original contract between king and people. This was more than misconduct. A grave and overruling necessity obliged them to take the step they took, and took with infinite reluctance, as under that most rigorous of all laws. Their trust for the future preservation of the constitution was not in future revolutions. The grand policy of all their regulations was to render it almost impracticable for any future sovereign to compel the states of the kingdom to have again recourse to those violent remedies. They left the crown what, in the eye and estimation of law, it had never been, perfectly irresponsible. In order to lighten the crown still further, they aggravated responsibility on ministers of state. By the statute of the 1st of King William, sess. 2nd, called "the act for declaring the rights and liberties of the subject, and for settling the succession to the crown," they enacted, that the ministers should serve the crown on the terms of that declaration. They secured soon after the frequent meetings of parliament, by which the whole government would be under the constant inspection and active control of the popular representative and of the magnates of the kingdom. In the next great constitutional act, that of the 12th and 13th of King William, for the further limitation of the crown, and better securing the rights and liberties of the subject, they provided, "that no pardon under the great seal of England should be pleadable to an impeachment by the Commons in parliament." The rule laid down for government in the Declaration of Right, the constant inspection of parliament, the practical claim of impeachment, they thought infinitely a better security not only for their constitutional liberty, but against the vices of administration, than the reservation of a right so difficult in the practice, so uncertain in the issue, and often so mischievous in the consequences, as that of "cashiering their governors."

Dr. Price, in his sermon, condemns very properly the practice of gross, adulatory addresses to kings. Instead of this fulsome style, he proposes that his Majesty should be told, on occasions of congratulation, that "he is to consider himself as more properly the servant than the sovereign of his people." For a compliment, this new form of address does not seem to be very soothing. Those who are servants in name, as well as in effect, do not like to be told of their situation, their duty, and their obligations. The slave, in the old play, tells his master, "*Hæc commemoratio est quasi exprobatio.*" It is not pleasant as compliment; it is not wholesome as instruction. After all, if the king were to bring himself to echo this new kind of address, to adopt it in terms, and even to take the appellation of Servant of the People as his royal style, how either he or we should be much mended by it, I cannot imagine. I have seen very assuming letters, signed, Your most obedient, humble servant. The proudest denomination that ever was endured on earth took a title of still greater humility than that which is now proposed for sovereigns by the Apostle of Liberty. Kings and nations were trampled upon by the foot of one calling himself "the Servant of Servants"; and mandates for deposing sovereigns were sealed with the signet of "the Fisherman."

I should have considered all this as no more than a sort of flippant, vain discourse, in which, as in an unsavoury fume, several persons suffer the spirit of liberty to evaporate, if it were not plainly in support of the idea, and a part of the scheme, of "cashiering kings for misconduct." In that light it is worth some observation.

Kings, in one sense, are undoubtedly the servants of the people, because their power has no other rational end than that of the general advantage; but it is not true that they are, in the ordinary sense, (by our constitution at least,) anything like servants; the essence of whose situation is to obey the commands of some other, and to be removable at pleasure. But the king of Great Britain obeys no other person; all other persons are individually, and collectively too, under him, and owe to him a legal obedience. The law, which knows neither to flatter nor to insult, calls this high magistrate, not our servant, as this humble divine calls him, but "our sovereign Lord the king;" and we, on our parts, have learned to speak only the primitive language of the law, and not the confused jargon of their Babylonian pulpits.

As he is not to obey us, but as we are to obey the law in him, our constitution has made no sort of provision towards rendering him, as a servant, in any degree responsible. Our constitution knows nothing of a magistrate like the Justicia of Arragon; nor of any court legally appointed, nor of any process legally settled, for submitting the king to the responsibility belonging to all servants. In this he is not distinguished from the Commons and the Lords; who, in their several public capacities, can never be called to an account for their conduct; although the Revolution Society chooses to assert, in direct opposition to one of the wisest and most beautiful parts of our constitution, that "a king is no more than the first servant of the public, created by it, and responsible to it."

Ill would our ancestors at the Revolution have deserved their fame for wisdom, if they had found no security for their freedom, but in rendering their government feeble in its operations, and precarious in its tenure; if they had been able to contrive no better remedy against arbitrary power than civil confusion. Let these gentlemen state who that representative public is to whom they will affirm the king, as a servant, to be responsible. It will then be time enough for me to produce to them the positive statute law which affirms that he is not.

Glossary

bottom: "rest" or "stand" (as on a foundation)

cashier: to be done with; expel

communi sponsione reipublicae: Latin for "the consent of the entire commonwealth"

Hæc commemoratio est quasi exprobatio: a line from a Roman comedy (*Andria*, by Terence), meaning, "this reminder is almost like a rebuke"

multosque per annos stat fortuna domus, et avi numerantur avorum: a quote from the Roman author Virgil, meaning roughly, "yet the stock remains immortal, and for many years the fortune of the house stands fast, and the grandfathers of grandfathers are counted"

Old Jewry: a reference to a noted Dissenting sermon delivered by Richard Price at a chapel in the Old Jewry, a London district established in medieval times

Privilegium non transit in exemplum: a maxim in Roman law, meaning, "the right of an individual does not translate into a general rule"

statute de tallagio non concedendo: a quote from the Magna Carta, referring to "a statute concerning certain liberties granted by the king to his commons"

Document Analysis and Themes

In this extract Burke outlines, and staunchly defends, the principle of hereditary succession to the English throne. He emphasizes the role played by the English Revolution of 1688 in confirming this principle through lineal descent and statute law. Burke's controversial interpretation challenged many political reformers, such as the Dissenting Minister Richard Price, who argued that the monarch of England required popular consent to rule as a servant of the people—the very consent that William of Orange had gained through Parliament prior to his joint enthronement with Queen Mary in 1688.

By contrast, in *Reflections*, Burke argues that the accession of William of Orange to the throne, though it represented "a small and a temporary deviation" from the *direct* hereditary line, was nevertheless a succession "derived from the same stock"—"hereditary descent qualified with Protestantism." Nowhere in the process, Burke contends, had the English people exercised a determining will or been required to give their consent. The lead-up to the English Revolution was, he suggests, a moment of great emergency, a litmus test on the constitutional footing of the monarchy. The passive acceptance by the public of William of Orange as joint sovereign confirmed *in perpetuity* the binding nature of hereditary royal succession.

According to Burke, not only had the deeds of the English Revolution and the acquiescence of the people confirmed this principle, but it also had a legal basis, enshrined by statute in the form of the "Declaration of Right," which confirmed a Protestant line of succession. Layering his argument still further but moving into his own century, Burke also suggests that the public acceptance of the Hanoverian line commencing with George I, despite all the "dangers and inconveniences" of a foreign monarch, had straightened what had been a brief but necessary hereditary deviation, by reestablishing a *direct* descent to James I, albeit through the female line.

Hereditary succession was necessary according to Burke, because it was the only way to provide political and social stability, which in turn generated wealth and happiness. Throughout *Reflections* but particularly in the extract, Burke is careful to draw a distinction between the concept of the hereditary right of succession by statute law and the "divine heredity and indefeasible right" claimed by monarchs in the past, most notably Charles I. Burke therefore positions himself as a moderate between two poles: the excesses of absolute monarchy associated with Louis XVI in France and the "new fanatics," or English political radicals who claimed that "popular election is the sole lawful source of authority."

In addition to defending hereditary monarchy, Burke also addresses the issue raised by Price of whether the people have a right to "cashier" or rebuke their governors or rulers for misconduct, while attacking his assertion that the king should consider himself "more properly the servant than the sovereign of his people." In Burke's view, this analogy is as pernicious as it is false, for the king is in no way subservient to his people, cannot be dismissed, and has the right to be obeyed. However, several pieces of legislation that had been passed under William and Mary already safeguarded the rights and liberties of subjects from arbitrary Crown rule, providing that "no pardon under the great seal of England should be pleadable to an impeachment by the Commons in parliament."

Burke's position in *Reflections on the Revolution in France* consists of a delicate and, some argue, contradictory balance between constitutional continuity and healthy correction. It hinges on the separation of the person of the monarch from the institution of the monarchy, for while a king could abdicate or forsake his crown in absentia as James II had done, the monarchy per se would continue in perpetuity. Burke's conservative sentiments in favor of hereditary monarchy and his antagonism toward the French Revolution—"the newest Paris Fashion of an improved liberty," as he sarcastically writes—surprised many contemporaries who remembered his progressive support for the American revolutionaries. However, his defection from the opposition to the government immediately prior to the writing of *Reflections* may partly explain this political shift.

—*Michael Shally-Jensen, PhD*
and Peter Robinson, PhD

Bibliography and Additional Reading

Bourke, Richard. *Empire and Revolution: The Political Life of Edmund Burke.* Princeton, NJ: Princeton University Press, 2015.

Burke, Edmund. *Reflections on the Revolution in France.* Edited by J. G. A. Pocock. Indianapolis: Hackett Publishing Co., 1987.

Norman, Jesse. *Edmund Burke: The First Conservative.* New York: Basic Books, 2013.

O'Brien, Connor Cruise. *The Great Melody: A Thematic Biography and Commentated Anthology of Edmund Burke.* Chicago: University of Chicago Press, 1993.

Olympe de Gouges: Declaration of the Rights of Woman and of the Female Citizen

Date: September 1791
Author: Olympe de Gouges
Genre: political tract

Summary Overview

Approximately two years after the Declaration of the Rights of Man and of the Citizen was promulgated as a binding law in France, Marie Gouze wrote the Declaration of the Rights of Woman and of the Female Citizen. A self-educated butcher's daughter from the south of France, she wrote a number of pamphlets, plays, and speeches under the name Olympe de Gouges. Her preamble was a call to arms to all women, including the queen of France, Marie-Antoinette. Calling on the Supreme Being for guidance, she lists seventeen rights of women and female citizens. Ending with a sample marriage contract designed to ensure more equitable treatment of women, the Declaration of the Rights of Woman and of the Female Citizen was never accepted or promulgated.

The Declaration of the Rights of Woman and of the Female Citizen was addressed to the nobility, including the queen, Marie-Antoinette, to married and unmarried women of all social ranks, and to revolutionaries who favored the implementation of rights for women.

Defining Moment

At the beginning of the eighteenth century, France experienced a period of expansion, population growth, and increased urbanization, and the newer colonial empires of France began to pay off. By the end of the century, the population surge had begun to press against the food supply. Land hunger and food shortages went hand in hand with increasing social dissatisfaction in the country. France was experiencing growing pains. Although France was changing, the structure of French society, a system of privilege, was not. The social structure was more than one hundred years old. The population was divided into three "estates," each with its own set of privileges, although the privileges were not equal. The First Estate was the clergy, the Second Estate consisted of the nobility, and the Third Estate included everyone else. The economic crises of 1787, 1788, and 1789 showed the weakness of the social order. This situation stimulated suspicions between the lower and the upper classes and between all classes and the government; it gave rise to an indefinite fear of complacency. Moreover, there was a general lack of confidence in the established social and political order.

The response of King Louis XVI was to call an Assembly of Notables, a meeting of select members of the nobility. In 1788 he invited them to come to his palace, Versailles, in the hope that the nobility would agree to gifts to the crown and to a new taxation structure. Thus the nobility, by acting in concert with the crown, would relieve the fiscal crisis faced by Louis XVI and the government. The assembly failed to produce the desired results, however, and Louis was forced to call a meeting of the Estates-General of France in 1789. This medieval representative institution in France had not met for 175 years before Louis XVI reconvened it on May 5, 1789, to deal with the looming financial crisis. France was on the verge of bankruptcy.

The meeting of the Estates-General provided those elected to it with the opportunity to present their grievances. On June 20, 1789, the members of the newly formed National Assembly took the Tennis Court Oath, pledging to remain together until they had drafted and passed a new constitution. The National Assembly, also called the Constituent Assembly, is what the Third Estate's delegation to the Estates-General decided to call itself when, on June

16, 1789, it proclaimed itself the sole legitimate representative of the French nation. The name stuck when, after a failed attempt to undo this clear usurpation of royal authority, Louis XVI ordered the noble and clerical delegations to join the National Assembly on June 27, 1789. (The National Assembly differed greatly from the Estates-General. The latter organization, which dated to the fourteenth century, was primarily a consultative assembly, convoked at the pleasure of the king.) These events marked the birth of the Patriot Party, resulting in part from the success of a small pamphlet published by Emmanuel-Joseph Sieyès in January 1789 titled "What Is the Third Estate?" It contains these stirring lines: "What is the Third Estate? *Everything*. What has it been until now in the political order? *Nothing*. What does it want to be? *Something*" (qtd. in Baker, p. 154). Sieyès's argument was based on the concepts of utility and nationalism. The Third Estate was the most useful class to the nation. The nobles constituted an *imperium in imperio*, or empire within an empire. The Third Estate's demands for equality were moderate. It was by itself the National Assembly and therefore should create a system that eliminated class privilege.

To put all of these events in context, a thumbnail summary of the key events of the French Revolution is necessary. The French Revolution actually began in the spring and summer of 1789, when food riots erupted throughout France. However, the traditional date marking the start of the Revolution is July 14, 1789, when revolutionaries stormed and seized the royal prison, the Bastille, in Paris. The next month, the National Assembly issued the Decrees Abolishing the Feudal System and the Declaration of the Rights of Man and of the Citizen. In October of that year, Parisian women marched on the king's palace at Versailles and forced him to return to Paris. But in June 1791 the royal family, fearing for their lives, attempted to flee France and were arrested at Varennes, France (the so-called "flight to Varennes"). Later, in October, the new Legislative Assembly met for the first time. By 1792 counterrevolutionary movements were forming, though in August of that year the king was imprisoned; that same month, the National Convention replaced the Legislative Assembly. The Revolution began to turn violent when prisoners, most of

First page of Declaration of the Rights of Woman and of the Female Citizen By Olympe de Gouges [Public domain], via Wikimedia Commons.

them aristocrats, were killed during the so-called September Massacres of 1792. In 1792 the monarchy was abolished, and the First French Republic was proclaimed. Louis XVI was executed on January 21, 1793, and in March the Revolutionary Tribunal was created, leading to the Reign of Terror under Maximilien de Robespierre and the radical Jacobins. Then, on October 16, 1793, Marie-Antoinette was executed. Further violence took place when Robespierre and other radicals were executed by moderates. By 1794 the Reign of Terror had come to an end.

The storming of the Bastille had few practical consequences, but symbolically it was of enormous significance. It represented the Revolution-inspired attack on the ancien régime. Today it is celebrated as Bastille Day, or French Independence Day. Shortly after the fall of the Bastille, in a series of disturbances in the countryside of France, rural peasants revolted against their feudal overlords during July and August 1789, a period known as the Great Fear. These revolts were occasioned by rumors of an aristocratic plot to hoard grain and drive up prices while sending gangs of bandits to ruin the peasants' crops in the countryside. France's economic crisis reached a peak in 1788 and 1789. The harvest of 1788 was terrible, leading to food shortages, high prices, and famine in 1789. Fearful that the peasants would next begin to attack the property of the bourgeois, or middle class, the National Assembly in August issued a series of decrees that, in effect, destroyed the ancien régime. Once they had agreed on the importance of drafting a declaration of rights, the deputies in the National Assembly faced the more difficult task of crafting a declaration that a majority could accept. They agreed on seventeen articles that laid out a new vision of government; the protection of natural rights replaced the will of the king as the justification for authority. The National Assembly deliberated carefully and on August 4, 1789, granted France the equality demanded by the bourgeois as Armand II, duke of Aiguillon, a liberal nobleman, renounced his rights, prerogatives, and dues in order to satisfy the peasants and restore order to the countryside. Effectively, this act ended the feudal system in France. On August 26, 1789, the assembly approved the Declaration of the Rights of Man and of the Citizen.

The declaration expresses the liberal and universal goal of the philosophes, the general term for those academics and intellectuals who became the leading voices of the French Enlightenment during the eighteenth century. The most important of these men were Voltaire, Jean-Jacques Rousseau, Denis Diderot, and Charles-Louis de Secondat, baron of Montesquieu. The two fundamental ideas of the Enlightenment were rationalism and relativism. Rationalism was the belief that through the power of reason, humans could arrive at truth and improve human society. The philosophes were eager to demonstrate that human reason was the best guide for organizing society and government. Relativism, a philosophy that different ideas, cultures, and beliefs had equal worth, gripped the European mind as the impact of the Age of Exploration demonstrated that adherence to this philosophy had practical and intellectual value in any societal program for reform. Europeans were exposed to a variety of cultures and peoples worldwide. The Declaration of the Rights of Man and of the Citizen also addressed the interests of the bourgeois, including their demands for government by the people and the idea that the aim of the government is to preserve the natural rights of the individual. The political ideas of John Locke and Montesquieu and Rousseau's work *The Social Contract*, along with Voltaire's thoughts on equality and an end to government censorship, spring from the pages of the document. In addition, the National Assembly helped businesses stop tariffs, ended the guild system, and decreed that French colonies trade only with France.

Following August 26, 1789, the National Assembly got the breathing space it needed and proceeded to rebuild France from the ground up. The Great Reforms of 1789–1791, all rooted in the ideological foundations of the declaration and the writings of the philosophes, fall roughly into three categories. First, the Patriots wanted to limit the government by decentralizing the administration and the judiciary. On December 14, 1789, the National Assembly established a structure for municipal governments throughout France. For this purpose it created a distinction between active citizens (men who paid yearly taxes equal to three days' wages) who could vote and passive citizens who could not vote. On December 22, 1789, the assembly established a structure for new departmental administration. The number of departments throughout France was reduced. The departments were subdivided into districts and cantons. In the cantons only active citizens could vote and then only for electors who would choose deputies to the National Assembly and district officials who had to pay yearly taxes equal to ten days' wages. Deputies to the National Assembly had to pay yearly taxes equal to a silver mark. On August 16, 1790, cantons, districts, and departments were given courts staffed by elected judges.

Second, to deal further with the bankruptcy problem, the National Assembly on December 19, 1789, authorized the issuance of paper money (assignats) to be backed by church lands and to be redeemable when they were sold. On February 13, 1790, the National Assembly suppressed the monastic orders, thus creating a supply of salable land. Members of the National Assembly did not wish to destroy the church, which they considered to be a useful source of popular moral inspiration. On July 12, 1790, they issued the Civil Constitution of the Clergy, making departments and dioceses coterminous. Bishops and priests were to be elected in the same fashion as other departmental and district officials; they were paid by the state. Moreover, they were required to pledge allegiance to the constitution of the nation. Only a few members of the clergy did so; most clergy became refractory, or nonaccepting, clergy. Many left France or went into hiding.

Finally, in more general financial and economic reforms, the National Assembly was strongly influenced by physiocratic doctrines (doctrines of utility or usefulness). In October 1790 it established a unified tariff for France. In November 1790 it set up two basic taxes—a contribution on land and a contribution on personal property. Also, on June 14, 1791, the National Assembly passed the Le Chapelier Law, which prohibited industrial and labor strikes. On May 21, 1791, the assembly established the metric system. The reorganization of France from the ground up was complete.

From the outset of the Revolution, there were scattered demands for women's rights. These demands were often rejected by revolutionary legislators, the vast majority of whom insisted that women were not fit to exercise political rights. Basing their rejection of women's rights on the very nature of woman herself, these legislators proclaimed that neither men nor women would receive any benefit from equality and full active participation on the part of women in the newly envisioned government of France. Clearly the idea of women's rights was constructed in disparaging and unequal terms in the revolutionary political discourse. Nevertheless, Gouges steadfastly appealed to women of all ranks to unite around her leadership in order to exert political power in the common interest for the common good. In order to redress the exclusion of women from the Declaration of the Rights of Man and of the Citizen, Gouges issued the Declaration of Rights of Woman and of the Female Citizen in September 1791. She was hopeful that the Legislative Assembly of 1791 would ratify the document.

Author Biography

Marie Gouze, the author of the Declaration of the Rights of Woman and of the Female Citizen, was a French author and activist. She was born in Montauban in southern France on December 31, 1748, to a modest family—her father was a butcher. Her mother was rumored to have had an affair with Jean-Jacques Lefranc, marquis de Pompignan, who some claimed was Marie's real father. A rebellious young woman, she married a French officer, Louis Aubrey, at age seventeen. Together they had a son. Louis Aubrey, who was much older than Marie, died three years into the marriage. Vowing never to abandon her son, she went to Paris seeking fame as a writer and taking the pen name Olympe de Gouges. Her career as a playwright brought her only modest success. Swept up in the political events of the 1780s in France, she initially took a somewhat moderate stance, arguing that reforms were intended to bring about change without sacrificing social stability. At first a supporter of the monarchy, she became impatient with the inaction of Louis XVI and Marie-Antoinette. She encouraged Louis to leave his throne and put in its place a regency government. The flight to Varennes in 1791 by the royal family forced her to break with Louis and side completely with the revolutionaries. Olympe de Gouges is best known for her Declaration of the Rights of Woman and of the Female Citizen, published in September 1791. She is considered a feminist pioneer, and her bold personality emerges strongly in her writings. Through the declaration she challenged the notion of male-female inequality. She used powerful language that was dangerous for her at the time; on November 3, 1793, she was executed for crimes against the government.

Historical Document

Declaration of the Rights of Woman and of the Female Citizen

Man, are you capable of being just? It is a woman who poses the question; you will not deprive her of that right at least. Tell me, what gives you sovereign empire to oppress my sex? Your strength? Your talents? Observe the Creator in his wisdom; survey in all her grandeur that nature with whom you seem to want to be in harmony, and give me, if you dare, an example of this tyrannical empire. Go back to animals, consult the elements, study plants, finally glance at all the modifications of organic matter, and surrender to the evidence when I offer you the means; search, probe, and distinguish, if you can, the sexes in the administration of nature. Everywhere you will find them mingled; everywhere they cooperate in harmonious togetherness in this immortal masterpiece.

Man alone has raised his exceptional circumstances to a principle. Bizarre, blind, bloated with science and degenerated—in a century of enlightenment and wisdom—into the crassest ignorance, he wants to command as a despot a sex which is in full possession of its intellectual faculties; he pretends to enjoy the Revolution and to claim his rights to equality in order to say nothing more about it.

For the National Assembly to decree in its last sessions, or in those of the next legislature:

Preamble. Mothers, daughters, sisters [and] representatives of the nation demand to be constituted into a national assembly. Believing that ignorance, omission, or scorn for the rights of woman are the only causes of public misfortunes and of the corruption of governments, [the women] have resolved to set forth a solemn declaration the natural, inalienable, and sacred rights of woman in order that this declaration, constantly exposed before all members of the society, will ceaselessly remind them of their rights and duties; in order that the authoritative acts of women and the authoritative acts of men may be at any moment compared with and respectful of the purpose of all political institutions; and in order that citizens' demands, henceforth based on simple and incontestable principles, will always support the constitution, good morals, and the happiness of all.

Consequently, the sex that is as superior in beauty as it is in courage during the sufferings of maternity recognizes and declares in the presence and under the auspices of the Supreme Being, the following Rights of Woman and of Female Citizens.

Article I. Woman is born free and lives equal to man in her rights. Social distinctions can be based only on the common utility.

Article II. The purpose of any political association is the conservation of the natural and impresciptible rights of woman and man; these rights are liberty property, security, and especially resistance to oppression.

Article III. The principle of all sovereignty rests essentially with the nation, which is nothing but the union of woman and man; no body and no individual can exercise any authority which does not come expressly from it (the nation).

Article IV. Liberty and justice consist of restoring all that belongs to others; thus, the only limits on the exercise of the natural rights of woman are perpetual male tyranny; these limits are to be reformed by the laws of nature and reason.

Article V. Laws of nature and reason proscribe all acts harmful to society; everything which is not prohibited by these wise and divine laws cannot be prevented, and no one can be constrained to do what they do not command.

Article VI. The law must be the expression of the general will; all female and male citizens must contribute either personally or through their representatives to its formation; it must be the same for all: male and female citizens, being equal in the eyes of the law, must be equally admitted to all honors, positions, and public employment according to their capacity and without other distinctions besides those of their virtues and talents.

Article VII. No woman is an exception; she is accused, arrested, and detained in cases determined by law. Women, like men, obey this rigorous law.

Article VIII. The law must establish only those penalties that are strictly and obviously necessary....

Article IX. Once any woman is declared guilty, complete rigor is exercised by law.

Article X. No one is to be disquieted for his very basic opinions; woman has the right to mount the scaffold; she must equally have the right to mount the rostrum, provided that her demonstrations do not disturb the legally established public order.

Article XI. The free communication of thoughts and opinions is one of the most precious rights of woman, since that liberty assures recognition of children by their fathers. Any female citizen thus may say freely, I am the mother of a child which belongs to you, without being forced by a barbarous prejudice to hide the truth; (an exception may be made) to respond to the abuse of this liberty in cases determined by law.

Article XII. The guarantee of the rights of woman and the female citizen implies a major benefit; this guarantee must be instituted for the advantage of all, and not for the particular benefit of those to whom it is entrusted.

Article XIII. For the support of the public force and the expenses of administration, the contributions of woman and man are equal; she shares all the duties and all the painful tasks; therefore, we must have the same share in the distribution of positions, employment, offices, honors, and jobs.

Article XIV. Female and male citizens have the right to verify, either by themselves of through their representatives, the necessity of the public contribution. This can only apply to women if they are granted an equal share, not only of wealth, but also of public administration, and in the determination of the proportion, the base, the collection, and the duration of the tax.

Article XV. The collectivity of women, joined for tax purposes to the aggregate of men, has the right to demand an accounting of his administration from any public agent.

Article XVI. No society has a constitution without the guarantee of rights and the separation of powers; the constitution is null if the majority of individuals comprising the nation have not cooperated in drafting it.

Article XVII. Property belongs to both sexes whether united or separate; for each it is an inviolable and sacred right; no one can be deprived of it, since it is the true patrimony of nature, unless the legally determined public need obviously dictates it, and then only with a just and prior indemnity.

Postscript. Woman, wake up; the tocsin of reason is being heard throughout the whole universe; discover your rights. The powerful empire of nature is no longer surrounded by prejudice, fanaticism, superstition, and lies. The flame of truth has dispersed all the clouds of folly and usurpation. Enslaved man has multiplied his strength and needs recourse to yours to break his chains. Having become free, he has become unjust to his companion. Oh, women, women! When will you cease to be blind? What advantage have you received from the Revolution? A more pronounced scorn, a more marked disdain. In the centuries of corruption you ruled only over the weakness of men. The reclamation of your patrimony, based on the wise decrees of nature-what have you to dread from such a fine undertaking? The bon mot of the legislator of the marriage of Cana? Do you fear that our French legislators, correctors of that morality, long ensnared by political practices now out of date, will only say again to you: women, what is there in common between you and us? Everything, you will have to answer. If they persist in their weakness in putting this non sequitur in contradiction to their principles, courageously oppose the force of reason to the empty pretentions of superiority; unite yourselves beneath the standards of philosophy; deploy all the energy of your character, and you will soon see these haughty men, not groveling at your feet as servile adorers, but proud to share with you the treasures of the Supreme Being. Regardless of what barriers confront you, it is in your power to free yourselves; you have only to want to.

Marriage is the tomb of trust and love. The married woman can with impunity give bastards to her husband and also give them the wealth which does not belong to them. The woman who is unmarried has only one feeble right; ancient and inhuman laws refuse to her for her children the right to the name and the wealth of their father; no new laws have been made in this matter. If it is considered a paradox and an impossibility on my part to try to give my sex an honorable and just consistency, I leave it to men to attain glory for dealing with this matter; but while we wait, the way can be prepared through national education, the restoration of morals, and conjugal conventions.

Form for a Social Contract between Man and Woman

We, _____ and _____, moved by our own will, unite ourselves for the duration of our lives, and for the duration of our mutual inclinations, under the following conditions: We intend and wish to make our wealth communal, meanwhile reserving to ourselves the right to divide it in favor of our children and of those toward whom we might have a particular inclination, mutually recognizing that our property belongs directly to our children, from whatever bed they come, and that all of them without distinction have the right to bear the name of the fathers and mothers who have acknowledged them, and we are charged to subscribe to the law which punishes the renunciation of one's own blood. We likewise obligate ourselves, in case of separation, to divide our wealth and to set aside in advance the portion the law indicates for our children, and in the event of a perfect union, the one who dies will divest himself of half his property in his children's favor, and if one dies childless, the survivor will inherit by right, unless the dying person has disposed of half the common property in favor of one whom he judged deserving.

That is approximately the formula for the marriage act I propose for execution. Upon reading this strange document, I see rising up against me the hypocrites, the prudes, the clergy, and the whole infernal sequence. But how it [my proposal] offers to the wise the moral means of achieving the perfection of a happy government! ...

Moreover, I would like a law which would assist widows and young girls deceived by the false promises of a man to whom they were attached; I would like, I say, this law to force an inconstant man to hold to his obligations or at least [to pay] an indemnity equal to his wealth. Again, I would like this law to be rigorous against women, at least those who have the effrontery to have recourse to a law which they themselves had violated by their misconduct, if proof of that were given. At the same time, as I showed in *Le Bonheur primitif de l'homme* in 1788, that prostitutes should be placed in designated quarters. It is not prostitutes who contribute the most to the depravity of morals, it is the women of society. In regenerating the latter, the former are changed. This link of fraternal union will first bring disorder, but in consequence it will produce at the end a perfect harmony.

I offer a foolproof way to elevate the soul of women; it is to join them to all the activities of man; if man persists in finding this way impractical, let him share his fortune with woman, not at his caprice, but by the wisdom of laws. Prejudice falls, morals are purified, and nature regains all her rights. Add to this the marriage of priests and the strengthening of the king on his throne, and the French government cannot fail.

[Source: From *Women in Revolutionary Paris, 1789–1795: Selected Documents Translated with Notes and Commentary.* Copyright 1979 by the Board of Trustees of the University of Illinois. Used with permission of the University of Illinois Press.]

Glossary

bon mot of the legislator of the marriage of Cana: a sarcastic allusion to the story in John 2:1–12; a connection between Jesus (the "legislator") to the author's point about women's rights entails an unsustainable stretch of reasoning

Le Bonheur primitif de l'homme: title of a pamphlet (English: *The Primitive Happiness of Man*) by Olympe de Gouges

Document Analysis

The Declaration of the Rights of Woman and of the Female Citizen, written by Olympe de Gouges, appeared as a pamphlet on September 14, 1791, and, like the Declaration of Rights of Man and of the Citizen, it embodied the ideas of the philosophes. Especially prevalent was the notion of the general will of Rousseau's *Social Contract*. Many concepts were likewise taken from the Cercle Social, a small band of supporters of women's rights. They launched a campaign for women's rights in 1790 and again in 1791, denouncing the prejudices against women that denied them equal rights in marriage and in education. While this group of women activists never formulated a specific plan, they published newspapers and pamphlets in order to foster a more egalitarian atmosphere for women and argued for more liberal divorce laws and reforms in inheritance laws. In her pamphlet Olympe de Gouges sought to redress the exclusion of women from political participation and from the guarantee of civil rights.

Preamble

In her preamble, Olympe de Gouges makes an impassioned plea to all women to join her in demanding to be constituted as a national assembly. Further asking for the rights afforded to men, her opening words embody the injustice felt by women as they clearly perceived the pain of exclusion: "Man are you capable of being just?" The preamble makes a positive statement of the need for women and men to be treated equally under the new laws of the New France. Until all were freed from oppression, none would truly have the freedoms set out in the Declaration of the Rights of Man and of the Citizen; Gouges provided the antidote, demanding a bill of rights for women.

Articles I–XVII

Divided into seventeen articles, the document follows closely the Declaration of the Rights of Man and of the Citizen. One notable exception is the first article, echoing and paraphrasing the words of Rousseau in the "Discourse on the Origin and Basis of Inequality among Men," modified for the female plea for equal rights: "Woman is born free and lives equal to man in her rights. Social distinctions can be based only on the common utility." This article, along with Article IV, articulates the feminist position of 1789–1791 that the only limits on the exercise of the natural rights of women were perpetual male tyranny. Gouges calls for a reform of this tyranny by employing natural law and reason, an embodiment of the two major themes of the French Enlightenment. The sixth article reiterates Rousseau's idea of the general will as the highest authority in the nation, adding that women and men must participate fully, and thus they must equally be allowed all honors, positions, and public employment. Carefully noting that an individual's capacity figures into the equation, de Gouges wants only virtues and talents to be used for making distinctions. There are no major diversions from the Declaration of the Rights of Man and of the Citizen from Article VI until Article XVII; here Gouges establishes the basis for a new set of inheritance laws and equal access to property.

Postscript

In her powerful postscript, Gouges addresses the plight of women in eighteenth-century society, calling on women to stand up for their rights and to protest the structure of the patriarchal society enslaving all French women. Drawing on prefeminist rhetoric, she tackles the political issues of divorce, child custody, property division, and women's participation in the political process, stating that "regardless of what barriers confront you, it is in your power to free yourselves; you have only to want to." Additionally, in this postscript she calls for an education act for women, to be supported and funded by the legislature. Further, she pleads for the recognition of the unmarried woman's right to the claim the "name and the wealth of their father" for her children. Thus, she addresses the status of women in domestic relations, property laws—equally dividing the family fortunes—conjugal agreements, and education. Her passion here for promulgating women's rights in eighteenth-century France earned her the title "rebel daughter."

Social Contract between Man and Woman

Appended to the declaration is a social contract between man and woman, designed to determine the equitable division of their property if one dies. Gouges calls for the fair treatment of children and for a fair law to "assist widows and young girls deceived ... by an inconstant man to hold to his obligations or at least [to pay] an indemnity equal to his wealth." Gouges concludes her contract by forcefully asserting that she has indeed "a foolproof way to elevate the soul of women; it is to join them to all the activities of man." She goes on to say that "if man persists in finding this way impractical, let him share his fortune with woman, not at his caprice, but by the wisdom of laws." Here Gouges is attempting to give a sort of social security to women in order to remove them from the uncertainty of subjection to the whims of men. In a radical last sentence, she advocates for "the marriage of priests and the strengthening of the king on his throne" (here revealing herself to be a constitutional monarchist), declaring that with these changes, along with the implementation of the Declaration of the Rights of Woman and of the Female Citizen, the government of France "cannot fail."

Essential Themes

The Declaration of the Rights of Woman and of the Female Citizen was never put into law, yet this should not deter an examination of its impact. Olympe de Gouges identified "woman as the other"; pled for women's rights, including sexual rights; decried the lack of political power of women; and created a feminist rhetoric to address the inequality between women and men. For women, the legacy of the French Revolution was contradictory. On the one hand, the unit of national sovereignty was declared to be a universal, abstract, rights-bearing individual; on the other hand, this human individual was almost immediately represented as a man. Gouges saw clearly that the attribution of citizenship to white male subjects complicated the project of claiming equal rights when these rights depended on physical characteristics.

—Anne York, PhD

Bibliography and Additional Reading

Baker, Keith Michael. *The Old Regime and the French Revolution.* Chicago: University of Chicago Press, 1987.

Best, Geoffrey, ed. *The Permanent Revolution: The French Revolution and Its Legacy, 1789–1989.* London: Fontana Press, 1988.

Doyle, William. *The French Revolution: A Very Short Introduction,* 2nd ed. Oxford, U.K.: Oxford UP, 2020.

Hunt, Lynn. *The French Revolution and Human Rights: A Brief Documentary History.* New York: Bedford Books, 1996.

"Liberty, Equality, Fraternity: Exploring the French Revolution." George Mason University Web site. http://chnm.gmu.edu/revolution.

Mason, Laura, and Tracey Rizzo. *The French Revolution: A Document Collection.* Boston: Houghton Mifflin, 1999.

Popkin, Jeremy. *A Short History of the French Revolution,* 7th ed. New York: Routledge, 2019.

Roberts, J. M. *The French Revolution,* 2nd ed. Oxford, U.K.: Oxford UP, 1997.

Maximilien Robespierre on the Ideals of the French Revolution

Date: 1794
Author: Maximilien Robespierre
Genre: political tract; speech

Summary Overview

The French revolutionary Maximilien Robespierre came to prominence during the National Convention (the French governing body) during the period of 1793–1794. Earlier he had served on the short-lived Estates-General, a body convened in 1789 by King Louis XVI as a concession to those calling for change. That same year he joined the Jacobins, a political club in Paris that initially did not seek the end of the monarchy but which became radicalized under Robespierre's leadership as the revolution proceeded. The Jacobins represented a minority section in the early National Convention but then mustered members of the Montagnards, a broadly radical group, to oppose the moderate Girondists, thus boosting their popularity. Also aiding the Jacobins in the beginning was their focus on establishing the principles of the revolution in France. "On the Principles of Political Morality" was Robespierre's address to the convention on February 5, 1794. In it, he justified the use of "terror" to control the numerous internal factions in France and to move sociopolitical reforms forward. The policy of "terror" was enacted through the Committee of Public Safety, which Robespierre dominated. Any vaunted principles he may have wished to see established, however, quickly descended into mere violence, as thousands of people were put to their death as enemies of the state.

Defining Moment

The French Revolution began in 1789 when underprivileged classes living under the monarchy of Louis XVI clamored for radical change. Although initially the revolutionaries aimed to establish a constitutional monarchy, by late 1792 that idea had been abandoned in favor of a self-standing republic. Divisions within the Estates-General of 1789 led to the formation of a National Assembly that largely excluded nobles and clergy and benefitted the "commons," or general populous. In 1791 the royal family attempted to escape, but Louis and his queen consort, Marie-Antoinette, were captured and imprisoned; a year later both were guillotined. Bitter factional struggles, riots, attacks by other nations, and counterrevolutionary uprisings helped to bring extremists to power along with a new governing body, the National Convention. The Jacobins, led by Maximilian Robespierre, represented the main extrem-

Portrait of Maximilien de Robespierre c. 1790 (anonymous). Image via Wikimedia Commons. [Public domain.]

ist group. Together with the Montagnards, they overthrew the moderate Girondist faction and, through the infamous Committee of Public Safety, instituted a policy of "terror" to maintain control of the country. In its bloody reign of terror, the Committee executed thousands of perceived enemies and counterrevolutionaries. Robespierre himself was viewed by some as less extreme than many of his cohorts, and his eloquent defense of democratic principles made him popular in Paris. His "On the Principles of Political Morality," excerpted here, illustrates his passion for reform and his zeal for achieving it—even if through the application of harsh measures.

Author Biography

Maximilian Robespierre (1758–1794) was born in Arras and attended school in Paris, where he studied classics and was influenced by the philosophical works of Montesquieu and Jean-Jacque Rousseau. After studying law at the Sorbonne and working as a lawyer, he was elected (1789) to the Estates-General, an assembly approved by King Louis XVI as a step toward liberalization; it included monarchists, nobles, clergy, and members of the third estate, or "the commons." Within two months of its creation, however, the assembly was challenged by deputies of the third estate, including Robespierre, who declared the establishment of a new National Assembly, thus moving the country toward revolution. In his speeches, Robespierre drew attention to the centrality of individual rights and was given the nickname "the Incorruptible" for his idealistic approach, even as he became increasingly radical in his views. Along with others of the left, he called for the death of Louis XVI and came to head the radical Jacobins against the right-wing republican Girondists in the reconstituted assembly called the National Convention (1792).

With the Girondists out, Robespierre was elected to the Committee of Public Safety, which acted essentially as a dictatorship operating under emergency conditions: not only did the revolution warrant such a label, but the country at that time was simultaneously engaged in war against several European powers for greater influence on the Continent. As violence, factional rivalries, and counterrevolutionary uprisings grew, the Committee of Public Safety, steered by Robespierre, instituted a bloody Reign of Terror to try to control the situation: thousands were put to the guillotine—although Robespierre personally ordered only about seventy-five executions. Robespierre's actions earned him many enemies, and a conspiracy eventually formed against him. In the conservative Thermidorian Reaction of 1794, he was pursued by opponents and tried to shoot himself, only to then be guillotined.

Recent scholarship paints a somewhat more generous picture of Robespierre and his social ideals than the bloodthirsty monster that he was made out to be in many earlier works.

Historical Document

We set forth, some time ago, the principles of our foreign policy. We came today to develop the principles of our domestic policy.

After operating for a long time at random and as if impelled by the movement of factions opposing one another, the representatives of the French people have finally shown a character and a government. A sudden change in the Nation's fortune told Europe that there had been a regeneration among the national representatives. But, up to the very moment when I am speaking, it must be agreed, we have been guided, in such stormy circumstances, by love of the good and by awareness of our country's needs rather than by a correct theory and precise rules of conduct, which we did not even have time to sketch.

It is time to mark clearly the aim of the revolution and the end we want to reach; it is time to take account of the obstacles which still separate us from it and of the means that we ought to adopt to attain it: a simple and important idea which seems never to have been noticed. Well, how could a weak and corrupt government have dared to implement it? A king, a proud senate, a Caesar, a Cromwell, must first of all cover their plans with a religious veil, compromise with all the vices, caress all the parties, crush the party of the good men, oppress or deceive the people, to attain the aim of their perfidious ambition. If we had not had a greater task to perform, if nothing were involved but interests of a faction or of a new aristocracy, we could have believed, like certain writers even more ignorant than they are perverse, that the plan of the French revolution was plainly written in the books of Tacitus and Machiavelli, and we could have looked for the duties of the people's representatives in the history of Augustus, Tiberius, or Vespasian, or even in that of certain French legislators; for, except for a few nuances of perfidy or cruelty, all tyrants are alike.

For our part, we come today to reveal to the whole world your political secrets, in order that all the friends of our country can rally to the voice of reason and the public interest; in order that the French nation and its representatives may be respected in all the countries where the knowledge of their real principles can be obtained; in order that the intriguers who are always to replace other intriguers may be judged by easy and certain rules.

Farsighted precautions are needed to make liberty's destiny depend on the truth, which is eternal, more than on men, who are ephemeral, so that if the government forgets the people's interests or if it falls back into the hands of corrupt men, in accordance with the natural course of things, the light of recognized principles will make clear its betrayals, and so that every new faction will meet death in the mere thought of crime.

Happy [are] the people who can reach that point! For, whatever new outrages are prepared against it, what resources are presented by an order of things in which the public reason is the guarantee of liberty!

What is the end toward which we are aiming? The peaceable enjoyment of liberty and equity; the reign of that eternal justice whose laws have been graven not on marble and stone but in the hearts of all men, even the slave who forgets them and the tyrant who denies them.

We want to substitute, in our land, morality for egotism; probity for honor; principles for customs; ethics for propriety; the rule of reason for the tyranny of fashion; disdain for vice for disdain for misfortune; self-respect for insolence; spiritual grandeur for vanity; love of glory for love of money; good men for good society; merit for intrigue; genius for wit; truth for brilliance; the charm of happiness for the boredom of sensual pleasure; human greatness for the pettiness of the great; a magnanimous, powerful, happy people for an easy, frivolous, and miserable people: that is, all the virtues and all the miracles of the republic for all the vices and all the absurdities of the monarchy.

What is the nature of the government that can effect these prodigies? Only that government which is democratic or republican: these two words are synonyms, despite the abuses of common diction; for aristocracy is no more republican than is monarchy. Democracy is not a state in which the whole people, continually assembled, itself rules on all public business, still less is it one in which a hundred thousand factions of the people decide, by unrelated, hasty, and contradictory measures, on the fate of the entire society; such a government has never existed, and it could exist only to lead the people back to despotism.

Democracy is a state in which the sovereign people, guided by laws which are its [i.e., their] own work, itself does all it can do well, and through delegates all it cannot do itself.

It is, then, in the principles of democratic government that you must look for the rules of your political conduct.

But to found and consolidate democracy, to achieve the peaceable reign of the constitutional laws, we must end the war of liberty against tyranny and pass safely across the storms of the revolution: such is the aim of the revolutionary system that you have enacted. Your conduct, then, ought also to be regulated by the stormy circumstances in which the republic is placed; and the plan of your administration must result from the spirit of the revolutionary government combined with the general principles of democracy.

Now, what is the fundamental principle of the democratic or popular government—that is, the essential spring which makes it move? It is virtue; I am speaking of the public virtue which effected so many prodigies in Greece and Rome and which ought to produce much more surprising ones in republican France; of that virtue which is nothing other than the love of country and of its laws.

But as the essence of the republic or of democracy is equality, it follows that the love of country necessarily includes the love of equality.

It is also true that this sublime sentiment assumes a preference for the public interest over every particular interest; hence the love of country presupposes or produces all the virtues: for what are they other than that spiritual strength which renders one capable of those sacrifices? And how could the slave of avarice or ambition, for example, sacrifice his idol to his country?

Not only is virtue the soul of democracy; it can exist only in that government...

Only in democracy is the state really the *patrie* of all the individuals who compose it and can it count as many interested defenders of its cause as it has citizens. That is the source of the superiority of free peoples over all others. If Athens and Sparta triumphed over the tyrants of Asia, and the Swiss over the tyrants of Spain and Austria, we need not look for any other cause.

But the French are the first people of the world who have established real democracy, by calling all men to equality and to the full rights of the citizen, and there, in my opinion, is the real reason why all the tyrants in league against the Republic will be vanquished.

There are great consequences to be drawn immediately from the principles that we have just set forth.

Since the soul of the Republic is virtue, equality, and since your aim is to found, to consolidate the Republic, it follows that the first rule of your political conduct must be to relate all your operations to the maintenance of equality and the development of virtue; for the first care of the legislator ought to be to fortify the principle of the government. Thus all that tends to stir the love of country, to purify morals and customs, to elevate souls, to direct the passions of the human heart toward the public interest, ought to be adopted or established by you. All that tends to concentrate them in the abjection of the personal self, to reawaken the infatuation for petty things and disdain for great things, ought to be rejected or suppressed. In the system of the French revolution, what is immoral is impolitic, what is corruptive is counter-revolutionary. Weakness, vice, prejudice are the road to royalty. Drawn along too often, perhaps by the weight of our old usages, as well as by the imperceptible tendency of human weakness, toward false ideas and pusillanimous feelings, we have to guard against excessive energy much less than against excessive weakness. Perhaps the greatest peril we have to avoid is not being fervent from zeal, but rather becoming tired of the good and intimidated by our own courage. So, turn ever tighter the spring of republican government, instead of letting it run down. I have no need to say here that I do not want to justify any excess. The most sacred principles are abused; it is for the government's wisdom to consider circumstances, to seize the right moment, to choose the method; to prepare great things is an essential part of doing them, as wisdom itself is part of virtue.

We do not claim to cast the French republic in the Spartan mold; we want neither the austerity nor the corruption of a cloister. What we have just presented to you, in all its purity, is the moral and political principle of popular government. You have a compass by which you can test all laws, all proposals, suggested to you. By ceaselessly comparing them with that principle, you can henceforward avoid the usual peril of great assemblies, the danger of being surprised and of hasty, incoherent, and contradictory measures. You can give all your operations the cohesion, unity, wisdom, and dignity that ought to distinguish the representatives of the first people of the world.

It is not the obvious consequences of the principle of democracy that need to be presented in detail; it is rather the simple and fertile principle itself that deserves to be expounded.

Republican virtue can be considered in relation to the people and in relation to the government; it is necessary in both. When only the government lacks virtue, there remains a resource in the people's virtue; but when the people itself is corrupted, liberty is already lost.

Fortunately virtue is natural to the people, notwithstanding aristocratic prejudices. A nation is truly corrupted when, having by degrees lost its character and its liberty, it passes from democracy to aristocracy or to monarchy, that is the decrepitude and death of the body politic....

But when, by prodigious efforts of courage and reason, a people breaks the chains of despotism to make them into trophies of liberty; when by the force of its moral temperament it comes, as it were, out of the arms of death, to recapture all the vigor of youth; when by turns it is sensitive and proud, intrepid and docile, and can be stopped neither by impregnable ramparts nor by the innumerable armies of the tyrants against it, but stops of itself upon confronting the law's image; then if it does not climb rapidly to the summit of its destinies, this can only be the fault of those who govern it.

Besides, in a sense, one can say that to love justice and equality, the people does not need great virtue; it has only to love itself.

But the magistrate is obliged to sacrifice his interest to the people's interest, and his pride, derived from power, to equality. The law must speak imperiously above all to him who is its voice. The government must weigh heavily on all its parts, to hold them in harmony. If there exists a representative body, a primary authority constituted by the people, it must exercise ceaseless surveillance and control over all the public functionaries. But what will control it, if not its own virtue? The higher the source of public order is placed, the purer it ought to be; the representative body, then, must begin in its own midst by subduing all private passions to the general passion for the public zeal. Fortunate are the representatives, when their glory and their interest itself, as much as their duties, attach them to the cause of liberty!

From all this let us deduce a great truth: the characteristic of popular government is confidence in the people and severity towards itself.

The whole development of our theory would end here if you had only to pilot the vessel of the Republic through calm waters; but the tempest roars, and the revolution imposes on you another task.

This great purity of the French revolution's basis, the very sublimity of its objective, is precisely what causes both our strength and our weakness. Our strength, because it gives to us truth's ascendancy over imposture, and the rights of the public interest over private interests; our weakness, because it rallies all vicious men against us, all those who in their hearts contemplated despoiling the people and all those who intend to let it be despoiled with impunity, both those who have rejected freedom as a personal calamity and those who have embraced the revolution as a career and the Republic as prey. Hence the defection of so many ambitious or greedy men who since the point of departure have abandoned us along the way because they did not begin the journey with the same destination in view. The two opposing spirits that have been represented in a struggle to rule nature might be said to be fighting in this great period of human history to fix irrevocably the world's destinies, and France is the scene of this fearful combat. Without, all the tyrants encircle you; within, all tyranny's friends conspire; they will conspire until hope is wrested from crime. We must smother the internal and external enemies of the Republic or perish with it; now in this situation, the first maxim of your policy ought to be to lead the people by reason and the people's enemies by terror.

If the spring of popular government in time of peace is virtue, the springs of popular government in revolution are at once *virtue and terror*: virtue, without which terror is fatal; terror, without which virtue is powerless. Terror is nothing other than justice, prompt, severe, inflexible; it is therefore an emanation of virtue; it is not so much a special principle as it is a consequence of the general principle of democracy applied to our country's most urgent needs.

It has been said that terror is the principle of despotic government. Does your government therefore resemble despotism? Yes, as the sword that gleams in the hands of the heroes of liberty resembles that with which the henchmen of tyranny are armed. Let the despot govern by terror his brutalized subjects; he is right, as a despot. Subdue by terror the enemies of liberty, and you will be right, as founders of the Republic. The government of the revolution is liberty's despotism against tyranny. Is force made only to protect crime? And is the thunderbolt not destined to strike the heads of the proud?

Nature imposes on every physical and moral being the law of striving for its own preservation: to reign, crime slaughters innocence; and in crime's hands, innocence resists with all its might....

And yet one or the other must succumb. Indulgence for the royalists, cry certain men, mercy for the villains! No! Mercy for the innocent, mercy for the weak, mercy for the weak, mercy for humanity.

Society owes protection only to peaceable citizens; the only citizens in the Republic are the republicans. For it, the royalists, the conspirators are null strangers or, rather, enemies. This terrible war waged by liberty against tyranny—is it not indivisible? Are the enemies within not the allies of the enemies without? The assassins who tear our country apart, the intriguers who buy the consciences that hold the people's mandate; the traitors who sell them; the mercenary pamphleteers hired to dishonor the people's cause, to kill public virtue, to stir up the fire of civil discord, and to prepare political counterrevolution—are all those men less guilty or less dangerous than the tyrants whom they serve? All who interpose their treasonous gentleness between those villains and the avenging sword of national justice resemble those who would throw themselves between the tyrants' henchmen and our soldiers' bayonets; all the impulses of their false sensitivity appear to me only sighs of longing for England and Austria....

With what good humor are we still duped by words! How aristocracy and moderatism still govern us through the murderous maxims they gave us!

Aristocracy defends itself better by intrigue than patriotism does by service. We try to control revolutions with the quibbles of the courtroom; we treat conspiracies against the Republic like lawsuits between individuals. Tyranny kills, and liberty argues; and the code made by the conspirators themselves is the law by which we judge them.

Though it involves our country's safety, general report cannot be substituted for the evidence of testimony, nor obviousness itself for literal proof.

Justice delayed means immunity from punishment; possible impunity encourages all the guilty; and yet there are complaints against the severity of justice; there are complaints against the imprisonment of enemies of the Republic. Examples are sought in the histories of tyrants, because those who complain do not want to choose them in the histories of peoples, nor derive them from the natural tendency of liberty threatened....

It is clemency to mankind to punish its oppressors; it is barbarism to pardon them. Tyrants' rigor has no principle but rigor; the republican government's rigor begins in charity....

What frivolity it would be to regard a few victories won by patriotism as the end of all our dangers. Glance at our real situation. You will be aware that you need vigilance and energy more than ever. Sullen ill-will everywhere acts contrary to the government's operations. The fatal influence of the foreign, while it is more effectively hidden, is thereby neither less active nor less deadly. Crime, intimidated, has done nothing but cover its operations more adroitly.

The internal enemies of the French people are divided into two factions like two army corps. They march under banners of different colors and by separate routes; but they are marching to the same destination: their purpose is the disorganization of popular government, the ruin of the Convention—that is, the triumph of tyranny. One of these two factions urges us to commit excesses; the other to be weak. One wants to change liberty into drunken frenzy, the other into prostitution.

One faction has been called the moderates, the other has been designated—more cleverly perhaps than precisely—as the ultra-revolutionaries. This denomination can in no case be applied to the men of good faith who may be carried away by zeal and ignorance to actions beyond the sound policy of the revolution and it does not characterize accurately the perfidious men whom tyranny hires to practice false and deadly applications that compromise the sacred principles of our revolution.

The false revolutionary is deficient more often than excessive in (his response to) the revolution. He is moderate or insanely patriotic, according to the circumstances. What he will think tomorrow is decided for him today by committees of Prussians, English, Austrians, even Muscovites. He opposes energetic measures and exaggerates them when he has been unable to block them. He is severe toward innocence but indulgent toward crime, accusing even the guilty who are not rich enough to purchase his silence nor important enough to merit his zeal, but carefully refraining from ever compromising himself to the point of defending virtue that has been slandered; now and then discovering plots that have already been discovered, ripping the masks off traitors who are already unmasked and even decapitated but extolling traitors who are living and still influential; always eager to embrace the opinion of the moment and as alert never to enlighten it, and above all never to clash with it; always ready to adopt bold measures provided they have many drawbacks; falsely attacking the measures that have only advantages, or adding all the amendments that can render them harmful; speaking the truth sparingly but as much as he must in order to acquire the right to lie with impunity; giving forth driblets of good and torrents of evil; full of fire for great resolutions which signify nothing; worse than indifferent to those which can honor the people's cause and save our country; giving much attention to the forms of patriotism; very much attached, like the devout whose enemy he declares himself to be, to formal observances, he would prefer to wear out a hundred red caps than to accomplish one good deed....

Do you want to put (such men) to the test? Ask them, not for oaths and declamations, but for real services.

Is action needed? They orate. Is deliberation required? They want to begin with action. Are the times peaceful? They will oppose every useful change. Are the times stormy? They will speak of reforming everything, in order to throw everything into confusion. Do you want to keep sedition in check? They remind you of Caesar's clemency. Do you want to deliver patriots from persecution? They propose to you as a model the firmness of Brutus. They discover that so-and-so was a noble when he is serving the Republic; they no longer remember this as soon as he betrays it. Is peace advantageous? They display the rewards of victory. Is war necessary? They praise the delights of peace. Must our territory be defended? They want to go and punish the tyrants beyond the mountains and seas. Must our forts be recaptured? They want to take the Churches by assault and scale heaven itself. They forget the Austrians in order to make war on the devout. Do we need the support of faithful allies? They will declaim against all the governments in the world and propose that you put on trial the great himself. Do the people go to the Capitol to give thanks to the gods for their victories? They intone lugubrious chants over our previous reverses. Is it a matter of winning new victories? In our midst they sow hatreds, divisions, persecutions, and discouragement. Must we make the sovereignty of the people a reality and concentrate its strength by a strong, respected government? They discover that the principles of government injure popular sovereignty. Must we call for the rights of the people oppressed by the government? They talk only of respect for the laws and of obedience owed to the constituted authorities.

They have found an admirable expedient for promoting the efforts of the republican government: it is to disorganize it, to degrade it completely, to make war on the patriots who have contributed to our successes....

Thus, for example, after having disseminated everywhere the germ of civil war by a violent attack on religious prejudices, they will seek to fortify fanaticism and aristocracy by the very measures, in favor of freedom of religious observances, that sound policy has prescribed to you. If you had left free play to the conspiracy, it would have produced, sooner or later, a terrible and universal reaction but if you stop it, they will still seek to turn this to their account by urging that you protect the priests and the moderates. You must not even be surprised if the authors of this strategy are the very priests who most boldly confess their charlatanism.

If the patriots, carried away by a pure but thoughtless zeal, have somewhere been made the dupes of their intrigues, they will throw all the blame upon the patriots; because the principal point of their Machiavellian doctrine is to ruin the Republic by ruining the republicans, as one conquers a country by overthrowing the army which defends it. One can thereby appreciate one of their favorite principles, which is: men must count as nothing—a maxim of royal origin, which means that all the friends of liberty must be abandoned to them.

It is to be noticed that the men who seek only the public good are to be the victims of those who seek to advance themselves, and this comes from two causes: first, that the intriguers attack using the vices of the old regime, second, that the patriots defend themselves only with the virtues of the new. Such an internal situation ought to appear worthy of all your attention, above all if you reflect that at the same time you have the tyrants of Europe to combat, 1,200,000 men under arms to maintain; and that the government is constantly obliged to repair, with energy and vigilance, all the evils which the innumerable multitude of our enemies has prepared for us during the course of five years.

What is the remedy for all these evils? We know no other than the extension of that mainspring of the Republic: virtue.

Democracy perishes by two kinds of excess: the aristocracy of those who govern or the people's scorn for the authorities whom the people itself has established, scorn which makes each clique, each individual take over the public power and lead the people, through excessive disorders, to its destruction or to the power of one man.

The double effort of the moderates and the false revolutionaries is to drive us back and forth perpetually between these two perils.

But the people's representatives can avoid them both, because government is always able to be just and wise; and when it has that character, it is sure of the confidence of the people....

It is a truth which ought to be regarded as commonplace in politics that a great body invested with the confidence of a great people can be lost only through its own failings. Your enemies know this; therefore you can be sure that they are applying themselves above all to reawaken in your midst all the passions which can further their sinister designs.

What can they do against the national representation if they do not succeed in beguiling it into politic acts which can supply pretexts for their criminal declamations? They are therefore necessarily obliged to obtain two kinds of agents, those who will seek to degrade it by their speeches and those, in its very midst, who will do their utmost to deceive it in order to compromise its glory and the interests of the Republic....

Far from us is the idea that there still exists in our midst a single man weakling enough to intend to serve the tyrants' cause! But farther from us still is the crime, for which we would not be pardoned, of deceiving the National Convention and betraying the French people by a culpable silence. For it is the good fortune of a free people that truth, which is the scourge of despots, is always its strength and salvation. Now it is true that there still exists a danger for our liberty, perhaps the only serious danger which remains for it to confront. That danger is a plan which has existed for rallying all the enemies of the Republic by reviving party spirit; for persecuting the patriots, defeating and disheartening the faithful agents of the republican government, rendering inadequate the most essential parts of public service. They have intended to deceive the Convention about men about conditions; they have sought to put it on the wrong track about the causes of abuses, which they have exaggerated so as to make them irremediable; they have studiously filled it with false terrors, in order to lead it astray or paralyze it; they seek to divide it above all to create division between the representatives sent out to the departments and the Committee of Public Safety. They have sought to influence those representatives to contradict the measures of the central authority, in order to make them the instruments of a cabal. The foreigners turn to their profit all private passions, even abused patriotism.

They first adopted the plan of going straight to their goal, by slandering the Committee of Public Safety; they flattered themselves aloud that it would succumb under the weight of its laborious duties. Victory and the good fortune of the French people defended it. Since that time they have adopted the plan of praising it while paralyzing it and destroying the results of its work. All those vague declamations against necessary agents of the Committee; all the proposals for disorganization, disguised under the name of reforms, already rejected by the Convention and reproduced today with a strange artificiality; that eagerness to extol the intriguers whom the committee of Public Safety was obliged to remove; that terror inspired in good citizens; that indulgence with which conspirators are favored; a man whom you have driven from your midst, is directed against the National Convention and tends to give effect to the resolutions of all the enemies of France.

It is since the time when this system was put forward in pamphlets and given effect in public acts that aristocracy and royalism have again begun to raise their insolent heads, that patriotism has again been persecuted in a part of the Republic, that the national authority has encountered a resistance which the intriguers had begun to abandon. If these indirect attacks had served only to divide the attention and energy of those who have to carry the immense burden that you have assigned them and distract them too often from the great measures for the public salvation in order to occupy themselves with thwarting dangerous intrigues; even so, they could be considered as a diversion useful to our enemies.

But let us be reassured, it is here that the truth has its sanctuary; it is here that the founders of the Republic reside, the avengers of humanity, and the destroyers of tyrants.

Here, to destroy an abuse it suffices to point it out. It suffices for us to appeal, in the name of our country, from counsels of self-love or from the weaknesses of individuals, to the virtue and the glory of the National Convention.

We call for a solemn debate upon all the subjects of its anxiety and upon everything that can influence the progress of the revolution. We adjure it not to permit any hidden particular interest to use ascendancy here over the general will of the assembly and indestructible power of reason.

We will limit ourselves today to proposing that by your formal approval you sanction the moral and political truths upon which your internal administration and the stability of the Republic ought to be founded, as you have already sanctioned the principles of your conduct toward foreign peoples. Thereby you will rally all good citizens, you will take hope away from the conspirators, you will assure your progress and confound the kings' intrigues and slanders, you will honor your cause and your character in the eyes of all people.

Give the French people this new gage of your zeal to protect patriotism, of your inflexible justice for the guilty, and of your devotion to the people's cause. Order that the moral and political principles which we have just expounded will be proclaimed, in your name, within and without the Republic.

Glossary

Augustus, Tiberius, or Vespasian: Roman emperors

clemency: an official act of leniency

lugubrious: mournful; brooding

Machiavelli: Italian diplomat and author; his *The Prince* lays out the tough positions that leaders must assume to maintain their authority

moderatism: the favoring of deliberate, incremental change over hasty action

patrie: homeland or "fatherland"

pusillanimous: lacking courage or resolve; timid

Tacitus: Roman historian and senator

Document Themes and Analysis

Robespierre starts his presentation by noting that after a period of factional infighting, the National Convention had decided on a new "domestic" policy—that is, a policy to address the internal needs of France, as opposed to foreign policy. In doing so, he says, the Convention members allowed themselves to be guided by a "love of the good," along with a keen awareness of the country's needs. For Robespierre, this resolute government had attempted something new in history, and he wanted to set out the "aim of the revolution" for all to hear in order to allow one to properly judge the actions taken so far, and perhaps those to come. The basic aim, says Robespierre, is the "peaceable enjoyment of liberty and equity" and the "reign" of "eternal justice" through laws that would create and sustain "happy" citizens. Such a goal can be realized only through the removal of the old guard (the monarchy and the *ancien régime* generally), together with the creation of a virtuous republic. Society's ills can be remedied only through a "democratic or republican" government: "a state in which the sovereign people, guided by laws which are its [i.e., their] own work, itself does all it can do well, and through delegates all it [or they] cannot do itself." (The French language objectification of "people" as "it" is at play here.) This means that the new French revolutionary government has acted in the interests of all the people (not just the king, nobility, and the clergy), and that government representatives have upheld their duty to act in the best interests of the people. According to Robespierre, such public interests include the need to consolidate the revolution's democratic principles, even as the ongoing "storms" of the revolutionary process continue to unfold.

To consolidate the principles of democracy for the French people, government has to use the ancient Greek notion of the love of country and law while promoting a love of equality and virtue in government. Government must also avoid the "weakness, vice, prejudice" of royalty by purifying "morals and customs" through the "maintenance of equality and the development of virtue." Robespierre warns against the "excessive energy" of factions within the revolution and the potential for such energy to turn into a "weakness" that might return France to the unjust ways of its past. France was then fighting both internal and external enemies. The internal enemies—moderates and ultra-revolutionaries—frequently deceived the people about the intentions of the National Convention, and wished either to destroy government (and the country) or to return it to monarchy. The external enemies were states such as England, Prussia, and Austria, which saw an opportunity to defeat a weakened France, avenge the execution of the king, and restore the status quo. Robespierre argues that these enemies wanted only to tyrannize France and destroy its democratic government, in the interest of asserting their own authority on the Continent.

In Robespierre's view, the way to defeat the will of France's domestic enemies is to not simply use the courts but to exact swift and severe justice by direct means. To save France from its internal foes and build confidence in the government, government representatives must utilize the "moral and political" principles of republican government. Some versions of this speech translate the phrase as "political morality," which suggests a certain necessity to act. While "the people" need only to love themselves ("itself") as citizens, government representatives have to sacrifice their interests for the people's interests in order to ensure public order, virtue, and liberty, thereby calming the "tempest" of the revolution and protecting France from its enemies at the same time. To control the passion-filled "tempest" requires both "virtue and terror," both moral excellence and targeted violence. Robespierre argues that terror is "nothing other than justice, prompt, severe, inflexible; it is therefore an emanation of virtue." Terror, for Robespierre, is a "general principle of democracy," used by a country when urgently required as a form of "political morality" to secure the goals of a revolution and establish a democratic form of government—in this instance, for the people of France. Ironically, this very same view was used to condemn Robespierre as an enemy of the state and subject him to the guillotine.

—*Michael Shally-Jensen, PhD*

Bibliography and Additional Reading

Israel, Jonathan. *Revolutionary Ideas: An Intellectual History of the French Revolution, from the Rights of Man to Robespierre.* Princeton, NJ: Princeton University Press, 2014.

McPhee, Peter. *Robespierre: A Revolutionary Life.* New Haven, CT: Yale University Press, 2012.

Popkin, Jeremy D. *A New World Begins: The History of the French Revolution.* New York: Basic Books, 2019.

Scurr, Ruth. *Robespierre: Fatal Purity.* New York: Metropolitan Books, 2006.

The Wider Americas in the Nineteenth Century

The Americas, with their diverse Indigenous populations, began to be colonized by Europeans in the fifteenth and sixteenth centuries. The conquistadores brought Spanish rule to much of the region, though Dutch and French settlements occurred in the Caribbean and elsewhere, and the Portuguese colonized Brazil. The Roman Catholic church became a dominant presence throughout the hemisphere, with its numerous missions and efforts to convert the natives. Colonists enslaved the Indigenous Indian population, whose numbers were decimated by disease and maltreatment. They also imported enslaved people from Africa to work the fields and groves and sustain the colonists in their lavish lifestyles.

In the early nineteenth century a series of movements for independence swept Latin America and French Haiti. These were led by Toussaint L'Ouverture and Jean-Jacques Dessalines in Haiti (1804); José de San Martín in Argentina (1812), Chile (1818), and Peru (1821); and Simón Bolívar in New Grenada (Colombia, Venezuela, and Ecuador), Upper Peru (Bolivia), and Peru. There were other, lesser movements and leaders, too. Federal republics were established across the region, yet many of the new countries soon succumbed to internal political strife and collapsed into dictatorships.

In Mexico, or New Spain as it was officially known, a rebellion (1811–1815) failed to win the day, but in 1821 Spain accepted independence for Mexico under the Treaty of Córdoba—which was not fully enacted until 1836 (the same year that Texas broke free of Mexico). Although a republic, by the 1850s Mexico had experienced considerable political turmoil and was in the hands of the dictator Antonio López de Santa Anna. Under a democratic reform movement led by Benito Juárez, Santa Anna was overthrown (1855) and a liberal constitution was drafted. Nevertheless, civil war and further dictatorships followed.

Even as most of Spain's possessions in the Americas transformed themselves into independent republics, Cuba remained a colony until the end of the nineteenth century. Slavery played a central role in maintaining the colony's profitable sugar economy. A ten-year war for independence between 1868 and 1878 proved inconclusive. Finally, in 1895, a new rebellion led by José Martí spawned the Spanish-American War (1898) and Cuba became a republic. Like Mexico, however, Cuba would end up suffering recurrent dictatorships, leading to the Communist revolution of the 1950s.

Meanwhile, in Canada, Anglo-French antagonism had led to the splitting of Quebec into English-speaking Upper Canada (now Ontario) and French-speaking Lower Canada (now Quebec). Revolts in both colonies erupted in 1837–1838, and the two were once again merged into Canada Province, a union that lasted until the creation, in 1867, of the self-governing Dominion of Canada.

Haitian Declaration of Independence

Date: January 1, 1804
Authors: Jean-Jacques Dessalines, Commander in Chief; Louis Boisrond-Tonnerre, Secretary to the Commander in Chief
Genre: charter; address

Summary Overview

At the time of the promulgation of the Haitian declaration of independence in 1804, France had been Haiti's colonial overseer since 1659. Slavery had largely defined the colony throughout its existence. In the event, Haiti's independence was won after several years of fighting, in which the slave population of the island rebelled against the white French slave owners and some of the mixed-race slave owning population. Independence was sought, especially, in order to free the people from particularly brutal French governors, who worked to reinstate slavery after France had banned the practice. The leader of the Haitian rebels, and author of the document printed here, was Jean-Jacques Dessalines. To this day, Dessalines is a controversial character in history—renowned for his brilliance in military strategy, but also for his brutality against the white population of Haiti after independence. Regardless of his legacy, the Haitian revolution is considered the only successful slave revolution in history and it made Haiti the first independent nation of all the colonized territories in the Americas after the United States.

Defining Moment

By 1776 the British colonies in what is now the eastern United States had declared their independence. Their sovereignty was won through a war that reached its conclusion in 1783. The achievement represented the first successful rebellion of a colony against its colonial power. Subsequently, in 1789, the French lower classes revolted against the aristocracy in the French Revolution. Although the denouement of the French Revolution was far less glorious than its predecessor, it and the American Revolution did encourage other colonies and marginalized peoples to push back against their rulers and control by foreign powers. In the case of Haiti, the French had operated in the region since 1625, importing slaves and French nationals to create massive sugarcane plantations. Living under the "Code Noir" or "Black Code," slaves in Saint-Domingue (the French name for Haiti) lived brutal and short lives. Sugar was a lucrative product in the eighteenth century, and businessmen would not risk their profits by providing a decent life to slaves. Formal colonial rule, from 1659, hardly improved matters. It was under such conditions that factions of slave rebels began to form against the established order and work toward the goal of freedom.

At first, many rebels did not intend to establish outright independence, but, inspired by ideas of the Enlightenment and particularly the French revolutionary ideals of *liberté, égalité, fraternité* ("liberty, equality, fraternity"), the rebels sought release from the bonds of slavery. The earliest efforts seemed to be working, too. In 1792, French administrators sent men to Haiti to deal with the rebel forces. What happened instead was that an alliance was made between various factions of Haitians, including white slave owners, members of the mixed-race social class, and some of the rebels. Consequently, slavery was abolished. Moreover, French Revolutionary leaders, the Jacobins, later extended the abolition to all French territories.

Yet, not all Haitians were satisfied with this development, as it relied on association with plantation owners and others of the governing class. Fighting continued for another decade in some places on the island. Indeed, there was little sense of unity among the factions until Napoleon Bonaparte assumed the French throne (1799). Putting his support behind the institution of slavery, Napoleon once again sent men

Deklarasyon Endepandans Ayiti. Haitian Declaration of Independence poster. Document MFQ 1/184. National Archives, U.K.

to Haiti. At this point, the rebels came together and faced the French head on. After the leader of the rebellion, Toussaint Louverture, was captured by French soldiers and deported to France for trial, Jean-Jacques Dessalines, future Governor-for-life and Emperor of Haiti, led the fight. The final battle of the rebellion took place at the Battle of Vertières on November 18, 1803.

The declaration of independence was delivered (as a speech) twice on January 1, 1804, first in Haitian Creole and then in French.

This document was created by the Commander in Chief, or senior general, of the Haitian people, Jean-Jacques Dessalines. Dessalines was, however, illiterate and spoke only Haitian Creole. Therefore, the actual writing and reading out of the declaration was put into the hands of Dessalines' secretary, Louis Boisrond-Tonnerre, who could speak French. The first proclamation to the Haitian people was given by Dessalines in Haitian Creole, while this version was presented in French.

Author Biography

Dessalines was born on September 20, 1758, as a slave on a plantation in Cormier. He had two brothers, but the identity of his parents is unknown. Dessalines, originally named Jean-Jacques Duclos after his first owner, eventually became the foreman of the plantation and then was sold to a free black man. This man was part of the *gens de couleur*, or the mixed-race inhabitants of Saint-Domingue. At this point, Dessalines' name was changed. In 1791, Dessalines joined in an ongoing slave rebellion. He fought against slave owners and French colonial officials and residents who controlled the island. However, when France abolished slavery (1793), he changed sides and worked for the French—alongside the famous freed slave and military commander Toussaint Louverture. Louverture became governor of Saint-Domingue and worked toward greater independence from French rule. Matters became more complicated, however, when the French under Napoleon Bonaparte decided to reinstate slavery in their colonies. Dessalines once again switched sides to fight against slavery, and famously defeated the French in the battle of Crête-à-Pierrot in 1802, defending a fort with 1,300 men against 18,000 Frenchmen.

Haitian rebels would not become unified until a brutal French governor forced them to put aside their differences and work together. After several decisive victories, Dessalines led his forces to victory and the French colonial army surrendered on December 4, 1803. By New Year's Day of 1804, Dessalines had declared himself Emperor of Haiti. Following the independence of Haiti, Dessalines began what is known as the 1804 Haiti massacre, during which he killed several thousand French men and women. Dessalines was assassinated on October 17, 1806, by members of his own cabinet after they had become disaffected with his rule.

Historical Document

Haitian Declaration of Independence

The Commander in Chief to the People of Haiti

Citizens:

It is not enough to have expelled the barbarians who have bloodied our land for two centuries; it is not enough to have restrained those ever-evolving factions that one after another mocked the specter of liberty that France dangled before you. We must, with one last act of national authority, forever assure the empire of liberty in the country of our birth; we must take any hope of re-enslaving us away from the inhuman government that for so long kept us in the most humiliating torpor. In the end we must live independent or die.

Independence or death…let these sacred words unite us and be the signal of battle and of our reunion.

Citizens, my countrymen, on this solemn day I have brought together those courageous soldiers who, as liberty lay dying, spilled their blood to save it; these generals who have guided your efforts against tyranny have not yet done enough for your happiness; the French name still haunts our land.

Everything revives the memories of the cruelties of this barbarous people: our laws, our habits, our towns, everything still carries the stamp of the French. Indeed! There are still French in our island, and you believe yourself free and independent of that Republic which, it is true, has fought all the nations, but which has never defeated those who wanted to be free.

What! Victims of our [own] credulity and indulgence for 14 years; defeated not by French armies, but by the pathetic eloquence of their agents' proclamations; when will we tire of breathing the air that they breathe? What do we have in common with this nation of executioners? The difference between its cruelty and our patient moderation, its color and ours the great seas that separate us, our avenging climate, all tell us plainly that they are not our brothers, that they never will be, and that if they find refuge among us, they will plot again to trouble and divide us.

Native citizens, men, women, girls, and children, let your gaze extend on all parts of this island: look there for your spouses, your husbands, your brothers, your sisters. Indeed! Look there for your children, your suckling infants, what have they become?… I shudder to say it … the prey of these vultures.

Instead of these dear victims, your alarmed gaze will see only their assassins, these tigers still dripping with their blood, whose terrible presence indicts your lack of feeling and your guilty slowness in avenging them. What are you waiting for before appeasing their spirits? Remember that you had wanted your remains to rest next to those of your fathers, after you defeated tyranny; will you descend into their tombs without having avenged them? No! Their bones would reject yours.

And you, precious men, intrepid generals, who, without concern for your own pain, have revived liberty by shedding all your blood, know that you have done nothing if you do not give the nations a terrible, but just example of the vengeance that must be wrought by a people proud to have recovered its liberty and jealous to maintain it let us frighten all those who would dare try to take it from us again; let us begin with the French. Let them tremble when they approach our coast, if not from the memory of those cruelties they perpetrated here, then from the terrible resolution that we will have made to put to death anyone born French whose profane foot soils the land of liberty.

We have dared to be free, let us be thus by ourselves and for ourselves. Let us imitate the grown child: his own weight breaks the boundary that has become an obstacle to him. What people fought for us? What people wanted to gather the fruits of our labor? And what dishonorable absurdity to conquer in order to be enslaved. Enslaved?... Let us leave this description for the French; they have conquered but are no longer free. Let us walk down another path; let us imitate those people who, extending their concern into the future, and dreading to leave an example of cowardice for posterity, preferred to be exterminated rather than lose their place as one of the world's free peoples.

Let us ensure, however, that a missionary spirit does not destroy our work; let us allow our neighbors to breathe in peace; may they live quietly under the laws that they have made for themselves, and let us not, as revolutionary firebrands, declare ourselves the lawgivers of the Caribbean, nor let our glory consist in troubling the peace of the neighboring islands. Unlike that which we inhabit, theirs has not been drenched in the innocent blood of its inhabitants; they have no vengeance to claim from the authority that protects them. Fortunate to have never known the ideals that have destroyed us, they can only have good wishes for our prosperity.

Peace to our neighbors; but let this be our cry: "Anathema to the French name! Eternal hatred of France!"; Natives of Haiti! My happy fate was to be one day the sentinel who would watch over the idol to which you sacrifice; I have watched, sometimes fighting alone, and if I have been so fortunate as to return to your hands the sacred trust you confided to me, know that it is now your task to preserve it. In fighting for your liberty, I was working for my own happiness. Before consolidating it with laws that will guarantee your free individuality, your leaders, who I have assembled here, and I, owe you the final proof of our devotion. Generals and you, leaders, collected here close to me for the good of our land, the day has come, the day which must make our glory, our independence, eternal.

If there could exist among us a lukewarm heart, let him distance himself and tremble to take the oath which must unite us. Let us vow to ourselves, to posterity, to the entire universe, to forever renounce France, and to die rather than live under its domination; to fight until our last breath for the independence of our country. And you, a people so long without good fortune, witness to the oath we take, remember that I counted on your constancy and courage when I threw myself into the career of liberty to fight the despotism and tyranny you had struggled against for 14 years.

Remember that I sacrificed everything to rally to your defense; family, children, fortune, and now I am rich only with your liberty; my name has become a horror to all those who want slavery. Despots and tyrants curse the day that I was born. If ever you refused or grumbled while receiving those laws that the spirit guarding your fate dictates to me for your own good, you would deserve the fate of an ungrateful people. But I reject that awful idea; you will sustain the liberty that you cherish and support the leader who commands you. Therefore, vow before me to live free and independent, and to prefer death to anything that will try to place you back in chains. Swear, finally, to pursue forever the traitors and enemies of your independence.

* * * * *

Done at the headquarters of Gonaives, the first day of January 1804, the first year of independence.

The Deed of independence

Native Army

Today, January 1st 1804, the general in chief of the native army, accompanied by the generals of the army, assembled in order to take measures that will insure the good of the country;

After having told the assembled generals his true intentions, to assure forever a stable government for the natives of Haiti, the object of his greatest concern, which he has accomplished in a speech which declares to foreign powers the decision to make the country independent, and to enjoy a liberty consecrated by the blood of the people of this island; and after having gathered their responses has asked that each of the assembled generals take a vow to forever renounce France, to die rather than live under its domination, and to fight for independence until their last breath. The generals, deeply moved by these sacred principles, after voting their unanimous attachment to the declared project of independence, have all sworn to posterity, to the universe, to forever renounce France, and to die rather than to live under its domination.

* * * * *

Translation by Laurent Dubois and John Garrigus

Glossary

anathema: a person or thing accursed or consigned to damnation or destruction

consecrated: to make something an object of honor or veneration; to devote or dedicate to some purpose

credulity: willingness to believe or trust too readily, especially without adequate evidence

firebrand: a person who kindles strife or encourages unrest; an agitator; troublemaker

posterity: following or future generations collectively

sentinel: a person or thing that watches or stands as if watching; someone standing guard

torpor: sluggish inactivity, inertia, apathy

Document Analysis

This document is the first of several parts of the Haitian Declaration of Independence, often referred to as the "proclamation" or introduction to the rest of the text. Within it, Dessalines, empowered by the rest of the generals who signed the document, calls for the people of Haiti to remember their lives of enslavement and never to allow anyone to enslave them again. He also denigrates the French and calls for further action against them; but at the same time, he ensures the people that he has no intention of taking their revolution beyond the borders of Haiti. The value of this document, in many ways, comes from the implicit way that Dessalines outlines the scope of the revolution and limits Haitian independence.

The opening lines of the text show that the rebels were not, at first, fighting for complete independence from France. They wanted only to end slavery. France actually created the push for independence when it reintroduced the prospect of reinstating slavery after having freed the people. Thus, Dessalines uses harsh language in his description of the French. On more than one occasion he calls them "barbarians," including in the opening line. This is a reversal, of course, of how the French would see things: for them, they were the "civilized" ones and the Haitians were the barbarians. Dessalines has turned that ideology on its head, using the reversal to glorify his own victory.

A second key element of the speech is its implicit description of what is left to be done and what will not be done, now that the Haitians are free. First off, the French must be dealt with. Dessalines cannot abide the idea that former slave owners might share the land with the rest of the people. Yet, he seems to caution restraint. As he explicitly states: "Let us ensure, however, that a missionary spirit does not destroy our work; let us allow our neighbors to breathe in peace..." He would like the people and the land to be safe, albeit through an arrangement of his own and essentially without the French; yet he will not invade any borders or force such changes on opponents. Because Haiti shares the island of Hispaniola with the Dominican Republic, which was then under Spanish control, this is an especially salient point.

Dessalines does call attention to the difference in status between Haiti and the rest of the slave colonies. When he states, "We have dared to be free," he explicitly draws attention to Haiti as the only successful slave rebellion. Haiti now stands alone, apart from its colonial origins and apart from other colonies. It was in statements such as this that Dessalines sought to unite the remnants of a fractured rebellion and to justify his place at the head of Haitian nationalism.

Essential Themes

Important to understanding and appreciating the declaration is in the legacy of Jean-Jacques Dessalines and the subsequent fate of the Haitian nation. As noted, Dessalines was a controversial figure then and remains one now. Never bothering to set up a republic or a democracy, he took dictatorial control of the new government. He even crowned himself Emperor, with the support of the seventeen generals who signed the declaration of independence alongside him. Even in the wording of this document, one can see Dessalines' violent intentions with respect to the French and the white Creoles remaining in Haiti. He was not satisfied simply to have won the war; he goes on to state that he does not want to be "breathing the air that they breathe." He draws a clear and brutal distinction between "us" and "them." He also says, "the terrible resolution that we will have made to put to death anyone born French whose profane foot soils the land of liberty...Therefore vow before me to live free and independent, and to prefer death to anything that will try to place you back in chains. Swear, finally, to pursue forever the traitors and enemies of your independence." In many ways, Dessalines was trying hard to ensure that his people remained free, but he suggests going about it in a violent way. The French reviled him as a murder, and his own people turned against him and viewed his rule with hatred after his death. It was not until the twentieth century that his actions and their role in shaping Haitian history came to be reexamined. Some people began to reframe his story in a more heroic light.

Dessalines was a man of his time. He experienced many of the worst aspects of being a person owned by another. Many of his ideas and his pleas were persuasive to those who followed him. This is evident at the end of the document, in its description of the signing ceremony: "The generals, deeply moved by these sacred principles," voted unanimously to sign the declaration. In so doing, they, along with Dessalines, set Haiti on a new course, one that would find echoes in later decades when selected Latin American colonies would gain their independence.

Unfortunately, after Dessalines' assassination, Haiti fell into civil war as his generals fought for control. Moreover, the idea that a slave population could overthrow their owners successfully may have been invigorating to slaves, but it was terrifying to other slave-owning nations, such as the United States and several European states. Haiti struggled to be recognized as independent by other nations, particularly those with their own colonies. Ironically, it was not until Haiti was charged 150 million francs for reparations to France (for "damages" wrought during the revolution) that it was recognized as an independent nation. The sum, nevertheless, was an outrageous one that could hardly be paid. Still, reparations payments were made, causing a hardship in Haiti that seemed to become the nation's common lot as the decades and centuries moved ahead.

—Anna Accettola, MA

Bibliography and Additional Reading

Geggus, David Patrick, ed. *The Impact of the Haitian Revolution in the Atlantic World*. London: Reaktion Books, 2001.

Girard, Philippe R. "Jean-Jacques Dessalines and the Atlantic system: A reappraisal." *The William and Mary Quarterly* 69.3 (2012): 549-582.

Heinl, Robert Debs, Nancy Gordon Heinl, and Michael Heinl. *Written in Blood: The Story of the Haitian People, 1492-1995*. Lanham, MD: UP of America, 2005.

Popkin, Jeremy D. *You Are All Free: The Haitian Revolution and the Abolition of Slavery*. New York: Cambridge UP, 2010.

Zavitz, Erin. "Revolutionary Commemorations: Jean-Jacques Dessalines and Haitian Independence Day, 1804–1904." The Haitian Declaration of Independence 221 (2016).

■ Cartagena Manifesto

Date: 1812
Author: Simón Bolívar
Genre: statement of political philosophy

Summary Overview

Simón Bolívar was one of the chief liberators of the nations of South America from Spanish rule, and his Cartagena Manifesto was a key document in the wars of independence that took place in Mexico and South America from 1808 to 1829. Bolívar was Venezuelan, but after the collapse of his nation's First Republic in 1812, he departed to live in exile in modern-day Colombia. In the city of Cartagena de Indias (Cartagena of the Indies), he wrote a manifesto outlining what he perceived to be the causes for the First Republic's collapse. In doing so, he implicitly outlined what he believed should be the shape of a future Venezuelan republic or of any South American republic. More explicitly, his goal in the Cartagena Manifesto was to seek support for an invasion of Venezuela to oust the Spanish.

Venezuela effectively achieved its independence in 1821, at least in part as a consequence of the Cartagena Manifesto and Bolívar's leadership. Bolívar also lent aid to revolutions in other countries, helping to liberate Peru, Chile, Bolivia, and Argentina and thus earning the sobriquet "Liberator of Five Nations." Because of his role and those of numerous other revolutionaries, Spanish rule in continental Central and South America came to an end after three centuries. After the early nineteenth century's wave of revolutionary activity, only Puerto Rico and Cuba remained under Spanish control, a state of affairs that lasted until the Spanish-American War of 1898.

Discussions of South American history during this period are complicated by the nomenclature used to refer to the states. In the modern world, the various nations of South America—Argentina, Bolivia, Colombia, Ecuador, Paraguay, Peru, Uruguay, Venezuela, and others—are established independent countries. In the eighteenth and early nineteenth centuries, however, these nations were in essence provinces of larger polities ruled by Spain. Borders were shifting, and Spain's territories were often carved up and recombined into new political entities. Venezuela, for example, began as a province of Spain's Viceroyalty of Peru. Later it was part of the Viceroyalty of New Granada and then what was called a captaincy general—all referring to administrative units of Spain's

Simón Bolívar; posthumous portrait by José Toro Moreno. Image via Wikimedia Commons. [Public domain.]

New World colonies. Accordingly, in historical context, modern country names such as "Venezuela" and "Peru" serve as shorthand devices for referring to the regions that would eventually become these nations.

The manifesto was Bolívar's first significant piece of political writing, and he used it to convince republicans of the errors they had made in forming the First Republic and confronting the challenges of uniting the provinces into a stable nation able to fend off its adversaries. Bolívar wrote the manifesto to ask the governing powers in New Granada for permission to lead a New Granada army into Venezuela. Bolívar believed that the defeat of the First Republic by royalist forces was in some measure his responsibility. Through the manifesto he wanted to rehabilitate his reputation among military leaders, for he was already planning his invasion of Venezuela, which would lead to the formation of the Second Republic.

Bolívar knew that like any infant country Venezuela would need aid from foreign nations, such as the United States and Great Britain; indeed, British and Irish troops would fight in Venezuela after the collapse of the First Republic. With his manifesto, Bolívar hoped to convince international leaders that the political leadership of a republican Venezuela—specifically he himself— would have the necessary political heft to forge and maintain a new nation, one worthy of assistance from other nations that support the goal of independence.

Defining Moment

As Spanish colonies in the New World expanded in the sixteenth century, they were divided into what were called viceroyalties, each under the command of a governor-general. The first two were the viceroyalties of New Spain and Peru. New Spain encompassed what is today California and the southwestern United States, Mexico, most of Central America, and the Caribbean islands. The Viceroyalty of Peru consisted essentially of all of Spain's South American holdings (with the notable exception of Brazil, which was a Portuguese colony). Later, in the eighteenth century, two additional viceroyalties were formed. In 1717 the Viceroyalty of New Granada was created out of what would become Panama, Columbia, Ecuador, and Venezuela. In 1776 the Viceroyalty of the Rio de la Plata was formed out of what would become Argentina, Bolivia, Uruguay, and Paraguay. Thus, by the eighteenth century, a map of Spain's New World colonies would extend all the way from the southern tip of South America up through most of western South America, through Central America and the western regions of North America.

Spain's relationships with its Atlantic colonies were rarely smooth. Spanish colonists in the New World grew to resent the high taxes they paid to the Spanish Crown as well as interference in their affairs by Spain, and they began to agitate for political independence. Many Latin American colonists were influenced by ideas coming out of the European Enlightenment, which, during the eighteenth century, questioned the legitimacy of hereditary succession and the divine right of kings to rule. These democratic notions began to gather momentum after England's American colonies declared their independence in 1776 and achieved victory in the Revolutionary War in 1783. Then, in 1789, the French Revolution overthrew the monarchy in France. The spirit of revolt moved to Central America with the Haitian Revolution, which began in 1791 and led to Haitian independence from France in 1804. The time was ripe for revolutionary movements to spread to Spain's American colonies.

A key event that triggered revolutionary movements in Latin America was the 1808 invasion of Spain by Napoleon Bonaparte in what is called the Peninsular War (referring to the Iberian Peninsula, which comprises Spain and Portugal). This campaign was part of a larger series of wars called the Napoleonic Wars, waged when Napoleon, having declared himself emperor of France, fought to topple hereditary monarchies and impose unified rule over Europe. The French invasion led to the complete breakdown of Spanish administration, both in Spain and in its colonies. What followed was a long period of warfare—both guerrilla and conventional— instability, turmoil, and uncertainty in Spain. The chief outcome of Napoleon's invasion, at least from the standpoint of the Americas, was a breakdown in communication between the colonies and Spain, which now no longer had the might necessary to enforce its control across the Atlantic.

Almost immediately, the Spanish colonies began to take action. The first effort to achieve independence in Venezuela occurred in 1810, when the municipal council in Caracas, the capital of the Captaincy General of Venezuela, launched a movement to depose the governor-general and set up a governing congress. Several of Venezuela's provinces quickly joined the "Caracas Junta," though numerous others did not. On July 5, 1811, the Venezuelan congress declared the nation's independence from Spain and established the First Republic. Meanwhile, revolutionary fervor spread to other Spanish colonies. In 1799 rebels in Mexico had launched an unsuccessful revolt called the Conspiracy of the Machetes. The spirit of rebellion survived in Mexico, and in September 1810 Mexico launched its war for independence from Spain, which it would achieve through the Treaty of Cordoba, signed in 1821. Also in 1810 the United Provinces of South America was formed. This state would become the United Provinces of the Rio de la Plata, which in turn would eventually become the nation of Argentina. The United Provinces deployed armies, including the Army of the North, to liberate northern Argentina and Upper Peru (modern-day Bolivia). On November 5, 1811, a rebellion called the Primer Grito de Independencia, or "First Shout of Independence," erupted in El Salvador. The Spanish Empire in the New World was crumbling.

In Venezuela, matters did not go well for the infant First Republic. Civil war erupted between republicans and those who wanted to remain loyal to the Spanish monarchy. Two major provinces, Maracaibo and Guiana, as well as the district of Coro, refused to recognize the rebellious junta in Caracas. The republicans launched a military operation to bring Coro and Guayana to heel, but the operation failed—though republican forces did succeed in suppressing a rebellion against the republicans in Valencia. Meanwhile Spain, now under Napoleon's brother Joseph Bonaparte, imposed a blockade. A further setback for the republican government was an earthquake on March 26, 1812, which hit republican areas particularly hard and killed some fifteen thousand to twenty thousand people. Amid all this turmoil, Francisco de Miranda, the First Republic's political leader, was able to assume dictatorial powers, but he was unable to stop the advance of royalist troops under the command of Domingo de Monteverde. On July 25, 1812, royalists dealt a decisive defeat to the republicans at the Battle of San Mateo. Miranda signed a cease-fire agreement with Monteverde, effectively ending the First Republic.

One of the key leaders of the republican movement was Simón Bolívar, a young aristocrat who supported complete independence from Spain. Bolívar regarded Miranda's surrender as an act of treason. He arrested Miranda and turned him over to Monteverde, who ignored the terms of the cease-fire and arrested and executed many of the rebels. To escape Monteverde's reprisals, Bolívar fled to Cartagena de Indias, where he wrote the Cartagena Manifesto and planned an invasion of Venezuela.

Author Biography

The author of the Cartagena Manifesto was Simón Jose Antonio de la Santisima Trinidad Bolívar y Palacios Ponte Blanco, known to history simply as Simón Bolívar. Bolívar was born in Caracas on July 24, 1783, to an aristocratic family that had made its immense fortune in sugar and mining, particularly of copper. He thus was a member of the caste called criollos, or people of pure Spanish descent born in the colonies. After completing his education in Spain and living for a time in France, he returned to Venezuela in 1807. After the Caracas Junta assumed control, he was dispatched to England as a diplomatic representative, but he returned to Venezuela in 1811. When republican forces surrendered to royalist forces in 1812, he fled to Cartagena, where he wrote the Cartagena Manifesto later that year.

Bolívar's life after 1812 was eventful. He was given a military command by the United Provinces of New Granada, and in 1813 he led an invasion of Venezuela known as the Admirable Campaign, liberating the provinces of Merida, Barinas, Trujillo, and Caracas from Spanish rule. When he seized Caracas on August 6, 1813, he proclaimed the Second Republic and served as its president until it collapsed in 1814. After a series of successes and setbacks, including the need to flee to Jamaica and then to Haiti, Bolívar returned to fight for the political independence of New Granada. He led military campaigns that liberated Venezuela and Ecuador and then established the nation known as Gran Colombia (comprising Venezuela, Colombia, Panama, and Ecuador) on December 17, 1819, serving as the nation's first president. He was able to witness his dream of a sovereign Venezuela after republican forces won the Battle of Carabobo on June 24, 1821, ensuring his nation's independence. A later victory in the Battle of Lake Maracaibo on July 24, 1823, drove out the last vestiges of the Spanish.

On August 6, 1825, the Congress of Upper Peru created the nation of Bolivia—one of the few nations in the world named after a person. Bolívar had difficulty governing, however, and had to assume dictatorial powers to maintain some semblance of control of the fragile state. He resigned his presidency on April 27, 1830, and died of tuberculosis on December 17 that year in Santa Marta, Gran Colombia (now Colombia).

Historical Document

Cartagena Manifesto

To spare New Granada the fate of Venezuela and save it from its present suffering are the objects of this report. Consent, my countrymen, to accept it with indulgence, in light of its praiseworthy intentions. I am, Granadans, a child of unhappy Caracas, who having miraculously escaped from the midst of her physical and political ruins, always faithful to the liberal and just system proclaimed by my country, have come here to follow the standards of independence, so gloriously waving in these states.

Motivated by a patriotic zeal, let me dare to address you, to outline for you the causes that led to Venezuela's destruction; flattering myself that the awful and exemplary lessons that extinguished Republic has given us persuade America to improve her conduct, correcting the errors of unity, strength, and energy that are manifested in her forms of government.

The gravest mistake Venezuela made, when they entered the political arena, was without a doubt the fatal adoption of a system of tolerance—a system that was rejected by the whole sensible world as weak and ineffective but that was held to tenaciously and with unexampled blindness until the end.

The first evidence that our government gave of its foolish weakness manifested with respect to the subject city of Coro, when it refused to recognize the city's legitimacy, pronounced it insurgent, and harassed it as an enemy.

Instead of subjugating that defenseless city, which was ready to surrender when our maritime forces arrived, the Supreme Council allowed it to fortify itself and to put on such a respectable facade that it later succeeded in subjugating the whole Confederation, almost as easily as we had previously done. The Council based its political policy on a mistaken understanding of humanity that does not allow any government to free by force stupid people who do not know the value of their rights.

The codes consulted by our magistrates were not those that could teach them the practical science of government but those that have formed certain visionaries who, imagining ethereal republics, have sought to attain political perfection, assuming the perfectibility of humankind. Thus we got philosophers for leaders; philanthropy for law, dialectics for tactics, and sophists for soldiers. With such a subversion of principles and things, the social order suffered enormously, and, of course, the state ran by leaps and bounds to a universal solution, which was soon realized.

Hence was born the impunity of crimes against the state committed brazenly by the discontented, and especially on the part of our born and implacable enemy, the Spanish Europeans, remained in our country with the malicious intent of causing constant unrest and promoting as many conspiracies as our forgiving judges allowed, even if their attacks were so enormous that the public well-being was threatened.

The doctrine supporting this behavior stemmed from the philanthropic maxims of certain writers who defend the notion that no one has to take the life of a man, even one who has committed a crime against the state. In the shelter of this pious doctrine, a pardon followed every conspiracy, and after every pardon came another conspiracy, which in turn was forgiven because liberal governments must be distinguished by leniency. But this clemency is criminal and contributed more than anything else to tearing down the machinery that had not yet quite been established!

From this source stemmed the determined opposition to the calling up of veteran troops, disciplined and able to appear in the battlefield, as instructed, to defend liberty with success and glory. Instead, countless undisciplined militia were established, which, in addition to exhausting the funds of the national treasury with huge salaries, destroyed agriculture, driving the peasants away from their homes and making hateful the government that had forced them to take up arms and abandon their families.

Our statesmen tell us, "Republics have no need of men paid to maintain their freedom. All citizens are soldiers when the enemy attacks us. Greece, Rome, Venice, Genoa, Switzerland, Holland, and recently North America defeated their opponents without the help of mercenary troops always ready to support despotism and subjugate their fellow citizens."

The simple-minded were fascinated by these impolitic and inaccurate arguments, but they failed to convince the wise, who knew well the vast difference between the peoples, times, and customs of those republics and ours. It is true that those republics paid no standing armies, but in ancient times it was for the reason that they did not have any and instead entrusted their salvation and the glory of the States to their political virtues, austere habits, and military character, qualities that we are very far from possessing. As for modern republics that have shaken off the yoke of tyrants, it is well known that they have maintained a considerable number of veterans to assure their security—except North America, which being at peace with everyone and bounded by the sea has not had the need in recent years to sustain a full complement of veteran troops to defend its borders and squares.

The result provided Venezuela with harsh evidence of the error of their calculation, because the militiamen who went to meet the enemy, ignorant of the use of weapons and not being accustomed to discipline and obedience, were overwhelmed at the start of the last campaign, despite the heroic and extraordinary efforts made by their leaders to lead them to victory. This produced a general feeling of discouragement among the soldiers and officers, because it is a military truth that only hardened armies are capable of overcoming the first fateful events of a campaign. The inexperienced soldier believes that everything is lost if he is once defeated, because experience has not proved that courage, skill, and perseverance make up for bad fortune.

The subdivision of the disputed province of Caracas, planned and sanctioned by the federal congress, awakened and fostered a bitter rivalry between the cities and outlying areas and the capital, which— so said the congressmen, ambitious to dominate their districts—was the tyranny of the cities and the leech of the State. In this way the flames of civil war were fanned in Valencia and were never put out, even with the defeat of that city. Secretly the torch was passed from adjacent towns to Coro and Maracaibo and grew in intensity, in this way facilitating the entry of the Spanish, who brought about the downfall of Venezuela.

The dissipation of public revenues on frivolous and harmful items—particularly in salaries for countless clerks, secretaries, judges, magistrates, provincial and federal legislators—dealt a fatal blow to the Republic because it was forced to resort to the dangerous expedient of establishing a paper currency, without other security than the strength and anticipated income of the Confederation. This new currency appeared in the eyes of most people to be a gross violation of property rights, because they saw themselves as being robbed of objects of intrinsic value in exchange for others whose price was uncertain and even imaginary. Paper money put the finishing touches on the discontent of the stolid people of the interior, who called upon the Commander of the Spanish troops to come and rescue them from a currency that they viewed with more horror than slavery.

But what weakened the government of Venezuela the most was the federal structure they adopted, following the most exaggerated notions of human rights. Authorizing each man to rule himself breaks the social compact and characterizes nations in anarchy. Such was the true state of the Confederation. Each province was governed independently and, following this example, each city sought to claim the same powers and adopt the theory that all men and all peoples have the prerogative to establish at will the government that suits them.

Although it is the most perfect and most capable of providing human happiness in society, the federal system is nonetheless the most contrary to the interests of our nascent states. Generally speaking, our citizens are not in a position to exert their rights fully, because they lack the political virtues that characterize the true republican—virtues that are not acquired in absolute governments, where the rights and duties of citizenship are not recognized.

On the other hand, what country in the world, no matter how temperate and Republican it is, will be able to rule itself, in the middle of internal strife and foreign warfare, by a system as complicated and weak as the federal government? No, it is not possible to maintain order in the turmoil of fighting and factions. The government needs to adjust itself, so to speak, to the nature of the circumstances, the times, and the men that surround it. If they are prosperous and serene, it should be temperate and protective, but if they are dire and turbulent, it has to be harsh and arm itself with strength equal to the dangers, with no regard for laws or constitutions until happiness and peace are restored.

Caracas had to suffer much in light of the defects of the Confederation, which, far from aiding her, exhausted her wealth and military supplies and, when danger came, abandoned her to her fate—without help, with the smallest contingent. Moreover, it augmented the problems by fostering competition between the federal and provincial powers, which allowed the enemy to get to the heart of the State, before it had resolved the question of which troops—federal or provincial—should be dispatched to drive them back, when they already had occupied a large portion of the province. This fatal disagreement produced a delay that was terrible for our forces. They were defeated in San Carlos before the reinforcements necessary for victory arrived.

I believe that as long as we do not centralize our American governments, our enemies will gain the most comprehensive advantages. We will be inevitably involved in the horrors of civil strife and abjectly defeated by the handful of bandits who infest our region.

Popular elections conducted by the rustics of the countryside and by those engaged in intrigue in the cities add a further obstacle to the practice of federation among us, because the former are so ignorant that they vote mechanically and the latter are so ambitious that they turn everything into factionalism. So in Venezuela a free and fair election has never been seen, which put government in the hands of men who are uncommitted to the cause, inept, and immoral. The party spirit decided all matters, thus creating more chaos than the circumstances dictated. Our own divisions and not the Spanish forces, has turned us to slavery.

The earthquake of March 26 certainly was as upsetting physically as psychically and can properly be called the immediate cause of the ruin of Venezuela. But this same event could have occurred without producing such deadly effect if Caracas had then been governed by a single authority that, acting with speed and force, could have repaired the damage unfettered by the hindrances and rivalries that retarded the effect of these measures until the destruction had become so devastating that it was beyond help.

If Caracas, instead of a languid and ineffectual Confederation, had set up a simple government— the kind it required for its political and military circumstances, you would exist today, O Venezuela, and you would enjoy freedom.

After the earthquake, the influence of the church played a large part in the uprising of the towns and cities and the introduction of the enemies into the country, sacrilegiously abusing the sanctity of its ministry in aid of the promoters of civil war. However, we must candidly confess that these traitorous priests were encouraged to commit the heinous crimes of which they are justly accused simply because impunity for their crimes was absolute, a condition that Congress shockingly aided. The situation came to such a pass that from the time of the insurrection of the city of Valencia—the pacification of which cost the lives of a thousand men—not a single rebel was given over to the vengeance of the law. All of them were left with their lives intact, and the majority also kept their property.

It follows from the foregoing that among the causes leading to the fall of Venezuela should be placed, first, the nature of its Constitution, which was, I repeat, as contrary to her own interests as it was favorable to those of her opponents. Second was the spirit of misanthropy that gripped our leaders. Third was the opposition to the establishment of a military force that could have saved the Republic and repelled the blows of the Spaniards. Fourth was the earthquake, accompanied by a fanaticism that succeeded in drawing from this phenomenon the most ominous interpretations. Finally, there were the internal factions that were, in fact, the deadly poison that had pushed the country into the grave. These examples of mistakes and misfortunes are not entirely without value for the peoples of South America, who aspire to freedom and independence.

New Granada has seen the demise of Venezuela, so it should avoid the pitfalls that have destroyed her. To this end, I advocate the reconquest of Caracas as an essential measure for securing the safety of New Granada. At first glance, this project might seem irrelevant, costly, and perhaps impractical, but if we examine it more closely, attentively, and with foresight, it is impossible to ignore the necessity and not to implement it once its utility is established.

The first thing that speaks in support of this operation is the origin of the destruction of Caracas, which was none other than the contempt with which the city regarded the existence of an enemy that seemed inconsequential. It was not, considered in its true light.

Coro certainly could never have competed with Caracas, when compared with Caracas in terms of its intrinsic strength. But because, in the order of human events, it is not always the largest physical entity that tilts the political balance, but the one that has superior moral force, should not the government of Venezuela therefore have refrained from removing an enemy who, though seemingly weak, had the support of the province of Maracaibo, including all those bound to the Regency; the gold; and the cooperation of our eternal enemies, the Europeans who live among us; the clerical party, always addicted to its supporter and partner, despotism; and, above all, the confirmed regard of the ignorant and superstitious within the boundaries of our states. So, to dismantle the machinery of state, it required only one traitorous official to call in the enemy, after which the unprecedented and patriotic efforts of the advocates of Caracas could not prevent the collapse of a structure already toppling from the blow of a single man.

Applying the example of Venezuela to New Granada and expressing it mathematically as a ratio, we find that Coro is to Caracas as Caracas is to all America; consequently, the danger that threatens this country is due to the aforementioned formula, because Spain, possessing the territory of Venezuela, can easily obtain men and munitions of war such that, under the direction of leaders with experience against the masters of war, the French, they can penetrate from the provinces of Barinas and Maracaibo to the ends of America South.

Spain has many ambitious and courageous general officers, who, accustomed to dangers and privations, yearn to come here to find an empire to replace the one she just lost.

It is very likely that upon the decline of the Peninsula, there will be a prodigious emigration of all sorts of men, particularly cardinals, archbishops, bishops, canons, and revolutionary clerics capable not only of subverting our tender and languid States but also entangling the entire New World in a frightful anarchy. The religious influence, the rule of civil and military domination, and all the prestige they can use to seduce the human spirit are so many instruments available to subjugate these regions. Nothing will prevent emigration from Spain.

England is likely to assist the emigration of a group that weakens Bonaparte's forces in Spain and augments and strengthens their own power in America. Neither France nor America can stop it. Neither can we do so on our own; all of our countries lacking a respectable navy, our attempts will be in vain.

These defectors will indeed find a favorable reception in the ports of Venezuela, as they are reinforcing the oppressors of that country and supplying the means to undertake the conquest of independent states.

They will raise a force of fifteen or twenty thousand men who will promptly be brought to order by their leaders, officers, sergeants, corporals, and veteran soldiers. This army will be followed by another, even more fearsome—one consisting of ministers, ambassadors, counselors, judges, the entire church hierarchy, and the grandees of Spain, whose profession is deceit and intrigue and who will be decorated with flashy titles well suited to dazzle the crowd. They will engulf everything like a torrent, right down to the seeds and even the roots of the tree of freedom in Colombia. The troops will fight on the field, and the others will wage war from their ministries by means of seduction and fanaticism.

Thus, we have no other recourse to guard against these calamities than to pacify our rebellious provinces and then to take up our weapons against the enemy and in this way to form soldiers and officials worthy to be called the pillars of the country.

Everything conspires to make us adopt this measure; without mentioning the urgent need for us to close the doors to the enemy, there are other very strong reasons for us to take the offensive. It would be an inexcusable political and military failure to fail to do so. We have been invaded, and we are therefore forced to drive the enemy back beyond the border. Moreover, it is a principle of the art of war that any defensive war is injurious and ruinous to the country that conducts it, because it weakens without hope of compensation. Conversely, fighting in enemy territory is always advantageous, for the sake of the good that results from harming the enemy. For this reason we must not, under any circumstances, go on the defensive.

We should also consider the current state of the enemy, which is in a very vulnerable position, having been deserted by most of its Creole soldiers and having, at just this time, to defend the patriotic garrison cities of Caracas, Puerto Cabello, La Guaira, Barcelona, Cumana and Margarita, where they have their supplies. They do not dare abandon these positions, fearing a general uprising when they leave. So it would be impossible for our troops to arrive at the gates of Caracas without engaging in a pitched battle.

It is certain that as soon as we arrive in Venezuela thousands of brave patriots who are longing for our arrival to help them shake off the yoke of their tyrants will join us, uniting their forces with ours to defend freedom.

The nature of this campaign gives us the advantage of approaching Maracaibo by way of Santa Marta and Barinas by way of Cucuta.

Let us therefore take hold of this propitious moment. Do not allow reinforcements that might arrive at any time from Spain to entirely alter this strategic balance. Do not lose, perhaps forever, the providential opportunity to ensure the fortune of these states.

The honor of New Granada absolutely requires us to chasten those audacious invaders, pursuing them to their last stronghold. Because her glory depends on our undertaking the enterprise of marching to Venezuela, to liberate the cradle of Colombian independence, its martyrs and the worthy people of Caracas, whose cries are directed only to their beloved compatriots of Granada, whom they eagerly await as their redeemers. Let us hasten to break the chains of those victims who groan in the dungeons, ever hopeful of rescue by us. Do not betray their confidence; do not be insensitive to the cries of your brothers. Fly to avenge the dead, to give life to the dying, ease to the oppressed, and freedom to all.

—*Cartagena de Indias, 15 December 1812*

Glossary

Creole: in this context, a Spanish American, born in the Americas

Peninsula: the Iberian Peninsula

Regency: French-dominated junta that briefly attempted to govern Spain's colonial possessions in South America

traitorous official: Francisco de Miranda

Document Analysis

Bolívar addresses his manifesto specifically to the people of New Granada. His goal is to outline his experiences in Venezuela, particularly the collapse of the First Republic, with a view to helping the people of New Granada escape the state's errors. Essentially, he outlines five major problems with the First Republic: the ineffectiveness of the army, poor administration of public revenues, reliance on a weak federal system, the Caracas earthquake of 1812, and the opposition of the Catholic Church to republican views. He then outlines his reasons for wanting to launch an invasion of Venezuela.

The first section of the manifesto is sharply critical of the republican military. After brief introductory paragraphs, Bolívar launches into a discussion of the failure of the First Republic's military campaigns, particularly against the district of Coro. His tone is harsh. He refers to "the fatal adoption of a system of tolerance" that allowed Coro to resist republican rule. He then makes a startling statement regarding the governing council in Caracas: "The Council based its political policy on a mistaken understanding of humanity that does not allow any government to free by force stupid people who do not know the value of their rights." Bolívar was a liberator, but he was by instinct an aristocrat, and as such he was willing to impose his political vision even on those who did not share it. He then discusses what he regarded as misplaced idealism, referring to "ethereal republics" and "pious doctrine" where philosophers supplanted leaders and philanthropy supplanted law. Crimes against the new state were tolerated, thus allowing royalist supporters free rein in Venezuela. One consequence of this tolerance was that unchecked opposition prevented the First Republic from calling up veteran troops, leading to the creation of undisciplined militias that were not equal to the fight at hand. And because these militias were formed from the local laboring populations, the impact on agriculture was severe. He rejects the view that because earlier nations, from ancient Greece and Rome to the fledgling United States, did not need mercenary armies, Venezuela did not need them either. He counters this view by arguing that these states had "political virtues, austere habits, and military character" that the Venezuelans did not possess.

The collective impact of these failures was twofold. In paragraph 13, Bolívar argues that the First Republic's military was simply ineffective; enlistees lacked discipline, obedience, and even knowledge of the use of weapons. The forces were thus doomed to defeat. In paragraph 14, Bolívar notes that the republic's unwillingness to take harsh measures led to problems in the city of Valencia; although the republic subdued Valencia, there resulted a rivalry between city and country that allowed the Spanish to regain a foothold in Venezuela.

Paragraph 15 briefly discusses the First Republic's poor administration of public revenues—"the dissipation of public revenues on frivolous and harmful items." For example, he cites the bloated salaries given to legions of public bureaucrats. The consequence of this overspending was that the First Republic had to issue its own paper currency. The currency, though, lacked the backing of goods and productive capacity. It was essentially worthless, with no "intrinsic value." Under such conditions of fiscal irresponsibility, many Venezuelans concluded that life was better under the Spanish than it was under the First Republic.

The core of Bolívar's argument is contained in this sequence of paragraphs. His chief objection to the First Republic was its "federal structure," a term that in Bolívar's usage means decentralization. In his view, too much power and authority were given to Venezuela's districts and cities, and not enough was reserved for the central government. Interestingly, the fledgling United States had faced the same problem. Under the original Articles of Confederation, the nation's first constitution, power was decentralized. The nation was less a unified polity than a "confederation" of states. Centrifugal forces threatened to drive the independent states apart until the U.S. Constitution, in the form in which it survives today, strengthened the federal government— while also planting the seeds of the American Civil War, when regional factionalism would overcome allegiance to the nation. Venezuela experienced the same kind of factionalism during the First Republic and beyond, as local economic interests trumped allegiance to the national government.

Bolívar's position is clear: "Authorizing each man to rule himself breaks the social compact and characterizes nations in anarchy." He goes on to write that despite its being ideal in certain respects, "the federal system is nonetheless the most contrary to the interests of our nascent states," especially since "our citizens are not in a position to exert their rights fully, because they lack the political virtues that characterize the true republican." He defends this notion by appealing to the nature of the times. When a country is "prosperous and serene," it can afford to relinquish power to its citizens. But when a country is fighting both internal factionalism and a foreign enemy, the times require it to exhibit strength. One of the practical consequences of this diffusion of power in the First Republic was that the federal government and provincial authorities quarreled in Caracas about who was going to deploy troops while the Spanish poised to strike. The result was certain defeat. A second practical consequence was ineffectual elections. In Bolívar's view, the federal system encouraged divisiveness, for "popular elections conducted by the rustics of the countryside and by those engaged in intrigue in the cities" become obstacles because the rustics "are so ignorant that they vote mechanically" while those in the cities "are so ambitious that they turn everything into factionalism."

In paragraphs 22 and 23, Bolívar makes reference to the Caracas earthquake, which struck on March 26, 1812, killing some fifteen to twenty thousand people and causing widespread property damage. Because the earthquake was centered in republican-controlled areas of Venezuela, it represented a serious setback to the First Republic. While Bolívar acknowledges that the earthquake was the "immediate cause" of the collapse of the republic, he goes on to argue that its effects would not have been as devastating if there had been a strong central government to address the crisis. In essence, the earthquake helped to expose the weaknesses of the federal system of government of the First Republic.

Paragraph 24 briefly apportions some of the blame for the collapse of the First Republic on the Catholic Church. Bolívar argues that Catholic priests aided those who promoted civil war and allowed the Spanish sanctuary in the country. He is particularly shocked by the fact that none of these "traitorous priests" were punished for their "heinous crimes"—again, a failing that he attributes to the weak and overly tolerant federal congress.

In the manifesto's final sequence of paragraphs, after reiterating the key points of his argument, Bolívar turns to the future by outlining how New Granada can learn from the mistakes made in Venezuela. He first insists that New Granada forces should invade and subdue Caracas. He draws his readers' attention again to the factionalism in Caracas, where distinct groups pursued their selfish ends at the expense of the republic, as had occurred in Coro. Bolívar argues that only by retaining control over Caracas could New Granada spread the spirit of revolution through South America. He then notes that because of events in Spain, it was likely that large numbers of Spanish immigrants would arrive in South America. These immigrants, acting in concert with seasoned military officers and soldiers, would be in a position to subvert South American independence. Bolívar goes on to claim that nothing can stop this immigration, and he raises the specter of a new Spanish army bent on conquest.

The only solution to this looming problem was "to pacify our rebellious provinces and then to take up our weapons against the enemy." He makes clear that fighting a purely defensive war would be ruinous to the country; the only alternative was to take the fight to the enemy. He calls the moment "propitious," for the Spanish were confined to their garrisons, which they had to defend. New Granada had to strike before Spanish reinforcements arrived. The manifesto closes with an inspirational call to action. Bolívar points out the obligation of New Granada to "chasten those audacious invaders" and "liberate the cradle of Colombian independence."

Essential Themes

In the short term, the Cartagena Manifesto had a profound impact. Bolívar won the support of New Granada and launched his Admirable Campaign on February 16, 1813. During the campaign, Bolívar issued a document called the Decree of War to the Death, in which he announced that any Spaniard who failed to support independence would be put to death. On July 22 his forces met and defeated the royalists at the Battle of Horcones. In August his army occupied Valencia and La Victoria, and the royalist government surrendered, leading to the formation of the Second Republic—which itself ended up collapsing less than a year later. From 1817 to 1819, Bolívar was head of a rump government that created a legislative body called the Congress of Angostura, which wrote a constitution for Venezuela in 1819. Later, in the Battle of Lake Maracaibo on July 24, 1823, republicans drove out the last vestiges of the Spanish. Thus, Bolívar's dream of an independent Venezuelan Republic was realized. The official, formal name of the country became and remains the Bolivarian Republic of Venezuela.

In the longer term, Bolívar's goal of a free, unified, prosperous South America proved harder to realize. Although several nations gained their independence—largely through the efforts of Bolívar and numerous other republicans—factionalism, caste, and power plays undermined attempts at South American unity. Gran Colombia collapsed within a decade, and in the ensuing years the nations of South America fell under the control of caudillos, a term often translated as "strongmen" or "warlords." Thus, throughout the 1800s, South American nations—excepting Brazil, a stable nation under the Portuguese until 1889—were ruled by authoritarian dictators, and the century was one of revolts, coups, civil wars, and wars between states.

—Michael J. O'Neal, PhD

Bibliography and Additional Reading

Chasteen, John Charles. *Americanos: Latin America's Struggle for Independence.* New York: Oxford UP, 2008.

Lynch, John. *Simón Bolívar: A Life.* New Haven, CT: Yale UP, 2007.

———. "Simón Bolívar and the Spanish Revolutions." *History Today* 33 Issue 7 (July 1983) www.historytoday.com/john-lynch/simon-bolivar-and-spanish-revolutions.

McFarlane, Anthony. *War and Independence in Spanish America.* New York: Routledge, 2008.

Rodriguez, Jaime E. *The Independence of Spanish America.* Cambridge: Cambridge UP, 1998.

■ Simón Bolívar: Address at Angostura

Date: February 15, 1819
Author: Simón Bolívar
Genre: address; speech

Summary Overview

Simón Bolívar played a central role in the wars for independence in South America during the first few decades of the nineteenth century. Spain had exercised imperial rule over much of the continent for centuries, but with disruptions back in Europe, these independence movements began and did not cease. After two Republics of Venezuela were briefly established and then overthrown, Bolívar started yet another military campaign against royalist forces allied with the Spanish crown. Amidst this campaign, the military leader convened the Congress of Angostura to set up a provisional government for the territories that were—and those that were soon to be—freed from Spanish rule. At this congress, Bolívar gave the speech that is reproduced (in translation) here. In it, he highlights his ideals as well as the type of government he thinks should replace imperial rule. He models such a government largely on that of Great Britain. The delegates at the congress did not agree to all of Bolívar's proposals, but they did elect him president. After the congress, the military campaign saw more victories, and Bolívar established the republic of Gran Colombia, encompassing a vast swath of the northern portion of South America. Two years later, the decisions made at the Congress of Cúcuta superseded the ones from the 1819 congress.

Defining Moment

Beginning at the end of the fifteenth century, European powers began colonizing the Americas. Spain and Portugal were the major European players colonizing South America. In 1494, the two imperial powers signed the Treaty of Tordesillas dividing the so-called New World along a border 370 leagues west of the Cape Verde islands, down the "bulge" of South America. Portugal laid claim to everything to the east of this line, which is why modern-day Brazilians speak Portuguese; Spain laid claim to everything to the west, the lion's share of the hemisphere. Although other European powers colonized parts of South America and various revolts arose, Spain was able to keep a firm grip most of South America until the turn of the nineteenth century.

In the early 1800s, the status quo of Spanish rule over the majority of South America was overturned. Back in France, Napoleon Bonaparte had risen to power and waged war against other European powers. In 1807, Napoleon invaded the Iberian peninsula, setting off the Peninsular War. In the following year he turned his attention from Portugal to Spain, disrupting the governing structure of the Spanish Empire. While the government of the Supreme Central and Governing Junta of the Kingdom temporarily took over the government in Spain proper, Spanish colonies in the Americas were setting up their own juntas and/or declaring their independence from the Spanish. Argentina, Chile, and Colombia declared their independence in 1810. Venezuelans set up the Supreme Junta of Caracas on April 19, 1810. On July 5, 1811, the majority of Venezuelan provinces declared their independence.

Meanwhile in Europe, Napoleon was defeated (for the first time) in 1814, and at this point Ferdinand VII, the son of Charles IV, the Bourbon king who reigned in Spain before the Peninsular War, assumed the Spanish throne. The following decade saw wars flare across the continent as the newly declared independent nations tried to solidify their independence against royalist forces attempting to retake these lands for the Spanish crown. In the south of the continent, José de San Martín helped Argentina confirm its independence, before crossing the Andes and doing the same for Chile and Peru. Meanwhile, up north, two short-lived Republics of Venezuela were put down by royalist forces.

In 1816, Simón Bolívar, who had taken part in the First Republic of Venezuela and led the Second Republic of Venezuela, returned to the region with military and financial aid from the Haitian president Alexandre Pétion. The revolutionaries' fight to retake the region was still ongoing when Simón Bolívar convened the Congress of Angostura in 1819. It was to this congress that Bolívar delivered the speech transcribed as this document. In the speech, Bolívar outlines the form of government he believed would be best for the region. The congress did not take up all the proposals he outlined in the speech, such as a hereditary senate; however, the delegates did elect Bolívar as president. Bolívar and his troops were victorious over the royalist forces in the war for independence that culminated with the Battle of Carabobo of 1821. In that same year, the Congress of Cúcuta superseded the previous Congress of Angostura and established Gran Colombia.

Bolívar spent the next several years continuing the fight against royalist Spanish forces as well as battling against separatist forces within Gran Colombia itself. At its height, Gran Colombia extended across the entire norther portion of South America, occupying all or parts of what are today the independent nations of Colombia, Venezuela, Ecuador, Panama, Peru, Guyana and Brazil. However, Gran Colombia proved fleeting. In 1830, with the strength of the separatists' movements growing, Bolívar resigned the presidency, and Gran Colombia dissolved into Venezuela, New Granada, and Ecuador. The government outlined in this document may have never come to fruition, and Gran Colombia may not have stayed together long, but the imperial rule of Spain in the region had been overthrown for good.

Author Biography

Simón Bolívar was a leading force in liberating Venezuela, Bolivia, Colombia, Ecuador, Peru, and Panama from Spanish imperial rule, earning himself the nickname *El Libertador*. Born on July 24, 1783 as Simón José Antonio de la Santísima Trinidad de Bolívar y Palacios in Caracas, Venezuela, Bolívar studied in Spain and spent much of his youth in Spain, France and around Europe. Upon returning to Venezuela, Bolívar played a prominent role in the establishment of the Supreme Junta of Caracas on April 19, 1810 and its declaration of independence from Spain in the following year. He took part in the delegation that recruited Francisco de Miranda back to his birth country. Miranda then established the short-lived First Republic of Venezuela. As Spanish royalists recovered Venezuela, Miranda and Bolívar split. Bolívar and other revolutionaries accused Miranda of treason and handed him over to their royalist enemies. Bolívar fought for the independent United Provinces of New Granada, in present day Colombia, recaptured Venezuela, and established the Second Republic of Venezuela. This republic, too, proved short-lived, and Bolívar left for Jamaica and from there onto Haiti. Receiving aid from Alexandre Pétion, the President of the newly formed Republic of Haiti, Bolívar returned to Venezuela, freed the slaves, and captured Angostura. He gave this speech there in 1819 and set back out on campaign against the Spanish royalists. Bolívar and his troops proved widely successful and took much of present day Colombia, Ecuador, and Peru. He founded the Republic of Bolivia, named after himself, and formed Gran Colombia out of the other vast lands he now controlled. Ceding to various separatist movements, Bolívar eventually resigned the presidency of Gran Colombia, which eventually dissolved into Venezuela, New Granada, and Ecuador. Bolívar died of tuberculosis on December 17, 1830 at the age of forty-seven.

Historical Document

Address at Angostura

We are not Europeans; we are not Indians; we are but a mixed species of aborigines and Spaniards. Americans by birth and Europeans by law, we find ourselves engaged in a dual conflict: we are disputing with the natives for titles of ownership, and at the same time we are struggling to maintain ourselves in the country that gave us birth against the opposition of the invaders. Thus our position is most extraordinary and complicated. But there is more. As our role has always been strictly passive and political existence nil, we find that our quest for liberty is now even more difficult of accomplishment; for we, having been placed in a state lower than slavery, had been robbed not only of our freedom but also of the right to exercise an active domestic tyranny.... We have been ruled more by deceit than by force, and we have been degraded more by vice than by superstition. Slavery is the daughter of darkness: an ignorant people is a blind instrument of its own destruction. Ambition and intrigue abuses the credulity and experience of men lacking all political, economic, and civic knowledge; they adopt pure illusion as reality; they take license for liberty, treachery for patriotism, and vengeance for justice. If a people, perverted by their training, succeed in achieving their liberty, they will soon lose it, for it would be of no avail to endeavor to explain to them that happiness consists in the practice of virtue; that the rule of law is more powerful than the rule of tyrants, because, as the laws are more inflexible, every one should submit to their beneficent austerity; that proper morals, and not force, are the bases of law; and that to practice justice is to practice liberty.

Although those people [North Americans], so lacking in many respects, are unique in the history of mankind, it is a marvel, I repeat, that so weak and complicated a government as the federal system has managed to govern them in the difficult and trying circumstances of their past. But, regardless of the effectiveness of this form of government with respect to North America, I must say that it has never for a moment entered my mind to compare the position and character of two states as dissimilar as the English-American and the Spanish-American. Would it not be most difficult to apply to Spain the English system of political, civil, and religious liberty: Hence, it would be even more difficult to adapt to Venezuela the laws of North America.

Nothing in our fundamental laws would have to be altered were we to adopt a legislative power similar to that held by the British Parliament. Like the North Americans, we have divided national representation into two chambers: that of Representatives and the Senate. The first is very wisely constituted. It enjoys all its proper functions, and it requires no essential revision, because the

Constitution, in creating it, gave it the form and powers which the people deemed necessary in order that they might be legally and properly represented. If the Senate were hereditary rather than elective, it would, in my opinion, be the basis, the tie, the very soul of our republic. In political storms this body would arrest the thunderbolts of the government and would repel any violent popular reaction. Devoted to the government because of a natural interest in its own preservation, a hereditary senate would always oppose any attempt on the part of the people to infringe upon the jurisdiction and authority of their magistrates...The creation of a hereditary senate would in no way be a violation of political equality. I do not solicit the establishment of a nobility, for as a celebrated republican has said, that would simultaneously destroy equality and liberty. What I propose is an office for which the candidates must prepare themselves, an office that demands great knowledge and the ability to acquire such knowledge. All should not be left to chance and the outcome of elections. The people are more easily deceived than is Nature perfected by art; and although these senators, it is true, would not be bred in an environment that is all virtue, it is equally true that they would be raised in an atmosphere of enlightened education. The hereditary senate will also serve as a counterweight to both government and people; and as a neutral power it will weaken the mutual attacks of these two eternally rival powers.

The British executive power possesses all the authority properly appertaining to a sovereign, but a triple line of dams, barriers, and stockades surrounds him. He is the head of government, but his ministers and subordinates rely more upon law than upon his authority, as they are personally responsible; and not even decrees of royal authority can exempt them from this responsibility. The executive is commander in chief of the army and navy; he makes peace and declares war; but Parliament annually determines what sums are to be paid to these military forces. While the courts and judges are dependent on the executive power, the laws originate in and are made by Parliament. Give Venezuela such an executive power in the person of a president chosen by the people or their representatives, and you will have taken a great step toward national happiness. No matter what citizen occupies this office, he will be aided by the Constitution, and therein being authorized to do good, he can do no harm, because his ministers will cooperate with him only insofar as he abides by the law. If he attempts to infringe upon the law, his own ministers will desert him, thereby isolating him from the Republic, and they will even bring charges against him in the Senate. The ministers, being responsible for any transgressions committed, will actually govern, since they must account for their actions.

A republican magistrate is an individual set apart from society, charged with checking the impulse of the people toward license and the propensity of judges and administrators toward abuse of the laws. He is directly subject to the legislative body, the senate, and the people: he is the one man who resists the combined pressure of the opinions, interests, and passions of the social state and who, as Carnot states, does little more than struggle constantly with the urge to dominate and the desire to escape domination. A strongly rooted force can only correct this weakness. It should be strongly proportioned to meet the resistance, which the executive must expect from the legislature, from the judiciary, and from the people of a republic. Unless the executive has easy access to all the administrative resources, fixed by a just distribution of powers, he inevitably becomes a nonentity or abuses his authority. By this I mean that the result will be the death of the government, whose heirs are anarchy, usurpation, and tyranny…Therefore, let the entire system of government be strengthened, and let the balance of power be drawn up in such a manner that it will be permanent and incapable of decay because of its own tenuity. Precisely because no form of government is so weak as the democratic, its framework must be firmer, and its institutions must be studied to determine their degree of stability…unless this is done, we will have to reckon with an ungovernable, tumultuous, and anarchic society, not with a social order where happiness, peace, and justice prevail.

Glossary

Carnot: Lazare Nicolas Marguerite, also known as Count Carnot, influential French revolutionary politician, military organizer, and writer

Document Analysis

This document is made up of excerpts from the transcription of a speech that Simón Bolívar gave to the Congress of Angostura when it came together in early 1819. The speech was given in Spanish, and the transcription has been translated into English. The war for independence from Spain was still ongoing, but the congress met to set up a provisional government. In his speech before the congress, Bolívar reveals his ideals and his nuanced perspective on what he believes this new government should look like.

Before getting to the specifics of his proposed government, Bolívar takes some time to place the infant nation in its proper context. He notes that the population is a mix of Europeans and Native Americans. Bolívar had recently played a large role in abolishing slavery and the race-based caste system put in place by the Spanish. He himself was an ardent abolitionist as this speech displays: "Slavery is the daughter of darkness." The changes that the revolution brought about created a heterogeneous population which Bolívar cites when theorizing the best form of rule to govern over it, as discussed below.

This speech was given several decades after the United States declared its own independence from Great Britain. Bolívar references the newly established nation to the north but only to argue that the democracy established there would not work for this nation: "But, regardless of the effectiveness of this form of government with respect to North America, I must say that it has never for a moment entered my mind to compare the position and character of two states as dissimilar as the English-American and the Spanish-American." He notes the northern system's "effectiveness" but argues this effectiveness is tied to the context in which the government was formed, which is quite different from the one in which he and his compatriots are operating. "Would it not be most difficult," he continues, "to apply to Spain the English system of political, civil, and religious liberty: Hence, it would be even more difficult to adapt to Venezuela the laws of North America." In this, the beginning portion of the speech, Bolívar, therefore, puts forward the particulars of the situation and the region's population for dismissing democracy as a favorable form of government.

Later in the document, however, Bolívar disparages democracy more generally. He does so by painting "the people" as easily deceived: "All should not be left to chance and the outcome of elections. The people are more easily deceived than is Nature perfected by art." Elections are put on the same register as chance, thanks to the unreliability of the people. Armed with this information from the latter part of the speech, we can better parse a statement from the beginning of the text. Early on Bolívar states that "An ignorant people is a blind instrument of its own destruction." Upon an initial reading, the reader might associate this thought with the call for an informed electorate, the cornerstone of any working democracy. However, given the negative thoughts of democracy that he expresses later, we may consider taking this sentence as a statement against democracy in general. He concludes the entire speech on a similar note: "Precisely because no form of government is so weak as the democratic, its framework must be firmer, and its institutions must be studied to determine their degree of stability…unless this is done, we will have to reckon with an ungovernable, tumultuous, and anarchic society, not with a social order where happiness, peace, and justice prevail." Given his focus on democracy in the speech, we can posit that the formation of a democracy was still quite possible at the time of a speech; the speaker was vigorously working to prevent this outcome.

With the United States' model of government dismissed, Bolívar turns to the very model against which the North Americans had revolted, Great Britain. He broaches the subject in this way: "Nothing in our fundamental laws would have to be altered were we to adopt a legislative power similar to that held by the British Parliament." By this, he means to establish a hereditary senate not dissimilar from the British House of Lords. He explains his reasoning at length, concluding, "The hereditary senate will also serve as a counterweight to both government and people; and as a neutral power it will weaken the mutual attacks of these two eternally rival powers." He also looks to the British system as a model for executive power: "The British executive power possesses all the authority properly appertaining to a sovereign, but a triple line of dams, barriers, and stockades surrounds him." Despite the mention of checks and balances, Bolívar chooses the British executive presumably because of the power that it wields. The delegates of the congress did not accept these proposals based on the British system, but the delegates did elect Bolívar as president.

Essential Themes

The speaker, Simón Bolívar, liberated much of South America from Spanish rule and, in so doing, earned himself the nickname *El Libertador*. It should therefore come as no surprise that he develops the theme of liberty throughout this speech. He mentions the word "liberty" an impressive four times in the opening paragraph, setting the tone for the entire speech. Right from the beginning, he references "our quest for liberty." This is how he articulates the primary mission for himself as well as for this congress. This first paragraph also includes the maxim: "to practice justice is to practice liberty." It is not just in the opening paragraph that Bolívar discusses liberty, but he returns to the topic throughout the speech. A particularly enlightening instance comes when he is discussing his proposal for the formation of a hereditary senate. He is careful to distinguish this senate from a nobility: "The creation of a hereditary senate would in no way be a violation of political equality. I do not solicit the establishment of a nobility, for as a celebrated republican has said, that would simultaneously destroy equality and liberty." His construction shows that the concepts of equality and liberty are intertwined. Although his abolitionist beliefs and opposition to Spanish rule fit together well with liberty, some may argue—and have argued—that the form of government he proposes in this speech does not particularly privilege liberty. He himself appears cognizant of this potential criticism and attempts to affirm explicitly his and his proposed government's commitment to this ideal.

—Anthony Vivian, MA

Bibliography and Additional Reading

Arana, Marie. *Bolivar: American Liberator*. New York: Simon & Schuster, 2014.

Bushnell, David. *Simon Bolivar: Liberation and Disappointment*. London: Pearson, 2003.

Langley, Lester D. *Simón Bolívar: Venezuelan Rebel, American Revolutionary*. Lanham, MD: Rowman & Littlefield Publishers, 2009.

McFarlane, Anthony. *War and Independence in Spanish America*. New York: Routledge, 2008.

Sherwell, Guillermo A. *Simon Bolivar, the Liberator*. Rockville, MD: Wildside Press, 2013.

■ Treaty of Córdoba

Date: August 24, 1821
Countries: Mexico; Spain
Genre: treaty

Summary Overview

Spain had controlled the territory that included nineteenth-century Mexico since 1521, and it ruled its New World subjects through a succession of viceroys. In the social hierarchy of Spanish Mexico (then territory within the viceroyalty of New Spain), the elites were Spanish-born peninsulars, while Mexican-born people of European descent, called criollos, held a slightly lower rank and became invested in Mexican independence when they believed it would elevate their status. Native Mexicans and those of mixed race, known as mestizos, were excluded from political and civic life to varying degrees and also looked to independence from Spain to improve their position.

The French invasion and occupation of Spain from 1808 to 1813 sparked a revolutionary movement in Mexico that led to an eleven-year war. After a combined force of indigenous, mixed-race, and criollo insurgents convinced the Spanish viceroy to accept terms, the revolution ended with the Treaty of Córdoba, signed on August 24, 1821, in Mexico. However, the treaty was not accepted by the Spanish government, which refused to recognize Mexican independence until December 1836.

Defining Moment

The Mexican War of Independence began with a criollo priest, Miguel Hidalgo y Costilla, whose indigenous and mixed-race parishioners suffered under Spanish colonial rule. With both the American Revolution and the French Revolution in recent memory, and Napoleon Bonaparte's French army occupying Spain, Hidalgo began meeting in secret with a group of insurgents determined to overthrow the colonial government in Mexico City. On September 16, 1810, Hidalgo issued a passionate call to arms, known as "Grito de Dolores" or "Cry of Dolores," calling for a radical redistribution of land and equality between indigenous people, criollos, and those of mixed race.

Despite leading a rapidly growing insurgent army toward Mexico City, Hidalgo was defeated and executed by firing squad on July 30, 1811. The insurgency continued under the leadership of José María Morelos y Pavón, Mariano Matamoros, and Vicente Guerrero, who continued to work to overthrow the Spanish colonial government and advocate for the rights of indigenous people and mestizos. During this phase of the revolution, most criollos opposed the in-

Signing the treaty on behalf of the Spanish government was Jefe Político Superior Juan O'Donojú. Image via Wikimedia Commons. [Public domain.]

TRATADOS CELEBRADOS

EN LA VILLA DE CORDOVA

el 24 del presente entre los Señores D. Juan O donojú, Teniente general de los Ejércitos de España, y D. Agustin de Iturbide, primer Gefe del Ejército Imperial Mejicano de las tres Garantías.

Pronunciada por Nueva España la Independencia de la antigua, teniendo un ejército que sostuviese este pronunciamiento, decididas por él las Provincias del reino, sitiada la Capital en donde se habia depuesto á la autoridad legítima, y cuando solo quedaban por el gobierno europeo las plazas de Veracruz y Acapulco, desguarnecidas y sin medios de resistir á un sitio bien dirigido y que durase algun tiempo; llegó al primer puerto el Teniente general D. Juan O donojú con el carácter y representacion de Capitan general, y Gefe superior político, de este reino nombrado por su M. C. quien deseoso de evitar los males que aflijen á los pueblos en alteraciones de esta clase, y tratando de consiliar los intereses de ambas españas, invitó á una entrevista al primer Gefe del Ejército Imperial D. Agustin de Iturbide, en la que se discutiese el gran negocio de la independencia, desatando sin romper los vínculos que unieron á los dos continentes. Verificóse la entrevista en la villa de Córdova el 24 de Agosto de 1821, y con la representacion de su carácter el primero, y la del Imperio Mejicano el segundo, despues de haber conferenciado detenidamente sobre lo que mas convenia á una y otra nacion atendido al estado actual, y las últimas ocurrencias, convinieron en los artículos siguientes que firmaron por duplicado, para darles toda la consolidacion de que son capaces esta clase de documentos, conservando un original cada uno en su poder para mayor seguridad y validacion.

1. Esta América se reconocerá por Nacion soberana é Independiente, y se llamará en lo sucesivo Imperio Mejicano.

Señor Infante D. Carlos; por su renuncia ó no admision el Serenísimo Señor Infante D. Francisco de Paula; por su renuncia ó no admision el Serenísimo Señor D. Carlos Luis Infante de España antes heredero de Etruria, hoy de Luca; y por renuncia ó no admision de este, el que las Córtes del Imperio designaren.

4. El Emperador fijará su Corte en Méjico que será la Capital del Imperio.

5. Se nombrarán dos Comisionados por el Excmo. Señor O donojú, los que pasarán á la Corte de España á poner en las Reales manos del Señor D. Fernando VII. cópia de este tratado, y exposicion que le acompañará para que sirva á S. M. de antecedente, mientras las Córtes del Imperio le ofrecen la corona con todas las formalidades y garantias, que asunto de tanta importancia exije; y suplicarán á S. M. que en el caso del artículo tercero se digne noticiarlo á los serenísimos Señores Infantes llamados en el mismo artículo por el órden que en él se nombran; interponiendo su benigno influjo para que sea una persona de las señaladas de su augusta casa la que venga á este imperio, por lo que se interesa en ello la prosperidad de ambas naciones, y por la satisfaccion que recibirán los mejicanos en añadir este vínculo á los demás de amistad, con que podrán, y quieren unirse á los españoles.

6. Se nombrará inmediatamente conforme al espíritu del plan de Iguala, una junta compuesta de los primeros hombres del Imperio por sus virtudes, por sus destinos, por sus fortunas, representacion y concepto, de aquellos que están designa-

Print version of the treaty signed in August 1821. Photo by Jaontiveros, via Wikimedia Commons.

surgency, as the redistribution of land and racial equality would cost them their relatively favorable social position as well.

Under the leadership of Morelos, a mestizo priest, delegates of provinces dedicated to the revolution convened a congress in Chilpancingo from September to November 1813. Though they declared independence from Spain and the seizure of Spanish lands, drawing up a constitution, Morelos was captured by the Spanish and executed for treason in 1815. The revolution struggled over the next five years, with sporadic guerilla warfare and pockets of resistance but no major victories against the Spanish.

In 1820, a liberal constitution went into force in Spain, changing the course of the revolution. The criollos decided that the time was right to support Mexican independence, as the Spanish constitution was not friendly to their interests and denied them full representation. The leader of the criollos, Agustín de Iturbide, met with the leader of the insurgency, Guerrero, and they issued a call to arms for all Mexicans in 1821, calling their combined force the Army of the Three Guarantees, which was representative of their goals that Mexico would be an independent monarchy, that criollos would have equal rights to the Spanish, and that Catholicism would be the established religion of an independent Mexico with the church retaining its rights and lands. These principals were outlined in an agreement signed in the city of Iguala, known as the Plan of Iguala. The establishment of an independent Mexico under the religious leadership of the Catholic Church was enough to bring the disparate factions together, and the combined army was able to force the Spanish viceroy to accept their terms. The Treaty of Córdoba, which formalized the Plan of Iguala, was signed on August 24, 1821, establishing an independent Mexico as a constitutional monarchy.

Co-signatory of the treaty, Agustín de Iturbide. Image via Wikimedia Commons. [Public domain.]

Document Information

The Treaty of Córdoba was signed on August 24, 1821, in Córdoba, Veracruz, Mexico. It was signed by Agustín de Iturbide, head of the Army of the Three Guarantees, and Juan O'Donojú, as a representative of the Spanish government. It was signed in duplicate, with each side retaining one original. The Spanish legislature did not accept the treaty or the Plan of Iguala upon which it was based until 1836.

Historical Document

Treaty of Córdoba

Agreement on the Independent Kingdom of Mexico

24 Aug 1821

Treaty concluded in the Town of Cordova on the 24th of August, 1821, between Don Juan O'Donnoju, Lieutenant-General of the Armies of Spain, and Don Augustin de Iturbide, First Chief of the Imperial Mexican Army of the "Three Guarantees."

New Spain having declared herself independent of the mother country; possessing an army to support this declaration; her provinces having decided in its favour; the capital wherein the legitimate authority had been deposed being besieged; the cities of Vera Cruz and Acapulco alone remaining to the European government ungarrisoned, and without the means of resisting a well directed siege of any duration, Lieut.-Gen. Don Juan O'Donnoju arrived at the first, named port in the character and quality of Captain General and first political chief of this kingdom, appointed by his most Catholic Majesty, and being desirous of avoiding the evils that necessarily fall upon the people in changes of this description, and of reconciling the interests of Old and New Spain, he invited the First Chief of the imperial army, Don Augustin de Iturbide to an interview in order to discuss the great question of independence, disentangling without destroying the bonds which had connected the two Continents. This interview took place in the town of Cordova, on the 24th of August, 1821, and the former under the character with which he came invested, and the latter as representing the Mexican empire, having conferred at large upon the interests of each nation, looking to their actual condition and to recent occurrences, agreed to the following Articles, which they signed in duplicate, for their better preservation, each party keeping an original for greater security and validity.

1st. This kingdom of America shall be recognised as a sovereign and independent nation; and shall, in future, be called the Mexican Empire.

2d. The government of the empire shall be monarchical, limited by a constitution.

3d. Ferdinand VII, catholic king of Spain, shall, in the first place, be called to the throne of the Mexican Empire, (on taking the oath prescribed in the 10th Article of the plan,) and on his refusal and denial, his brother, the most serene infante Don Carlos; on his refusal and denial, the most serene infante Don Francisco de Paula; on his refusal and denial, the most serene Don Carlos Luis, infante of Spain, formely heir of Tuscany, now of Lucca; and upon his renunciation and denial, the person whom thp cortes of the empire shall designate.

4th. The emperor shall fix his court in Mexico, which shall be the capital of the empire.

5th. Two commissioners shall be named by his excellency Senor O'Donnoju, and these shall proceed to the court of Spain, and place in the hands of his Majesty king Ferdinand VII, a copy of this treaty, and a memorial which shall accompany it, for the purpose of affording information to his Majesty with respect to antecedent circumstances, whilst the cortes of the empire offier him the crown with all the formalities and guarantees which a matter of so much importance requires; and they supplicate his Majesty, that on the occurrence of the case provided for in Article 3, he would be pleased to communicate it to the most serene infantes called to the crown in the same article, in the order in which they are so named; and that his Majesty would be pleased to interpose his influence and prevail on one of the members of his august family to proceed to this empire, inasmuch as the prosperity of both nations would be thereby promoted, and as the Mexicans would feel satisfaction in thus strengthening the bands of friendship, with which they may be, and wish to see themselves, united to the Spaniards.

6th. Conformably to the spirit of the "Plan of Iguala," an assembly shall be immediately named, composed of men the most eminent in the empire for their virtues, their station, rank, fortune, and influence; men marked out by the general opinion, whose number may be stifficiently considerable to insure by their collective knowledge the safety of the resolutions which they may take in pursuance of the powers and authority granted them by the following articles.

7th. The assembly mentioned in the preceding article shall be called the 11 Provisional Junta of Government."

8th. Lientenant-General Don Juan O'Donnoju shall be a member of the Provisional Junta of Government, in consideration of its being expedient that a person of his rank should take an active and immediate part in the government, and of the indispensable necessity of excluding some of the individuals mentioned in the above Plan of Iguala, conformably to its own spirit.

9th. The Provisional Junta of Government shall have a president elected by itself from its own body, or from without it, to be determined by the absolute plurality of votes; and if on the first scrutiny the votes be found equal, a second scrutiny shall take place, which shall embrace those two who shall have received the greatest number of votes. sdct

10th. The first act of the Provisional Junta shall be the drawing up of a manifesto of its installation, and the motives of its assemblage, together with whatever explanations it may deem convenient and proper for the information of the country, with respect to the public interests, and the mode to be adopted in the election of deputies for the cortes, of which more shall be said hereafter.

11th. The Provisional Junta of Government after the election of its president, shall name a regency composed of three persons selected from its own body, or from without it, in whom shall be vested the executive power, and who shall govern in the name and on behalf of the monarch till the vacant throne be filled.

12th. The Provisional Junta as soon as it is installed, shall govern ad interim according to the existing laws, so far as they may not be contrary to the "Plan of Iguala," and until the cortes shall have framed the constitution of the state.

13th. The regency immediately on its nomination, shall proceed to the convocation of the cortes in the manner which shall be prescribed by the Provisional Junta of Government, conformably to the spirit of Article No. 7 in the aforesaid "Plan."

14th. The executive power is vested in the regency, and the legislative in the cortes; but as some time must elapse before the latter can assemble, and in order that the executive and legislative powers should not remain in the hands of one body, the junta shall be empowered to legislate; in the first place, where cases occur which are too pressing to wait till the assemblage of the cortes, and then the junta shall proceed in concert with the regency; and, in the second place, to assist the regency in its determinations in the character of an auxiliary and consultative body.

15th. Every individual who is domiciled amongst any community, shall, on an alteration taking place in the system of government, or on the country passing under the dominion of another prince, be at full liberty to remove himself, together with his effects, to whatever country he chooses, without any person having the right to deprive him of such liberty, unless he have contracted some obligation with the community to which lie had belonged, by the commission of a crime, or by any other of those modes which publicists have laid down; this applies to the Europeans residing in New Spain, and to the Americans residing in the Peninsula. Consequently it will be at their option to remain, adopting either country, or to demand their passports, (which cannot be denied them,) for permission to leave the kingdom at such time as may be appointed before-hand, carrying with them their families and property; but paying on the latter the regular export duties now in force, or which may hereafter be established by the competent authority.

16th. The option granted in the foregoing article shall not extend to persons in public situations, whether civil or military, known to be disaffected to Mexican independence; such persons shall necessarily quits the empire within the time which shall be allotted by the regency, taking with them their effects after having paid the duties, as stated in the preceding article.

17th. The occupation of the capital by the Peninsular troops being an obstacle to the execution of this treaty, it is indispensable to have it removed. But as the Commander-in-Chief of the imperial army fully participating in the sentiments of the Mexican nation, does not wish to attain this object by force, for which, however, he has more than ample means at his command, notwithstanding the known valour and constancy of the Peninsular troops, who are not in a situation to maintain themselves against the system adopted by the nation at large, Don Juan O'Donnoju agrees to exercise his authority for the evacuation of the capital by the said troops without loss of blood, and upon the terms of an honourable capitulation.

AGUSTIN DE ITURBIDE, JUAN O'DONNOJU. (A true copy.)

JOSE DOMINGUEZ.
Dated in the Town of Cordova,
24th August, 1821 *sdct*

Document Analysis

The Treaty of Córdoba begins with a declaration of Mexican independence and the assurance of the military strength to defend the claim. The introduction then provides context for the declaration, explaining that the provinces have decided in favor of independence, the capital is under siege, and there are only two cities that have not yet capitulated. Under these circumstances, O'Donojú and Iturbide, as representatives of the two sides and their armies, have met and agreed to the articles that make up the remainder of the treaty.

The first articles lay out the structure of the new "Mexican Empire." It is to be a sovereign, independent nation governed by a constitutional monarch—preferably King Ferdinand of Spain, but if he will not accept, any of his brothers or another member of his family. The document goes on to emphasize that the selection of a Spanish monarch for Mexico will allow some measure of unity with Spain, though Mexico will continue to be an independent nation.

While the nation waits to formally install its monarch and present King Ferdinand with the treaty, Mexico will be run by a Provisional Governing Junta, "composed of men the most eminent in the empire for their virtues, their station, rank, fortune, and influence." Members will select a president for the junta as well as regents until the question of which Spanish royal will be sent to rule is settled. Lengthy articles outline the responsibilities of the junta, which will have executive power through its designated regents if an emperor is not sent over fairly quickly; these duties include exercising legislative power until the parliament has its next meeting.

The final articles detail the freedom of movement allowed for Mexicans in Spain and vice versa, and calls for the evacuation of Mexico City by Spanish troops, who "are not in a situation to maintain themselves against the system adopted by the nation at large," in order to ensure a peaceful settlement.

Essential Themes

On September 27, 1821, the Army of the Three Guarantees, under the command of Iturbide, marched triumphantly into Mexico City. Iturbide acted quickly to consolidate the power of the criollos, and the coalition that had won Mexico its independence quickly unraveled. The "Mexican Empire" was still without an emperor, and after the Spanish legislature refused to recognize the validity of the Treaty of Córdoba, Iturbide declared himself the emperor of Mexico as Agustin I. As he was a deeply unpopular ruler, however, opposition to his reign coalesced around Antonio López de Santa Anna, who opposed Iturbide's refusal to adhere to the new Mexican constitution. Santa Anna joined forces with Iturbide's former allies in the insurgency and called for the overthrow of the emperor and the establishment of an independent republic. Iturbide abdicated and fled to Europe in March 1823 but returned to Mexico in 1824. He was captured and executed on July 15, 1824, and the first Mexican Republic was established by Santa Anna.

Spain repeatedly attempted to reconquer Mexico. In September 1829, the Battle of Pueblo Viejo was a disastrous loss for the Spanish and marked the last attempt to return the former colony to Spain. Seven years later, on December 28, 1836, the Santa María–Calatrava Treaty recognized Mexican independence. Mexico was the first Spanish colony to successfully free itself of Spanish control.

—*Bethany Groff Dorau, MA*

Bibliography and Additional Reading

Henderson, Timothy J. *The Mexican Wars for Independence*. New York: Hill, 2009.

McFarlane, Anthony. *War and Independence in Spanish America*. New York: Routledge, 2008.

Young, Eric Van. *The Other Rebellion: Popular Violence, Ideology, and the Mexican Struggle for Independence, 1810–1821*. Stanford: Stanford UP, 2001.

■ Documents relating to the Canadian Rebellions, 1837-1838

Date: 1837-1838
Authors: Various
Genre: letter; charter

Summary Overview

In the late 1830s, both Upper Canada (much of modern-day Ontario) and Lower Canada (much of modern-day Quebec and Labrador) saw an armed insurgency against the British Crown and calls for greater political power among the people in the colonies. Although they were separate events led by leaders with separate agendas, these two insurgencies helped forge a national identity that ultimately led to a more unified Canadian identity. Beginning in the 1820s in Lower Canada, Louis-Joseph Papineau led a group of French Canadian nationalists known as the Patriotes in a sometimes violent effort to advocate for an elected legislature. In Upper Canada, meanwhile, a Scottish immigrant named William Lyon Mackenzie and his followers sought a government less beholden to immigrants coming from Britain, advocating instead land rights for those already living in Canada.

What united the two movements was the push for so-called responsible government: government for the benefit of the people rather than for the benefit of the mother country. Though neither of the revolts immediately achieved their aims, and although both Upper and Lower Canada had large numbers of residents who supported the British Crown, they did eventually lead to the significant reforms contained in 1) the 1839 Durham Report, which recommended responsible government and the unification of the two colonies; 2) the 1840 British North America Act, which accomplished that unification and began the process of establishing responsible government; and, eventually, 3) the 1867 British North America Act, which created Canada as a separate nation.

William Lyon MacKenzie, c. 1850. Photo via Wikimedia Commons. [Public domain.]

Defining Moment

In both parts of Canada, Upper Canada (much of modern-day Ontario) and Lower Canada (much of modern-day Quebec), the British crown authorities, represented by the Lieutenant-Governor and other office holders, were seen by many of the ordinary residents as being aligned with the wealthy families of the colonies. To combat the power of the oligarchy, opposition seeking popular reform emerged in Upper Canada in the guise of William Lyon Mackenzie, and in Lower Canada under the leadership of Louis-Joseph Papineau. Both wanted to see a government more aligned with the democratic ideals that were sweeping through both the Americas and much of Europe during the early nineteenth century. The response to the rebellion in Lower Canada was the imposition of absolute rule by the Crown authorities, which only exacerbated the conflict. In Upper Canada, elections in 1836 saw accusations of fraud on the part of Lieutenant-Governor, Sir Francis Bond Head, which saw reformers such as Mackenzie and Lount lose seats to which they claimed to have been fairly elected. These actions only reinforced the idea that the British Crown governments of the two colonies were not legitimate representatives of the people.

At this same time, an economic downturn caused many farmers in the region to fall upon hard times, and banks calling in the debts they owed only made the situation worse. The banks, and by extension the families that ran them, were seen as enemies of the people and were acting for the oligarchy against the people. In both colonies, rebel leaders organized groups to speak out against this oppression. In Lower Canada, the Patriotes organized into the Société des Fils de la Liberté (translated the "Sons of Liberty" – the same name as the prominent group in the years before the American Revolution), and in Upper Canada, Mackenzie started the Toronto Political Union. These groups educated people on the issues, encouraged protests, and finally led them into rebellion.

In Lower Canada, Papineau and the Patriotes demanded that the revenue and expenditures of the colony be controlled by the people rather than by the Crown government and the Château Clique. The idea of Responsible Government – government that sought to benefit all of the people – went against the British system of nobility, and they were rejected both by the Crown government in Canada and the British government. Protests began in earnest during the 1830s, and armed battles between the Patriotes and a combination of British troops and English-speaking volunteers. However, the Patriotes were not well-organized, and they were quickly defeated, and the Patriote leaders – including Papineau – fled to the United States. They sought to regain their momentum with the help of American volunteers in November 1838, but were again defeated.

The main figure in the rebellion in Upper Canada, Mackenzie, was inspired by the rebels in Lower Canada, and used his position as a newspaper publisher to

Louis-Joseph Papineau; portrait, c. 1840. Image by Napoléon Aubin, via Wikimedia Commons.

spread news and opinion regarding the Crown government and the Family Compact. Favoring closer ties with the United States rather than Britain, Mackenzie quickly ran afoul of the Colonial government. In 1837, Mackenzie and his followers attempted to take control of the colony and declare a new nation. However, the rebels were poorly-armed, and were quickly dispersed by militia loyal to the Crown government. Like the leaders of the rebellion in Lower Canada, Mackenzie and other leaders fled to the United States, where they continued to launch attacks against the Crown government in Upper Canada. However, the rebellion gradually subsided after Mackenzie left for the U.S.

Author Biography

The variety of documents presented here precludes making blanket statements regarding their origins,

The Battle of Saint-Eustache, a decisive battle in the Lower Canada Rebellion, 1837. Image via Wikimedia Commons. [Public domain.]

as each of them is the product of different authors writing for different reasons. Robert Nelson, the author of the Declaration of Independence of the Republic of Lower Canada, was a physician and one of the Anglo leaders of the Patriotes. The author of the letter from "James Buchanan" to Sir George Arthur, the Lieutenant Governor of Upper Canada, could have either been the future U.S. President (who was, at that time, a U.S. Senator from Pennsylvania) or a British lawyer who served as the British Consul at New York from 1816 until 1843. The anonymous author of the letter to Arthur was clearly opposed to the system of British patronage represented by the so-called Family Compact. The notes taken in the Executive Council Minute come from Arthur's own papers. The Chief Justice referenced in the letters is Sir John Beverley Robinson, who served as Chief Justice of Upper Canada from 1829 until Upper Canada transformed into Canada West in 1841. Finally, Lord Glenelg was the British Secretary of State for War and the Colonies during 1835-1839.

Historical Document

Declaration of Independence of the Republic of Lower Canada

November 4, 1838

Whereas the solemn compact made with the people of Lower Canada and registered in the book of statutes of the United Kingdom of Great Britain and Ireland, the 31st chapter of the Acts passed in the 31st year of the reign of George III, has been continually violated by the British Government and our rights usurped; and whereas our humble petitions, addresses, protests, and complaints against this prejudicial and unconstitutional conduct have been in vain; and whereas the British government has disposed of our revenue without the constitutional consent of our local legislature, that it has pillaged our treasury, that it has arrested and imprisoned a great number of our fellow citizens, that it has spread throughout the country a mercenary army whose presence is accompanied by consternation and alarm, whose path has been reddened by the blood of our people, that has reduced our villages to ashes, profaned the temples, and spread terror and desolation throughout the land; and whereas we can no longer put up with the repeated violations of our most cherished rights or patiently bear the multiple outrages and cruelties of the government of Lower Canada; We, in the name of the people of Lower Canada, recognizing the decrees of Divine Providence that permit us to overthrow a government that has violated the object and the intention of its creation, and to choose the form of government that will re-establish the reign of justice, assure domestic tranquillity, assure the common defense, increase general well-being, and guarantee for ourselves and our posterity the advantages of civil and religious freedom;

Solemnly declare:

That from this day forward the people of Lower Canada are absolved of all allegiance to Great Britain, and that all political ties between that power and Lower Canada have ceased as of this day;

That Lower Canada shall take the form of a republican government and, as such, declare itself a Republic;

That under the free Government of Lower Canada all citizens will have the same rights; the savages will cease being subjected to any form of civil disqualifications and will enjoy the same rights as the other citizens of the State of Lower Canada;

That all ties between Church and State are declared abolished, and every person has the right to freely exercise the religion and the beliefs dictated to him by his conscience;

That feudal and *Seigneurial* tenure are abolished in fact, as if they never existed in this country;

That any person who bears or will bear arms, or will furnish the means of assistance to the Canadian People in its struggle for emancipation, is relieved of all debts or obligations, real or supposed, towards *Seigneurs*, and for *arriérages** in virtue of *Seigneurial* laws* that formerly existed.

That the *douaire coutoumier* is, in future, entirely abolished and prohibited;

That imprisonment for debt will no longer exist, except in cases of obvious fraud, which will be specified in an act of the Legislature of Lower Canada to that effect;

That the death penalty will be pronounced in cases of murder alone, and no other;

That all mortgages on lands must be special and, in order to be valid, must be registered in Offices created to that effect by an act of the legislature of Lower Canada;

That there will be full and entire freedom of the press in all public affairs and matters;

That trial by jury is guaranteed to the People of the State in criminal trials to its most liberal extent, and in civil affairs to the sum of an amount to be determined by the legislature of the State of Lower Canada;

That as a necessity and obligation of the Government towards the people, public and general education will be put in operation and encouraged in a special manner, as soon as circumstances permit;

That in order to ensure the franchise and electoral freedom, all elections will be held in the form of a ballot;

That as soon as circumstances permit, the People will choose its Delegates following the current division of the country in cities, towns and counties, which will constitute a Convention or Legislative body, in order to found and establish a constitution, according to the needs of the country and in conformity with the conditions of this Declaration, subject to modification according to the will of the people;

That any male person over the age of 21 will have the right to vote as above mentioned, for the election of the above-named delegates;

That those lands called Crown lands, as well as those called Reservations of the Clergy and those nominally in the possession of a certain company of speculators in England, called the "Company of the Lands of British North America" shall become by law the property of the State of Lower Canada, except for those portions of land that are in the possession of farmers who hold them in good faith, for which we guarantee the title in virtue of a law which will be passed in order to legalize the possession of such lots of land situated in the Townships which are now under cultivation;

That French and English will be used in all public matters.

And for the support of this declaration, and the success of the Patriotic cause that we support, we, confident of the protection of the All-Powerful and of the justice of our line of conduct, engage by these present, mutually and solemnly the ones towards the others, our lives, our fortunes, and our most sacred honor.

By order of the Provisional Government

Robert Nelson
President

**arriérages:* The amount due on the rent of a farm.

*Seigneurial laws: That which the husband assigns to the wife for her use should she survive him.

Documents concerning the Rebellion in Upper Canada

[LETTER *from James Buchanan to Sir George Arthur, Lieutenant-Governor of Upper Canada (March 10, 1838; Marked "private Confidential")*]

I question whether my Loyalty would lead me to take this liberty, yet did I regard British interests more than my private interests, I would run the risk, of speaking openly for where are [sic] your Excellency to look but to those deeply interested in the success of your Measures, - I have stated no man is more interested in the general prosperity - others have family interests to promote, other have office or power in View, all of these I disclaim but my firm Conviction is, that the Colony will be lost to the Empire, if the people are not led to believe that the Queen Governs, and not - the family - Independent Men will keep aloft from your Excellency - You have all the tools to work with, which have too long prevailed, and without appearing to oppose, they will thwart every act, which is not in accordance with the interests of those who pull the same rope - I feel in the duty I owe my Sovereign and my family, I have done my duty in this Very frank statement; had I done less I might have reproached myself - I ventured to name Mr. Neilson he is too independent and will not obtrude upon your Excellency, but perhaps no other Man in Upper Canada stands so free from all parties - his determination is to leave the Province unless he sees a change - I do not know who he is aquatinted with at Toronto. - his address is The Honl. Robert Neilson Lake View Stoney Creek near Hamilton, - he wants no office, favor or Appointments for any, and if he leaves the province the Consequence will be that many will also withdraw.

Pardon Sir this letter - I shall never again presume to repeat these Sentiments- I feel I have done my duty, - and I pray your Excellency to pardon the Manner of doing it...

[P.S.] The family Compact: Robinsons, Jones's, McCauleys [sic], Bo[u]ltons, Archdean Strachan - Majors; All men in office in the Province through the above influence Legislative Council Included - Minors.

[LETTER from Anonymous to Sir George Arthur, Lieutenant-Governor of Upper Canada (Toronto, March 27, 1838)]

The errors of your predecessors, and more particularly Sir Francis Bond Head, have all originated in holding to a certain party in this Province which has been its ruin. I pray that you may be able to discern that Party, and all other Parties, and avoid them, do equal justice to all act upon the broad Principles of impartiality and you will make us a Contented People, and you will heal the sore wounds which have been inflicted upon this unfortunate Colony by Sir F. B. Head, Hagerman, Draper and Co - You will be surrounded by them, and their cunning devices to entrap you, Beware of them, they are unwise, and treacherous professors full of deceit. They are latent enemies of our enlightened ministry who have sent you here. The Chief Justice is at the head of what is called the Family Compact, which is as overbearing as it is wicked. You have unsafe Executive Councillors, Mr. Sullivan who is the first, is a man without character or influence, who has been amongst the Ranks of the worst of Radicals, elevated by Sir Francis Bond Head from the very dregs of Society, who should not have been any other than the trade of a Tallow Chandler, whose father was in a very small way not many years ago. The Comfort, the prosperity of us depends on you, and if you avoid The Shoals of the Family Compact, you will find your situation a happy one - Beware of the Smooth and Silvery tongue of the Chief Justice, Keep your eye on Hagerman, Draper, Robinson's and Boulton's. Pause, and look well before you act on their opinions, for on every case, rest assured they have their own purposes to serve. - The Chief Justice wrote the "address to Sir Francis Bond Head" for the Legislative Council, on hearing of your appointment to this Government, and also the state of the Province, and Hagerman wrote the state of the Province for the House of Assembly. Read these documents. In truth these People plunged the Province into Rebellion, and Sir Francis Bond Head has been a Tool in their hands. I warn you again to beware of them, and remember that you have Mr. Joseph about you Son in Law to this Mr. Hagerman. It is a misfortune which the Province hope and trust you will remove. He is an unfit person for such a situation, all that transpires will be communicated to the Party.

I am in sincerity Your well wisher and Subject.

[EXECUTIVE COUNCIL MINUTE (Toronto, March 31, 1838)]

...The Honorable The Chief Justice being in attendance was called in, and His Excellency having communicated to him the Documents above enumerated, was pleased to request his Opinion as to the necessity of Capital punishments for High Treason, commited during the late revolt and to what extent the actual State of the Province required that such punishment should be inflicted, and also as to the time when it would be most calculated to be of public benefit to carry the Sentences of the Courts into effect in cases in which it would be considered that the Royal mercy ought not to be extended. The Chief Justice stated, that in his Opinion is was necessary for the ends of Justice, and due to the Loyal Inhabitants of the Province, that some examples should be made in the way of Capital punishments. He also said that he conceived the extent to which this was actually required to be done would be very limited. The Chief Justice was of Opinion that all the good to arise from carrying Sentences of death into effect, would be lost by the delay which must take place, if references were had to Her Majesty and that however his feelings might lead him to give the unfortunate Convicts every chance of Mercy, he felt himself bound by an imperative sense of public duty, not to advise such a reference in all cases.

His Excellency was pleased to ask the Opinion of The Chief Justice as to whether it would be legal or proper for the Government after selecting for prosecution and punishment those whose cases might be considered as most Aggravated and requiring exemplary punishment to direct a Stay of proceedings against others until the pleasure of Her Majesty should be known?

The Chief Justice answered, that an interference with the ordinary course of Justice, on the part of the Government and without Parliamentary Sanction was liable to many objections, but that before giving any decided recommendation he would take pains to inform himself more fully as to the course usually pursued on like occasions, and that he would if it was His Excellency's pleasure, wait upon His Excellency in Council at such time as His Excellency should desire his attendance.

Upon which The Lieutenant Governor informed the Chief Justice that it was his intention to meet his Council on Monday next at Noon and would feel obliged by Chief Justice's attendance.

His Excellency was pleased to require the attendance of the Attorney General, and on that Officer appearing, His Excellency proposed to him the same questions as had been before asked of the Chief Justice, and moreover directed his attention to the Cases of the two Convicts reported by the Chief Justice to be under Sentences of death.

[Chief Justice's Address to Samuel Lount and Peter Matthews (Christian Guardian, Toronto, April 4, 1838)]

On Thursday, the 29th March instant, SAMUEL LOUNT and PETER MATTHEWS, who on the preceding Monday had pleaded GUILTY to the Indictment preferred against them for HIGH TREASON, were again placed at the BAR, when the ATTORNEY GENERAL moved for Judgement against them. Silence having been proclaimed, HIS HONOR, the CHIEF JUSTICE, pronounced the awful sentence of the LAW, preceded by the following impressive Address:

SAMUEL LOUNT and PETER MATTHEWS!

You have been arraigned upon several indictments charging you with High Treason. In accordance with the humane provisions of our law, many days have necessaraly elapsed between the time of your being indicted and arraigned; and in that interval you were furnished with full and exact copies of charges preferred against you, together with lists of the witnesses by whom those charges were to be proved, and with the names of the jurors who were to pronounce upon the awful question of your guilt or innocence. Having had all these advantadges for disproving the charge, if that were possible, you have each of you upon your arraignment pleaded "guilty"; that is, you have confessed that upon the day named in the indictments, you were in arms against your SOVEREIGH, and did traitorously levy war in this Province, for the purpose of subverting the constitution and government.

We have no discretion to exercise. The awful sentence of death must follow your conviction. But although a power to pardon resides only in the SOVEREIGN whose authority you endeavoured to subvert, if I could conscientiously encourage in you a hope that pardon would be extended, I should gladly do so - .. I know no grounds, however, on which I can venture to hold out such a hope; and I do therefore most earnestly exhort you to prepare yourselves for the execution of the sentence which is about to be pronounced. In the short time which may remain to you, I pray that you may be brought to a deep sense of the guilt of the crime of which you are convicted; and that may be enabled to address yourselves in humble and earnest sincerity to the infinite mercy of the SAVIOUR whose divine commands you have transgressed...

[LETTER from Sir George Arthur, Lieutenant-Governor of Upper Canada to Sir John Colborne (Toronto, April 5, 1838; marked "Private")]

...With such a body of Prisoners in Jail, and such numbers out on bail; together with the embarrassment which arises from the terms of the Proclamation which have been issued; and the Act of the Provincial Parliament which has been passed- the strong desire of many that the severest punishment should be inflicted, and the wish of others that it should be mitigated - you may imagine that the commencement of my campaign here is at least troublesome and anxious.

After a week's anxious consideration in the Executive Council, I hope a Majority of Members are brought over to the opinion that it is possible, consistently with a due regard to Public justice, to extend Pardons very largely, and not to proceed to trial with the Multitude of cases which have been presented by the Grand Jury. In some cases, however, in which the Prisoners were actually parties to Murder and arson, the Law must take its course, and two of the most guilty are now under sentence and will be executed on the 12th Inst.

...Sir Francis Head persuaded himself that there was a general loyal feeling here - Certainly there was a gratifying exhibition of Loyalty at the moment to put down that worthless creature McKenzie; and, no doubt there is a very considerable body of excellent persons well affected towards the Constitution - but, what has become of the Numbers who for years have been known as Reformers, and very disaffected ones too? Where are the persons who returned a Majority of Reformers to the House of Assembly, and elected McKenzie Mayor of Toronto?...

[LETTER from Anonymous to Sir George Arthur, Lieutenant-Governor of Upper Canada (Toronto, April 26, 1838)]

Revenge Revenge I Say
Bee gon Bee gon I Say
Or I Will Putt you in that
Place Whare you Will never return
you shall die a villains deth you
are marker out for mark that Shall
Bee onerd by a Pill Whitch Shall make
Hole in your body

I am Sir Your Most Obedient Friend

[DISPATCH from Lord Glenelg to Sir George Arthur (London, May 30, 1838)]

I have received your despatch of the 14th April last, reporting the execution, on the 12th of that month, of Lount and Matthews, who had been convicted, on their own confession, of "high treason," and explaining, at considerable length, the views adopted by yourself and the Executive Council with regard to these prisoners, and the considerations which appeared to you imperatively to demand that the law in this case should be allowed to take its course.

Her Majesty's Government regret extremely that a paramount necessity should have arisen for these examples of severity. They are, however, fully convinced that you did not consent to the execution of these individuals without having given the most ample consideration to all the circumstances of the case, and they have no reason to doubt the necessity of the course which, with the entire concurrence of the Executive Council, you felt it your duty to adopt.

With respect to the disposal of the other prisoners, Her Majesty's Government cannot give you any specific instructions, until they shall have received the report which you lead me to expect. But I cannot defer expressing our earnest hope that, with respect to these persons, your opinion that no further capital punishments will be necessary, may have been acted on. Nothing would cause, her Majesty's Goverment, more sincere regret than an unnecessary recourse to the punishment of death, and I am persuaded that the same feeling will influence not only yourself, but the Executive Council. The examples which have been made in the case of the most guilty will be sufficient to warn others of the consequences to which they render themselves liable by such crimes, and this object having been accomplished, no further advantage could be gained by inflicting the extreme penalty of the law on any of their associates.

Glossary

civil disqualifications: removal of social and political rights, such as voting

douaire coutoumier: a practice in Lower Candada that granted property to upper-class widows, while freeing her from any debts incurred by her husband

seigneurial tenure: a system of land ownership dominated by nobles

usurp: to take away, unfairly, a power that rightly belongs to someone else

Document Analysis

The documents presented speak both to the aims of the rebellions in Upper and Lower Canada, as well as to the reactions to the rebellions both from the Crown officials in Canada and the members of the British government itself. Upper and Lower Canada differed in many ways – especially in the desire of many in Lower Canada for independence based upon a differing linguistic and ethnic background. However both governments represented the Crown of Great Britain, and were modeled on the British idea of a balance between the power of the monarchy (represented by the Lieutenant-Governor of the colony), the aristocracy (represented by the oligarchy of the leading families in the colony, known as the Family Compact in Upper Canada and the Château Clique in Lower Canada), and democratic institutions to represent the interests of the people. The rebels in both colonies considered that the present governments of Upper and Lower Canada were beholden to the Crown and the oligarchs, and did not represent the will and welfare of the people in any meaningful ways.

The Declaration of Independence of Lower Canada was written by an English-speaking resident of predominately French-speaking Lower Canada (modern-day Quebec), Robert Nelson. Nelson articulated what he and the other leaders of the rebellion, such as Louis-Joseph Papineau, were working to accomplish, namely independence from the British crown. However, it also went on to enumerate the rights of the residents of Lower Canada. Largely modeled on the United States Declaration of Independence, it outlined what the Patriotes saw as the basic rights of citizenship, such as a separation of Church and State, the doing away with of forms of property holding that smacked of patronage and rights of the nobility, the banning of imprisonment for fraud, and the limitation of the death penalty. It also included many of the guarantees contained in many such documents of the late eighteenth and early nineteenth centuries: freedom of the press, trial by jury, the government's role in promoting the welfare of the people, the right to vote, and the formation of a legislative body to represent the people.

The two letters to Sir George Arthur, Lieutenant-Governor of Upper Canada written during March 1838 were both written to encourage Arthur to do something about the system of patronage against which William Lyon Mackenzie and his followers were rebelling. Both letters refer to the Family Compact, the system of the granting of both public position and land rights to families of wealth, who saw themselves as the Canadian equivalent to the British nobility. Opposition to the Family Compact is one of the foremost commonalities between rebels in Upper and Lower Canada.

In both the Executive Council Minute and the Chief Justice's Address, the Crown officials in Canada are discussing what should be done with the leaders of the rebellions. The Chief Justice of Upper Canada, Sir John Beverley Robinson, was the head of one of the notable families benefitting from the Family Compact, and his view of the rebel leaders was that they had committed treason against the British Crown and should be executed. Robinson then addresses two of the leaders, Samuel Lount and Peter Matthews, informing them of their death sentence and again condemning their actions.

George Arthur's letter to Sir John Colborne shows that Arthur realizes that a large-scale punishment of the people who participated with Mackenzie's rebellion would be untenable and should be avoided. At the same time, however, Arthur is wary of the reassertion of rebel ideas held by many of the residents of Upper Canada. This is only reinforced by the anonymous letter to Arthur on April 26, 1838, which articulates a desire for revenge among some in the Canadian public.

Finally, in the aftermath of the rebellions, Lord Glenelg writes to Arthur to reinforce to him the support of the British Crown for the actions he undertook to subdue the rebellions. Specifically, Glenelg comments upon the execution of the rebel leaders, stating that the British government was "fully convinced that you did not consent to the execution of these individuals without having given the most ample consideration to all the circumstances of the case, and they have no reason to doubt the necessity of the course which, with the entire concurrence of the Executive Council, you felt it your duty to adopt." That said,

Glenelg tells Arthur that he hopes that no further executions will be necessary, and that the examples made of the rebel leaders will serve the purpose of restoring order in the colony.

Essential Themes

The rebellions of 1838 in Upper and Lower Canada resulted in approximately 300 rebel deaths and the deaths of 27 British soldiers. Rebel leaders on both sides were exiled in the United States, with Mackenzie living in New York from 1838 until 1849, when he was granted a pardon and allowed to return to Canada. Papineau left initially for the United States, eventually resettling in exile in Paris. As the rebellions took place, a British Whig politician named John George Lambton (First Earl of Durham) arrived in Canada to investigate. The report he produced, known as the Durham Report, outlined the motives of the two rebellions and what they sought to achieve. Though he underestimated the democratic impulse of the Lower Canada rebellion, attributing it primarily to linguistic and ethnic differences, he outlined the need for Responsible Government in both of the colonies.

The rebellions in Upper and Lower Canada both reflected a divided population, much as the American Revolution exacerbated the differences between the patriots and the loyalists. In Lower Canada, many supported Papineau and his Patriotes, largely because of the impact of the economic downturn on the farmers of the colony. The group of supporters of Mackenzie's rebellion in Upper Canada was much smaller and largely located in Toronto, which helps explain why the rebellion was subdued much more easily.

In the end, however, the rebellions and the Durham Report that grew out of them were instrumental in the eventual adoption of Responsible Government and other reforms, as well as, eventually, the independence of Canada some thirty years later. Durham recommended the two colonies be combined and that the government be more representative of the people. Though it would be later reformers such as Louis-Hippolyte LaFontaine and Robert Baldwin who would work to create a democratic and united Canada, the ideas that carried the nation to independence in 1867 began with earlier rebel leaders such as Papineau and Mackenzie.

—*Steven L. Danver, PhD*

Bibliography and Additional Reading

Buckner, P.A. *The Transition to Responsible Government: British Policy in British North America 1815-1850.* Westport, CT: Greenwood Press, 1985.

Cameron, David R. "Lord Durham Then and Now." *Journal of Canadian Studies/Revue d'Études Canadiennes* 25:1 (1990).

Greer, Allan. *The Patriots and the People: The Rebellion of 1837 in Rural Lower Canada.* Toronto: University of Toronto Press, 1993.

Martin, Ged. *The Durham Report and British policy: A Critical Essay.* London: Cambridge UP, 1972.

Morton, Desmond. *Rebellions in Canada.* Toronto: Grolier, 1979.

Read, Colin. *The Rising in Western Upper Canada, 1837-8: The Duncombe Revolt and After.* Toronto: University of Toronto Press, 1982.

Read, Colin and Ronald J. Stagg, eds. *The Rebellion of 1837 in Upper Canada: A Collection of Documents.* Ottawa: The Champlain Society and Carleton UP, 1985.

Benito Juárez on *La Reforma*

Date: ca. 1857
Author: Benito Juárez
Genre: autobiography; essay; letter

Summary Overview

Benito Juárez was one of the central figures of La Reforma, *or the political events in Mexico surrounding reform efforts in the mid-nineteenth century and a push to establish a new constitution culminating in a civil war. On the opposite side of Juárez was the conservative president, Antonio López de Santa Anna, also commonly known as Santa Anna. The document reproduced here represents the private autobiographical notes of Benito Juárez, supposedly written for his children. The period of time discussed in the document is during the early years of Juárez's involvement in the military movement against Santa Anna. Instead of describing battles or strategy, the text describes the build up to the outbreak of war and Juárez's own involvement within the existing governmental structure. Juárez held various political and judicial offices before becoming the 26th president of Mexico. This document seems to have been written just before he took presidential office, possibly while he was serving as Governor of Oaxaca or as President of the Supreme Court, but before* La Reforma *would have reached its conclusion.*

Defining Moment

Benito Juárez is considered to be the founding father of modern Mexico. During his life, he fought for a Mexico that was independent from the tensions remaining from colonial ownership and worked to overcome the scars from the deep-seated racism that Europeans had used to support their own aggressive imperial aspirations. Moreover, Juárez, although born of the indigenous people of Mexico, broke from some of the more traditional aspects of Indian and Hispanic culture, specifically with respect to the power of the church to control all aspects of everyday life. In place of the military's and the church's control over Mexican affairs, Juárez instituted a new federal constitution with a bill of rights for Mexican citizens. Eventually, he was able to put the military under civilian control (instead of under the control of the Mexican leader, as in the case of Santa Anna) and to cut back not only the power of the church but also its property, redistributing the land and offering civil rights to the people.

Benito Juarez, c. 1872. Photo via Wikimedia Commons. [Public domain.]

Liberals posing with a copy of the Constitution of 1857. Photo courtesy of Instituto Nacional de Antropología e Historia, via Wikimedia Commons.

This document was written right at the beginning of this time period and largely reflects on the events that led to *La Reforma,* also called the Liberal Reform. Juárez generally explains events that he witnessed or that were relatively well-known during the time period. While Mexico had already gained its independence from Spain, in 1821, an internal revolution was then afoot. Juárez's words highlight the growing tensions within Mexican society, as it was split between the conservatives and the church on the one hand and the liberals and their reforms on the other. These same tensions played out in a number of other European colonies and in the European homeland, as well. Witness the Revolutions of 1848 in Europe, for example, and the various independence movements elsewhere in Latin America. People across the world were fighting back against the ideology that required the mass of people to be less free in order to support the small but influential aristocracy. In the case of Mexico, the wealthy and the members of the clergy held privileged positions in society, to the detriment of the poor and the indigenous populations. Juárez's text shows the growing concern the author felt over the state of the country and his own internal struggle to find a way to aid his people. At first, he remained part of the system, working in his profession and trying to keep his people from falling into civil war. As time continued, however, Juárez found that more drastic action was needed in order to protect the people from a conservative government that did not, in his view, have their best interests at heart.

Author Biography

Benito Juárez was born on March 21, 1806 in the Oaxaca region of Mexico. His parents and grandparents died when he was a young child, leaving him to be raised by an uncle. They were Zapotec, the name of the indigenous people of Mexico (especially southern Mexico), and worked in fields or as herders. His formal education did not begin until after age twelve, when a Franciscan scholar noticed his intelligence and enrolled him in the local seminary school. Even though Juárez had no interest in becoming a priest or a monk, he used the opportunity to learn as much as he could before pursuing law at the newly founded Institute of Sciences and Art. His largely liberal education at the Institute allowed him to then enter politics and begin a legal career. By the time he married Margarita Maza in 1843, he had already held positions on the local city council and as a judge.

His marriage is of historical significance, because an indigenous man marrying a socially higher-class "white" woman (her family had European descent) was highly unusual at the time, as Mexico was separated into a type of caste system based on skin color and ethnic descent. Juárez and his wife had twelve children together, in addition to his two children from another relationship before his marriage. Between the years of 1855 and 1872, Juárez held numerous positions within the new reformed government, including Secretary of Public Education, Governor of Oaxaca, Secretary of the Interior, President of the Mexican Supreme Court, and President of Mexico. Juárez and Maza were married until Maza's death in 1871. Juárez passed a year later, on July 18, 1872, while serving as president.

Historical Document

Benito Juárez, Apuntes Para Mis Hijos
[Notes for My Children] (ca. 1857)

In the year 1845, there were held elections of the deputies to the departmental assembly, and I appeared as one of the many candidates who offered themselves to the public. The electors nominated me and I was unanimously elected. Early in 1846, the departmental assembly was dissolved as a result of the military sedition led by General Paredes, who, under orders from the President, don José Joaquín de Herrera to march to the frontier threatened by the American army, pronounced in the hacienda of the Penasco in the state of San Luis Potosí, and countermarched towards the capital of the Republic, in order to seize the government, which he did, submitting himself completely to the direction of the monarchist-conservative party. The liberal party did not concede defeat. Aided by the Santa Anna party, it worked actively until it succeeded in overturning the reactionary administration of Paredes and in installing General don Mariano Salas provisionally in the Presidency of the Republic.

In Oaxaca, the movement against Paredes was supported by General don Juan Bautista Díaz; there was named a Legislative Committee and an Executive Power of three persons who were named by a Committee of Notables. The election fell on don Luis Fernández del Campo, don José Simeon Arteaga, and myself, and we began at once to fulfill the duties with which we had been honored. Informed of this arrangement, the general government decided to dissolve the Legislative Committee, and to entrust the executive power of the state to don José Simeon Arteaga alone. I had to return to my legal post in the prosecutor's office, but Governor Arteaga dissolved it in order to reorganize it with other personnel, and in consequence he proceeded to its reorganization, naming me President or Regent—as at that time was named the presiding officer—of the Tribunal of Justice of the state.

The general government called on the nation to elect its representatives with full powers to revise the constitution of 1824, and I was one of those named for Oaxaca, and so proceeded to the capital of the Republic, to fulfill my new duties, early in December of the same year of 1846. At this time the Republic was already invaded by forces of the United States of the North; the government lacked funds sufficient to set up a defense, and it was necessary for the Congress to afford the means of acquiring them. The deputy for Oaxaca, don Tiburcio Canas, took the initiative in authorizing the government to mortgage part of the properties administered by the clergy, in order to provide resources for the war. The proposal was admitted and then turned over to a special commission, to which I belonged, with the recommendation that it be given prompt attention. On January 10, 1847, a report was made on this matter, advising the adoption of this method, and it was brought up immediately for discussion. The debate was extremely long and heated, because the moderate party, which had a large majority in the chamber, put up a strong opposition to the project. At two in the morning of the 11th, however, the report was approved in general, but in the discussion of the particulars, the opposition presented a multitude of amendments to each of the articles, with the unpatriotic purpose that even when it was finally approved the act would have so many hobbles that it would not produce the result that the congress proposed. At ten in the morning the discussion came to a close with the passage of the law, but for the reasons stated it did not issue with the desired amplitude...

From that moment, the clergy, the moderates, and the conservatives redoubled their efforts to destroy the law and to eject from the Presidency of the Republic don Valentín Gómez Farías, whom they considered the leader of the liberal party. In a few days they succeeded in realizing their desires by inciting to rebellion a part of the city at the moment when our troops were fighting for the nation's independence on the northern frontier and in the city of Veracruz. This mutiny, which was called that of the Polkos, was viewed with indignation by most of the people; and the rebels, thinking that their plan could not succeed by force of their arms, resorted to subversion, and succeeded in winning over General Santa Anna, who commanded the army that had defeated the enemy at La Angostura, and whom the liberal party had just named President of the Republic over the opposition of the moderate and conservative party; but Santa Anna, inconsistent as always, abandoned his men and rushed to Mexico to give the victory to the rebels. These went to the Villa of Guadalupe to receive their protector, with their chests covered with badges of membership in religious orders and relics of saints, as "defenders of religion and the exemptions." Don Valentín Gómez Farías was removed from the Vice-Presidency of the Republic, and the liberal deputies were attacked and denied the reimbursement that the law allowed them for their subsistence in the capital. We deputies from Oaxaca could not receive any help from our state because there the legislature had been destroyed and replaced by those who supported the rebellion of the Polkos; and as a matter of fact the congress was not holding sessions because it lacked a quorum. I decided to go home and dedicate myself to the practice of my profession.

In August of [1847] I arrived in Oaxaca. Although they were persecuted, the liberals were working actively to reestablish the legal order, and in this effort they were authorized by law, for there existed a decree that, on my motion and that of my associates in the deputation from Oaxaca, was passed and sent by the general congress, condemning the mutiny that had occurred in this state and refusing to recognize the authorities established by the rebels; nor did I hesitate to help in any way that I found possible those who worked for the fulfillment of the law, which has always been my sword and my shield.

On November 23rd, we succeeded very well in a movement against the intruding authorities. The President of the Court of Justice, Lic. don Marcos Pérez, took charge of the government; the legislature met and named me Governor pro tempore of the state.

Glossary

pro tempore: temporarily; temporary; for the time being.

quorum: the number of members of a group or organization required to be present to transact business legally, usually a majority.

Document Analysis

This text is the memoir of a man who actively participated in the internal revolution of his government, believing in the ideas of representative leadership and the betterment of the lives of each individual Mexican who had suffered under the burden of poverty and strict social hierarchies. Juárez's description of the events before *La Reforma* fall into two types, those of a local nature and those of a larger, federal nature. Juárez was from Oaxaca and held many positions in the local government, but he was also involved in the movement against the Conservative leadership of the federal Mexican government. He would eventually blend those two capacities in becoming president of Mexico.

In Oaxaca, and in many other Mexican states, the independent governance of the region was often troubled by larger issues within the Mexican government. Once such incident is related at the beginning of this text, when Juárez explains that his duties to his government were suspended during a military coup. Often in the period after the declaration of Mexican Independence in 1821, the rivalries between the conservative and liberal factions would cause turmoil inside and outside the government. The opening paragraphs of this text are full of instances where the government swings between parties, rarely settling under one for any length of time. In addition, each party was likely to declare the other as rebels or acting illegally.

Later, after he was elected as a representative for Oaxaca to the federal government to revise the 1824 constitution, Juárez recounts his view of the renewed Conservative push against a liberal government. "From that moment, the clergy, the moderates, and the conservatives redoubled their efforts to destroy the law and to eject from the Presidency of the Republic don Valentín Gómez Farías, whom they considered the leader of the liberal party." In particular, he states that they intended "to destroy the law." This is an interesting phrase and falls in line with the idea that each faction would see the other as acting illegally. But the terminology itself goes far to show that at this point in his life, Juárez still believed in the power of the law and the governmental system in Mexico. He may not agree with all the decisions made or even with the ideology of the people in power, but he also is not willing to endorse, even implicitly, the instability and/or violence that typically came with rebellion.

At the end of this text, Juárez returns home again to take up his legal practice. "In August of [1847] I arrived in Oaxaca. Although they were persecuted, the liberals were working actively to reestablish the legal order, and in this effort they were authorized by law..." Again, Juárez promotes the idea that legality is a strong factor in his decision making process. In this context, however, the matter is a little more complicated, because with a conservative leader in power, the liberals were by definition the disruptors. They were the rebels. But according to Juárez, he and his fellow lawmakers had passed regional Oaxacan laws in order to promote the liberal cause. In so doing, he finds a way to subvert the very governmental system within which he was working.

Finally, Juárez follows the previous statement with one of his most famous lines: "nor did I hesitate to help in any way that I found possible those who worked *for the fulfillment of the law, which has always been my sword and my shield...*" In declaring the law both a "sword" and a "shield," Juárez shows that he intends to use the law as both an active tool of attack and a form of defensive protection. The phrase is both aggressive and passive in its imagery. Overall, it fits with a man who at times worked within a conservative government in order to protect his people, as well as to overturn that same government—a man who eventually came to lead his country.

Essential Themes

In the years following *La Reforma*, Juárez faced numerous problems both from within Mexico and without. Among the many policies initiated at this time, one policy of *La Reforma* tried to redistribute land in small parcels to the poor and landless. However, this failed rather dramatically, with many wealthy landowners simply buying up the land, increasing their holdings and their influence, and showing little regard for the plight of others. Then, in 1862, the French attempted to assert colonial control over Mexico, now that Spain had lost its sovereignty. After siding with the conservative faction against Juárez, the French eventually withdrew, allowing Juárez to be reelected president in 1867. Unfortunately, an economic recession and day-to-day conditions for many Mexicans did not improve in the following years, and Juárez began to be more and more dictatorial. Members of his own party grew increasingly dissatisfied with his rule, in part because the dream of a better Mexico had failed to materialize under their leadership.

La Reforma is an interesting occurrence in history, mainly because the revolution did not come entirely from outside the government. Instead, a liberal party faction rose up from within and took control. Juárez's reforms nevertheless faced significant trouble, and, over time, those who once supported him turned against him. Porfirio Díaz, once a supporter of Juárez, revolted against Juárez's successor after Juárez's death in 1872. Díaz was perturbed by the lack of dramatic change under the new regime and eventually ran for president himself, holding the position from 1877–80 and again in 1884–1911. Under Díaz, Mexico became a centralized and militaristic state, nominally run on democratic principles, but mostly falling back on authoritarian rule.

—Anna Accettola, MA

Bibliography and Additional Reading

Brittsan, Zachary. *Popular Politics and Rebellion in Mexico Manuel Lozada and La Reforma, 1855-1876.* Nashville: Vanderbilt University Press, 2015.

Guardino, Peter F. *Peasants, Politics, and the Formation of Mexico's National State: Guerrero, 1800-1857.* Redwood City: Stanford University Press, 2001.

Hamnett, *Brian R. Juárez: Profiles in Power.* London: Longman, 1997.

Powell, T. G. "Priests and Peasants in Central Mexico: Social Conflict during 'La Reforma.'" *The Hispanic American Historical Review,* vol. 57, no. 2, 1977, pp. 296–313.

Montecristi Manifesto

Date: March 25, 1895
Authors: José Martí; Máximo Gómez
Genre: manifesto

Summary Overview

As a colony of Spain, Cuba in the second half of the nineteenth century saw three wars fought in the name of independence. The Cuban revolutionaries called for the abolition of slavery and for the end of Spain's exploitative occupation of the island. The first two wars fell short of their stated goal, as Spain persistently retained its rule over the island. Both José Martí and Máximo Gómez, the two authors of this document, fought on behalf of Cuban independence starting in the first war, which later came to be known as the Ten Years' War. The two men were very different: Martí was at this time a teenage poet, while Gómez was already a hardened military commander. When the Cuban rebels were unable to set up an autonomous nation in this war, the two men were separately forced to leave the island. They continued to work on behalf of Cuban independence from abroad. In early 1895, almost three full decades after the first war had begun, the two men met at Montecristi in the Dominican Republic. The Cuban rebels were now gearing up for the third and final war for independence, and Martí and Gómez composed the manifesto reprinted (in translation) here to articulate why they were fighting and what they were hoping to achieve. In the event, the Cuban people were finally able to shake off the yoke of Spain; however, the nearby United States opportunistically stepped in during the Spanish-American War (1898) to postpone the full realization of Cuban independence.

Defining Moment

The fight for Cuban Independence spanned multiple decades and three separate wars. On October 10, 1868, Cuba attempted to declare its independence and set off what later came to be known as the Ten Years' War, the first of the wars for Cuban independence. Slavery had long been practiced on the island, but an abolitionist tide was rising. Moreover, Spain's exploitative imperial rule over Cuba had left local inhabitants disaffected. Carlos Manuel de Céspedes, a wealthy planter, took up a leadership role in the revolt. He freed his own slaves and issued the 10th of October manifesto which articulated the wrongs of Spain and the aims of the revolt. The fighting carried on for a full decade with wide bloodshed but no clear victor. The Pact of Zanjón was signed on February 10, 1878. The Cubans did not achieve independence, but they did win some concessions from Spain, including a constitution and the freeing of some slaves.

The Cuban coat of arms. Image via Wikimedia Commons. [Public domain.]

The peace did not last long. Calixto García had fought on the side of the revolutionaries in the Ten Years' War and had been captured. He was released after the Pact of Zanjón, went abroad, and immediately began plotting a renewal of hostilities. The second of Cuba's wars for independence broke out on August 26th, 1879, about a year and a half after the cessation of the previous war. This encounter was the most one-sided of the three. The rebels were outnumbered, out-resourced, and outmatched. The war ended a little over a year after it began, which is why it is today known as the Little War. The Spanish legislature did outlaw slavery in 1880; however, the repeal came with a period of *patronato* for freed slaves, which essentially amounted to indentured servitude. However, on October 7, 1886, slavery was finally abolished on Cuba, and the practice of *patronato* was made illegal.

The abolition of slavery achieved one of the primary goals of the Cuban independence movement, but it did not mollify the movement itself. The iniquities of the imperial rule over the island exasperated economic woes. The third and final war, also known as the Cuban War of Independence, began on February 24, 1895, with a widespread revolt erupting across the island. José Martí was in exile in the United States at the time, helping to stir up an anti-Spanish sentiment among the population of Florida. He traveled to the Dominican Republic and penned this document with Máximo Gómez, one of the revolutionaries' military leaders, on March 25, 1895. The fight carried on for several with the Cuban rebels seeing greater success than they had in the previous two wars. By 1898, the rebels were in control of the eastern portion of the island and taking the fight to the colonialists who only controlled a few cities on the island's western half.

Stemming from a complex nexus of factors, such as earlier efforts like those of Martí, the sinking of the USS Maine on February 15, 1898, and a sustained campaign of yellow journalism, the United States declared war on Spain and entered the conflict in Cuba in the spring of that year. The Teller Amendment was added to the congressional approval for the war. Introduced by and named after Senator Henry Moore Teller, the Teller Amendment prevented the United States from annexing Cuba after the war. Some claim that this amendment was rooted in pushback against American imperial expansionist tendencies; others more cynically point to the fact that Teller did not want Cuban sugar to compete with sugar producers from his home state.

With the United States pressing Spain in Cuba and in the Pacific, the War for Cuban Independence only lasted for a few more months. On August 12, 1898, Spain and the United States agreed to a peace in which Spain assented to relinquish claims on Cuba. This arrangement was ratified later that year in the Treaty of Paris, signed on December 10, 1898. Tellingly, the Cuban revolutionaries were not invited to sign the Treaty of Paris. Through a decades-long struggle and three wars, Cuba won its independence from Spain. However, the United States opportunistically stepped into the vacuum created by Spain's absence. The foreign power occupied Cuba until 1902. Before they left, the United States Congress passed the Platt Amendment on March 2, 1901. Although it

José Martí, 1892. Photo via Wikimedia Commons. [Public domain.]

did not annex Cuba directly, it did place Cuba in a subservient role to the United States. Cuba had thrown off Spain's direct rule only for it to be replaced by the indirect rule of the United States.

Author Biography

The poet José Martí and the military commander Máximo Gómez composed this document together.

José Martí struggled for Cuban independence throughout his life, a cause which his writing helped articulate. He was born January 28, 1853, in Havana, Cuba to a father of Spanish descent and a mother who was from the Canary Islands. When the first war for Cuban Independence, the Ten Years' War, broke out, Martí took up the cause of independence vigorously. He composed and published poems, such as *Abdala* and *10 de Octubre*, advocating independence. Only sixteen years old, Martí was arrested on charges of treason and bribery and eventually exiled to Spain. He was able to finish his schooling in Spain and continued to write prolifically. From there he returned to the Americas and traveled profusely, spending significant time in Mexico, the United States, Guatemala, and Venezuela. All the while, he used his writing to advocate an anti-imperialist message. He argued not only against Spanish imperialism in Cuba but also the expansionism of the United States that threatened all of Latin America. His primary passion was Cuban independence. In early 1895, Martí traveled to Montecristi in the Dominican Republic to rendezvous with Máximo Gómez and help plan the revolt. There the two coauthored this document. The poet turned soldier took part in a campaign that landed on Cuba in early April. He was killed on May 19, 1985 at the Battle of Dos Ríos, dying for the cause to which had devoted much of his life.

As a military commander, Máximo Gómez was one of the strongest forces fighting for Cuban independence. He was born on November 18, 1836, in Baní, Dominican Republic. He attended the Zaragoza Military Academy and fought for the Spanish army against Haitian incursions and in the Dominican Annexation War. He moved to Cuba, and at

Máximo Gómez, c. 1890s. Photo via Wikimedia Commons. [Public domain.]

the beginning of the Ten Years' War in 1868 joined the rebel cause. He brought much needed experience to the revolution. He rose up the ranks of the rebel military command and led important campaigns in the Ten Years' War. After the Spanish were able to retain control of Cuba at the end of this war, Gómez lived in exile but continued to work towards Cuban independence. It was in his homeland of the Dominican Republic that he wrote this document along with José Martí. By the time of Cuban War of Independence in the 1890s, Gómez had become the commander of the rebel army, and he helped lead his cause to victory. After the war, he retired outside of Havana. In 1901, he was offered the presidential nomination but refused, abhorring the machinations of politics. He died on June 17, 1905, at his home outside of Havana.

Historical Document

Montecristi Manifesto

The Cuban Revolutionary Party Addresses Cuba

Cuba's revolution of independence, initiated in Yara, has now, after a glorious and bloody preparation, entered a new period of war, by virtue of the order and agreements of the Revolutionary Party both in and outside the Island, and of the exemplary presence within that party of all elements consecrated to the betterment and emancipation of the country, for the good of America and of the world. Without usurping the accent and declarations that are appropriate only to the majesty of a fully constituted republic, the elected representatives of the revolution that is reaffirmed today recognize and respect their duty to repeat before the patria, which must not be bloodied without reason or without just hope of triumph, the precise aims, born of good judgment and foreign to all thought of vengeance, for which the inextinguishable war that today in moving and prudent democracy leads all elements of Cuban society into combat was initiated and will reach its rational victory.

In the serene minds of those who represent it today and the responsible public revolution that elected them, this war is not the insane triumph of one Cuban party over another, or even the humiliation of a group of mistaken Cubans, but the solemn demonstration of the will of a country that endured far too much in the previous war to plunge lightly into a conflict that can end only in victory or the grave, without causes sufficiently profound to overcome human cowardice and its several disguises, and without a determination so estimable-for it is certified by death-that it must silence those less fortunate Cubans who do not have equal faith in the capacities of their nation or equal valor by which to emancipate it from its servitude.

This war is not a capricious attempt at an independence that would be more fearsome than useful-which only those who manifest the virtuous aim of conducting it to a more viable and certain independence can stave off or do away with, and which must not in truth tempt a people that cannot endure it-but the disciplined product of the resolve of solid men, who in the repose of experience have decided to face once more the dangers they well know, and of a cordial assembly of Cubans of the most diverse origins, all convinced that the virtues necessary for the maintenance of liberty are better acquired in the conquest of liberty than in abject dispiritedness.

This is not a war against the Spaniard, who, secure among his own children and in his deference to the patria they win for themselves, will enjoy, respected and even beloved, the liberty that will sweep away only those imprudent individuals who seek to block its path. This war will not be a cradle of tyranny or of disorder, which is alien to the proven moderation of the Cuban spirit. Those who promoted it, and who can still raise their voices and speak, affirm in its name, before the patria, their freedom from all hatred, their fraternal indulgence toward timid or mistaken Cubans, their radical respect for the dignity of man, which is the catalyst of combat and the cement of the republic, and their certainty that this war can be conducted in a way that contains the redemption that inspires it, and the ongoing relations in which a people must live among others, alongside the reality of what war is. They must express, as well, their categorical determination to respect, and to ensure that all respect, the neutral and honorable Spaniard during and after the war, and to be merciful toward the repentant, and inflexible only toward vice, crime, and inhumanity. In the war that has just begun again in Cuba the revolution does not see cause for a jubilation that could commandeer an unreflecting heroism, but only the responsibilities that must preoccupy the founders of nations.

Cuba is embarking upon this war in the full certainty, unacceptable only to halfhearted, sedentary Cubans, of the ability of its sons to win a victory through the energy of the thoughtful and magnanimous revolution, and the ability of the Cuban people, developed during those ten early years of sublime fusion and in the modern practices of work and government, to save the patria at its origin from the trials and troubles that were necessary at the beginning of the century in the feudal or theoretical republics of Hispano-America, which were without communication and without preparation. Inexcusable ignorance or perfidy it would be to remain unaware of the often glorious and now generally remedied causes for those American upheavals, which arose from the error of trying to adapt foreign models of uncertain dogma, related only to their place of origin, to the ingenious reality of countries that knew nothing of liberty except their own eagerness to attain it and the pride that they won while fighting for it. The concentration of a merely literary culture in the capitals, the erroneous adherence of the republics to the lordly habits of the colony, the creation of rival caudillos as a consequence of the distrustful and inadequate treatment of remote areas, the rudimentary state of the only industry, which was farming or cattle herding, and the abandonment and distain of the fertile indigenous race amid the disputes between creed or locales that these causes for the upheavals in the nations of America carried on-these are in no way the problems of Cuban society. Cuba returns to war with a democratic and educated people, zealously aware of its own rights and those of others, and with even the humblest of its populace far more educated than the masses of plainsmen or Indians by whom, at the voice of the supreme heroes of emancipation, the silent colonies of America were transformed from herds of cattle into nations.

[...] The civic-mindedness of Cuba's warriors, the skill and benevolence of her craftsmen, the real and modern employment of a vast number of her minds and fortunes, the peculiar moderation of the campesino seasoned by exile and war, the intimate and daily contact and rapid and inevitable unification of the diverse sectors of the country, the reciprocal admiration for the virtues equally distributed among Cubans who passed directly from the differences of slavery to the brotherhood of sacrifice, and the benevolence and growing capability of the freed slave, far more common than the rare examples of his deviation or rancor, all ensure Cuba, without unwarranted illusions, a future in which the conditions of stability and immediate labor for a fruitful people in a just republic will exceed those of dissociation and partiality stemming from the laziness or arrogance that war sometimes breeds, from the offensive rancor of a minority of masters stripped for their privileges, from the censurable haste with which a still invisible minority of discontented freed slaves might aspire, in disastrous violation of free will and human nature, to the social respect that solely and surely must come to them by their proven equality of talent and virtue, or from the sudden and widespread loss by the literate inhabitants of the cities of the relative sumptuousness or abundance that they derive today from the colony's immoral and facile sinecures and the positions that liberty will cause to disappear.

A free nation, where work is open to all, positioned at the very mouth of the rich and industrial universe, will without obstacle and with some advantage replace, after a war inspired by the purest self-sacrifice and carried out in keeping with it, the shameful nation where well-being is obtained only in exchange for an express or tacit complicity with the tyranny of the grasping foreigners who bleed and corrupt it. We have no doubts about Cuba or its ability to obtain and govern its independence, we who, in the heroism of death and the silent foundation of the patria, see continually shining forth among the great and the humble its gifts of harmony and wisdom, which are only imperceptible to those who, living outside the real soul of their country, judge it, in their own arrogant concept of themselves, to possess no greater power of rebellion and creation than that which it timidly displays in the servitude of its colonial tasks.

And there is another fear from which cowardice, disguised as prudence, may wish to profit just now: the senseless and, in Cuba, always unjustified fear of the black race. The revolution, with all its martyrs and generous subordinate warriors, denies indignantly, as the long experience of those in exile and those on the island during the truce denies, the slanderous notion of a threat by the Negro race, which has been wickedly employed to the benefit of those who profit from the Spanish regime to stir up fear of the revolution. There are already Cubans in Cuba, of one color or another, who have forgotten forever-through the emancipating war and the work they carry on together-the hatred by which slavery may have divided them. The novelty and asperity of social relations following the sudden transformation of the man who belonged to another into his own man are less important than the sincere esteem of the white Cuban for the equal soul, painstaking education, freeman's fervor, and lovable character of his black compatriot. And if vile demagogues are born to the race, or avid souls whose own impatience incites that of their race, or in whom pity for their own people is transformed into injustice toward others, then out of their gratitude and prudence and love for the patria, out of their conviction of the need to disprove by a manifest demonstration of the intelligence and virtue of the black Cuban the still prevailing opinion of his incapacity for those two qualities, and in their possession of all the reality of human rights and the consolation and strength of their esteem for whatever element of justice and generosity there is in the white Cubans, the black race itself will expatriate the black menace in Cuba without a single white hand having to be raised to the task. The revolution knows this and proclaims it; those in exile proclaim it as well. The Cuban black has no schools of wrath there, and in the war not a single black was punished for arrogance or insubordination. Upon the shoulders of the black man, the republic, which he has never attacked, moved in safety. Only those who hate the black see hatred in the black, and those who traffic in such unjust fears do so in order to subjugate the hands that could be raised to expel the corrupting occupier from Cuban soil.

From the Spanish inhabitants of Cuba, the revolution, which neither flatters nor fears, hopes to receive, instead of the dishonorable wrath of the first war, such affectionate neutrality or truthful assistance as to make the war shorter, its disasters lesser, and the peace in which fathers and sons must live together easier and friendlier. We Cubans are starting the war, and Cubans and Spaniards will finish it together. If they do not mistreat us, we will not mistreat them. If the show respect, we will respect them. The blade is answered with the blade, and friendship is answered with friendship.

[...] What fate will the Spaniards choose: relentless war, open or concealed, that threatens and further disturbs the country's perennially turbulent and violent relations, or definitive peace, which will never be achieved in Cuba except by independence: Will the Spaniards who have roots in Cuba provoke a war in which they may be vanquished? And by what right would the Spaniards hate us, when we Cubans do not hate them? The revolution makes use of this language without fear because the mandate to emancipate Cuba once and for all from the irremediable ineptitude and corruption of the Spanish government, and to open it forthrightly to all men of the new world, is as absolute as our will to welcome to Cuban citizenship, without faint hearts or bitter memories, the Spaniards who in their passion for liberty help us to victory in Cuba, as well as those other Spaniards who by their respect for today's war redeem the blood that in yesterday's war coursed, under their blows, from the chests of their sons.

The forms the revolution takes will provide no pretext for reproach to the vigilant cowards, fully aware of its selflessness, who in the formal errors or scant republicanism of the nascent country might have found some reason for which to deny it the blood they owe it. Pure patriotism will have no cause to fear for the dignity and future fate of the patria. The difficulty of America's wars of independence and of its first nationalities has not lain primarily in any discord among its heroes or the emulation and mistrust inherent in mankind, but rather in the lack of a form that could contain both the spirit of redemption which, supported by lesser incentives, promotes and nourishes the war, and the practices necessary to war, which the war must sustain and not encumber. In its initiatory war, a country must find a manner of government that can satisfy both the mature and cautious intelligence of its literate sons and the necessary conditions for the assistance and respect of its other peoples, and that does not hinder but enables the full development and rapid conclusion of the war that was calamitously necessary to the public happiness. From its origin, the patria must be constituted in viable forms, forms born of itself, so that a government without reality or sanction does not lead it into biases or tyranny. [...] It will be governed to ensure that a powerful and effective war will quickly establish a stable home for the new republic.

The war, healthy and vigorous from the start, which Cuba begins again today, with all the advantages of its experience and victory at last guaranteed to the unyielding resolve and lofty efforts of its unfading heroes, whose memory is always blessed, is not merely a pious longing to give full life to the nation that, beneath the immoral occupation of an inept master, is crumbling and losing its great strength both within the suffocating patria and scattered abroad in exile. This war is not an inadequate drive to conquer Cuba, for political independence would have no right to ask Cubans for their help if it did not bring with it the hope of creating one patria more for freedom of thought, equality of treatment, and peaceful labor. The war of independence in Cuba, the knot that binds the sheaf of islands where shortly the commerce of the continents must pass through, is a far-reaching human event and a timely service that the judicious heroism of the Antilles lends to the stability and just interaction of the American nations and to the still unsteady equilibrium of the world. It honors and moves us to think that when a warrior for independence falls on Cuban soil, perhaps abandoned by the heedless or indifferent peoples for whom he sacrifices himself, he falls for the greater good of mankind, for the confirmation of a moral republicanism in America, and for the creation of a free archipelago through which the respectful nations will pour a wealth that must, at its passage, spill over into the crossroads of the world. Hardly can it be believed that with such martyrs and such a future there could be Cubans who would bind Cuba to the corrupt and provincial monarchy of Spain and its sluggish, vice-ridden wretchedness! Tomorrow the revolution will have to explain anew to its country and to the nations the local causes, universal in concept and interest, by which for the progress and service of humanity the emancipating nation of Yara and Guáimaro begins again a war that, in its unswerving idea of the rights of man and its abhorrence of sterile vengeance and futile devastation, deserves the respect of its enemies and the support of the nations. Today, as we proclaim from the threshold of the earth, in veneration of the spirit and doctrines that produce and animate the wholehearted and humanitarian war for which the people of Cuba unite once more, invincible and indivisible, it is fitting that we evoke, as guides and helpers to our people, the magnanimous founders whose labor the grateful country takes up once again, and the honor that must prevent Cubans from wounding by word or deed those who gave their lives for them. And thus, making this declaration in the name of the patria and deposing before her and her free faculty of constitution the identical labor of two generations, the Delegate of the Cuban Revolutionary Party, created to organize and support the current war, and the Commander in Chief elected by all the active members of the Liberating army, in their shared responsibility to those they represent and in demonstration of the unity and solidity of the Cuban revolution, sign this declaration together.

José Martí

Máximo Gómez

Montecristi (Dominical Republic), March 25, 1895

Document Analysis

José Martí and Máximo Gómez composed this document at the very beginning of the War for Cuban Independence, which was, in fact, the third and final war fought for the sake of Cuban liberty. The manifesto has been translated from the original Spanish. The authors articulate their cause by describing their enemy, the recent history of the region, and the divisions that still remained amidst the Cuban population.

At the time of composition, the most recent war for Cuban independence had just ignited; however, the conflict had been raging for decades. The authors use the opportunity of the beginning of this new war to try to describe whom exactly the rebels are fighting against—and whom they are not: "This is not a war against the Spaniard, who, secure among his own children and in his deference to the patria they win for themselves, will enjoy, respected and even beloved, the liberty that will sweep away only those imprudent individuals who seek to block its path." The authors express no enmity against the Spaniards themselves. They indicate the security of the Spanish people as a way to say that the independence and the security of Spain are not at risk, nor were they ever a primary factor in this conflict. The implication is that the Cubans simply want the same thing for their island and their citizens as the Spanish already enjoy for themselves.

The authors also delve into the recent history of the region. The independence of Cuba, they argue, will be different from other problematic attempts at freedom across the Americas: "Cuba is embarking upon this war in the full certainty… to save the patria at its origin from the trials and troubles that were necessary at the beginning of the century in the feudal or theoretical republics of Hispano-America, which were without communication and without preparation." They continue, describing the ways in which these previous revolutions fell short: "Inexcusable ignorance or perfidy it would be to remain unaware of the often glorious and now generally remedied causes for those American upheavals, which arose from the error of trying to adapt foreign models of uncertain dogma, related only to their place of origin." Lack of preparation and the attempt to force foreign ill-fitting models upon local peoples doomed these earlier attempts, so this reckoning goes. The argument assumes that Cuba's bid for independence is much better prepped and thought-out and that the autonomous nation that results will not rely upon foreign, out-of-place models.

Finally, the authors touch upon an axis which still has the potential to divide Cubans, the subject of race. Slavery had recently been abolished, but race remained a tense subject. The authors hope that by taking up the subject they can help stave off a deeper division. While bringing up the topic, the authors make clear where they stand. They discuss "the senseless and, in Cuba, always unjustified fear of the black race… the slanderous notion of a threat by the Negro race, which has been wickedly employed to the benefit of those who profit from the Spanish regime to stir up fear of the revolution." They go on to vehemently defend black Cubans: "Upon the shoulders of the black man, the republic, which he has never attacked, moved in safety. Only those who hate the black see hatred in the black, and those who traffic in such unjust fears do so in order to subjugate the hands that could be raised to expel the corrupting occupier from Cuban soil." Like elsewhere in the Americas where the slave trade had operated for centuries, race had the potential to be exploited by bad actors as a means to divide. The authors recognize this fact and attempt to unite their nation as it prepares to face off against its imperial oppressors by way of defending black Cubans.

Essential Themes

As one might expect from the manifesto of an independence movement, the authors elaborate upon the themes of liberty and freedom repeatedly throughout this document. The document is in many ways a call to arms for the Cuban people. As such, it argues against inertia and apathy. To do so, it strikes upon the theme of liberty: "The virtues necessary for the maintenance of liberty are better acquired in the conquest of liberty than in abject dispiritedness." The more or less synonymous themes of liberty and freedom are then used repeatedly throughout the document. Later in the text, the authors summarize what the war hopes to accomplish: "A free nation, where work is open to all, positioned at the very mouth of the rich and industrial universe, will without obstacle and with some advantage replace, after a war inspired by the purest self-sacrifice and carried out in keeping with it, the shameful nation where well-being is obtained only in exchange for an express or tacit complicity with the tyranny of the grasping foreigners who bleed and corrupt it." A free nation will replace a shameful nation. By contrasting the adjectives of "free" and "shameful," the authors reveal the high value they place on freedom. They believe that putting forward these ideals will inspire their fellow citizens and steel them for the fight ahead.

—Anthony Vivian, MA

Bibliography and Additional Reading

Brenner, Philip & Peter Eisner. *Cuba Libre: A 500-Year Quest for Independence.* Lanham, MD: Rowman & Littlefield Publishers, 2017.

García De La Torre, Armando. *José Martí and the Global Origins of Cuban Independence.* Kingston, Jamaica: University of West Indies Press, 2015.

Martí, José. *Selected Writings,* trans. Esther Allen. London: Penguin Classics, 2002.

Muller, Dalia Antonia. *Cuban Émigrés and Independence in the Nineteenth-Century Gulf World.* Chapel Hill: University of North Carolina Press, 2017.

The European Revolutions of 1848—Before and After

Even after the French Revolution, the French Revolutionary Wars, and the Napoleonic Wars during the period 1789–1815, France was not done with revolution as the nineteenth century advanced. With the monarchy restored (under the Bourbon Restoration, 1814–1830), an insurrection in July 1830 (the July Revolution) resulted in the abdication of the increasingly unpopular King Charles X and his replacement by Louis-Phillippe, who was supported especially by the wealthy bourgeoise (as opposed to the nobles and clergy). Yet political factions remained, with some upholding the new king's power and others hoping to diminish it. An uprising in Paris in June 1832, memorialized in Victor Hugo's famous novel *Les Misérables,* saw rebels make a stand at the barricades for a day and night before they were violently disbursed by the army and national guard. However, increasing dissatisfaction with the policies of Louis-Phillippe and his foreign minister, François Guizot, along with worsening conditions for the working class, led to the February Revolution of 1848 in France. This widespread action proved successful in the removal of the monarchy and the creation of a provisional republican government. Yet, once again, internal hostility between right and left factions resulted in the government's collapse and the ascendancy of Prince Louis Napoleon (Napoleon III).

The February Revolution, at its outset, at least, helped fuel other budding revolutions across Europe. Eruptions occurred in the German and Italian states (both not unified at the time) and the Austrian empire (under the Hapsburgs). The liberal Frankfurt Parliament, swept into power in 1848, sought the unification of Germany, but the effort foundered within a year. In Italy, the Risorgimento, or nationalist movement, sought to reject Hapsburg influence and unite the peninsula; it enjoyed only selected success, and unity would not occur until later in the century. Throughout the Hapsburg empire revolutionists demanded greater autonomy, and in Central Europe liberal political reform met with some success, if only briefly. A counterreaction among monarchist forces led to the reestablishment of traditional authority and the dissipation of any serious reforms.

■ June Rebellion of 1832 as described in *Les Misérables* (1862)

Date: 1862 (reflecting on events of 1832)
Author: Victor Hugo
Genre: novel

Summary Overview

Les Misérables, *Victor Hugo's great novel from 1862, addresses events and characters that develop over decades, beginning in 1815. It reaches its climax with the June Rebellion of 1832, in which republican citizens of Paris rise up against the monarchy of King Louis-Philippe I, who had taken control of France in the July Revolution of 1830. It is a sprawling story, comprising five volumes and covering over a thousand pages, and contains numerous lengthy diversions into various topics such as history, architecture, and political philosophy. In the excerpts presented here, we see an example of this, as characters expound upon the progressive nature of technology and political thought. The events described in the novel, while happening in 1832, also reflected Hugo's criticism of France's government at the time—the Second Empire under the control of Napoleon III.* Les Misérables *combines personal stories of love and redemption with a broader political message, cementing it as one of the most beloved stories in modern European literature.*

Defining Moment

On June 5 and 6, 1832, around 3,000 anti-monarchist republicans in Paris rose up in an attempt to topple the government of King Louis-Philippe I (reigned 1830–48). This was the last gasp of violence in a period of French history that was filled with contention over the form the government of the country would take as well as who would be in charge of it. This event had its beginnings in the July Revolution of 1830, when King Charles X (r. 1824–30). Facing political resistance from the Chamber of Deputies (which was an elected body), Charles dissolved it, hoping that with new elections, there would be new Deputies more amenable to his wishes. Many politically liberal members of the French bourgeois as well as more radical republicans in France—particularly in Paris—believed that Charles was undermining the constitution (called the *Charte*) that had been established when the French monarchy had been restored. When opposition to his policies erupted in the summer of 1830, Charles cracked down on the freedom of the press, dissolving the newly-elected Chamber, and restricting voting rights in upcoming elections with a number of emergency orders issued on July 26, 1830.

Victor Hugo in 1861. Photo via Wikimedia Commons. [Public domain.]

An 1870 illustration depicting the rebellion. Image via Wikimedia Commons. [Public domain.]

The radicals of Paris began constructing barricades and arming themselves. By the 29th, the city was under the control of the rebels and Charles X had fled France. The Chamber of Deputies established a new Constitutional Monarchy headed by Louis-Philippe (Charles's cousin), who had a reputation for being more liberal. Despite this, there was contention between Royalists who wanted a return to more conservative policies, those who supported Louis-Philippe, and the working-class radicals of Paris. Contributing to the chaos was an economic crisis that included food shortages and inflation as well as a cholera outbreak in Paris in early 1832, killing 100,000 in France, with nearly 20,000 of these in Paris—mostly among the poor.

Republican groups (on which Hugo modeled the "Friends of the ABC' in *Les Misérables*) began to plan riots and demonstrations, beginning their operations on June 5 at the funeral of popular General Jean Lamarque. 3,000 insurgents, mounting a defense behind barricades near the center of Paris, faced 20,000 troops from the National Guard militia. By the end of June 6, the rebels had taken nearly 300 casualties, including 93 killed.

This was a brief insurrection and Louis-Philippe's resolve in the face of the uprising (as opposed to Charles X's flight from France and found support from many French citizens, particularly the middle classes. Victor Hugo was living in Paris at the time and found himself caught on the streets on June 5. His observations and experiences would become part of the extensive descriptions contained in *Les Misérables*.

Author Biography

Victor Hugo was born in France on February 26, 1802. He was a poet, playwright, and novelist with *The Hunchback of Notre Dame* (published in 1831) and *Les Misérables* (published in 1862) being among the most well-regarded of the nineteenth century. In addition to his writing career, Hugo he became involved in politics—a strand of his life particularly significant in the examination of this selection from *Les*

Misérables. In 1845, King Louis-Philippe appointed Hugo a Peer of France, entitling him to a seat in the upper chamber of the National Assembly. While in that position he was outspoken on several issues—most notably his opposition to the death penalty. Following the Revolution of 1848 and the establishment of the Second Republic, Hugo continued his political service, being elected the National Assembly where he continued his critique of social injustice, supporting widespread voting rights and increased access to education.

In 1851, a coup d'état placed Napoleon III in control of France. Hugo denounced the new Emperor as a traitor and left France, eventually living as a political exile on the island of Guernsey. It was on Guernsey that Hugo not only wrote political pamphlets condemning Napoleon III but also *Les Misérables*, which—as can be seen from the excerpts here—reflects Hugo's political and social views. While it is set during the Rebellion of June 1832, its political themes were relevant to the France of 1862. Hugo would not return to France until 1870, after Napoleon was driven from power during the Franco-Prussian War. He failed to be elected to the National Assembly in 1872, but was elected to the Senate in 1876. He died following a struggle with pneumonia on May 22, 1885, at 83 years old.

Napoleon III, in 1852. Hugo's oppostion to this new Emperor is reflected in the views espoused in Les Miserables. Photo via Wikimedia Commons. [Public domain.]

Historical Document

Excerpts from *Les Misérables*

Chapter V—The Horizon Which One Beholds from the Summit of a Barricade

The situation of all in that fatal hour and that pitiless place, had as result and culminating point Enjolras' supreme melancholy. ...Enjolras was standing erect on the staircase of paving-stones, one elbow resting on the stock of his gun. He was engaged in thought; he quivered, as at the passage of prophetic breaths; places where death is have these effects of tripods. A sort of stifled fire darted from his eyes, which were filled with an inward look. All at once he threw back his head, his blond locks fell back like those of an angel on the sombre quadriga made of stars, they were like the mane of a startled lion in the flaming of an halo, and Enjolras cried:

"Citizens, do you picture the future to yourselves? The streets of cities inundated with light, green branches on the thresholds, nations sisters, men just, old men blessing children, the past loving the present, thinkers entirely at liberty, believers on terms of full equality, for religion heaven, God the direct priest, human conscience become an altar, no more hatreds, the fraternity of the workshop and the school, for sole penalty and recompense fame, work for all, right for all, peace over all, no more bloodshed, no more wars, happy mothers! To conquer matter is the first step; to realize the ideal is the second. Reflect on what progress has already accomplished. Formerly, the first human races beheld with terror the hydra pass before their eyes, breathing on the waters, the dragon which vomited flame, the griffin who was the monster of the air, and who flew with the wings of an eagle and the talons of a tiger; fearful beasts which were above man. Man, nevertheless, spread his snares, consecrated by intelligence, and finally conquered these monsters. We have vanquished the hydra, and it is called the locomotive; we are on the point of vanquishing the griffin, we already grasp it, and it is called the balloon. On the day when this Promethean task shall be accomplished, and when man shall have definitely harnessed to his will the triple Chimæra of antiquity, the hydra, the dragon and the griffin, he will be the master of water, fire, and of air, and he will be for the rest of animated creation that which the ancient gods formerly were to him. Courage, and onward! Citizens, whither are we going? To science made government, to the force of things become the sole public force, to the natural law, having in itself its sanction and its penalty and promulgating itself by evidence, to a dawn of truth corresponding to a dawn of day. We are advancing to the union of peoples; we are advancing to the unity of man. No more fictions; no more parasites. The real governed by the true, that is the goal. Civilization will hold its assizes at the summit of Europe, and, later on, at the centre of

continents, in a grand parliament of the intelligence. Something similar has already been seen. The amphictyons had two sittings a year, one at Delphos the seat of the gods, the other at Thermopylæ, the place of heroes. Europe will have her amphictyons; the globe will have its amphictyons. France bears this sublime future in her breast. This is the gestation of the nineteenth century. That which Greece sketched out is worthy of being finished by France. Listen to me, you, Feuilly, valiant artisan, man of the people. I revere you. Yes, you clearly behold the future, yes, you are right. You had neither father nor mother, Feuilly; you adopted humanity for your mother and right for your father. You are about to die, that is to say to triumph, here. Citizens, whatever happens to-day, through our defeat as well as through our victory, it is a revolution that we are about to create. As conflagrations light up a whole city, so revolutions illuminate the whole human race. And what is the revolution that we shall cause? I have just told you, the Revolution of the True. From a political point of view, there is but a single principle; the sovereignty of man over himself. This sovereignty of myself over myself is called Liberty. Where two or three of these sovereignties are combined, the state begins. But in that association there is no abdication. Each sovereignty concedes a certain quantity of itself, for the purpose of forming the common right. This quantity is the same for all of us. This identity of concession which each makes to all, is called Equality. Common right is nothing else than the protection of all beaming on the right of each. This protection of all over each is called Fraternity. The point of intersection of all these assembled sovereignties is called society. This intersection being a junction, this point is a knot. Hence what is called the social bond. Some say social contract; which is the same thing, the word contract being etymologically formed with the idea of a bond. Let us come to an understanding about equality; for, if liberty is the summit, equality is the base. Equality, citizens, is not wholly a surface vegetation, a society of great blades of grass and tiny oaks; a proximity of jealousies which render each other null and void; legally speaking, it is all aptitudes possessed of the same opportunity; politically, it is all votes possessed of the same weight; religiously, it is all consciences possessed of the same right. Equality has an organ: gratuitous and obligatory instruction. The right to the alphabet, that is where the beginning must be made. The primary school imposed on all, the secondary school offered to all, that is the law. From an identical school, an identical society will spring. Yes, instruction! light! light! everything comes from light, and to it everything returns. Citizens, the nineteenth century is great, but the twentieth century will be happy. Then, there will be nothing more like the history of old, we shall no longer, as to-day, have to fear a conquest, an invasion, a usurpation, a rivalry of nations, arms in hand, an interruption of civilization depending on a marriage of kings, on a birth in hereditary tyrannies, a partition of peoples by a congress, a dismemberment because of the failure of a dynasty, a combat of two religions meeting face to face, like two bucks in the dark, on the bridge of the infinite; we shall no longer have to fear famine, farming out, prostitution arising from distress, misery from the failure of work and the scaffold and the sword, and battles and the ruffianism of chance in the forest of events. One might almost say: There will be no more events. We shall be happy. The hu-

man race will accomplish its law, as the terrestrial globe accomplishes its law; harmony will be re-established between the soul and the star; the soul will gravitate around the truth, as the planet around the light. Friends, the present hour in which I am addressing you, is a gloomy hour; but these are terrible purchases of the future. A revolution is a toll. Oh! the human race will be delivered, raised up, consoled! We affirm it on this barrier. Whence should proceed that cry of love, if not from the heights of sacrifice? Oh my brothers, this is the point of junction, of those who think and of those who suffer; this barricade is not made of paving-stones, nor of joists, nor of bits of iron; it is made of two heaps, a heap of ideas, and a heap of woes. Here misery meets the ideal. The day embraces the night, and says to it: 'I am about to die, and thou shalt be born again with me.' From the embrace of all desolations faith leaps forth. Sufferings bring hither their agony and ideas their immortality. This agony and this immortality are about to join and constitute our death. Brothers, he who dies here dies in the radiance of the future, and we are entering a tomb all flooded with the dawn."

Enjolras paused rather than became silent; his lips continued to move silently, as though he were talking to himself, which caused them all to gaze attentively at him, in the endeavor to hear more. There was no applause; but they whispered together for a long time. Speech being a breath, the rustling of intelligences resembles the rustling of leaves. ...

Chapter VII—The Situation Becomes Aggravated

The daylight was increasing rapidly. Not a window was opened, not a door stood ajar; it was the dawn but not the awaking. The end of the Rue de la Chanvrerie, opposite the barricade, had been evacuated by the troops, as we have stated, it seemed to be free, and presented itself to passers-by with a sinister tranquillity. The Rue Saint-Denis was as dumb as the avenue of Sphinxes at Thebes. Not a living being in the crossroads, which gleamed white in the light of the sun. Nothing is so mournful as this light in deserted streets. Nothing was to be seen, but there was something to be heard. A mysterious movement was going on at a certain distance. It was evident that the critical moment was approaching. As on the previous evening, the sentinels had come in; but this time all had come.

The barricade was stronger than on the occasion of the first attack. Since the departure of the five, they had increased its height still further.

On the advice of the sentinel who had examined the region of the Halles, Enjolras, for fear of a surprise in the rear, came to a serious decision. He had the small gut of the Mondétour lane, which had been left open up to that time, barricaded. For this purpose, they tore up the pavement for the length of several houses more. In this manner, the barricade, walled on three streets, in front on the Rue de la Chanvrerie, to the left on the Rues du Cygne and de la

Petite Truanderie, to the right on the Rue Mondétour, was really almost impregnable; it is true that they were fatally hemmed in there. It had three fronts, but no exit.—"A fortress but a rat hole too," said Courfeyrac with a laugh.

Enjolras had about thirty paving-stones "torn up in excess," said Bossuet, piled up near the door of the wine-shop.

The silence was now so profound in the quarter whence the attack must needs come, that Enjolras had each man resume his post of battle.

An allowance of brandy was doled out to each.

Nothing is more curious than a barricade preparing for an assault. Each man selects his place as though at the theatre. They jostle, and elbow and crowd each other. There are some who make stalls of paving-stones. Here is a corner of the wall which is in the way, it is removed; here is a redan which may afford protection, they take shelter behind it. Left-handed men are precious; they take the places that are inconvenient to the rest. Many arrange to fight in a sitting posture. They wish to be at ease to kill, and to die comfortably. In the sad war of June, 1848, an insurgent who was a formidable marksman, and who was firing from the top of a terrace upon a roof, had a reclining-chair brought there for his use; a charge of grape-shot found him out there.

As soon as the leader has given the order to clear the decks for action, all disorderly movements cease; there is no more pulling from one another; there are no more coteries; no more asides, there is no more holding aloof; everything in their spirits converges in, and changes into, a waiting for the assailants. A barricade before the arrival of danger is chaos; in danger, it is discipline itself. Peril produces order.

As soon as Enjolras had seized his double-barrelled rifle, and had placed himself in a sort of embrasure which he had reserved for himself, all the rest held their peace. A series of faint, sharp noises resounded confusedly along the wall of paving-stones. It was the men cocking their guns.

Moreover, their attitudes were prouder, more confident than ever; the excess of sacrifice strengthens; they no longer cherished any hope, but they had despair, despair,—the last weapon, which sometimes gives victory; Virgil has said so. Supreme resources spring from extreme resolutions. To embark in death is sometimes the means of escaping a shipwreck; and the lid of the coffin becomes a plank of safety.

As on the preceding evening, the attention of all was directed, we might almost say leaned upon, the end of the street, now lighted up and visible.

They had not long to wait. A stir began distinctly in the Saint-Leu quarter, but it did not resemble the movement of the first attack. A clashing of chains, the uneasy jolting of a mass, the click of brass skipping along the pavement, a sort of solemn uproar, announced that some sinister construction of iron was approaching. There arose a tremor in the bosoms of these peaceful old streets, pierced and built for the fertile circulation of interests and ideas, and which are not made for the horrible rumble of the wheels of war.

The fixity of eye in all the combatants upon the extremity of the street became ferocious.

A cannon made its appearance.

Artillery-men were pushing the piece; it was in firing trim; the fore-carriage had been detached; two upheld the gun-carriage, four were at the wheels; others followed with the caisson. They could see the smoke of the burning lint-stock.

"Fire!" shouted Enjolras.

The whole barricade fired, the report was terrible; an avalanche of smoke covered and effaced both cannon and men; after a few seconds, the cloud dispersed, and the cannon and men reappeared; the gun-crew had just finished rolling it slowly, correctly, without haste, into position facing the barricade. Not one of them had been struck. Then the captain of the piece, bearing down upon the breech in order to raise the muzzle, began to point the cannon with the gravity of an astronomer levelling a telescope.

"Bravo for the cannoneers!" cried Bossuet.

And the whole barricade clapped their hands.

A moment later, squarely planted in the very middle of the street, astride of the gutter, the piece was ready for action. A formidable pair of jaws yawned on the barricade.

"Come, merrily now!" ejaculated Courfeyrac. "That's the brutal part of it. After the fillip on the nose, the blow from the fist. The army is reaching out its big paw to us. The barricade is going to be severely shaken up. The fusillade tries, the cannon takes."

"It is a piece of eight, new model, brass," added Combeferre. "Those pieces are liable to burst as soon as the proportion of ten parts of tin to one hundred of brass is exceeded. The excess of tin renders them too tender. Then it comes to pass that they have caves and chambers when looked at from the vent hole. In order to obviate this danger, and to render it possible to force the charge, it may become necessary to return to the process of the fourteenth century, hooping, and to encircle the piece on the outside with a series of unwelded steel bands, from the breech to the trunnions. In the meantime, they remedy this defect as best they may; they manage to discover where the holes are located in the vent of a cannon, by means of a searcher. But there is a better method, with Gribeauval's movable star."

"In the sixteenth century," remarked Bossuet, "they used to rifle cannon."

"Yes," replied Combeferre, "that augments the projectile force, but diminishes the accuracy of the firing. In firing at short range, the trajectory is not as rigid as could be desired, the parabola is exaggerated, the line of the projectile is no longer sufficiently rectilinear to allow of its striking intervening objects, which is, nevertheless, a necessity of battle, the importance of which increases with the proximity of the enemy and the precipitation of the discharge. This defect of the tension of the curve of the projectile in the rifled cannon of the sixteenth century arose from the smallness of the charge; small charges for that sort of engine are imposed by the ballistic necessities, such, for instance, as the preservation of the gun-carriage. In short, that despot, the cannon, cannot do all that it desires; force is a great weakness. A cannon-ball only travels six hundred leagues an hour; light travels seventy thousand leagues a second. Such is the superiority of Jesus Christ over Napoleon."

"Reload your guns," said Enjolras.

How was the casing of the barricade going to behave under the cannon-balls? Would they effect a breach? That was the question. While the insurgents were reloading their guns, the artillery-men were loading the cannon.

The anxiety in the redoubt was profound.

The shot sped the report burst forth.

"Present!" shouted a joyous voice.

And Gavroche flung himself into the barricade just as the ball dashed against it.

He came from the direction of the Rue du Cygne, and he had nimbly climbed over the auxiliary barricade which fronted on the labyrinth of the Rue de la Petite Truanderie.

Gavroche produced a greater sensation in the barricade than the cannon-ball.

The ball buried itself in the mass of rubbish. At the most there was an omnibus wheel broken, and the old Anceau cart was demolished. On seeing this, the barricade burst into a laugh.

"Go on!" shouted Bossuet to the artillerists.

Chapter VIII—The Artillery-Men Compel People to Take Them Seriously

They flocked round Gavroche. But he had no time to tell anything. Marius drew him aside with a shudder.

"What are you doing here?"

"Hullo!" said the child, "what are you doing here yourself?"

And he stared at Marius intently with his epic effrontery. His eyes grew larger with the proud light within them.

It was with an accent of severity that Marius continued:

"Who told you to come back? Did you deliver my letter at the address?"

Gavroche was not without some compunctions in the matter of that letter. In his haste to return to the barricade, he had got rid of it rather than delivered it. He was forced to acknowledge to himself that he had confided it rather lightly to that stranger whose face he had not been able to make out. It is true that the man was barcheaded, but that was not sufficient. In short, he had been administering to himself little inward remonstrances and he feared Marius' reproaches. In order to extricate himself from the predicament, he took the simplest course; he lied abominably.

"Citizen, I delivered the letter to the porter. The lady was asleep. She will have the letter when she wakes up."

Marius had had two objects in sending that letter: to bid farewell to Cosette and to save Gavroche. He was obliged to content himself with the half of his desire.

The despatch of his letter and the presence of M. Fauchelevent in the barricade, was a coincidence which occurred to him. He pointed out M. Fauchelevent to Gavroche.

"Do you know that man?"

"No," said Gavroche.

Gavroche had, in fact, as we have just mentioned, seen Jean Valjean only at night.

The troubled and unhealthy conjectures which had outlined themselves in Marius' mind were dissipated. Did he know M. Fauchelevent's opinions? Perhaps M. Fauchelevent was a republican. Hence his very natural presence in this combat.

In the meanwhile, Gavroche was shouting, at the other end of the barricade: "My gun!"

Courfeyrac had it returned to him.

Gavroche warned "his comrades" as he called them, that the barricade was blocked. He had had great difficulty in reaching it. A battalion of the line whose arms were piled in the Rue de la Petite Truanderie was on the watch on the side of the Rue du Cygne; on the opposite side, the municipal guard occupied the Rue des Prêcheurs. The bulk of the army was facing them in front.

This information given, Gavroche added:

"I authorize you to hit 'em a tremendous whack."

Meanwhile, Enjolras was straining his ears and watching at his embrasure.

The assailants, dissatisfied, no doubt, with their shot, had not repeated it.

A company of infantry of the line had come up and occupied the end of the street behind the piece of ordnance. The soldiers were tearing up the pavement and constructing with the stones a small, low wall, a sort of side-work not more than eighteen inches high, and facing the barricade. In the angle at the left of this epaulement, there was visible the head of the column of a battalion from the suburbs massed in the Rue Saint-Denis.

Enjolras, on the watch, thought he distinguished the peculiar sound which is produced when the shells of grape-shot are drawn from the caissons, and he saw the commander of the piece change the elevation and incline the mouth of the cannon slightly to the left. Then the cannoneers began to load the piece. The chief seized the lint-stock himself and lowered it to the vent.

"Down with your heads, hug the wall!" shouted Enjolras, "and all on your knees along the barricade!"

The insurgents who were straggling in front of the wine-shop, and who had quitted their posts of combat on Gavroche's arrival, rushed pell-mell towards the barricade; but before Enjolras' order could be executed, the discharge took place with the terrifying rattle of a round of grape-shot. This is what it was, in fact.

The charge had been aimed at the cut in the redoubt, and had there rebounded from the wall; and this terrible rebound had produced two dead and three wounded.

If this were continued, the barricade was no longer tenable. The grape-shot made its way in.

A murmur of consternation arose.

"Let us prevent the second discharge," said Enjolras.

And, lowering his rifle, he took aim at the captain of the gun, who, at that moment, was bearing down on the breach of his gun and rectifying and definitely fixing its pointing.

The captain of the piece was a handsome sergeant of artillery, very young, blond, with a very gentle face, and the intelligent air peculiar to that predestined and redoubtable weapon which, by dint of perfecting itself in horror, must end in killing war.

Combeferre, who was standing beside Enjolras, scrutinized this young man.

"What a pity!" said Combeferre. "What hideous things these butcheries are! Come, when there are no more kings, there will be no more war. Enjolras, you are taking aim at that sergeant, you are not looking at him. Fancy, he is a charming young man; he is intrepid; it is evident that he is thoughtful; those young artillery-men are very well educated; he has a father, a mother, a family; he is probably in love; he is not more than five and twenty at the most; he might be your brother."

"He is," said Enjolras.

"Yes," replied Combeferre, "he is mine too. Well, let us not kill him."

"Let me alone. It must be done."

And a tear trickled slowly down Enjolras' marble cheek.

At the same moment, he pressed the trigger of his rifle. The flame leaped forth. The artillery-man turned round twice, his arms extended in front of him, his head uplifted, as though for breath, then he fell with his side on the gun, and lay there motionless. They could see his back, from the centre of which there flowed directly a stream of blood. The ball had traversed his breast from side to side. He was dead.

He had to be carried away and replaced by another. Several minutes were thus gained, in fact.

Glossary

Amphictyons: a council of leaders of the ancient Greek city states

breach: a break in the formation of troops caused by cannon-fire

pell-mell: in a disorderly fashion

Piece of Eight: a reference to a cannon that fires eight-pound projectiles

quadriga: a chariot pulled by four horses

Virgil: Classical Roman poet

Document Analysis

The excerpts from *Les Misérables* presented here are comprised of three chapters—chapters five, seven, and eight from the first book of the fifth and final volume. These chapters feature three characters whose stories are among those traced in the book. Enjolras is a radical republican and the leader of the Friends of the ABC, a fictionalized group of radical students based on the groups that had fomented the June Rebellion of 1832. Enjolas is in command of the barricade on the Rue de la Chanvrerie, which is where we first meet him. Gavroche, who enters this excerpt near the end of chapter seven, is a street urchin who joins the rebels in the climactic battle at the barricade. Marius Pontmercy is a student revolutionary, in love with Cosette. When we meet Marius in this excerpt, he believes he has lost Cosette, and he has entrusted Gavroche with a letter to her explaining that he plans to give up his life for her.

In chapter five ("The Horizon which one Beholds from the Summit of a Barricade"), we encounter Enjolras who arises to address his fellow rebels manning the barricade on the Rue de la Chanvrerie. His theme is the future—a future their uprising can help bring about. Enjolras's vision of the future is in line with the radical nature of his political and philosophical beliefs. He envisions a future where nations are "sisters" and where freedom of expression and of belief is a reality. In particular, he promotes the idea of a religion freed from the strictures of a religious hierarchy ("for religion heaven, God the direct priest, human conscience become an altar"). There will be an end to war and bloodshed. He then explains that there is a relationship between material progress and political or social progress. He argues that humanity is well on its way to conquering "matter" with locomotives and balloon flight. The next step is "science made government" and a new state free of "parasites." Enjolras explains that whether or not the uprising is successful, there revolution will continue.

In the second portion of the chapter, Enjolas expounds on the nature of political equality ("legally speaking, it is all aptitudes possessed of the same opportunity; politically, it is all votes possessed of the same weight; religiously, it is all consciences pos-

The death of Éponine during the June Rebellion, illustration from the novel. Image via Wikimedia Commons. [Public domain.]

sessed of the same right.") and of the benefits that would result including education for all children. The key to this is the political remaking not just of France but of the world.

Chapter seven ("The Situation Becomes Aggravated") provides an example of the kind of historical, architectural, and technical digressions that are one of the features that characterize the novel. The barricade had weathered an attack and was preparing for the next one. Hugo describes the preparations, including details such as the value of left-handed fighters who can be stationed where right-handed fighters cannot. There is also an example of Hugo inserting details that date from *after* the action being described in the narrative. In this case, he provides an example from "the sad war of June, 1848," which would take place over a decade later.

As the fighting begins, Hugo provides two paragraphs of characters (Bossuet and Combeferre) explaining the history of cannon technology and tactics. The dialogue with which Hugo's characters present this information seems a bit stilted and unrealistic, but it provides another example of the wide array of information that pervade the novel. Chapter seven ends with the enemy firing their cannon at the barricade as the street urchin Gavroche suddenly arrives.

Chapter eight ("The Artillery-men Compel the People to take them Seriously") begins with Marius asking Gavroche if he had been able to deliver his letter to Cosette. Gavroche, in reality, had given the letter to Jean Valjean, but lies to Marius, telling him that since Cosette was asleep, he had given the letter to the porter to deliver.

Gavroche joins the fighters at the barricade, providing information on enemy troop positions. The barricade suffers a successful shot from the enemy artillery. Enjolras prepares to shoot the captain of the enemy artillery, hoping to forestall another assault. But he and his comrade Combeferre agonize over the horror of killing, even when the enemy is the target. Enjolras fires, weeping as he does so, killing the enemy soldier.

Essential Themes

There are three key themes that emerge in this excerpt from *Les Misérables*. The first is manner in which Hugo's political and philosophical views are expressed through the character of Enjolras. The speech he gives in chapter five is representative of republican political thought in nineteenth century France and is part of a tradition that stretches back to the Enlightenment and the French Revolution of 1789. Enjolras defines liberty and explains the state very succinctly, saying, "From a political point of view, there is but a single principle; the sovereignty of man over himself. This sovereignty of myself over myself is called Liberty. Where two or three of these sovereignties are combined, the state begins."

This expression of individual sovereignty and its role as the foundation of the states is only part of the story. The second major theme of these excerpts is the idea of progress. Hugo, through Enjolras, also expresses the profound and abiding sense of optimism and progress that was part of liberal politics throughout Europe at the time. Enjolras links political progress to material progress, citing the technological achievements of the early industrial age. He also predicts a future none too different than liberal politicians and thinkers would predict throughout the 1800s. His declaration that "the nineteenth century is great, but the twentieth century will be happy" is evocative of the prevalent attitude that in the future, as the character claims, there "will be nothing more like the history of old." Wars, famine, hunger, ignorance, all will pass away.

The third theme that emerges in these chapters is the unfortunate necessity of revolutionary violence to accomplish these ends and to bring about the new future. Hugo is very careful here to ensure that characters like Enjolras and Combeferre do not revel in the violence necessary to secure their safety and that of their rebellion. On the contrary, they seem to abhor it, viewing it as an unfortunate consequence and a necessary evil rather than presenting the violence as an end unto itself.

—*Aaron John Gulyas, MA*

Bibliography and Additional Reading

Harsin, Jill. *Barricades: The War of the Streets in Revolutionary Paris, 1830–1848*. New York: Palgrave, 2002.

Mansel, Philip. *Paris Between Empires: Monarchy and Revolution 1814–1852*. New York: St. Martin's Press, 2003.

Robb, Graham. *Victor Hugo: A Biography*. New York: Norton, 1999.

Traugott, Mark. *The Insurgent Barricade*. Berkley: University of California Press, 2010.

The Communist Manifesto

Date: February 1848
Authors: Karl Marx; Friedrich Engels
Genre: political tract

Summary Overview

In The Communist Manifesto, German philosophers Karl Marx and Friedrich Engels set forth the precepts of the early Communist movement, framing history as the product of a conflict between economic classes. The book analyzed the historical progression of politics and economics that led to the dominance of capitalism, characterized throughout by the struggle of workers, or the proletariat, against those who control the means of production, or the bourgeoisie. The Manifesto stated that human life was transformed by industry and economic development and that the ultimate victory of the proletariat through socialist revolution was inevitable.

Though the document initially had little impact, socialism and Communism became increasingly influential in the twentieth century and the work eventually came to be regarded as one of the most important political statements of all time. It spawned the philosophy known as Marxism that applied class-conscious analysis to virtually every realm of society and culture. Communism itself evolved into various branches, with perhaps none more influential than the authoritarian style of government promoted by the Soviet Union and the People's Republic of China.

Defining Moment

In the nineteenth century Europe experienced great changes. Advances in science led to rapid technological and economic progress as the Industrial Revolution began. This brought about greater urbanization and professional specialization and the development of the modern middle class. In turn, the political landscape began to shift. Particularly after the defeat of Napoleon in 1815 numerous underground revolutionary groups existed under the conservative, often repressive governments of Europe. Middle-class or "bourgeois" movements, empowered by industrial wealth, were increasingly successful in challenging

Cover of The Communist Manifesto's initial publication in February 1848 in London. Image via Wikimedia Commons. [Public domain.]

the aristocratic domination of the old feudal system, principally in Britain, France, and the German states.

The new industrial economic system became known as capitalism. Yet some thinkers and activists, generally considered radicals, saw this system as flawed and even repressive in a new way. A diverse set of ideas labeled "socialism" arose in critique of capitalism, with advocates of different factions endorsing different economic and political values. These ideas had roots in the Enlightenment and the French Revolution of 1789 but began to fully coalesce in urban centers in the mid-1800s. Some of the most radical socialists, including those who became known as Communists, supported ideas such as the redistribution of property and the complete abolition of the market system to avoid economic inequality. Groups such as the Communist League, founded in 1847 and which included the philosophers Karl Marx and Friedrich Engels as members, arose to promote their political and economic views. Such radical groups were the target of much persecution by the established European governments they criticized.

The globalizing impulse of capitalism was of concern to many radical socialist students and scholars, who witnessed the imperial expansion of European power and the dominance of international trade. For example, the first Opium War between Britain and China from 1839 to 1842 forced the Chinese to open their markets not just to British-grown opium, but to British manufactured goods as well. The bourgeois capitalist system of Europe appeared to be spreading over the whole world.

Author Biography and Document Information

Karl Marx (1818–1883) came from a middle-class family with Jewish roots. He received a German university education and became involved in radical politics. He met Friedrich Engels (1820–1895), the

Karl Marx and Friedrich Engels. Photo via Wikimedia Commons. [Public domain.]

rebellious scion of a German family of textile manufacturers, in Paris, France, in 1844, and the two became close associates. Marx was both persecuted by the Prussian government and expelled from France in 1845; he and Engels both settled in Brussels, Belgium. There they became involved with the radical secret society the League of the Just in 1847.

That group soon evolved into the more open Communist League and tasked Marx with writing its manifesto, or public statement of its beliefs and aims. Working with Engels he produced the Communist Manifesto for publication in 1848. The work was originally published in German but translations into several languages soon appeared as Marx and Engels targeted a Europe-wide audience of workers and revolutionaries. Marx would go on to author several other highly influential works that shaped Marxism and Communism, including the multivolume *Das Kapital* (1867, 1885, 1894; *Capital: A Critique of Political Economy*, 1886, 1907, 1909).

Historical Document

Manifesto of the Communist Party

A spectre is haunting Europe—the spectre of communism. All the powers of old Europe have entered into a holy alliance to exorcise this spectre: Pope and Tsar, Metternich and Guizot, French Radicals and German police-spies.

Where is the party in opposition that has not been decried as communistic by its opponents in power? Where is the opposition that has not hurled back the branding reproach of communism, against the more advanced opposition parties, as well as against its reactionary adversaries?

Two things result from this fact:

I. Communism is already acknowledged by all European powers to be itself a power.

II. It is high time that Communists should openly, in the face of the whole world, publish their views, their aims, their tendencies, and meet this nursery tale of the Spectre of Communism with a manifesto of the party itself.

To this end, Communists of various nationalities have assembled in London and sketched the following manifesto, to be published in the English, French, German, Italian, Flemish and Danish languages.

I. Bourgeois and Proletarians*

The history of all hitherto existing society† is the history of class struggles.

Freeman and slave, patrician and plebeian, lord and serf, guild-master and journeyman, in a word, oppressor and oppressed, stood in constant opposition to one another, carried on an uninterrupted, now hidden, now open fight, a fight that each time ended, either in a revolutionary reconstitution of society at large, or in the common ruin of the contending classes.

In the earlier epochs of history, we find almost everywhere a complicated arrangement of society into various orders, a manifold gradation of social rank. In ancient Rome we have patricians, knights, plebeians, slaves; in the Middle Ages, feudal lords, vassals, guild-masters, journeymen, apprentices, serfs; in almost all of these classes, again, subordinate gradations.

The modern bourgeois society that has sprouted from the ruins of feudal society has not done away with class antagonisms. It has but established new classes, new conditions of oppression, new forms of struggle in place of the old ones.

Our epoch, the epoch of the bourgeoisie, possesses, however, this distinct feature: it has simplified class antagonisms. Society as a whole is more and more splitting up into two great hostile camps, into two great classes directly facing each other—Bourgeoisie and Proletariat.

From the serfs of the Middle Ages sprang the chartered burghers of the earliest towns. From these burgesses the first elements of the bourgeoisie were developed.

The discovery of America, the rounding of the Cape, opened up fresh ground for the rising bourgeoisie. The East-Indian and Chinese markets, the colonisation of America, trade with the colonies, the increase in the means of exchange and in commodities generally, gave to commerce, to navigation, to industry, an impulse never before known, and thereby, to the revolutionary element in the tottering feudal society, a rapid development.

The feudal system of industry, in which industrial production was monopolised by closed guilds, now no longer sufficed for the growing wants of the new markets. The manufacturing system took its place. The guild-masters were pushed on one side by the manufacturing middle class; division of labour between the different corporate guilds vanished in the face of division of labour in each single workshop.

Meantime the markets kept ever growing, the demand ever rising. Even manufacturer no longer sufficed. Thereupon, steam and machinery revolutionised industrial production. The place of manufacture was taken by the giant, Modern Industry; the place of the industrial middle class by industrial millionaires, the leaders of the whole industrial armies, the modern bourgeois.

Modern industry has established the world market, for which the discovery of America paved the way. This market has given an immense development to commerce, to navigation, to communication by land. This development has, in its turn, reacted on the extension of industry; and in proportion as industry, commerce, navigation, railways extended, in the same proportion the bourgeoisie developed, increased its capital, and pushed into the background every class handed down from the Middle Ages.

We see, therefore, how the modern bourgeoisie is itself the product of a long course of development, of a series of revolutions in the modes of production and of exchange.

Each step in the development of the bourgeoisie was accompanied by a corresponding political advance of that class. An oppressed class under the sway of the feudal nobility, an armed and self-governing association in the medieval commune*: here independent urban republic (as in Italy and Germany); there taxable "third estate" of the monarchy (as in France); afterwards, in the period of manufacturing proper, serving either the semi-feudal or the absolute monarchy as a counterpoise against the nobility, and, in fact, cornerstone of the great monarchies in general, the bourgeoisie has at last, since the establishment of Modern Industry and of the world market, conquered for itself, in the modern representative State, exclusive political sway. The executive of the modern state is but a committee for managing the common affairs of the whole bourgeoisie.

The bourgeoisie, historically, has played a most revolutionary part.

The bourgeoisie, wherever it has got the upper hand, has put an end to all feudal, patriarchal, idyllic relations. It has pitilessly torn asunder the motley feudal ties that bound man to his "natural superiors", and has left remaining no other nexus between man and man than naked self-interest, than callous "cash payment". It has drowned the most heavenly ecstasies of religious fervour, of chivalrous enthusiasm, of philistine sentimentalism, in the icy water of egotistical calculation. It has resolved personal worth into exchange value, and in place of the numberless indefeasible chartered freedoms, has set up that single, unconscionable freedom—Free Trade. In one word, for exploitation, veiled by religious and political illusions, it has substituted naked, shameless, direct, brutal exploitation.

* * *

The bourgeoisie, during its rule of scarce one hundred years, has created more massive and more colossal productive forces than have all preceding generations together. Subjection of Nature's forces to man, machinery, application of chemistry to industry and agriculture, steam-navigation, railways, electric telegraphs, clearing of whole continents for cultivation, canalisation of rivers, whole populations conjured out of the ground—what earlier century had even a presentiment that such productive forces slumbered in the lap of social labour?

We see then: the means of production and of exchange, on whose foundation the bourgeoisie built itself up, were generated in feudal society. At a certain stage in the development of these means of production and of exchange, the conditions under which feudal society produced and exchanged, the feudal organisation of agriculture and manufacturing industry, in one word, the feudal relations of property became no longer compatible with the already developed productive forces; they became so many fetters. They had to be burst asunder; they were burst asunder.

Into their place stepped free competition, accompanied by a social and political constitution adapted in it, and the economic and political sway of the bourgeois class.

* * *

II. Proletarians and Communists

In what relation do the Communists stand to the proletarians as a whole?

The Communists do not form a separate party opposed to the other working-class parties.

They have no interests separate and apart from those of the proletariat as a whole.

They do not set up any sectarian principles of their own, by which to shape and mould the proletarian movement.

The Communists are distinguished from the other working-class parties by this only: 1. In the national struggles of the proletarians of the different countries, they point out and bring to the front the common interests of the entire proletariat, independently of all nationality. 2. In the various stages of development which the struggle of the working class against the bourgeoisie has to pass through, they always and everywhere represent the interests of the movement as a whole.

The Communists, therefore, are on the one hand, practically, the most advanced and resolute section of the working-class parties of every country, that section which pushes forward all others; on the other hand, theoretically, they have over the great mass of the proletariat the advantage of clearly understanding the line of march, the conditions, and the ultimate general results of the proletarian movement.

The immediate aim of the Communists is the same as that of all other proletarian parties: formation of the proletariat into a class, overthrow of the bourgeois supremacy, conquest of political power by the proletariat.

The theoretical conclusions of the Communists are in no way based on ideas or principles that have been invented, or discovered, by this or that would-be universal reformer.

* * *

By freedom is meant, under the present bourgeois conditions of production, free trade, free selling and buying.

But if selling and buying disappears, free selling and buying disappears also. This talk about free selling and buying, and all the other "brave words" of our bourgeois about freedom in general, have a meaning, if any, only in contrast with restricted selling and buying, with the fettered traders of the Middle Ages, but have no meaning when opposed to the Communistic abolition of buying and selling, of the bourgeois conditions of production, and of the bourgeoisie itself.

You are horrified at our intending to do away with private property. But in your existing society, private property is already done away with for nine-tenths of the population; its existence for the few is solely due to its non-existence in the hands of those nine-tenths. You reproach us, therefore, with intending to do away with a form of property, the necessary condition for whose existence is the non-existence of any property for the immense majority of society.

In one word, you reproach us with intending to do away with your property. Precisely so; that is just what we intend.

* * *

The charges against Communism made from a religious, a philosophical and, generally, from an ideological standpoint, are not deserving of serious examination.

Does it require deep intuition to comprehend that man's ideas, views, and conception, in one word, man's consciousness, changes with every change in the conditions of his material existence, in his social relations and in his social life?

What else does the history of ideas prove, than that intellectual production changes its character in proportion as material production is changed? The ruling ideas of each age have ever been the ideas of its ruling class.

When people speak of the ideas that revolutionise society, they do but express that fact that within the old society the elements of a new one have been created, and that the dissolution of the old ideas keeps even pace with the dissolution of the old conditions of existence.

When the ancient world was in its last throes, the ancient religions were overcome by Christianity. When Christian ideas succumbed in the 18th century to rationalist ideas, feudal society fought its death battle with the then revolutionary bourgeoisie. The ideas of religious liberty and freedom of conscience merely gave expression to the sway of free competition within the domain of knowledge.

* * *

The proletariat will use its political supremacy to wrest, by degree, all capital from the bourgeoisie, to centralise all instruments of production in the hands of the State, i.e., of the proletariat organised as the ruling class; and to increase the total productive forces as rapidly as possible.

Of course, in the beginning, this cannot be effected except by means of despotic inroads on the rights of property, and on the conditions of bourgeois production; by means of measures, therefore, which appear economically insufficient and untenable, but which, in the course of the movement, outstrip themselves, necessitate further inroads upon the old social order, and are unavoidable as a means of entirely revolutionising the mode of production.

These measures will, of course, be different in different countries.

Nevertheless, in most advanced countries, the following will be pretty generally applicable.

Abolition of property in land and application of all rents of land to public purposes.

A heavy progressive or graduated income tax.

Abolition of all rights of inheritance.

Confiscation of the property of all emigrants and rebels.

Centralisation of credit in the hands of the state, by means of a national bank with State capital and an exclusive monopoly.

Centralisation of the means of communication and transport in the hands of the State.

Extension of factories and instruments of production owned by the State; the bringing into cultivation of waste-lands, and the improvement of the soil generally in accordance with a common plan.

Equal liability of all to work. Establishment of industrial armies, especially for agriculture.

Combination of agriculture with manufacturing industries; gradual abolition of all the distinction between town and country by a more equable distribution of the populace over the country.

Free education for all children in public schools. Abolition of children's factory labour in its present form. Combination of education with industrial production, &c, &c.

When, in the course of development, class distinctions have disappeared, and all production has been concentrated in the hands of a vast association of the whole nation, the public power will lose its political character. Political power, properly so called, is merely the organised power of one class for oppressing another. If the proletariat during its contest with the bourgeoisie is compelled, by the force of circumstances, to organise itself as a class, if, by means of a revolution, it makes itself the ruling class, and, as such, sweeps away by force the old conditions of production, then it will, along with these conditions, have swept away the conditions for the existence of class antagonisms and of classes generally, and will thereby have abolished its own supremacy as a class.

In place of the old bourgeois society, with its classes and class antagonisms, we shall have an association, in which the free development of each is the condition for the free development of all.

Document Analysis

The key concept for Marx and Engels is the idea of history as a struggle between economically defined classes. One struggle is between the aristocracy, whose power is based on the control of agricultural land, and the bourgeoisie. This is a struggle that the bourgeoisie have all but won through the power of industrialization and free trade and translated into political power through the transformation of the "great monarchies" into the "modern representative state." However, the authors argue that bourgeois victory over the aristocracy is only a precursor to the more important struggle between the bourgeoisie and the proletariat. This struggle is unique, they claim, in that victory for the workers will end class struggle entirely.

The authors argue that broad economic forces are the drivers of change even before technological development. For example, steam manufacturing emerged because markets had grown so large traditional methods no longer served. The dynamism of industrial civilization is connected to the possibility of real radical social change—not the transfer of power from one exploitive class to another, as seen in previous revolutions, but the abolition of exploitation entirely. Industrial workers constitute the revolutionary class.

The Communist Manifesto advocates for revolution as the only way to truly change the system. Marx and Engels have little faith in reformism or gradual change. The kinds of reforms promoted by socialist labor unions, for example, they claim are ultimately doomed to be defeated, although the struggle itself is valuable in giving workers experience of organization and campaigning. The Manifesto also repudiates the revolutionary sectarianism and emphasis on small underground groups characteristic of the early nineteenth-century political left. The closing statement that the "Communists disdain to conceal their views and aims," is a declaration that the movement intends to openly contend for political power rather than plot secretively. Marx and Engels put their faith in the mobilization of masses of industrial workers, not the workings of a handful of underground revolutionaries. They also show little interest in nationalism, believing that the conflict between bourgeoisie and proletariat is an international struggle transcending homelands.

Marx and Engels are concerned with establishing the superiority of their brand of socialism to the many competing varieties. One way they do this is to associate other socialisms with social classes other than the proletariat. Some forms of socialism are identified with the reactionary aristocracy, who share an enemy, the bourgeoisie, with the proletariat but have no shared goals. In other cases the authors acknowledge that members of the bourgeoisie espouse socialist messages, but claim this is only "to secure the continued existence of the bourgeois society." One of Marx and Engels's chief rivals, French socialist Pierre Proudhon, is characterized in this way, ready to take the benefits of social improvement but against true revolution. Marx and Engels also have little interest in the type of socialism that involves intellectuals laying out blueprints for an ideal society, known as utopian socialism.

The Manifesto says little about the nature of the society that the authors believe will come to replace capitalism. General steps for the revolutionary process, which will vary in each society, are given and include things such as the abolition of private property and inheritance, centralization of power in the government, even population distribution, and free public education for all. However, the document is mainly a survey of past and present conditions rather than a detailed plan for the future.

Essential Themes

The publication of the Communist Manifesto was followed by a period of revolution in many European cities, although the impact of the document itself was initially minimal. Marx was active in the revolutionary movements in Germany but most revolutionaries were not followers of his ideas. The revolutions in Germany failed and the Communist League itself broke up a few years later.

Marxism, as the philosophy of the Manifesto became known, would be a greater success in the long run. The Marxist brand of socialism and Communism defeated its rivals in most European socialist movements in the second half of the nineteenth century. It was particularly strong in Germany, which by the end of the century was the home of the world's largest socialist party, one based on industrial workers in the classical Marxist model. Although Marx never lost faith in the idea of a working-class revolution, the revolutionary optimism of the Communist Manifesto was replaced in his later writings with a more pessimistic attitude over the prospect of immediate change.

The first revolution to establish a state following Marxist Communism did not take place in an advanced industrial economy like Germany or Great Britain but in comparatively rural Russia, with the October Revolution of 1917 that brought the Bolsheviks to power. Subsequent Communist revolutions followed this pattern by mostly taking place in countries with an undeveloped, rather than extensively developed, industrial sector, and have frequently drawn on the power of peasants, who Marx did not regard as revolutionary, rather than the industrial working class. Bolshevik Russia became part of the authoritarian Communist Soviet Union, which dominated world politics for much of the twentieth century as a nuclear superpower. Other Communist states, such as China and Cuba, remained active into the twenty-first century, demonstrating the lasting impact of Marxism.

Many of the themes addressed in the Communist Manifesto, such as class conflict and revolutionary transformation, continue to be relevant. It remains one of the most widely read pieces of Marxist literature, frequently taught in survey courses in modern history or political theory and considered one of the most influential documents of all time.

—William E. Burns, PhD

Bibliography and Additional Reading

Carver, Terrell and James Farr, eds. *The Cambridge Companion to the Communist Manifesto.* New York: Cambridge UP, 2015.

Marxists Internet Archive. Marxists Internet Archive, n.d.

Smaldone, William. *European Socialism: A Concise History with Documents.* Lanham: Rowman, 2014.

Sperber, Jonathan. *Karl Marx: A Nineteenth-Century Life.* New York: Liveright, 2014.

Louis Kossuth—Speech at a Dinner Given in His Honor by the U.S. Congress in Washington, D.C.

Date: January 7, 1852
Author: Louis Kossuth
Genre: speech; address

Summary Overview

In the early part of the sixteenth century, Hungarian forces were beaten by the Ottoman army at the battle of Mohacs and their king, Louis Jagiellon, was killed—heirless. The proud historical kingdom of Hungary ceased to exist: part of it fell under the Ottoman yoke, part remained semi-independent as the duchy of Transylvania, and part of it was incorporated into Habsburg lands as the kingdom of Hungary—under that foreign dynasty. At the end of seventeenth century, as a result of the peace of Karlowitz (1699), the majority of Hungarian lands were united under the Habsburg scepter. This meant the diminishment of freedoms and privileges, and the domination wrought under Viennese centralism merged with absolutism. On top of that, Hungarians were not a significant majority in their own part of Habsburg lands.

After the Napoleonic Wars of the early nineteenth century and the rise of nationalism in various European countries, the Habsburgs became more conciliatory toward the Hungarians, agreeing to work with the Hungarian Diet, or legislature. (After all, the Hungarian nobility had a well-developed system of provincial self-governments—more than fifty such governments operated within the territory—and estate representation.) Hungarian demands for national autonomy, the use of the Hungarian language, and wider participation in state structures were on the rise. The emperor Francis initially opposed these demands but, in 1825, he summoned the parliament to launch a set of reforms. Hungarians seized the opportunity and started presenting new demands as well as working toward the creation of a Hungarian national front. Among the activists of this time was Louis (Lajos) Kossuth, who, after his arrest and confinement in the years 1837–40, became one of the leaders of the national struggle.

In March 1848 a wave of revolutions, which started in France, swept through Europe, not bypassing the Austrian empire. A revolution also started in Pest (now part of Budapest), and Hungarians called for the creation of a national government. Louis Kossuth took an active part in the revolution, and in April 1849 he was chosen by Hungarians to lead their cause in the Hungarian War of Independence. The war, in the end, was lost owing to the military intervention of Tsar Nicholas I of Russia. Many of the Hungarian revolutionary leaders, soldiers, and patriots—those who were not killed or arrested—found safety abroad. Louis Kossuth was among them.

Defining Moment

Following the defeat in the War of Independence, Louis Kossuth with a large group of other patriots and soldiers left the country. He escaped to the Ottoman Empire, and soon afterward a death sentence was placed on him by the Austrian court. After a short stay in Turkey, Kossuth was invited by the U.S. Congress to visit the United States. He travelled by ship to the south of France, but was denied entry and passage through Louis Napoleon's country. He had to continue by sea.

In his travels Kossuth visited Great Britain for about three weeks, where he was welcomed with some enthusiasm, except by the governmental and legal circles. After that he continued his sea trip to the United States with his wife and a few colleagues. In December 1851, they landed in America and Kossuth began an eight-month-long tour of the country. He was hoping perhaps to secure American help for the continuation of the Hungarian struggle against absolutism, centralism, and Habsburg rule. He met with various organizations, politicians, religious figures, and others. Five weeks after his arrival, Kossuth was the guest of honor at a dinner organized by the U.S. Congress. The dinner took place on January 7, 1852 in Washington D.C. It was here, that Kossuth delivered his speech.

Author Biography

Louis (Lajos) Kossuth (1802–1894) was a Hungarian nobleman, lawyer, journalist, and politician. He became a lawyer in 1825 and was active as a politician, serving as a deputy to the Hungarian parliament in the years 1825–1827, 1832–1836, and 1847–1848. In the parliament he represented the national, liberal wing. In 1837 he was accused of treason and sentenced to three years in prison. While in prison he taught himself English using Shakespeare and the King James's Bible. Once out of captivity he started publishing a national-liberal periodical, *Pesti Hírlap*, which became the most important newspaper of the opposition. Among other things, it advocated a joint struggle of the nobles with other estates for the national cause. Hungarians achieved limited success in 1840 and 1844, when the Viennese government agreed to the use of the Hungarian language in parliament (replacing Latin). At that time Kossuth undoubtedly was the most popular opposition leader. He did not, however, see the need to work toward autonomy for other national groups, in particular the Slavic ones.

Lajos Kossuth's reception among businessmen industrialists and bankers in the Guildhall above the Bargate.

In March 1848, with the outbreak of the revolution, Kossuth demanded the transformation of the empire into a constitutional state. In October 1848 Hungarians formed their own government under the premiership of Lajos Batthyány. Kossuth held the ministry of finance and the presidency of military affairs within the government. He became one of the most popular Hungarian leaders, proposing to end serfdom and liquidate the nobles' privileges. He was also co-organizer of Hungarian army units. When on March 7, 1849 the newly crowned emperor, Franz Joseph, issued a new constitution for Hungary, it was rejected by Hungarians. On April 14, 1849 Hungarians, under Kossuth's leadership declared independence. He was elected Hungarian leader—"Governing President"—with practically absolute power.

The initial military successes ended with the interference of the Russian troops. The Hungarian War of Independence was crushed and those who survived and were not captured fled abroad. Kossuth fled to the Ottoman Empire. He spent some time under home arrest in Turkey, leaving for Britain in October 1851. He was feted there and held numerous meetings. Three weeks later he took a ship to America. His trip to America was a great personal and ideological success, for he received verbal backings for his championing of the cause of democratic struggle; and yet he won no real financial, diplo-

Louis Kossuth, 1852. Photo via Wikimedia Commons. [Public domain.]

matic, or military help. Arriving back in England, he continued his work but met with no great success. He lived and worked in Italy organizing a Hungarian legion to fight against the Austrians. When Austria expanded into Austria-Hungary and the emperor was crowned king of Hungary, Kossuth refused to return to his home country. When he died in Turin in 1894, Franz Joseph had him buried in Budapest.

Historical Document

Sir, though I have the noble pride of my principles, and though I have the inspiration of a just cause, still I have also the consciousness of my personal humility. Never will I forget what is due from me to the sovereign source of my public capacity. This I owe to my nation's dignity; [good! good!] and therefore, respectfully thanking this highly distinguished assembly in my country's name, I have the boldness to say that Hungary well deserves your sympathy; that Hungary has a claim to protection because it has a claim to justice. But, as to my own humble self, permit me humbly to express that I am well aware not to have in all these honors any personal share. Nay, I know that even that which might seem to be personal in your toast, is only an acknowledgment of a historical fact, very instructively connected with a principle valuable and dear to every republican heart in the United States of America. ...

We Hungarians are very fond of the principle of municipal self-government, and we have a natural horror against the principle of centralization. That fond attachment to municipal self-government without which there is no provincial freedom possible, is a fundamental feature of our national character. We brought it with us from far Asia a thousand years ago, and we conserved it throughout the vicissitudes of ten centuries. No nation has perhaps so much struggled and suffered from the civilized Christian world as we. We do not complain of this lot. It may be heavy, but it is not inglorious. Where the cradle of our Savior stood, and where his divine doctrine was founded, there now another faith rules, and the whole of Europe's armed pilgrimage could not avert this fate from that sacred spot, nor stop the rushing waves of Islamism absorbing the Christian empire of Constantine. We stopped these rushing waves. The breast of my nation proved a breakwater to them. We guarded Christendom, that Luthers and Calvins might reform it. It was a dangerous time, and the dangers of the time often placed the confidence of all my nation into one man's hand, and that confidence gave power into his hands to become ambitious. ... At the head of the army, circumstances placed him in the capacity to ruin his country. But he never had the people's confidence. So even he is no contradiction to the historical truth that no Hungarian whom his nation honored with its confidence was ever seduced by ambition to become dangerous to his country's liberty. ... Our nation, through all its history, was educated in the school of municipal self-government, and in such a country ambition having no field, has also no place in man's character.

The truth of this doctrine becomes yet more illustrated by a quite contrary historical fact in France. Whatever have been the changes of government in that great country—and many they have been, to be sure—we have seen a Convention, a Directorate, Consuls, and one Consul, and an Emperor, and the Restoration, and the Citizen King, and the Republic; through all these different experiments centralization was the fundamental tone of the institutions of France—power always centralized; omnipotence always vested somewhere. And, remarkably indeed, France has never yet raised one single man to the seat of power who has not sacrificed his country's freedom to his personal ambition!

It is sorrowful, indeed, but it is natural. It is in the garden of centralization where the venomous plant of ambition thrives. I dare confidently affirm, that in your great country there exists not a single man through whose brain has ever passed the thought that he would wish to raise the seat of his ambition upon the ruins of your country's liberty, if he could. Such a wish is impossible in the United States. ...

With self-government is freedom, and with freedom is justice and patriotism. With centralization is ambition, and with ambition dwells despotism. Happy your great country, sir, for being so warmly addicted to that great principle of self-government. Upon this foundation your fathers raised a home to freedom more glorious than the world has ever seen. Upon this foundation you have developed it to a living wonder of the world. ...

This is my confident hope. Then will at once subside the fluctuations of Germany's fate. It will become the heart of Europe; not by melting North Germany into a Southern frame, or the South into a Northern; not by absorbing historical peculiarities by centralized omnipotence; not by mixing in one State, but by federating several sovereign States into a Union like yours.

Upon a similar basis will take place the national regeneration of the Slavonic States, and not upon the sacrilegious idea of Panslavism, equivalent to the omnipotence of the Czar. [Applause.] Upon a similar basis will we see fair Italy independent and free. Not unity, but union will and must become the watchword of national bodies, severed into desecrated limbs to provincial rivalries, out of which a flock of despots and common servitude arose. To be sure, it will be a noble joy to this your great Republic, to feel that the moral influence of your glorious example has operated this happy development in mankind's destiny, and I have not the slightest doubt of the efficacy of your example's influence.

But there is one thing indispensable to it, without which there is no hope for this happy issue. This indispensable thing is, that the oppressed nations of Europe become the masters of their future, free to regulate their own domestic concerns. And to this, nothing is wanted but to have that "fair play" to all, for all, which you, sir, in your toast, were pleased to pronounce as a right of my nation, alike sanctioned by the law of nations as by the dictates of eternal justice. Without this "fair play" there is no hope for Europe - no hope of seeing your principles spread.

Yours is a happy country, gentlemen. You had more than fair play. You had active operative aid from Europe in your struggle for independence, which, once achieved, you so wisely used as to become a prodigy of freedom, and welfare and a book of life to nations. But we in Europe—we, unhappily, have no such fair play. With us, against every palpitation of liberty all despots are united in a common league; and you may be sure that despots will never yield to the moral influence of your great example. They hate the very existence of this example. It is the sorrow of their thoughts, and the incubus [nightmare] of their dreams. To stop its moral influence abroad, and to check its spreading development at home, is what they wish, instead of yielding to its influence.

Alas! Europe can no more secure to Europe fair play. Albion [England] only remains; but even Albion casts a sorrowful glance over the waves. Still we will stand our place, "sink or swim, live or die." You know the word; it is your own. We will follow it; it will be a bloody path to tread. Despots have conspired against the world. Terror spreads over Europe, and, anticipating persecution, rules. From Paris to Pesth [Budapest] there is a gloomy silence, like the silence of Nature before the terrors of a hurricane. ... The very sympathy which I met in England, and was expected to meet here, throws my sisters into the dungeons of Austria. [Cries of Shame! shame! throughout the room.] Well, God's will be done! The heart may break, but duty will be done. We will stand in our place, though to us in Europe there be no "fair play". ...

Sir, I most fervently thank you for the acknowledgment that my country has proved worthy to be free. Yes, gentlemen, I feel proud at my nation's character, heroism, love of freedom and vitality, and I bow with reverential awe before the decree of Providence which placed my country in a position that, without its restoration to independence, there is no possibility for freedom and the independence of nations on the European continent. Even what now in France is about to pass proves the truth of this. Every disappointed hope with which Europe looked toward France is a degree more added to the importance of Hungary to the world. Upon our plains were fought the decisive battles for christendom; [sic] there will be fought the decisive battles for the independence of nations, for State rights, for international law, and for democratic liberty. We will live free, or die like men; but should my people be doomed to die, it will be the first whose death will not be recorded as suicide, but as a martyrdom for the world, and future ages will mourn over the sad fate of the Magyar race, doomed to perish, [sensation,] not because we deserved it, but because in the nineteenth century there was nobody to protect the laws of nature and of nature's God.

...Once in my life I supposed a principle to exist in a certain quarter where indeed no principle proved to exist. It was a horrible mistake, and resulted in a horrible issue. The present condition of Europe is a very consequence of it. But precisely this condition of Europe proves that I did not wantonly suppose a principle to exist there, where I found none. Would it have existed, the consequences could not have failed to arrive as I have contemplated them. Well, there is a providence in every fact. [Applause.] Without this mistake the principles of American republicanism would for a long time yet not found a fertile soil on that continent, where it was considered wisdom to belong to the French school. Now matters stand thus: that either the continent of Europe has no future at all, or this future is American republicanism. And who could believe that two hundred million of that continent, which is the mother of a civilization, are not to have any future at all? Such a doubt would be almost blasphemy against Providence indeed—a just, a bountiful Providence. I trust with the piety of my religion in it.

I confidently trust that the nations of Europe have a future. I am aware that this future is contradicted by bayonets of absolutism; but I know that bayonets may support, but afford no chair to sit upon. I trust to the future of my native land, because I know that it is worthy to have it; and it is necessary to the destinies of humanity. I trust to the principles of republicanism; and, whatever be my personal fate, so much I know, that my country will conserve to you and your glorious land an everlasting gratitude.

Glossary

Albion: an ancient name for the Island of Great Britain

citizen-king: a notion from the French Revolution meaning a king who seeks to serve the interests of the people; this title was used, for example, in reference to Louis Philippe (1830–1848) in the early years of his reign

consul: a title of magistrates in the ancient Roman Republic; here it refers to the positions created in France after Napoleonic coup of 1799

Convention (French: *Convention nationale*): the first government in France during the French revolution, formed after the passing of the first constitution in 1791 and the August insurrection of 1792

Directorate: the French Directory was a five-person government that ruled France between 1795 and 1799

Panslavism: a political ideology promoting the integrity and unity of Slavic peoples

Pesth (Pest): one of the two parts of Hungary's capital based on the left (eastern) bank of the Danube; it had been an independent city before merging with Óbuda and Buda in 1873 to form Budapest

Slavonic States: any of the states or territories inhabited by Slavic peoples

Document Analysis

This speech is devoted to the issue of the Hungarian struggle for autonomy, or independence. At the very beginning Kossuth states that, "We Hungarians are very fond of the principle of municipal self-government, and we have a natural horror against the principle of centralization." Developing this idea, he maintains that this self-government has been cultivated by his nation for over a thousand. Instead of adopting the idea and implementing it, however, European states have done nothing for Hungary. This was so, even though it was Hungarians who defended Europe from the early threat of Islamism. Kossuth further contrasts this age-old idea of self-government to events taking place in France, the supposed flagship of revolution and democracy. Here he points to the issue of centralism versus self-government, maintaining that all of the various French governments (Convention, Directory, Consulate) abused their power out of self-interest, rather than serving the interests of the people. Being a guest of U.S. Congress, he flatters the American political system, saying, "Your fathers raised a home to freedom more glorious than the world has ever seen." Unfortunately, Kossuth does not see such a possibility in Europe ("there is no hope for Europe—no hope of seeing your principles spread"), where the centralized authoritarian states too often unite to put down liberalizing aspirations (including those of the Slavic nations).

Interesting in this regard is Kossuth's reference to fair play in politics. He stresses the fact that, in the American War of Independence, the colonies had the support of outside parties from Europe in their defeat of Great Britain (which did not have such help). He is making an oblique reference here to the crushing of Hungary's insurrection by Russian forces, which came, as a third party, to the aid of the ruling Habsburgs. "With us," he says, "against every palpitation of liberty all despots are united in a common league"—describing the cooperation of European monarchies in suppressing the revolutions of the Spring of Nations. He goes on to stress that Hungarians do have a right to freedom, and that he is grateful that his hosts acknowledge that. Being proud of his countrymen's achievements and sacrifice, he promises that they will continue fighting for "the independence of nations, for State rights, for international law, and for democratic liberty." "We will live free, or die like men" he continues.

By the end of the speech Kossuth is far from optimistic. He does not see a chance for Europe or Europeans to win the struggle for freedom and self-government. He goes as far as to maintain that the French model has gone bankrupt, and the only possibility for European freedom is the adoption of American democratic-republican system. He becomes very emotional: "Who could believe that two hundred million of that continent [Europe], which is the mother of a civilization, are not to have any future at all?" Finally, he states that against all odds, and against "bayonets of absolutism," he believes in Europe having a future, and that this future is connected with the principles of (American-style) republicanism.

Essential Themes

Louis Kossuth's visit to the United States had a very concrete aim. He was hoping to secure American backing for his countrymen's struggle for independence, but also to collect money to raise an army, which could undertake a military struggle. In light of those aims, his speech to Congress is of a part of the rest of his eight-month tour in America. It is to promote the Hungarian cause and find outside supporters. The whole speech is devoted to the issue of self-government, in particular the right of Hungarians to govern themselves outside of Habsburg Viennese centralism. On the one hand, Kossuth criticizes European states and leaders for not accepting liberal, self-governing ideas, and fighting in unity with the Hungarians. On the other hand, he flatters the Americans and their republican system. In Europe, he claims, there is no self-government, not even in France. Even Great Britain, which prides itself in having a democratic political system, has not stood up to defend the struggle against centralism and absolutism.

Kossuth held many more meetings and delivered other speeches during his visit to the United States. Most of them had the same aim, and described the

Hungarian struggle against the Habsburgs. His visit and speeches were received very well in the United States. Many residents learned who Hungarians were, what their struggle was, and what the situation in Central Europe was. His words stressed the need to carry on the good fight for principles and ideas that had spread throughout the United States yet remained distant in many parts of Europe. Donald S. Spencer examined Kossuth's impact in America in the latter part of the nineteenth century. Although he was much more widely known then than he is now, he left a small legacy of liberal thought as regards the problem of sectionalism (localism or regionalism as against nationalism) and the development of foreign policy. He is also said to have influenced such distant fields as American fashion!; indeed, even babies were named after him.

As for Kossuth's aims and dreams, however, they did not pan out as planned. He never managed to secure American diplomatic or military support for the Hungarian cause. During his visit, funds were collected in numerous places for supporting Hungarian emigration and possible military struggle. Unfortunately, much of what was collected was used to finance Kossuth's fund-raising efforts—the travel, the welcome ceremonies, the dinners, and so on. Kossuth left the United States under a false name to avoid detection by European (Austrian, Russian) spies or agents.

—*Jakub Basista, PhD, DLitt*

Bibliography and Additional Reading

Deak, Istvan. *Lawful Revolution: Louis Kossuth and the Hungarians 1848–1849*. New York: Columbia University Press, 1979.

Kossuth, Lajos, Francis W. Newman. *Selected Speeches of Kossuth*. London: Turner & Co., 1853.

Okey, Robin. *The Habsburg Monarchy, c. 1765–1918: From Enlightenment to Eclipse*. London and New York: Palgrave Macmillan, 2000.

Spencer, Donald S. *Louis Kossuth and Young America: A Study of Sectionalism and Foreign Policy, 1848–1852*. Columbia, MO: University of Missouri Press, 1977.

Várdy, Steven B. "Louis Kossuth. A Celebrated, Disillusioned Hungarian Revolutionary's Visit to Pittsburgh in 1852," *Western Pennsylvania History*, volume 91, no. 1, spring 2008; pp. 18–31.

■ Manifesto of the Paris Commune

Date: April 19, 1871
Author: The Leadership of the Paris Commune
Genre: political manifesto

Summary Overview

During the nineteenth century, France endured a number of wars, rebellions, and changes of government. The 1870–1871 war with a confederation of German states, led by Prussia, led to the end of the Second Empire and the creation of the Third Republic. In the midst of the war and the shift in government, the city of Paris was besieged by enemy forces. When the war ended, the radical working class of Paris—who had defended the city during the siege—took control of the city and denied the legitimacy of the new Third Republic government. This movement, known as the Paris Commune, issued a manifesto in late April 1871 in which they outlined their demands and their vision for a new France—a France in which the political power was ultimately in the hands of the people rather than kings, emperors, or even parliaments.

While historians have categorized the Paris Commune as the first extensive revolution by the working class, it was not a long-lived phenomenon. Despite the brevity of the Commune, it had significant influence on the thinking of radical revolutionary figures such as Karl Marx. This Manifesto of the revolution provides a fascinating glimpse at the blueprint for a France that would never truly come into being but would serve as an inspiration in the future.

Defining Moment

From July 19, 1870, to May 10, 1871, France fought a war against the North German Confederation, under the leadership of Prussia and its King, Wilhelm I. While this war was a crucial step in the formation of a unified German Empire, it was also significant for the political chaos it brought to France.

Over September 1 and 2, 1870, the German army defeated French forces at the battle of Sedan and Captured the French Emperor, Napoleon III. When news of the French surrender reached Paris, the Empress fled the capital and the government of the Empire collapsed. A group of deputies, or representatives, of the French National Assembly established a new government (a government of "national defense") and vowed to continue the fight against the Prussian-led Germans. The enemy forces, following their victory at Sedan, marched on Paris and had the city surrounded on September 20. With the German forces a little over a mile from the French capital, the city's defense was largely in the hands of the National Guard (*Garde Nationale*, in French).

The National Guard was a citizen militia that had existed since the time of the French Revolution of 1789. Since it was made up of citizens of the city, rather than being a professional military force, the National Guard was diverse in its makeup. During the Siege of Paris, the National Guard had significant numbers of working class troops who were often politically radical. The political radicalization was part of the wider social context of France at the time. Urban areas—like Paris and other large cities—were home to being supporters of democratic government and labor unions, and engaging in demonstrations against the national government. The countryside, with its smaller villages and towns, were more conservative.

Leading up to the siege, radical groups inside Paris lost confidence in the new government and its ability to defend Paris (and itself). Demonstrators called for a new, communal, city government. During the siege, word got through to Paris that the French army had suffered setbacks and demonstrations by radical groups within the city continued. As the people of Paris suffered in the late autumn of 1870, cold and hungry, the new national government was determined

The Manifesto as it appeared in April 1871. Photo courtesy of BNF, via Wikimedia Commons.

to continue the war, despite an absence of support from other European nations. In January, 1871, the German forces pushed for a resolution—launching artillery attacks against the city. By the middle of the month, the French forces were near collapse. Radicals and National Guard troops continued to demand a new government in Paris. During a demonstration on January 22, the national government retaliated, fighting broke out, protestors were killed, and the government banned radical newspapers.

Elections for the new government took place in February, with the new assembly split between conservatives who supported the Emperor, moderates who favored a republic, and radical republicans and socialists. It was this radical group that dominated Paris. The new leader of the French government was Adolph Theirs, who urged an end to the war. A cease-fire was agreed to on February 24 and, following the fighting, conflict between the city of Paris and the national government escalated. This was triggered by an agreement that the German forces could occupy Paris and an attempt by the national government to confiscate cannons that had been used by the National Guard to defend the city. A rebellion began and, on March 26, 1871, a citizens government—the Paris Commune—was the result.

The Communards (as the residents of the Commune were known) were divided between militant revolutionaries and more moderate socialists. New laws and regulations withdrew financial support for the Roman Catholic church, established limits on working hours, and allowed for financial relief from the effects of the siege, such as cancelling out back rent payments, other debts, and the return of items that had been pawned. As the Manifesto of April 19 attempted to proclaim the Commune's vision to the people of France, the people of the Commune labored to defend themselves against assault by the national government of France.

Author Biography

The Manifesto is unsigned, but contains elements that would have been acceptable to both the radical and the more moderate elements of the Commune. There are strident calls for revolution and armed resistance to the national government—as well as a sense that this uprising should be a model for others—but there also exists a vision for moving forward following the fighting; of a nation of "communes" working together.

The Manifesto was published in the news paper *Paris Libre*, one of several publications that emerged during the period of the Commune. These papers were vital for spreading news and promoting the vision of the Commune, since many national papers refused to give space to radical views or, indeed, had been actively suppressed by the national government. *Paris Libre* was established and edited by Pierre Vésinier and was published from April 12 to May 24, 1871. Vésinier was an established figure in the Commune, having been arrested for seizing control of government facilities during the turmoil of late 1870. He was elected to the council that led the Commune.

Historical Document

To the French people:

In the painful and terrible conflict that again threatens Paris with the horrors of a siege and bombardment; that causes French blood to flow, sparing neither our brothers, our wives nor our children; crushed beneath cannonballs and rifle shot, it is necessary that public opinion not be divided, that the national conscience be troubled.

Paris and the entire nation must know the nature, the reason, and the goal of the revolution that is being carried out. Finally, it is only just that the responsibility for the deaths, the suffering, and the misfortunes of which we are the victims fall on those who, after having betrayed France and delivered Paris to the foreigners, pursue with a blind and cruel obstinacy the ruin of the great city in order to bury, in the disaster of the republic and liberty, the dual testimony to their treason and their crime.

The Commune has the obligation to affirm and determine the aspirations and wishes of the populace of Paris, to define the character of the movement of March 18, misunderstood, unknown and slandered by the politicians seated at Versailles.

Once again, Paris works and suffers for all of France, for whom it prepares, through its combats and sacrifices, the intellectual, moral, administrative and economic regeneration, its glory and prosperity.

What does it ask for?

The recognition and consolidation of the Republic, the only form of government compatible with the rights of the people and the normal and free development of society.

The absolute autonomy of the Commune extended to all localities in France and assuring to each one its full rights, and to every Frenchman the full exercise of his faculties and abilities as man, citizen and producer.

The only limit to the autonomy of the Commune should be the equal right to autonomy for all communes adhering to the contract, whose association shall insure French unity.

The inherent rights of the Commune are:

The vote on communal budgets, receipts and expenses; the fixing and distribution of taxes; the direction of public services; the organization of its magistracy, internal police and education; the administration of goods belonging to the Commune.

The choice by election or competition of magistrates and communal functionaries of all orders, as well as the permanent right of control and revocation.

The absolute guarantee of individual freedom and freedom of conscience.

The permanent intervention of citizens in communal affairs by the free manifestation of their ideas, the free defense of their interests, with guarantees given for these manifestations by the Commune, which alone is charged with overseeing and assuring the free and fair exercise of the right to gather and publicize.

The organization of urban defense and the National Guard, which elects its chiefs and alone watches over the maintenance of order in the city.

Paris wants nothing else as a local guarantee, on condition, of course, of finding in the great central administration—the delegation of federated Communes—the realization and the practice of the same principles.

But as an element of its autonomy, and profiting by its freedom of action, within its borders it reserves to itself the right to operate the administrative and economic reforms called for by the populace as it wills; to create the institutions needed to develop and spread instruction, production, exchange and credit; to universalize power and property in keeping with the needs of the moment, the wishes of those concerned and the facts furnished by experience.

Our enemies are fooling themselves or are fooling the country when they accuse Paris of wanting to impose its will or its supremacy over the rest of the nation and to pretend to a dictatorship, which would be a veritable attack on the independence and sovereignty of other communes.

They are fooling themselves or are fooling the country when they accuse Paris of pursuing the destruction of that French unity constituted by the Revolution to the acclaim of our fathers, who hastened to the Fête de la Fédération from all corners of the old France.

Unity, as it has been imposed on us until today by the Empire, the monarchy or parliamentarism is nothing but unintelligent, arbitrary or onerous centralization.

Political unity, as Paris wants it, is the voluntary association of all local initiatives, the spontaneous and free concourse of all individual energies in view of a common goal: the well-being, the freedom and the security of all.

The communal revolution, begun by popular initiative on March 18, begins a new era of experimental, positive, scientific politics.

It's the need of the old governmental and clerical world, of militarism and *fonctionnarisme*, of exploitation, speculation, monopolies and privileges to which the proletariat owe their servitude and the Fatherland its misfortunes and disasters.

Let this beloved and great country—fooled by lies and calumnies- be reassured! The fight between Paris and Versailles is one of those that cannot be ended through illusory compromises. The end cannot be in doubt. Victory, pursued with an indomitable energy by the National Guard, will go to the idea and to right.

We call on France.

Warned that Paris in arms possesses as much calm as bravery, that it supports order with as much energy as enthusiasm, that it sacrifices itself with as much reason as energy, that it only armed itself in devotion to the liberty and glory of all: let France cease this bloody conflict.

It is up to France to disarm Versailles through the solemn manifestation of its irresistible will.

Called upon to benefit by our conquests, let it declare itself in solidarity with our efforts. Let it be our ally in this combat that can only end in the triumph of the communal idea or the ruin of Paris.

As for us, citizens of Paris, our mission is the accomplishing of the modern Revolution, the largest and must fecund of all those which have illuminated history.

It is our obligation to fight and to win.

April 19, 1871 the Paris Commune

Published in *Paris Libre*, April 21, 1871

Translated by Mitch Abidor

Glossary

autonomy: political independence

calumnies: outrageous lies that aim at damaging someone's or something's reputation

"the foreigners": the German forces which had recently defeated France in the Franco-Prussian War.

fonctionnarisme: bureaucracy, the civil service

magistracy, magistrates: courts and judges

parliamentarism: rule of a nation by an elected legislature

Document Analysis

As stated at the outset, the purpose of the April 19th manifesto is to "trouble" the "national conscience" to make the entirety of France aware of the violence and bloodshed that are being visited upon the Commune. In doing so, the goal is to unify public opinion. In order to make this possible, the public needs to be made aware of the "nature, the reason, and the goal" of the revolution in Paris. The authors of the manifesto also wish to make it clear that those who are responsible for the death and destruction of those in the Commune are also those who lost the war against Germany. They hope "to bury, in the disaster of the republic and liberty, the dual testimony to their treason and their crime." That is, the attack on the Paris Commune is intended to serve as a distraction from the disastrous Franco-Prussian War. The purpose of the manifesto is also to set the record straight on the "aspirations and wishes of the populace of Paris." Those aspirations and wishes have been poorly understood or misrepresented by political leaders. In truth, the people of the Paris Commune are fighting for the "intellectual, moral, administrative, and economic regeneration" for the entire nation.

Following this preamble, the writers of the Manifesto transition into their demands. They begin with their demand for a Republican form of government in France as opposed to a restoration of monarchy. However, in their second demand, they push for the recognition of the "absolute autonomy" of the Commune to be "extended to all localities in France," tying this recognition and expansion) of the Communes to the fundamental rights of French citizens. The next paragraph explains that the autonomy, or independence, of all the communes will result in the unity of France as a whole.

Next, the authors outline what they see as the "inherent rights" of the Commune. Taken together, the assertion of rights in these five paragraphs among to a desire for local affairs with in the city to be entirely under the control of the people of that city, including taxation, election of all officials, management of police, and military defense. In addition, the manifesto calls for absolute individual freedom and freedom of conscience—as reflected in the dismantling of the religious hierarchy and state support of the Roman Catholic church undertaken by the Paris Commune. The manifesto also calls for the "permanent intervention of citizens" in the life of the Commune—a more direct form of citizen participation than currently existed. The commune "wants nothing else" but makes that conditional on these principles of communal control being exercised throughout the nation. They also discuss the importance of a "central administration" made up of representation of all the "federated Communes." Further, each commune asserts that its autonomy involves "the right to operate the administrative reforms called for by the populace as it wills." The people of the commune will, presumably, be the ultimate authority for the policies and procedures that are put in place.

The final section of the manifesto details what they perceive as the unjust and inaccurate claims made against them. They reject the idea that Paris is "wanting to impose its will" on all of France or that it is attempting to establish a dictatorship. They deny that they are attempting to destroy the unity of the French people. On the contrary, they argue, they are seeking a true unity—a unity not imposed by a monarch or an emperor, or even a parliament. The unity desired by the Paris Commune is "the voluntary association of all local initiatives." It is a unity fostered from the bottom up rather than the top down.

The concluding paragraphs call for all of France to join the fight and that this is a fight that will not be won through "illusory compromises." The revolution must spread beyond Paris to other cities and to the countryside. Finally, the citizens of the Commune have an "obligation to fight and win."

Essential Themes

The manifesto goes into detail about the nature of the autonomy it is asserting. The authors emphasize that the management of the Commune is determined by the will of the people and the "needs of the moment" as well as the "facts furnished by experience." This reflects a desire for a fast-moving, revolutionary government, unfettered by the constraints of monarchy or even traditional representative republican forms of government as opposed to a more measured, deliberative body. This type of flexibility was a reasonable need, since during April fighting with the national government intensified.

Perhaps most significant in this brief manifesto is not only a desire to break with the notion of a monarchical or imperial government, but also a rejection of the moderate, liberal middle-class parliamentary government established by the Third Republic. The Communes represent something new—the mobilization of the urban, industrial masses and a desire not only to remake government, but to reject "the old governmental and clerical world, of militarism and *fonctionnarisme*, of exploitation, speculation, monopolies and privileges to which the proletariat owe their servitude." It is this world and its characteristics which must bear the responsibility for the "misfortunes and disasters" that France and its people had suffered.

This new form of government and its desire to unify France under a coalition of locally-controlled peoples' governments would not last. One month after the Manifesto of the Paris Commune was published in *Paris Libre* the army of the national government breached the city's defenses. Brutal street-by-street, neighborhood-by-neighborhood fighting took place, and on May 24, the Commune's leaders, including chief executive Delescluze made plans to escape the city, torching their headquarters numerous other government buildings. Discipline within the National Guard broke down and resistance collapsed by May 28.

Despite the short-lived nature of the Commune, it would continue to serve as an inspiration for radicals. Karl Marx and other communist theorists pointed to the Paris Commune—and the notions outlined in its Manifesto—as an example of the "dictatorship of the proletariat."

—*Aaron John Gulyas, MA*

Bibliography and Additional Reading

Gluckstein, Donny. *The Paris Communie: A Revolution in Democracy.* Chicago: Haymarket Books, 2011.

Gullickson, Gay. *Unruly Women of Paris: Images of the Commune.* Ithaca: Cornell UP, 1996.

Horne, Alistair. *The Fall of Paris: The Siege and the Commune.* New York: Penguin, 2007.

Merriman, John. *Massacre: The Life and Death of the Paris Commune.* New York: Basic Books, 2014.

King Victor Emmanuel II: Address to Parliament

Date: November 27, 1871
Author: Victor Emmanuel II
Genre: address; speech

Summary Overview

The Italian peninsula in the nineteenth century was the scene of numerous demonstrations, uprisings, and military campaigns aimed at promoting and advancing the political unity of the Italian people—and at putting down those who stood in the way. Italian lands had been divided into independent states since the Middle Ages. Following the Napoleonic wars and the Congress of Vienna (1815), this division was represented by such separate states as the Kingdom of the Two Sicilies, the Papal State, the Kingdom of Sardinia, Tuscany, Parma, Modena, and the Northern Provinces under Habsburg rule. The process of unification, referred to as Risorgimento ("rebirth," "resurgence," or "revival"), had numerous faces, actors, and aims. Even today historians understand the term—and the era—in a variety of ways. In any case it is applied to the unification of Italy in the decades between 1815 and 1871.

Following three Italian wars of independence—1848–49, 1859, and 1866—the peninsula was united under the rule of the Savoy dynasty, hitherto overseeing the kingdom of Sardinia. In 1861 Victor Emmanuel II of Sardinia was proclaimed the first king of united Italy, which did not include the regions of Venice, Trento, and, most importantly, the capital city of Rome. Rome remained under papal rule and the protection of Napoleon III's French army. Turin was the Italian state capital in the years 1861–64, followed by Florence in 1864–1871. After the Third War of Independence, in 1866, Venice was incorporated into Italy, with Rome still outside the Italian borders. In 1870, taking advantage of French defeats in the Franco-Prussian War, Italian forces entered Rome and incorporated it into Italy against the pope's protests. The address presented here was given by King Victor Emmanuel II to the Italian Parliament at its first session in the new capital of Rome on the occasion of the final unification of the nation.

Defining Moment

Following the Third War of Independence, in which Italians allied themselves with Prussia against Austria, a peace treaty was signed in Vienna in October 1866. The Italian army did not have any successes in the war; nevertheless, Austria decided to give up the province of Venice—it was passed to Napoleon III of France, who held a plebiscite in Venice and handed it over to Italy. Italians failed to gain any additional territories. In particular Rome remained a papal domain, outside Italy's borders and protected by Napoleon against the Italians.

An attempt to by forces under General Giuseppe Garibaldi to enter Rome in November 1867 failed. With the outbreak of the Franco-Prussian war in 1870, Napoleon III had his army retreat from Rome, which was left under the protection of small and inefficient papal forces. With the surrender of Napoleon III to Prussians at Sedan, the Italian government decided to ignore the earlier agreements with France and enter Rome. A special corps entered the city on September 20, 1870, through the destroyed Aurelian Wall close to Porta Pia and advanced against symbolic opposition of papal troops. The city was taken without real fighting, and its population decided on the incorporation into Italy in a plebiscite carried out in October 1870.

At first the Città Leonita, surrounding the Vatican was not entered, but soon Italian troops moved in. The pope, Pius IX, refused to negotiate and locked himself in the Vatican. He excommunicated all who took part in the plebiscite and waited for outside help. The Italian parliament passed the "Law of Guarantees" for papal sovereignty, immunity, and annual income, which was rejected by Pius who promptly excommunication of the Savoy dynasty and all who took part in the unification of Italy. He claimed to be a prisoner.

On July 2, 1871 Rome was proclaimed the capital of Italy and the seat of the Italian monarch, government, and parliament. The address by Victor Emmanuel was given to the Italian Parliament in recognition of the newly united country. On November 27, 1871 the two chambers of parliament convened for the first time in modern history in Rome. The second session of the XI Legislature was initiated in the great hall of the Palazzo Montecitorio in Rome, which remains the seat of parliament today. Although by then most of Italy had been united for a decade, the incorporation of Rome, the removal of papal rule there, and the withdrawal of French troops was a momentous occasion, as is indicated in the address.

Author Biography

Victor Emmanuel II (1820–1878) was the king of Sardinia and the first king of united Italy. He was born in Turin to Charles Albert, prince of Savoy, who in 1831 became the king of Sardinia. He was brought up in a courtly atmosphere, albeit one that was very rigid, religious, and not inclined to modern intellectual trends. Being kept away from politics, Victor Emmanuel was active in the military. His marriage to the Austrian princess Adelaide in 1842 was a step toward improved relations with the Habsburg neighbors. In 1848, during the First War of Independence, he was given the command of a division. In combat he fought bravely but proved to be a poor commander. After the total defeat of the Sardinian army in 1849 at Novara, his father abdicated in favor of Victor Emmanuel.

The new ruler managed to keep the constitution in place despite pressures to the contrary, and in 1852 he chose Count Camillo Cavour as the new prime minister. Cavour's skillful rule helped stabilized the domestic situation, restore state finances, and modernize administration and the army. The privileged church courts were abolished under protest by the clergy and the pope. In the 1850s Sardinia joined Britain and France in the Crimean war, gaining their

Victor Emmanuel II, c. 1861. Photo via Wikimedia Commons. [Public domain.]

support and friendship. At the end of 1855 Victor Emmanuel visited Western Europe, meeting with Napoleon III and Queen Victoria and seeking support for Italian cause.

In the Third War of Independence, Sardinia allied itself with France to push Austrians out of Italy. Victor Emmanuel commanded Piedmontese troops in person in the battles of Magenta and Solferino. He signed the treaty of Villafrance and secretly encouraged Guiseppe Garibaldi's expedition south to the kingdom of Two Sicilies. As a consequence of the military action, and the plebiscites that followed, Italy was united (albeit without Venice, Trente and Rome) and Victor Emmanuel became king. After Cavour's death in 1861, Victor Emmanuel became more active in politics. In 1866 he allied with Prussia against Austria, which resulted in the acquisition of Venice, despite the Italian army's defeats. Four years later he took advantage of the Franco-Prussian war and the withdrawal of the French garrison to enter Rome. In September 1870 Victor Emmanuel's Italian army began the occupation of Rome, against Pius IX's protests. On July 2, 1871, Victor Emmanuel made an official entry into Rome, and his government proclaimed it the capital city. Pius IX never recognized the new state, and he and Victor Emmanuel never reconciled, never meeting in person despite the monarch's attempts to end the crisis. Victor Emmanuel II spent the rest of his life in royal duties, devoting more time to foreign than to domestic policy. He died on January 9, 1878, and with Pius IX's permission was buried in the Pantheon. He was succeeded by his son Humbert.

Historical Document

Senators and Deputies, gentlemen!

The work to which we consecrated our life is accomplished. After long trials of expiation Italy is restored to herself and to Rome. Here, where our people, after centuries of separation, find themselves for the first time solemnly reunited in the person of their representatives: here where we recognize the fatherland of our dreams, everything speaks to us of greatness; but at the same time it all reminds us of our duties. The joy that we experience must not let us forget them. ...

We have proclaimed the separation of Church and State. Having recognized the absolute independence of the spiritual authority, we are convinced that Rome, the capital of Italy, will continue to be the peaceful and respected seat of the Pontificate. ...

Economic and financial affairs, moreover, claim our most careful attention. Now that Italy is established, it is necessary to make it prosperous by putting in order its finances; we shall succeed in this only by persevering in the virtues which have been the source of our national regeneration. Good finances will be the means of re-enforcing our military organization. Our most ardent desire is for peace, and nothing can make us believe that it can be troubled. But the organization of the army and the navy, the supply of arms, the works for the defense of the national territory, demand long and profound study. ...

Senators and deputies, a vast range of activity opens before you; the national unity which is today attained will have, I hope, the effect of rendering less bitter the struggles of parties, the rivalry of which will have henceforth no other end than the development of the productive forces of the nation.

I rejoice to see that our population already gives unequivocal proofs of its love of work. The economic awakening is closely associated with the political awakening. The banks multiply, as do the commercial institutions, the expositions of the products of art and industry, and the congresses of the learned. We ought, you and I, to favor this productive movement while giving to professional and scientific education more attention and efficiency, and opening to commerce new avenues of communication and new outlets.

The tunnel of Mont Cenis is completed; we are on the point of undertaking that of the St. Gotthard. The commercial route, which, crossing Italy, terminates at Brindisi and brings Europe near to India, will thus have three ways open to railway traffic across the Alps. The rapidity of the journeys, the facility of exchanges, will increase the amicable relations which already unite us to other nations, and will make more productive than ever the legitimate competition of labor and the national rivalry in advancing civilization.

A brilliant future opens before us. It remains for us to respond to the blessings of Providence by showing ourselves worthy of bearing among the nations the glorious names of Italy and Rome.

Glossary

Brindisi: an Italian seaport and town in south east Italy on the Adriatic shore

Mont Cenis: a massif and a pass in the Cottian and Graian Alps, which connects France (Val-Cenis) with Italy (Susa)

St. Gotthard: a mountain pass in the Alps traversing the Saint-Gotthard Massif between Airolo in the Italian-speaking canton of Ticino, and Andermatt in the German-speaking canton of Uri

Document Analysis

The two chambers of the Italian parliament assembled for the first time in modern history in Rome on November 27, 1871. It was the second session of the XI Legislature of the Chamber of Deputies, which earlier had met in Turin and Florence. The session was opened by Victor Emmanuel II, the king of Italy, who delivered the speech.

Two main elements stand out in this speech. The first is the expression of great joy and satisfaction, even a sense of triumph related to seeing Italy finally united with the acquisition of Rome (1870) and to making Rome, once again, the capital of the nation. The second element that stands out is the idea of working toward the continuing development and modernization of Italy as a state. The king expresses his satisfaction, but at the same time asks for intense work directed toward the welfare and growth of the young state.

The speech opens with a triumphant statement about having reached such a point in history: "The work to which we consecrated our life is accomplished"; but it is also stated that the work is not done yet and numerous tasks await the deputies. Before moving on to a discussion of the economic, social, and logistic tasks awaiting the parliament and the government, the monarch stresses the execution of the separation of the State and the Church. The pope will be allowed to reside in Rome, he notes, and will enjoy full freedom and respect—but will not have any say in civic affairs. This is a new development in Italian affairs.

The remaining part of the address is devoted to a short, yet wide and ambitious program of national development. A country can survive and be strong only if it has strong and well-armed military forces, he notes. A desire for peace cannot stop the development and modernizing of the army and the navy. Banks, industry, commercial institutions, and the sciences must be developed too, he states. In the last part of the speech, Victor Emmanuel provides concrete examples of the task facing them. He foresees an Italy situated in a wider, European, and world context. Such an achievement must be accomplished through the development of mutual contacts between nations: "The rapidity of the journeys, the facility of exchanges, will increase the amicable relations which already unite us to other nations." He stresses the necessity of development and civilizational achievements through exchange, but also through competition and rivalry.

After describing how new train lines would be constructed to connect Northern Europe with the seaport of Brindisi and allow for a fast connection with India (through the Mediterranean and the Suez Canal), the king completes his short speech with statement of hope about how the Italians will prove themselves worthy of the gift they have been given by Providence and lead their country into bright future.

Essential Themes

At the end of the eighteenth century Napoleon entered the Italian peninsula, changing the political order, altering borders, and disrupting the status of the Italian states. In many of these states he introduced French-like constitutions and his new civic code. These actions produced a break with the old medieval and early modern structures. When the Congress of Vienna in 1815 restored components of the *ancien régime*, many Italians longed for more liberal and democratic changes, for constitutions. In various Italian cities activities erupted initiating the process of *Risorgimento*, the awakening, which soon was connected with a longing for national unity.

Historians speak of three Italian Wars of Independence. In reality, one can see a continuous move toward change in the years 1815–1871. The first step was taken after in 1860, when almost the whole peninsula was united under the Savoy dynasty. Still, Venice, Trento, and, most importantly, Rome remained outside the Italian state. Venice was annexed in 1866, Rome in 1870. It was Victor Emmanuel II, who as king of Sardinia in the moment of unification became the first king of a united Italy (although he did not change the "II" in his title). Five years later, in 1870, he entered Rome and made it his capital. In doing so he—together with all Italians—usurped the pope, the office of which had resided in Rome since antiquity, and whose power in Rome was not only spiritual but political as well.

Victor Emmanuel's address to the joint session of the Italian parliament is a very special address because it takes place in Rome, at parliament's first session after the incorporation of the capital. It is, then, an emotional speech, delivered at a unique moment in history. The king stresses how relations with the hitherto papal city will be maintained (full separation) and what needs to be done to make the united Italy a strong international state. The monarch sees the need to reinforce the army, but also to develop industry and infrastructure as Italy embarked on its future as a unified state.

—*Jakub Basista, PhD, DLitt*

Bibliography and Additional Reading

A transcript of the speech in Italian can be found here: storia.camera.it/regno/lavori/leg11/sed000B.pdf

Beales, Derek, and Eugenio F. Biagini. *The Risorgimento and the Unification of Italy*. London and New York: Routledge 2002.

Forester, Cecil Scott. *Victor Emmanuel II: And the Union of Italy*. N.p.: Simon Publications 2001.

Riall, Lucy. *Risorgimento: The History of Italy from Napoleon to Nation State*. Basingstoke, U.K.: Palgrave Macmillan 2009.

Japan and Korea

The Meiji period (1868–1912) in Japan was one of revolutionary change, modernization, and westernization. During the preceding 250 years, the Tokugawa shogunate had ruled over Japan; the country remained more or less at peace internally but was isolated and relatively stagnant culturally and intellectually. In 1863, the U.S. commodore Matthew C. Perry entered Japan and, through gunboat diplomacy, forced the opening of trade with the West. One result was that samurai groups opposed to the Tokugawa took up arms and announced the restoration of the Meiji emperor. By 1869 the shogunate had collapsed. Under the Meiji the feudal domains and old class system were abolished, and a new Meiji constitution was enacted. Unequal treaties with western powers were modified, and Japan modernized its industry and military to reflect its status as an emerging world power.

In consequence of its newfound strength, Japan during this period undertook to annex Taiwan following the Sino-Japanese War (1894–1895); to exert force in Korea and ultimately annex it (1910) as well; and to take some lands from Russia after its defeat of that country in the Russo-Japanese War (1904–1905). Japan was now an imperialist nation.

In Korea (or the Kingdom of Choson) the Yi dynasty had ruled since 1392 from its capital in Hanyang (Seoul). Korea too remained relatively isolated, but in 1876 Japan forced it to open its ports for trade. During the Sino-Japanese War and the Russo-Japanese War, Japan moved troops into Korea. Following the latter war, Japan formally annexed the country. After World War I, members of the March 1st movement declared independence from Japan, but the movement was brutally put down. All that was left for the opposition was to create a government in exile and wait for Japanese control to end, which it did in 1945. Korea was now divided into two zones of occupation, one in the north (Russian/Communist) and the other in the south (United States/Republic). It remains that way today.

Meiji Charter Oath

Date: April 7, 1868
Author: Yuri Kimimasa; Fukuoka Takachika; Kido Takayoshi
Genre: charter

Summary Overview

Also known as the Oath of Five Articles, the Meiji Charter Oath established the principles that were to guide the new Japanese government during a time of great change in the second half of the nineteenth century. After centuries of practical rule by a shogun, or military dictator, and nominal rule by the emperor (dynastic monarch), these goals made Emperor Meiji the de facto ruler in 1868. The reforms inspired by this charter radically transformed Japan into a modern nation-state instead of a feudal country that zealously guarded its isolation from foreign powers. These changes were a response both to internal and external factors. Aggressive foreign intrusion, especially after the American Commodore Matthew C. Perry appeared in Edo Bay with warships to force Japan to open for trade, along with terrible earthquakes and political upheavals contributed to the end of the longstanding Tokugawa shogunate. Imperial restoration, inspired by the principles stated in this oath, marked a period of intense militarization, industrialization, and political consolidation that made Japan a world power to be reckoned with at the end of the nineteenth century and into the twentieth.

Defining Moment

Commodore Perry's aggressive display of American maritime force did more than open up Japanese markets to foreign interests in 1853: it was a catalyst for the instability that would lead to the end of the Tokugawa shogunate and the restoration of imperial power. It was originally because of foreign influences and the threat they posed to domestic stability that Tokugawa Iemitsu, Shogun of Japan, issued a series of edicts in the 1630s to create an official policy of isolation. Before this anti-European reaction, some daimyō, i.e. feudal lords subordinate to the shogun, like Oda Nobunaga were tolerant of Christian missionaries and especially favored the influx of trade and European products. However, the Tokugawa shogunate began to distrust that this interaction was merely economic or religious after the Spanish conquest of the Philippines in the second half of the sixteenth century. Consequently, the Sakoku Edict of 1635 was intended to prevent this and secure Tokugawa power domestically. This decree prevented the Japanese from leaving the country, forbade the practice of Catholicism, and restricted foreign trade to a few ports and from select countries. The Shimabara Rebellion from 1637-8, which resulted from unrest over excessive taxation and famine, provided the shogunate proof that Christian influence was detrimental, since many of the rebelling peasants were Catholic converts. A rare episode of upheaval during the relatively peaceful Tokugawa shogunate, the Shimabara Rebellion ended with the beheading of the region's daimyō: this dire punishment signaled how seriously the shogunate took its desire to drive out foreign influences and resist imperialism.

European and American fleets would attempt occasionally over the next two hundred years to challenge Japanese seclusion (*sakoku*), but the arrival in Edo Bay of Commodore Perry's four ships fitted with cannons that could shoot explosive shells changed this pattern. Faced with an unprecedented threat from the Americans and an incapacitated shogun, top councilors in the shogunate could not come to a consensus about how to act. Left with few viable options, Japan signed the Treaty of Peace and Amity in 1854 with the United States. By signing this treaty, Japan avoided immediate confrontation and the United States gained diplomatic relations with Japan. The

Treaty of Amity and Commerce in 1858 between the United States and Japan showed the shogunate how quickly the Americans would work to benefit themselves at Japan's cost: Japan was forced to grant Americans residents extraterritoriality privileges, to open new ports, and to grant the Americans any rights that the Japanese granted to any other foreign nation.

Daimyō immediately sensed the weakness of central shogunate leadership, and turmoil wrecked the last years, known as Bakumatsu. Ii Naosuke, Chief Minister of the shogunate and a proponent of the opening of Japan, played a central role at the beginning of this upheaval. Ii attempted to rid the higher levels of shogunate administration of opponents of Westernization in the Ansei Purge from 1859-60, but he was himself assassinated on March 24, 1860 in the Sakuradamon Incident. During the same period, foreigners and sympathetic Japanese nationals were routinely targeted on the street. Emperor Kōmei, asserting more power than his traditionally ceremonial role had used in centuries, issued *an edict to "expel the barbarians" in 1863. The slogan sonnō jōi* ("revere the emperor, expel the barbarians") created a wedge between the emperor and the shogun, as well as between the shogunate and imperial-supporting daimyō. In particular, the Satsuma and Chōshū provinces supported the emperor and were two of the strongest domains in Japan. The violent opposition of the Sat-Chō Alliance to the shogunate and foreigners invited retaliatory attacks from the Americans, British, and French; the success of the foreign powers in crushing imperial opposition forces allowed the shogunate to regain a measure of its prior power over the country in 1864.

This period of renewed shogunate control did not last for long. The Western powers that helped crush the imperial rebellions demanded Japan pay indemnities that the shogunate could not afford; the central government also realized that it needed to modernize the country's weaponry if the Japanese hoped to withstand any future confrontation with the Europeans or Americans. Westernizing daimyō, like the leaders of Satsuma and Chōshū, also learned the value of Western arms as a tactical advantage and began to modernize their regional armies as well. As the shogunate attempted to reassert its power over the domains, a second attempt to punish Chōshū for its militant behavior in 1866 undercut all of the shogunate's progress. Although the new shogun Tokugawa Yoshinobu (also known as Keiki) negotiated a ceasefire, the more modernized Chōshū troops actually had outclassed and defeated the shogunate armies.

A last push to modernize the shogunate army ensued, but the loss of authority was too great. Yoshinobu attempted to consolidate power, but a con-

The Charter Oath as officially published. Photo via Wikimedia Commons. [Public domain.]

ference of daimyō in November 1867 convinced him to preemptively surrender his power to the emperor, thus ending the shogunate. For the next year, however, conflict raged between Sat-Chō and shogunate forces in the Boshin War: the pro-imperial Sat-Chō forces advanced on Kyoto and Edo to formalize the restoration of imperial power; Yoshinobu attempted to reverse the restoration of the emperor, and shogunate forces attempted again to attack Satsuma and Chōshū strongholds in retaliation. Under Saigo Takamori, an influential commander from Satsuma, imperial forces eventually surrounded the capital Edo in May 1868 and forced the shogunate to surrender for the last time. Although some naval shogunate forces in the north continued to resist, the emperor's residence was transferred from Kyoto to Edo late in 1868: this symbolic move represented the country's unification under one leader and the dawn of a new era.

Author Biography

Several different men from the victorious domains composed the Meiji Charter Oath. Yuri Kimimasa (1829-1912), a man of samurai rank from Echizen, provided a draft that used more inclusive wording to make the new government seem as if it were open to men from all ranks; Fukuoka Takachika (1835-1919) from Tosa, also of samurai rank, preferred more moderate language to suit the social status quo. Kido Takayoshi (1833-77) from Chōshū reworked the final draft with broad language that would assuage the fears of domains that had not supported the imperial restoration, provide the hope of opportunity for men of more moderate rank, and protect the prerogatives of those in official ranks.

At the time that the oath was proclaimed, the emperor was only fifteen years old. His father, Emperor

Emperor Meiji; portrait by Edoardo Chiossone, c.?1888. Photo via Wikimedia Commons. [Public domain.]

Kōmei, had died suddenly in 1867 at the height of the fighting between the imperial domains and the shogunate; the young Mutsuhito continued his education at the time, and was likely not involved in the political decisions being made, nor would he be much more involved in the governmental changes that followed, other than issuing official proclamations and attending cabinet meetings. His regime name "Meiji" means "enlightened rule," and he presided over a period of great cultural and institutional change for Japan.

Historical Document

Meiji Charter Oath

By this oath we set up as our aim the establishment of the national weal on a broad basis and the framing of a constitution and laws.

Deliberative assemblies shall be widely established and all matters decided by public discussion.

All classes, high and low, shall unite in vigorously carrying out the administration of affairs of state.

The common people, no less than the civil and military officials, shall each be allowed to pursue his own calling so that there may be no discontent.

Evil customs of the past shall be broken off and everything based upon the just laws of Nature.

Knowledge shall be sought throughout the world so as to strengthen the foundations of imperial rule.

[*Source:* Sources of Japanese Tradition, *volume II, compiled by Ryusaku Tsunoda, Wm. Theodore de Bary and Donald Keene (N.Y.: Columbia UP, 1958) p. 137.*]

Document Analysis

The success of the Meiji Charter Oath was in its uniquely general phrasing: this has allowed it to be read in different ways by different audiences throughout Japanese history. It reflects the motives of its composers at the time, however, who hoped to strike a balance between the more progressive desires of moderate rank samurai and the fears of daimyō who did not want to see the status quo overturned.

Each of the five points illustrates this ambiguousness between established order and a democratizing influence. In the first article, the authors have left the definition of "deliberative assemblies" and "public discussion" unclear: this could refer to traditional discussions between daimyō as under the shogunate, or it could refer to more modernizing ideas about representative assemblies that incorporate all people. The second article states that "all classes" can participate in the government, but the clarification "high and low" indicates that a class structure will still exist. The third article uses a similar tactic. Commoners and other officials are each allowed "to pursue his own calling'": this could mean that lower class men could pursue work based on their talents, or that higher class men could continue in the same level of work as their families. The eradication of "evil customs" in article four assures modernizers that the state will undertake changes, but the oath then asserts that new customs will be "based upon the just laws of Nature," which could refer to Confucian theory. Finally, the last article combines the perspective of both modernizers who looked to the West for models and to more conservative individuals. Although the Japanese government will seek knowledge "throughout the world," all of that knowledge will be in service of one of the longest-lasting traditions in Japanese history, imperial rule.

The openness of the language in the oath contributed to its longevity during a transformative period for Japan. The Charter Oath promises both reform and stability for its audience after years of civil unrest, which made it a particularly notable achievement of compromise for a country comprised for many years of many different and sometimes diametrically opposed autonomous domains.

Essential Themes

The Meiji Charter Oath became the unofficial blueprint around which future politicians structured policy or reinforced national identity. Out of the language in the oath about creating "deliberative assemblies," the new leaders of the Meiji era created the *genr ō*, or "elder statesman," who were all men from lower ranking samurai families; the *genr ō* were unofficial imperial advisors who could later nominate the prime minister, who held supreme political power in the state; experienced statesmen within this group could also serve in imperial posts at the emperor's discretion. Additionally, the Meiji Constitution of 1890 used the oath as a preamble to its more detailed articles that expanded on the promises within the oath's five points. Although the final constitutional reflected the influence of the Western constitutions that the composers had studied, once again, the generalizing language of the oath permitted different interpretations by the political factions of the 1870s and 1880s that competed for their own interpretation of constitutional government to prevail. The incorporation of the Meiji Charter Oath in the new constitution also allowed the composers to assert that the new treatise was fundamentally Japanese in identity and not a copy of European thought.

Another figure in Japanese history also used the Charter Oath in a surprising context in order to assert Japanese democratic identity. Emperor Hirohito cited the oath at the beginning of his imperial rescript on January 1, 1946, which has also been called the Humanity Declaration. For the Allied Powers who required this rescript, the most important message was the emperor's admission that he was not a living god. However, the use of the Charter Oath allowed the emperor to reassert to his audience that the defining quality of the Japanese state had always been democratic in spirit since the days of the imperial restoration. As Japan transitioned to a new constitution for the postwar era, the reminder of the Charter Oath allowed the shapers of a new constitution to see their task as a continuation of the past rather than an abrupt and humiliating break from tradition.

—Ashleigh Fata, MA

Bibliography and Additional Reading

Hellyer, Robert, ed. *The Meiji Restoration: Japan as a Global Nation.* New York: Cambridge UP, 2019.

Hillsborough, Romulus. *Samurai Revolution: The Dawn of Modern Japan Seen Through the Eyes of the Shogun's Last Samurai.* North Clarendon, VT: Tuttle Publishing, 2014.

Jansen, Marius B. *The Making of Modern Japan.* Cambridge, MA: Harvard UP, 2002.

Wert, Michael. *Meiji Restoration Losers: Memory and Tokugawa Supporters in Modern Japan.* Cambridge, MA: Harvard University Asia Center, 2013.

Wilson, George M. *Patriots and Redeemers in Japan: Motives in Meiji Restoration.* Chicago: University of Chicago Press, 1992.

Korean Declaration of Independence

Date: March 1, 1919
Author: Choe Nam-seon
Genre: political tract

Summary Overview

In the period leading up to the Korean Declaration of Independence, Japan had formally ruled Korea since 1910, although the Japanese had been a dominate force in Korean affairs since 1904. Buoyed by the post–World War I ideal of national self-determination, Korean leaders sought this for their nation too. Thirty-three leaders signed the Korean Declaration of Independence, seeking to end Japanese rule. What became known as the March First Movement was ultimately unsuccessful in ending Japanese rule. Yet the document reproduced here (in translation) did make the plight of the Korean people known to the world, and some believe that it indirectly produced better conditions for the Koreans. Although Japan had conducted few military operations as part of the Allied nations (or Entente powers), its leaders had positioned the nation to play a significant role in the postwar talks. The Korean leaders hoped that Japan's desire to be a full partner among the global powers might make its leaders open to changes in the relationship between their two peoples. They were mistaken.

Defining Moment

Once Japan had formal political control of the Korean peninsula, the Japanese government instituted a military government for the territory. Strict controls were placed upon the population in all areas of life. Although the Korea government had been strongly influenced by foreign powers (usually the Chinese) for hundreds of years, the nation had generally been at least nominally independent. Generally, the Korean population believed that the officials who had submitted to Japanese rule in 1910 were traitors. Thus, the former national leaders were not the individuals who instituted and led the push for independence in 1919. The push was from a broader base, with religious leaders playing a key role.

With widespread support for ridding the country of its Japanese rulers, there was a debate as to what means should be used. One faction sought to inspire a militant uprising, using the numerical superiority of the Korean population to overcome the superior weapons of the Japanese military and police. They believed that a rapid unified strike against the Japanese would be successful. However, the other major group among the individuals pushing for independence believed that this would be only a short term victory. They asserted that Japan would send thousands more troops to Korea and then would slaughter the population. This group also believed that if the Korean people initiated the violence by killing all the Japanese soldiers stationed in Korea, then there would be no international support for their cause when Japan responded with even greater violence.

In the end, the non-violent faction carried the day among those pushing for independence. They created this document and had thirty-three of the nation's religious/cultural leaders sign it for the general population. As those pushing for independence (and a republic) did not represent traditional Korean thought, those signing this document were not traditional religious leaders. Intentionally, the leaders' religious affiliations were split: fifteen Christian leaders, fifteen Chondokyo (or Chondogyo), and three Buddhists. Chondogyo was an indigenous Korean nineteenth religious/political movement opposed to Christian missionaries/theology and the imperial court's version of Confucian teachings. On March 1st, a Saturday, the thirty-three signatories gathered in Seoul to publically sign the document declaring independence, while others within the movement led

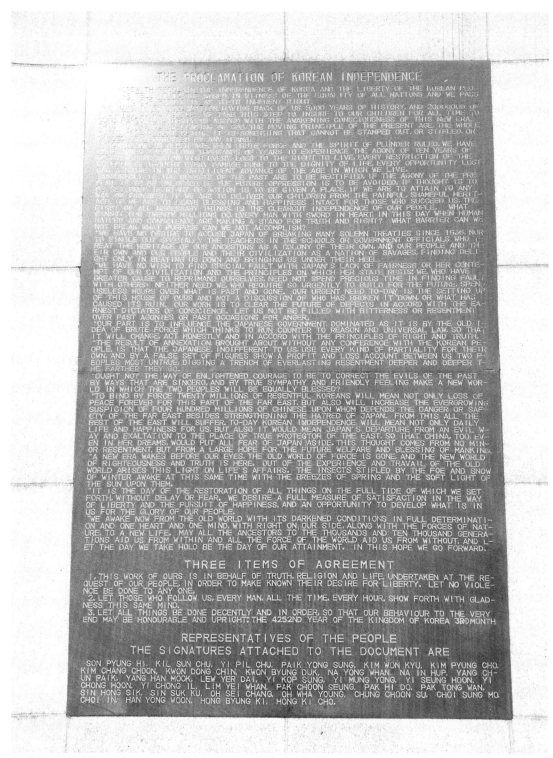

English version of the Proclamation of Korean Independence, displayed in Tapgol Park in Seoul. Photo by Seudo, via Wikimedia Commons.

massive demonstrations in many cities throughout the peninsula. It has been estimated that about two million Koreans (ten percent of the population) participated in anti-Japanese demonstrations. Various demonstrations were held in the next six weeks, during which time the Japanese government had applied enough pressure on the population to end this push for independence. Although the movement failed to gain independence for Korea, or strong international support for their cause, it was the first major twentieth century attempt to use non-violent protest as a political tool against repressive foreign rule.

Author Biography

Choe Nam-seon (1890-1957) was one of the founders of the March First Movement. Born in Seoul and educated in Japan, Choe was a leading figure in literary circles, which included his developing a new style of Korean poetry. He also did extensive historical work focusing on Korean culture. Politically, he believed that the revolution should be led by young people and would ultimately end with Korea as the foremost nation in the world. After imprisonment for his participation in the March First Movement, Choe continued an academic and literary career, at times collaborating with the Japanese rulers. (He exhorted Koreans to join the Japanese army during World War II.) After World War II, his trial on this charge was eventually suspended. His positive legacy as a historian, poet, publisher, and leader of the March First Movement has been tarnished by his acceptance of Japanese rule in the 1930s and 1940s.

Historical Document

Korean Declaration of Independence
[March 1, 1919]

We herewith proclaim the independence of Korea and the liberty of the Korean people. This we proclaim to all the nations of the world in witness of human equality. This we proclaim to our descendants so that they may enjoy in perpetuity their inherent right to nationhood. Inasmuch as this proclamation originates from our five-thousand-year history, inasmuch as it springs from the loyalty of twenty million people, inasmuch as it affirms our yearning for the advancement of everlasting liberty, inasmuch as it expresses our desire to take part in the global reform rooted in human conscience, it is the solemn will of heaven, the great tide of our age, and a just act necessary for the co-existence of all humankind. Therefore, no power in this world can obstruct or suppress it! Victims of the outdated notions of aggression and brute force, we have now suffered for a decade, for the first time in our long history, under foreign tyranny; our right to existence deprived, our spiritual growth stunted, our national pride and honor damaged, and our opportunity to make our own creative contribution to the progress of world civilization lost. Surely, if we are to eradicate our longstanding sense of injustice, if we are to extricate ourselves from today's pain, if we are to forestall tomorrow's threat, if we are to resuscitate our trampled national pride, if we as individuals are to reach our full potential, if we are to deliver our children from the legacy of shame, if we are to bequeath to our future generations blessing and prosperity, our first and foremost duty is to secure the independence of our people. If each and every twenty million of us carry a sword in our hearts and if we are supported by today's shared human conscience ready to stand by us equipped with arms of justice and morality, what can stop us from pressing forward to defeat the strongest? If we regroup and build up our strength, what aim can we not accomplish?

Though Japan has repeatedly violated its promises since the Treaty of 1876, we do not here condemn its perfidy. Though its scholars and government officials dismiss our great dynastic achievements in order to prop up its claim that our history began as a foreign colony with a primitive civilization, though it merely seeks a conqueror's gratification willfully ignoring the ancient foundation and the outstanding characteristics of our people, we do not here take it to task. We are pressed to reprimand ourselves, and thus have little time to reproach others. Busy with today's work, we have little time to chastise yesterday's actions.

Today, our only duty is to rebuild ourselves, not to demolish others. It is to explore our new destiny according to the solemn dictates of our conscience, not to squabble with others over fleeting grudges and old animosities. It is to restore our natural, rational foundation by rectifying the unnatural, irrational ambition of the Japanese politicians in the grip of obsolete ideas. The annexation made without national consensus has inevitably led to intimidation used as a temporary measure, inequality caused by discrimination, and statistics falsified to justify it. Just look at the result today! The chasm of rancor has grown so wide that bridging the two peoples with differing interests seems all but impossible.

To boldly right old wrongs, opening a new relationship based on true mutual understating, is certainly the best way for both countries to avert disaster and foster amity. To forcibly bind twenty million people filled with bitterness and enmity will not secure lasting peace. Moreover, it will exacerbate the apprehension and distrust of four hundred million Chinese people who hold the key to East Asian stability, which will undoubtedly lead to the unrest and eventual downfall of the entire region. Therefore, establishing Korean independence today will permit Koreans to return to their rightful lives, will enable the Japanese to break away from their wrongful path and concentrate on their responsibility as a major player in East Asia, and will free the Chinese from their nightmare of uncertainty and anxiety about Japan. Korean independence will indeed be an indispensable step toward the stability of East Asia, which will in turn contribute to the attainment of world peace. With the well-being of all humanity at stake, the establishment of Korean independence is a grave issue that transcends mere animosity between two nations.

Behold! A new world is approaching before our very eyes! The age of might has receded, and the age of morality has arrived. The spirit of humanism cultivated throughout the past century now begins to throw its light on a new chapter in world history. Just as a new spring has come, hastening the rebirth of every living thing, our pulse, once frozen in the bitter cold and snow, now quickens in the warm breeze and sunshine. The good fortune of heaven and earth has returned to us, and we ride the changing tide of the world. Do not hesitate or flinch! By protecting our inalienable individual right to freedom, we will enjoy our lives to the full. By realizing our bountiful creativity, our national civilization will flower in the warmth of spring that pervades the world.

We hereby rise up! Conscience is on our side, and truth marches with us. Men and women, young and old, leave your darkened corners and partake in the joyful resurrection along with all creation! The spirit of our many ancestors protects us from within, and the tide of the new world from without. To begin is to succeed! Let us march straight into the light!

We hereby pledge the following:

Today's undertaking reflects the demands of our people for justice, morality, survival, and prosperity. Therefore, we will act solely in the spirit of liberty, never in the spirit of enmity.

To the last person and to the last moment, we will forthrightly express the will of the Korean people.

We will respect order in all our actions and ensure that our demeanor and claims are always honorable and upright.

The first day of the third month of the 4252nd year of the founding of Korea,

[signed]

Glossary

perfidy: treachery, intentionally breaking a trust

shared human conscience: a reference to the ideals of progressivism and national self-determination.

Document Themes and Analysis

When the thirty-three individuals met at the Taehwagwan Restaurant in Seoul to sign the Declaration of Independence, they made clear not only their goal, but the means by which they sought to attain it. The goal of independence was made clear in the first sentence, while the means was expressed in the three points which closed the document. In between, there were assertions regarding the justification for the push, as well as lofty rhetoric regarding what the new era of total independence would bring for Korea and the world.

For the leaders of the Korean independence movement, change was not only going to happen in an unusual manner, but would be propelled by the vision of what might be, rather than hatred and rejection of what had been. Although the second paragraph recounted some of the steps Japan took in taking control of Korea, it ended with the exhortation not to "chastise yesterday's actions." In other sections of the document, the desire to rebuild or to "seek a new relationship" was emphasized, rather than focusing on the destruction of the old. Hopes were expressed that the "age of morality has arrived." Rather than a few leaders, or the ruling class of past generations, confronting the Japanese government, the First of March Movement exhorted all twenty million Koreans to be the non-violent force that will bring about this transformation. Independence would be the result not of skills in the martial arts; rather it would the swords in the hearts of all Koreans which would give the strength for victory.

Choe, in writing this document, understood the realities of the world, while his, and the movement's, idealism gave hope that a substantial change would occur. Thus, while the movement sought to expel Japan from Korea, the leaders understood that Japan was a regional power. While the annexation of Korea by Japan needed to end, by not pushing enmity between the two nations or peoples, the movement's leaders hoped that stability in East Asia could be attained. The implication was that balancing the powers of Japan, China, and an independent Korea, would create stability and peace in the region and help to implement the common goal of world peace. The peaceful uprising of the Korean people meant the end of the "age of might" and the implementation of the "age of morality."

Through the development of the new Korean state, the world would be touched by Korean ideals and culture, as they flowered in this new era of independence. The ideals of self-determination, "global reform" based in the new "human consciousness," would be illustrated for the world community by Korea's non-violent push to transform its situation. The "honorable and upright" manner in which independence would be attained, as well as a similar description of the movement's goal, would show the world what was possible when a nation unified itself against an oppressor. Unfortunately for the Korean people, the goal of the movement was not attained. Although the movement adheres to many of its ideals, the lack of support from other nations that professed that national self-determination should be a global norm doomed the March First Movement. Several thousand Koreans were killed and tens of thousands arrested. With no change in sight, the internal push for independence faded, leaving only exiles in secure locations to continue to sound the message. After the initial repression, Japan did respond to the situation in Korea by establishing a civilian police force, rather than using mainly military policy, and greater freedom was granted to Korean publications. Korea was never able to unilaterally force Japan to leave the country. It was only after Japan's defeat in World War II that the goals of the 1919 March First Movement were reached. However, with the division of the nation into North and South Korea, the "good fortune of heaven and earth" which was foreseen by the movement, did not come with independence.

—Donald A. Watt, PhD

Bibliography and Additional Reading

Arirang News. "Korea's March 1st 'Samil' Movement hits 87th anniversary." *YouTube*. Seoul: Arirang News, 2016.

Breen, Mike. "The March 1 Uprising: New Nation, New Leaders." *The Korea Times*. Seoul: Hankook Ilbo, 2018.

Institute of Korean Independence Movement Studies. *The History of the Korean Independence Movement.* Cheonan City, Rep. of Korea: The Institute/Independence Hall, 2014.

Shin, Michael. *Korean National Identity under Japanese Colonial Rule: Yi Gwangsu and the March First Movement of 1919.* (Routledge Studies in the Modern History of Asia). London: Routledge, 2018.

The Mexican Revolution

The Mexican Revolution (1910–1920), like the French Revolution, was a complicated, lengthy struggle that involved many different phases, factions, and leading figures. During the thirty-five years prior, the country was ruled with an iron fist by Porfirio Díaz, who brought stability and economic growth to Mexico but at the price of government corruption and the concentration of wealth in the hands of the few. Growing public dissatisfaction with Díaz led to the rise of various revolutionary movements and leaders, among them Emiliano Zapata, Francisco "Pancho" Villa, Pascual Orozco, and Francisco Madera. These men came together in order to overthrow Díaz (1911) and replace him with Madera. Once in office, however, Madera alienated his former allies and hardened his foes against him. He was overthrown in 1913 by a former Díaz general, Victoriano Huerta. Huerta instituted a repressive military dictatorship—one vehemently opposed by the United States. Constitutional forces inside Mexico, led by Alvaro Óbregon and Venustiano Carranza, and aided by Villa, toppled the Huerta regime in 1914. Carranza declared himself president, thus ending Villa's support. After further bloodshed, Carranza presented a liberal constitution in 1917, which laid the foundation for reform but was not fully implemented. A rebellion against his increasingly reactionary policies resulted in his removal in 1920, with Óbregon assuming the presidency. Although sporadic clashes continued, the revolutionary period is considered to have ended at this point. Óbregon was able to bring relative peace and prosperity to Mexico. He was reelected in 1928 yet killed before resuming office.

Plan de San Luis de Potosi

Date: October 5, 1910
Author: Francisco Madero
Genre: political tract

Summary Overview

By the time of this document's publication in 1910, Porfirio Díaz had ruled Mexico for decades. His administration had brought peace and stability after a period of chaos and foreign intervention. However, these positive effects came with a loss of civil liberties and an expanding gap between rich and poor. Although Díaz first campaigned on the ideal that the president should not be reelected for a second term, he himself served seven full terms. When he stood for an eighth term, his country had had enough. Francisco Madero, the author of this document, ran against Díaz in the presidential election of 1910. Fearing the rising popularity of his rival, Díaz had Madero and many of his partisans arrested and imprisoned before the election. Madero escaped from prison and issued this document as a call for revolution. In the document, Madero details the injustices of the Díaz administration and evokes lofty ideals to encourage action. The document and revolution were successful. Díaz was forced into exile, and Madero was elected in a new presidential in 1911. Madero's victory, however, was short-lived.

Defining Moment

José de la Cruz Porfirio Díaz Mori, more commonly known as Porfirio Díaz, first became the president of Mexico in 1877. It had been a tumultuous time for Mexico. The liberal reforms of the 1850s did not sit well with the nation's conservatives, who rose up in the War of Reform. The conservatives were defeated in this war; however, they invited in foreign assistance from France to overcome their liberal compatriots. France, with help from these conservatives, placed Maximilian I in power, who reigned from 1863 to 1867. Mexico's liberals retook the country and executed Maximilian. Benito Juárez had been president before the French intervention, and although he never officially relinquished his title, the ascendance of Mexican liberals allowed him to retake his role as the country's executive. After Juárez died of a heart attack in 1872, Sebastian Lerdo de Tejada became president and was formally elected to his own term later that year. Lerdo won reelection in 1876; however, Díaz opposed Lerdo on the grounds of "No Reelection." Also a liberal and an accomplished general, Díaz forced Lerdo into exile and was elected president in new elections in early 1877.

Porfirio Díaz, c.?1910. Photo via Wikimedia Commons. [Public domain.]

Francisco Madero, c. 1910. Photo via Wikimedia Commons. [Public domain.]

It is ironic that Díaz first took power by championing the tenet of "No Reelection" considering he would go on to serve seven terms as president. After his first term, he abided by his tenet on a technicality; he did not run for reelection but positioned his trustworthy lieutenant Manuel González to succeed him while he retained a position of power behind the scenes. When González's presidency struggled, Díaz threw off all pretensions and ran for election in 1884. He won that year and his five following reelection campaigns, six if you include his final controversial electoral victory. Díaz was and remains a polarizing figure. His rule ended years of tumult and ushered in the period sometimes dubbed the *Pax Porfiriana*. This phrase translates to the Peace of Porfirio and references the *Pax Romana*, the period of stability experienced under the Roman Empire. However, the stability brought with it certain injustices. To retain power, his administration restricted many civil liberties including freedom of the press. His economic policies showed favoritism and exacerbated the gap between rich and poor. These injustices paved the way for Francisco Madero's political rise and overthrow of Díaz's rule.

Born into a wealthy family, Madero did not enter politics until his rapid ascendance in the first decade of the twentieth century. Opposed to Díaz's ongoing rule, he largely funded his own candidacy for president and set himself up as Díaz's main rival. After declaring that he would not run for an eighth term in 1910, the aging Díaz changed his mind. Díaz had Madero imprisoned prior to the election to solidify his own reelection. Madero wrote this document while in prison, and published it upon his escape and flight over the U.S. border. It was named after the city where he was held captive and dated to his final day in the city. With the document as his call to arms, Madero led the first stage of the Mexican revolution. The revolutionaries won a decisive battle at Ciudad Juárez on May 21, 1911. Díaz agreed to resign and went into exile. Madero was elected president of Mexico in an election held later that year. He did not serve long, however. He was assassinated in February of 1913 in a reactionary coup d'état led by Victoriano Huerta. He, in turn, was forced out in the following year, and the tumult of revolution persisted for the remainder of the decade.

Author Biography

Francisco Madero was a Mexican revolutionary and, subsequently, the president of Mexico. He was born on October 30, 1873, to a very wealthy family in Coahuila, a region in northern Mexico. He studied at the *École des Hautes Études Commerciales* in Paris and then the University of California at Berkeley before returning to the family's diverse business empire in Mexico. He did not enter politics until the early twentieth century where he took a hardline stance against Porfirio Díaz, who had by then occupied the presidency for decades and continuously consolidated power. Madero helped form the Anti-Reelectionist Party whose primary goal was to oust Díaz from power. In April 1910, the party selected Madero as their nominee to face off against Díaz for the presidency. Funded in large part by his family's own fortune, Madero threatened Díaz's hold on power and was arrested along with thousands of his fellow partisans. Díaz won reelection with Madero in prison, in what was widely regarded as a fraudulent election. Madero escaped from imprisonment, crossed the U.S. border, and issued this document as a rallying cry for revolution. Understanding that he was losing his grip on power, Díaz fled to Europe, and after the brief interim presidency of León de la Barra, Madero was overwhelmingly elected president in October of 1911. However, he only ruled for a little over a year. General Victoriano Huerta led a reactionary coup d'état and oversaw Madero's assassination on February 22, 1913.

Historical Document

Peoples, in their constant efforts for the triumph of the ideal of liberty and justice, are forced, at precise historical moments, to make their greatest sacrifices.

Our beloved country has reached one of those moments. A force of tyranny, which we Mexicans were not accustomed to suffer after we won our independence, oppresses us in such a manner that it has become intolerable. In exchange for that tyranny we are offered peace, but peace full of shame for the Mexican nation, because its basis is not law, but force; because its object is not the aggrandizement and prosperity of the country, but to enrich a small group who, abusing their influence, have converted the public charges into fountains of exclusively personal benefit, unscrupulously exploiting the manner of lucrative concessions and contracts.

The legislative and judicial powers are completely subordinated to the executive; the division of powers, the sovereignty of the States, the liberty of the common councils, and the rights of the citizens exist only in writing in our great charter; but, as a fact, it may almost be said that martial law constantly exists in Mexico; the administration of justice, instead of imparting protection to the weak, merely serves to legalize the plundering committed by the strong; the judges instead of being the representatives of justice, are the agents of the executive, whose interests they faithfully serve; the chambers of the union have no other will than that of the dictator; the governors of the States are designated by him and they in their turn designate and impose in like manner the municipal authorities.

From this it results that the whole administrative, judicial, and legislative machinery obeys a single will, the caprice of General Porfirio Díaz, who during his long administration has shown that the principal motive that guides him is to maintain himself in power and at any cost.

For many years profound discontent has been felt throughout the Republic, due to such a system of government, but General Díaz with great cunning and perseverance, has succeeded in annihilating all independent elements, so that it was not possible to organize any sort of movement to take from him the power of which he made such bad use. The evil constantly became worse, and the decided eagerness of General Díaz to impose a successor upon the nations in the person of Mr. Ramon Corral carried that evil to its limit and caused many of us Mexicans, although lacking recognized political standing, since it had been impossible to acquire it during the 36 years of dictatorship, to throw ourselves into the struggle to recover the sovereignty of the people and their rights on purely democratic grounds....

In Mexico, as a democratic Republic, the public power can have no other origin nor other basis than the will of the people, and the latter can not be subordinated to formulas to be executed in a fraudulent manner...

For this reason the Mexican people have protested against the illegality of the last election and, desiring to use successively all the recourses offered by the laws of the Republic, in due form asked for the nullification of the election by the Chamber of Deputies, notwithstanding they recognized no legal origin in said body and knew beforehand that, as its members were not the representatives of the people, they would carry out the will of General Diaz, to whom exclusively they owe their investiture.

In such a state of affairs the people, who are the only sovereign, also protested energetically against the election in imposing manifestations in different parts of the Republic; and if the latter were not general throughout the national territory, It was due to the terrible pressure exercised by the Government, which always quenches in blood any democratic manifestation, as happened in Puebla, Vera Cruz, Tlaxcala, and in other places.

But this violent and illegal system can no longer subsist.

I have very well realized that if the people have designated me as their candidate for the Presidency it is not because they have had an opportunity to discover in me the qualities of a statesman or of a ruler, but the virility of the patriot determined to sacrifice himself, if need be, to obtain liberty and to help the people free themselves from the odious tyranny that oppresses them.

From the moment I threw myself into the democratic struggle I very well knew that General Díaz would not bow to the will of the nation, and the noble Mexican people, in following me to the polls, also knew perfectly the outrage that awaited them; but in spite of it, the people gave the cause of liberty a numerous contingent of martyrs when they were necessary and with wonderful stoicism went to the polls and received every sort of molestation.

But such conduct was indispensable to show to the whole world that the Mexican people are fit for democracy, that they are thirsty for liberty, and that their present rulers do not measure up to their aspirations.

Besides, the attitude of the people before and during the election, as well as afterwards, shows clearly that they reject with energy the Government of General Díaz and that, if those electoral rights had been respected, I would have been elected for President of the Republic.

Therefore, and in echo of the national will, I declare the late election illegal and, the Republic being accordingly without rulers, provisionally assume the Presidency of the Republic until the people designate their rulers pursuant to the law. In order to attain this end, it is necessary to eject from power the audacious usurpers whose only title of legality involves a scandalous and immoral fraud.

With all honesty I declare that it would be a weakness on my part and treason to the people, who have placed their confidence in me, not to put myself at the front of my fellow citizens, who anxiously call me from all parts of the country, to compel General Díaz by force of arms, to respect the national will.

Document Themes and Analysis

In this document, which has been excerpted and translated from its original Spanish, Francisco Madero declares the recent reelection of Porfirio Díaz illegal and states that he will assume the presidency provisionally until another election can be held. The document develops the theme of injustice associated with the Díaz campaign as well as the high-minded themes of liberty and duty in order to encourage action from Madero's supporters.

The majority of the first half of the document paints the Díaz regime as unjust and violent. Madero calls this regime a tyranny: "A force of tyranny, which we Mexicans were not accustomed to suffer after we won our independence, oppresses us in such a manner that it has become intolerable." Madero elaborates upon this idea, showing in what way Díaz has turned the government into a tyranny centered around his own person: "From this it results that the whole administrative, judicial, and legislative machinery obeys a single will, the caprice of General Porfirio Díaz, who during his long administration has shown that the principal motive that guides him is to maintain himself in power and at any cost." After detailing the injustices at length, the author reveals why he is spending so much time on them: "But this violent and illegal system can no longer subsist." The injustice of the prior regime, the document argues, is why action is required.

In juxtaposition to the illegality, injustice, and violence of the Díaz administration, Madero develops the themes of liberty and duty. These two themes are introduced from the very first line: "Peoples, in their constant efforts for the triumph of the ideal of liberty and justice, are forced, at precise historical moments, to make their greatest sacrifices." The author explicitly names the concept of liberty and alludes to duty by calling for his audience to make their greatest sacrifices. The author directly names the theme of liberty four more times in the document. Liberty is what the Díaz regime is stifling and what the revolutionaries are being called upon to defend. The author does not only evoke the duty of his audience but also strongly declares duty as the reason for his own actions. He ends the document, asserting, "With all honesty I declare that it would be a weakness on my part and treason to the people, who have placed their confidence in me, not to put myself at the front of my fellow citizens, who anxiously call me from all parts of the country, to compel General Díaz by force of arms, to respect the national will." Madero is taking strong, revolutionary steps and employing lofty ideals as the grounds for taking them.

—Anthony Vivian, MA

Bibliography and Additional Reading

Brenner, Anita. *The Wind that Swept Mexico: The History of the Mexican Revolution of 1910-1942*. Austin, TX: University of Texas Press, 1984.

Buchenau, Jügen, and Timothy Henderson. *The Mexican Revolution: A Documentary History*. Indianapolis: Hackett Publishing Co., 2022.

Knight, Alan. *The Mexican Revolution: A Very Short Introduction*. New York: Oxford UP, 2016.

Ross. Stanley R. *Francisco I. Madero: Apostle of Mexican Democracy*. New York: Columbia UP, 1955.

Plan of Ayala

Date: November 25, 1911
Author: Emiliano Zapata
Genre: political tract

Summary Overview

The 1910s were a tumultuous time for Mexicans as the Mexican Revolution raged on. Revolutionaries overturned the longstanding administration of Porfirio Díaz, resulting in the Francisco Madero Administration. Next, a reactionary coup d'état under Victoriano Huerte pushed out Madero but was itself overthrown by another group of revolutionaries. Throughout these cycles, Emiliano Zapata became a cult figure in his home state of Morelos and beyond. Zapata's primary concern was land inequality as large estates continued to grow at the expense of small landowners. In this document, he details his plan for land reform and rails against Madero, his former ally. Madero had recently risen to power but made it clear to Zapata that he was uninterested in enacting significant land reform. Zapata and his forces allied with and fought against different factions of the revolution, all in effort to put into practice the land reform outlined here.

Defining Moment

The long administration of Porfirio Díaz was labelled by some as the *Pax Porfiriana*, or Peace of Porifirio. However, whatever peace and stability this administration ushered in came with a price, especially for the rural peasants of Mexico. *Haciendas*, or large plantations, expanded rapidly and gobbled up land from smaller land owners. The large landowners profiting from the changes were well-connected to the Díaz administration, who aided and accelerated the process. Meanwhile, many of the peasants became landless—often racked with debt—working land owned by others.

In the presidential election of 1910, Francisco Madero ran against Díaz as the latter ran for his eighth term in office. Although Madero came from a wealthy background, he campaigned on a promise of reform. Meanwhile, Emiliano Zapata, president of the council of Anenecuilco, a village in Morelos in Southern Mexico, worked to stem the expansion of *haciendas* in his region. He backed Madero's campaign hoping that a change of administration would bring with it tangible land reform. Feeling threatened by Madero's rising popularity, Díaz had him jailed and ordered the election go ahead on schedule. When the results came in,

Emiliano Zapata, 1914. Photo via Wikimedia Commons. [Public domain.]

Plan of Ayala (1911), Emiliano Zapata's manuscript. Photo by Luis Alvaz, via Wikimedia Commons.

Díaz won reelection nearly unanimously despite Madero's large support. People immediately viewed the results as fraudulent, and the outrage sparked the Mexican Revolution. Madero escaped from jail and issued the Plan de San Luis de Potosi, a call to revolution. At the inception of the revolution, Zapata continued his support for Madero, despite Madero's less revolutionary stance on land reform. Zapata's forces, dubbed Zapatistas, defeated the forces of Díaz in the Battle of Cuautla in Morelos in May of 1911. This victory, coupled with the revolutionary victory at Ciudad Juárez, caused Díaz to capitulate.

In the summer of 1911, Zapata's and Madero's alliance soured. Despite Zapata's greatest efforts, it became clear to him that Madero had no intention of instituting the type of land reforms for which Zapata advocated. Shortly after Madero was elected president, Zapata issued this document, which strongly denounces Madero, declares the revolution not over, and lays out Zapata's plans for land reform. Zapata allied with fellow revolutionaries, such as Pascual Orozco and Emiliano Vázquez Gómez and fought against Madero's recently formed administration. Zapata and his Zapatistas saw success against Madero's forces, and victory appeared to be in sight. However, before they got the chance, General Victoriano Huerte led a coup d'état and toppled Madero's administration in February of 1913. Huerte had risen the ranks of the military under Díaz, and his coup d'état was a reactionary one. He was even more ideologically opposed to Zapata and his fellow revolutionaries than Madero had been.

A spectrum of different revolutionaries continued the fight, now against Huerte's administration. Zapata and his forces took control of the state of Morelos as Huerte focused his attention elsewhere. In July, 1914, Venustiano Carranza, Álvaro Obregón and Francisco Villa deposed Huerte's government. The different revolutionary factions met at the Convention of Aguascalientes to try to reconcile their differences and form a government. They were unable to reach an agreement, and Villa broke with Carranza and Obregón. Unable to convince Carranza on the importance of the Plan of Ayala, Zapata sided with Villa. Zapata consolidated control over Morelos; however, as Carranza's power became more stable elsewhere he asserted more pressure on the region. On April 10, 1919, one of Carranza's generals invited Zapata to a meeting, claiming that he wanted to desert Carranza and join Zapata's cause. However, as soon as Zapata arrived, he was ambushed and killed.

The ambitious land reform laid out in this document was never realized. However, the efforts of Zapata, the document's author, had a deep effect on Mexican politics. The Plan of Ayala had a direct influence on Article 27 of the 1917 Mexican Constitution. After his death, Zapata became a martyr for his cause. His memory contributed to southern Mexico's independent inclination. He also posthumously inspired the land reform of Lázaro Cárdenas, the Mexican President during the 1930s.

Author Biography

Emiliano Zapata was the leader of the peasant revolts in Morelos and an influential figure in the wider Mexican Revolution. Zapata was born on August 8, 1879, in Morelos, Mexico. Under the long administration of Porfirio Díaz, the *haciendas*, or large plantations, of the region had expanded greatly. In 1910, when the Díaz administration was shaken by revolution across Mexico, Zapata led a peasants' revolt in Morelos. He banded together with the other rebel leaders to help defeat Díaz's forces and exile him from the country. Zapata soon grew frustrated with Mexico's new leader Francisco Madero and his unwillingness to enact Zapata's proposed land reforms. He issued this document, denouncing Madero and articulating his extensive land reform. After a reactionary coup d'état under Victoriano Huerte overthrew Madero's government, a group of revolutionaries under Zapata, Venustiano Carranza, and others toppled Huerte's government. Shortly after the victory, Carranaza and Zapata split, with the former assuming the presidency and the latter consolidating his power in Morelos. A group of Carranza's men invited Zapata to a rendezvous, ambushed, and killed him on April 10, 1919. He was thirty-nine years old.

Historical Document

Plan of Ayala

Liberating Plan of the sons of the State of Morelos, affiliated with the Insurgent Army that defends the fulfillment of the Plan of San Luis, with the reforms which it has believed proper to add in benefit of the Mexican Fatherland.

We who undersign, constituted in a revolutionary junta to sustain and carry out the promises which the revolution of November 20, 1910, just past, made to the country, declare solemnly before the face of the civilized world which judges us and before the nation to which we belong and which we call [sic, love], propositions which we have formulated to end the tyranny which oppresses us and redeem the fatherland from the dictatorships which are imposed on us, which [propositions] are determined in the following plan:

Taking into consideration that the Mexican people led by Don Francisco I. Madero went to shed their blood to reconquer liberties and recover their rights which had been trampled on, and for a man to take possession of power, violating the sacred principles which he took an oath to defend under the slogan "Effective Suffrage and No Reelection," outraging thus the faith, the cause, the justice, and the liberties of the people: taking into consideration that that man to whom we refer is Don Francisco I. Madero, the same who initiated the above-cited revolution, who imposed his will and influence as a governing norm on the Provisional Government of the ex-President of the Republic Attorney Francisco L. de Barra [sic], causing with this deed repeated shedding of blood and multiple misfortunes for the fatherland in a manner deceitful and ridiculous, having no intentions other than satisfying his personal ambitions, his boundless instincts as a tyrant, and his profound disrespect for the fulfillment of the preexisting laws emanating from the immortal code of '57 [Constitution of 1857], written with the revolutionary blood of Ayutla;

Taking into account that the so-called Chief of the Liberating Revolution of Mexico, Don Francisco I. Madero, through lack of integrity and the highest weakness, did not carry to a happy end the revolution which gloriously he initiated with the help of God and the people, since he left standing most of the governing powers and corrupted elements of oppression of the dictatorial government of Porfirio Díaz, which are not nor can in any way be the representation of National Sovereignty, and which, for being most bitter adversaries of ours and of the principles which even now we defend, are provoking the discomfort of the country and opening new wounds in the bosom of the fatherland, to give it its own blood to drink; taking also into account that the aforementioned Sr. Francisco I. Madero, present President of the Republic, tries to avoid the fulfillment of the promises which he made to the Nation in the Plan of San Luis Potosí, being [sic, restricting] the above-cited promises to the agreements of Ciudad Juárez, by means of false promises and numerous intrigues against the Nation nullifying, pursuing, jailing, or killing revolutionary elements who helped him to occupy the high post of President of the Republic;

Taking into consideration that the so-often-repeated Francisco I. Madero has tried with the brute force of bayonets to shut up and to drown in blood the pueblos who ask, solicit, or demand from him the fulfillment of the promises of the revolution, calling them bandits and rebels, condemning them to a war of extermination without conceding or granting a single one of the guarantees which reason, justice, and the law prescribe; taking equally into consideration that the President of the Republic Francisco I. Madero has made of Effective Suffrage a bloody trick on the people, already against the will of the same people imposing Attorney José M. Pino Suárez in the Vice-Presidency of the Republic, or [imposing as] Governors of the States [men] designated by him, like the so-called General Ambrosio Figueroa, scourge and tyrant of the people of Morelos, or entering into chains and follow the pattern of a new dictatorship more shameful and more terrible than that of Porfirio Díaz, for it has been clear and patent that he has outraged the sovereignty of the States, trampling on the laws without any respect for lives or interests, as has happened in the State of Morelos, and others, leading them to the most horrendous anarchy which contemporary history registers.

For these considerations we declare the aforementioned Francisco I. Madero inept at realizing the promises of the revolution of which he was the author, because he has betrayed the principles with which he tricked the will of the people and was able to get into power: incapable of governing, because he has no respect for the law and justice of the pueblos, and a traitor to the fatherland, because he is humiliating in blood and fire, Mexicans who want liberties, so as to please the científicos, landlords, and bosses who enslave us, and from today on we begin to continue the revolution begun by him, until we achieve the overthrow of the dictatorial powers which exist.

Recognition is withdrawn from S. Francisco I. Madero as Chief of the Revolution and as President of the Republic, for the reasons which before were expressed, it being attempted to overthrow this official.

Recognized as Chief of the Liberating Revolution is the illustrious General Pascual Orozco, the second of the Leader Don Francisco I. Madero, and in case he does not accept this delicate post, recognition as Chief of the Revolution will go to General Don Emiliano Zapata.

The Revolutionary Junta of the State of Morelos manifests to the Nation under formal oath: that it makes its own the plan of San Luis Potosí, with the additions which are expressed below in benefit of the oppressed pueblos, and it will make itself the defender of the principles it defends until victory or death.

The Revolutionary Junta of the State of Morelos will admit no transactions or compromises until it achieves the overthrow of the dictatorial elements of Porfirio Díaz and Francisco I. Madero, for the nation is tired of false men and traitors who make promises like liberators and who on arriving in power forget them and constitute themselves tyrants.

As an additional part of the plan, we invoke, we give notice: that [regarding] the fields, timber, and water which the landlords, científicos, or bosses have usurped, the pueblos or citizens who have the titles corresponding to those properties will immediately enter into possession of that real estate of which they have been despoiled by the bad faith of our oppressors, maintain at any cost with arms in hand the mentioned possession; and the usurpers who consider themselves with a right to them [those properties] will deduce it before the special tribunals which will be established on the triumph of the revolution.

In virtue of the fact that the immense majority of Mexican pueblos and citizens are owners of no more than the land they walk on, suffering the horrors of poverty without being able to improve their social condition in any way or to dedicate themselves to Industry or Agriculture, because lands, timber, and water are monopolized in a few hands, for this cause there will be expropriated the third part of those monopolies from the powerful proprietors of them, with prior indemnization, in order that the pueblos and citizens of Mexico may obtain ejidos, colonies, and foundations for pueblos, or fields for sowing or laboring, and the Mexicans' lack of prosperity and well-being may improve in all and for all.

[Regarding] The landlords, científicos, or bosses who oppose the present plan directly or indirectly, their goods will be nationalized and the two-third parts which [otherwise would] belong to them will go for indemnizations of war, pensions for widows and orphans of the victims who succumb in the struggle for the present plan.

In order to execute the procedures regarding the properties aforementioned, the laws of disamortization and nationalization will be applied as they fit, for serving us as norm and example can be those laws put in force by the immortal Juárez on ecclesiastical properties, which punished the despots and conservatives who in every time have tried to impose on us the ignominious yoke of oppression and backwardness.

The insurgent military chiefs of the Republic who rose up with arms in hand at the voice of Don Francisco I. Madero to defend the plan of San Luis Potosí, and who oppose with armed force the present plan, will be judged traitors to the cause which they defended and to the fatherland, since at present many of them, to humor the tyrants, for a fistful of coins, or for bribes or connivance, are shedding the blood of their brothers who claim the fulfillment of the promises which Don Francisco I. Madero made to the nation.

The expenses of war will be taken in conformity with Article 11 of the Plan of San Luis Potosí, and all procedures employed in the revolution we undertake will be in conformity with the same instructions, which the said plan determines.

Once triumphant the revolution which we carry into the path of reality, a Junta of the principal revolutionary chiefs from the different States will name or designate an interim President of the Republic, who will convoke elections for the organization of the federal powers.

The principal revolutionary chiefs of each State will designate in Junta the Governor of the State to which they belong, and this appointed official will convoke elections for the due organization of the public powers, the object being to avoid compulsory appointments which work the misfortune of the pueblos, like the so-well-known appointment of Ambrosio Figueroa in the State of Morelos and others who drive us to the precipice of bloody conflicts sustained by the caprice of the dictator Madero and the circle of científicos and landlords who have influenced him.

If President Madero and other dictatorial elements of the present and former regime want to avoid the immense misfortunes which afflict the fatherland, and [if they] possess true sentiments of love for it, let them make immediate renunciation of the posts they occupy and with that they will with something staunch the grave wounds which they have opened in the bosom of the fatherland, since, if they do not do so, on their heads will fall the blood and the anathema of our brothers.

Mexicans: consider that the cunning and bad faith of one man is shedding blood in a scandalous manner, because he is incapable of governing; consider that his system of government is choking the fatherland and trampling with the brute force of bayonets on our institutions; and thus, as we raised up our weapons to elevate him to power, we again raise them up against him for defaulting on his promises to the Mexican people and for having betrayed the revolution initiated by him, we are not personalists, we are partisans of principles and not of men!

Mexican People, support this plan with arms in hand and you will make the prosperity and well-being of the fatherland.

Ayala, November 25, 1911

Liberty, Justice and Law

Signed, General in Chief Emiliano Zapata; Generals Eufemio Zapata, Francisco Mendoza, Jesús Morales, Jesús Navarro, Otilio E. Montaño, José Trinidad Ruiz, Próculo Capistrán; Colonels...; Captains... [This] is a true copy taken from the original. Camp in the Mountains of Puebla, December 11, 1911. Signed General in Chief Emiliano Zapata.

[Source: John Womack, *Zapata and the Mexican Revolution* (New York: Knopf, 1969), pp. 400-404. Translation by John Womack]

Glossary

científicos: administrators who believed in governing by "scientific" principles

indemnization: compensation

junta: a military body or council in control of a government

suffrage: the vote; voting rights

Document Themes and Analysis

This document details Francisco Madero's duplicity, expounds the importance of land reform, and uses violent imagery to underline the urgency of the time.

The document is broken up into fifteen numbered provisions, the first of which is by far the longest. After a number of sentences beginning with "Taking into consideration..." or similar variants, this first provision builds up to the following payoff: "For these considerations we declare the aforementioned Francisco I. Madero inept at realizing the promises of the revolution of which he was the author, because he has betrayed the principles with which he tricked the will of the people and was able to get into power." In total, the document explicitly mentions the name of Madero a full seventeen times. Madero and Emiliano Zapata, the author of this document, had fought together against the government of Porfirio Díaz. However, shortly before the composition of the document was penned, the two split; a major aim of the document is for Zapata to outline why he broke with Madero.

The other major aim of this document is for Zapata to explain his proposed land reform. Among other components, the pulp of the land reform is stated in provision seven: "[T]here will be expropriated the third part of those monopolies from the powerful proprietors of them, with prior indemnization, in order that the pueblos and citizens of Mexico may obtain ejidos, colonies, and foundations for pueblos, or fields for sowing or laboring, and the Mexicans' lack of prosperity and well-being may improve in all and for all." In the years before, large *haciendas*, or plantations ("those monopolies" in the quotation above), had been rapidly expanding. Although reappropriating a third of the land from these monopolies may not seem radical, it proved radical enough to frighten off Madero and, later, Venustiano Carranza. These men were, like Zapata, revolutionaries but still unwilling to support the policy outlined here.

The document uses violent imagery to underline its points and stir its audience to action. The first provision alone mentions "blood" seven times. The first sentence of the provision describes how the Mexican people had shed blood *for* Madero: "Taking into consideration that the Mexican people led by Don Francisco I. Madero went to shed their blood to reconquer liberties." Yet before long, the author is explaining how Madero has turned against the Mexican people and now spills their blood as enemies: "Francisco I. Madero has tried with the brute force of bayonets to shut up and to drown in blood the pueblos." The document uses this imagery to depict the graphic urgency of the situation. Yet it does not only use violent imagery to showcase the ways in which the Mexican people have already suffered. It uses these injustices to incite its audience to fight. It ends with a succinct call to arms: "Mexican People, support this plan with arms in hand and you will make the prosperity and well-being of the fatherland."

—Anthony Vivian, MA

Bibliography and Additional Reading

Brenner, Anita. *The Wind that Swept Mexico: The History of the Mexican Revolution of 1910-1942.* Austin, TX: University of Texas Press, 1984.

Knight, Alan. *The Mexican Revolution: A Very Short Introduction.* Oxford: Oxford UP, 2016.

McLynn, Frank. *Villa and Zapata: A History of the Mexican Revolution.* New York: Basic Books, 2002.

Womack, John. *Zapata and the Mexican Revolution.* New York: Vintage, 1970.

Ireland

From at least the sixteenth century, when England sought to expand Protestantism in Catholic Ireland, religious rivalry and conflict has recurred on the island. In the north (Ulster), Catholic landowners fled English persecution and were replaced by English and Scottish Protestants. Through the Act of Union (1801), the United Kingdom of Great Britain and Ireland was established, with Ireland gaining representation in (British) Parliament. The Great Famine in Ireland (1845–1852), in which the population fell by nearly 25 percent due to starvation, disease, and migration, led to increased agitation for Home Rule, or self-government for Ireland. The first two Home Rule bills in Parliament (1886, 1893) were defeated. The third (1912) passed the House of Commons but was altered by the House of Lords to exclude Ulster, since threats by Unionists there of an uprising against Home Rule were taken seriously.

In Republican (pro-independence) Ireland, meanwhile, agitation for an Irish Free State continued. The 1916 Easter Rising in Dublin saw about 1,800 Republicans and members of the more radical Sinn Féin raise arms against British troops. After five days of fighting, the rebellion was put down and many of its leaders tried and executed. Sinn Féin, however, emerged as a dominant force. A larger Irish war of independence (1919–1921), pitting the Irish Republican Army against British and Unionist forces, followed. Britain in 1920 concluded a new home rule law, the Anglo-Irish Treaty, which formally separated Northern Ireland from the Irish Free State that makes up the bulk of the island to the south. Even as the new Provisional Government of Ireland was getting underway, anti-Treaty forces in the Irish Republican Army launched a civil war (1922–1923) against it as too accommodationist; they demanded an independent republic. A 1922 treaty granted dominion status to Ireland, bringing an end to the Irish revolutionary period (but not to the old animosities).

John Morley on Irish Home Rule

Date: 1887
Author: John Morley
Genre: magazine articles

Summary Overview

The question of Ireland and its place within the United Kingdom was a troubling one throughout the nineteenth century and into the twentieth. For some, the best compromise between utter subjugation and complete independence was Home Rule, a term used to mean self-government under the British crown. For numerous reasons—political, security-based, economic, especially religious—the idea of Irish Home Rule was considered appalling by many among the Victorian British establishment.

Those, on the other hand, who had worked in Ireland and seen its people's poverty, sense of injustice, and seething rage up close harbored different opinions. One such was John Morley, a Liberal Party member of Parliament and the Chief Secretary of Ireland in 1886. Morley was a journalist of uncommon skill who had made a name for himself in the Liberal Party at the point when the party split over the idea of pursuing Home Rule for Ireland. In response to a law professor's arguments as to the illegal and irresponsible nature of the concept of the Irish running their own government, Morley wrote a pair of articles published in the intellectual journal Nineteenth Century, excerpted here. He argued that Home Rule was the only true alternative to independence or subjugation, neither of which were palatable alternatives to the change considered necessary in Ireland in the 1880s.

Defining Moment

In 1801, an Act of Union made Ireland a fully-fledged member of the United Kingdom, on equal status with England, Scotland and Wales. At least, that was the Act's purported goal; as the people of Scotland and Wales could attest, no nation in the United Kingdom was taken as anything close to an equal to England, where the monarch sat and the UK's economy was centered. The real reason for the Union was security. The Irish had rebelled against British rule in 1798 in the midst of the Napoleonic Wars, and the British government decided that its best policy was to fully integrate Ireland into the United Kingdom and try to remake the island of Ireland and its people in the im-

John Morley. Photo via Wikimedia Commons. [Public domain.]

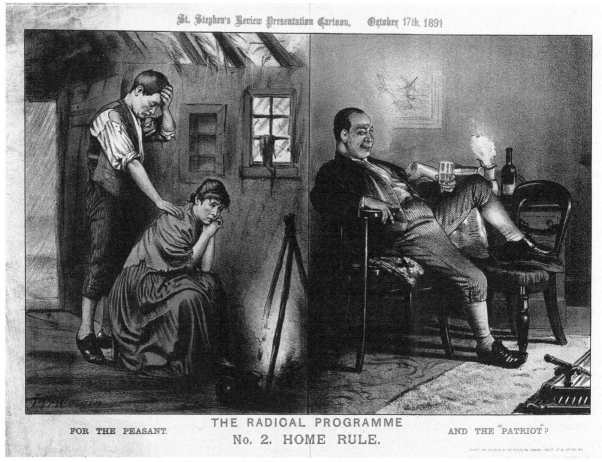

Anti-Home Rule cartoon, 1891: it claims that Home Rule will bring economic benefits to middle class "patriots", but ruin to the peasantry. Image by Wellcome Images, via Wikimedia Commons.

age of the English. It had not worked for the previous 225 years, but maybe this time, and in this way, it would be different.

Of course, that was not the case. The English crown had maintained a presence and power in Ireland since 1179 and had never been able to determine exactly how Ireland fit into the United Kingdom—as an equal to the other nations, as an occupied European nation, or as a colony. This problem became dangerous with the Protestant Reformation and King Henry VIII's establishment of the Church of England as Protestant. The Irish people remained predominantly Catholic and despised the English now not just as their economic and political overseers but as their religious enemies. English settlement schemes launched under Elizabeth I and Oliver Cromwell had brought Protestant settlers to Ireland, mainly Presbyterian Scots in the far northern province of Ulster; some Anglican settlers arrived in the east, and a few Irishmen gave in to Protestant coercion and became members of the Church of Ireland, as the Anglican Church was called there. Most Irishmen did not convert, however. They hated the Protestant Ascendancy—the laws and people privileging Protestantism on a Catholic island—and the effort it represented towards turning the Catholic Irish into an alien people in their own land. The rebellion in 1798 had been launched with the hope of attracting the Catholic French to invade Ireland and overthrow English rule. This was exactly the kind of action that made the English realize even more that they needed to subdue the Irish once and for all, or risk invasion from enemies on their west coast. Thus was the Act of Union of 1801 promulgated.

From the very beginning the Act of Union was a disaster. It was one thing for the English to enlist the Welsh and Scots to fight and die in imperial armies and surrender their resources to economic exploitation; it was quite another to expect the Irish to fall in line easily and do the same thing. Catholic Irishmen indeed enlisted in British armies and gave up their agricultural wealth for English profit, but they hated the English for it, launching rebellions, fomenting crime waves, and especially killing Protestant Irishmen given just about any opportunity. Within 25 years a repeal movement arose, led by the lawyer and orator Daniel O'Connell—though O'Connell himself advocated peace, many of his younger followers wanted violent resistance, and trouble loomed in the 1840s.

At precisely this point, a famine swept Ireland; a crop fungus from North America destroyed the potato crop that the Irish relied upon to supply their nutrition needs. While Irish peasant farmers produced other crops like wheat, that was also the way they paid their rent to their Protestant landlords, so if they used it for flour and bread, they would lose their land and livelihoods. The result was mass starvation. A million and a half Irish died from famine and disease between 1846 and 1851, and another million and a half Irish emigrated to the United States and other places in the English-speaking world. The British government bought cheap grain for sale to the Irish, removed tariffs on grain, passed laws to improve care for the poor, but the one thing they would not do was hand the Irish food to eat or demand that the landlords give up their profits—throughout the entire famine, Ireland was a net exporter of food. Instead, the English blamed Catholic Irish suffering on the Irish peasantry's poor economic planning and no government official ever even ventured to visit the island to see the peoples' misery for themselves. So much for union.

Not surprisingly, those Irish intellectuals and activists who survived the famine were determined to remove themselves from the Union at whatever cost necessary. Some of O'Connell's followers launched a rebellion in 1848. Since it failed, many moved to America to raise money and planned further acts of rebellion and terrorism, calling themselves the Fenian Brotherhood after an old Celtic Irish myth of legendary warriors from the pre-Christian era. By the 1860s, bombings in London, Dublin and other British cities announced the Fenians' intentions. In the 1870s, land agents such as Charles Boycott saw Irish peasants organize themselves to avoid working as tenants on their properties, plunging them into bankruptcy; the idea of being "boycotted" entered the English language for the first time, and landlords feared for their livelihoods in Ireland. Most of all, though, a sizeable number of sympathetic Protestant Irishmen—the only Irishmen who could meet the property requirement to vote—organized themselves into political parties and ran for office in the British Parliament, with the goal of effecting the best solution of all to Ireland's problems: independence. Realizing that such a goal was likely impossible to achieve, considering English prejudices and fears of Catholic invasion, their alternative was Home Rule.

Home Rule was in most respects just like the government of an American state in the United States. Local issues such as education, infrastructure, law and order and welfare would be in the hands of the Irish people, whereas any nationally-relevant issue like foreign policy, defense and international commerce would be handled by Parliament in London. In the modern United Kingdom, this has been implemented through a process called devolution; Scotland, Wales and Northern Ireland all have their own national governments. Yet even today, there is fear of what this process means to the security and economy of the United Kingdom—Scotland held a referendum on outright independence in 2014. In the late nineteenth century, when the history of Irish relations with England was littered with legalized prejudices favoring Protestants over Catholics and Catholics slaughtering Protestants given any opportunity, the idea of giving a predominantly Catholic Ireland the chance to run its own affairs was considered insane by most English politicians and voters. In the 1880s alone, numerous land agents had been killed and the government's Chief Secretary for Ireland and his top civil servant had been stabbed to death on the streets of Dublin.

At the same time, however, it was abundantly clear that British government had never treated Ireland as an equal within the boundaries of the United Kingdom, that most of its reforms had been selfish, ignorant and poorly implemented, that those Protestants who clung to their Ascendancy were just as violently inclined as their Catholic counterparts and most of all, nothing else had worked to pacify the Irish people. Home Rule stood a chance of keeping Ireland in the British fold while reducing the island's violence and the security threat it represented to England, which was why it was being discussed seriously in Parliament. Most English politicians, intellectuals, journalists and scholars opposed the idea; indeed, the Liberal Party itself split over the issue in 1886, a third of the party asserting its independence as the Unionist Party during the election held in that year. Among these Liberal Unionists was a famed constitutional scholar named Andrew Venn Dicey. Dicey wrote a series of books in opposition to Home Rule, the first of which, *England's Case Against Home Rule*, came out in 1887. His former Liberal allies attacked Dicey's position in a hastily assembled series of articles published in the same year, called *Handbook of Home Rule*. One of the most persuasive of the chapters in the Handbook was the one written by the most recent Liberal Chief Secretary of Ireland, John Morley, called "Some Arguments Considered," In it, Morley combined two articles he had written in the journal *Nineteenth Century* attacking Dicey's arguments.

Author Biography

John Morley was born in Blackburn in 1838 and went to school with the intention of becoming an Anglican clergyman, at the apparent wishes of his father. Instead, he and his father had a falling out over his abandonment of a religious career, and he became a journalist, working for the *Saturday Review of Politics, Literature, Science, and Art*, a prestigious Conservative intellectual journal in its day. Morley did not share the *Saturday Review*'s politics; rather, he sympathized with William Gladstone, a one-time Tory who became an adherent to the more flexible ideological libertarianism and paternalism of the Liberal Party. Morley moved on to become the editor of the Liberal equivalent of the *Saturday Review*, the *Fortnightly Review*, becoming known for his support of Gladstone. His journal published articles by Matthew Arnold, Thomas Huxley, John Stuart Mill and Herbert Spencer, while Morley himself wrote biographies of Enlightenment philosophers like Voltaire and Rousseau. By the 1870s Morley was one of the best known Liberal journalists and intellectuals in Britain.

Morley ran for Parliament unsuccessfully in 1880; he instead became editor of the *Pall Mall Gazette* and transformed it into a Liberal newspaper. With this added profile, he finally won political office as one of the members of Parliament for Newcastle upon Tyne in 1883. Due to his impeccable Liberal credentials, he quickly became a confidant of Gladstone, then the prime minister. In 1886, he became a member of Gladstone's Cabinet as the Secretary of State for Ireland. At the time, the Liberals were allied with the Irish Parliamentary Party led by Charles Stuart Parnell; in return for Parnell's support in Ireland during the 1886 election, Gladstone and Morley drew up the first Irish Home Rule Bill. The bill failed in the Commons, instead splitting the Liberal Party along religious lines, and Gladstone's Cabinet was turned out in another election in the same year.

Morley's career became somewhat defined by Ireland, and colonial issues in general. He returned to the Cabinet as Chief Secretary for Ireland again in 1892; the second Home Rule Bill passed the House of Commons but failed in the Lords, and the Cabinet was turned out of office again in 1895. When the Liberals came back to power in 1906, Morley was made Secretary of State for India, a Cabinet position that concentrated solely on the Indian colony. Like with Ireland, Morley worked to give the Indian people more control over their own governance in a series of reforms he passed in concert with the Indian Viceroy, Lord Minto. In 1908, he was given a peerage and moved to the House of Lords as Lord Morley, and soon became the leading Liberal voice in the Lords. He only resigned from office in August 1914, in protest at the idea of fighting the Great War to support the autocratic Russian tsarist state. He lived long enough to see Ireland become mostly independent in 1922 and died in 1923.

Historical Document

John Morley on Irish Home Rule

It is a favourite line of argument to show that we have no choice between the maintenance of the Union and the concession to Ireland of national independence. The evils of Irish independence are universally reckoned by Englishmen to be so intolerable that we shall never agree to it. The evils of Home Rule are even more intolerable still. Therefore, it is said, if we shall never willingly bring the latter upon our heads, *à fortiori* we ought on no account to invite the former. The business in hand, however, is not a theorem, but a problem; it is not a thesis to be proved, but a malady to be cured; and the world will thank only the reasoner who winds up, not with Q.E.D., but with Q.E.F. To reason that a patient ought not to take a given medicine because it may possibly cause him more pain than some other medicine which he has no intention of taking, is curiously oblique logic. The question is not oblique; it is direct. Will the operation do more harm to his constitution than the slow corrosions of a disorder grown inveterate? Are the conditions of the connection between England and Ireland, as laid down in the Act of Union, incapable of improvement? Is the present working of these conditions more prosperous and hopeful, or happier for Irish order and for English institutions, than any practicable proposal that it is within the compass of statesmanship to devise, and of civic sense to accept and to work? That is the question.

Some people contend that the burden of making out a case rests on the advocate of change, and not on those who support things as they are. But who supports things as they are? Things as they are have become insupportable. If you make any of the constitutional changes that have been proposed, we are told, parliamentary government, as Englishmen now know it, is at an end; and our critic stands amazed at those "who deem it a slighter danger to innovate on the Act of Union than to remodel the procedure of the House of Commons." As if that were the alternative. Great changes in the rules may do other good things, but no single competent authority believes that in this particular they will do the thing that we want. We cannot avoid constitutional changes. It is made matter of crushing rebuke that the Irish proposals of the late Government were an innovation on the old constitution of the realm. But everybody knows that, while ancient forms have survived, the last hundred years have witnessed a long succession of silent but most profound innovations. It was shortsighted to assume that the redistribution of political power that took place in 1884–5 was the last chapter of the history of constitutional change. It ought to have been foreseen that new possessors of power, both Irish and British, would press for objects the pursuit of which would certainly involve further novelties in the methods and machinery of government.

Every given innovation must be rigorously scrutinized, but in the mere change or in the fact of innovation there is no valid reproach. When one of the plans for the better government of Ireland is described as depriving parliamentary institutions of their elasticity and strength, as weakening the Executive at home, and lessening the power of the country to resist foreign attack, no careful observer of the events of the last seven years can fail to see that all this evil has already got its grip upon us. Mr. Dicey himself admits it. "Great Britain," he says, "if left to herself, could act with all the force, consistency, and energy given by unity of sentiment and community of interests. The obstruction and the uncertainty of our political aims, the feebleness and inconsistency with which they are pursued, arise in part at least from the connection with Ireland." So then, after all, it is feebleness and inconsistency, not elasticity and strength, that mark our institutions as they stand; feebleness and inconsistency, distraction and uncertainty. The supporter of things as they are is decidedly as much concerned in making out a case as the advocate of change.

The strength of the argument from Nationality is great, and full of significance; but Nationality is not the whole essence of either the argument from History or the argument from Self-government. Their force lies in considerations of political expediency as tested by practical experience.

The point of the argument from the lessons of History is that for some reason or another the international concern, whose unlucky affairs we are now trying to unravel, has always been carried on at a loss: the point of the argument from Self-government is that the loss would have been avoided if the Irish shareholders had for a certain number of the transactions been more influentially represented on the Board. That is quite apart from the sentiment of pure nationality. The failure has come about, not simply because the laws were not made by Irishmen as such, but because they were not made by the men who knew most about Ireland. The vice of the connection between the two countries has been the stupidity of governing a country without regard to the interests or customs, the peculiar objects and peculiar experiences, of the great majority of the people who live in it. It is not enough to say that the failures of England in Ireland have to a great extent flowed from causes too general to be identified with the intentional wrong-doing either of rulers or of subjects. We readily admit that, but it is not the point. It is not enough to insist that James I., in his plantations and transplantations, probably meant well to his Irish subjects. Probably he did. That is not the question. If it is "absolutely certain that his policy worked gross wrong," what is the explanation and the defence? We are quite content with Mr. Dicey's own answer. "Ignorance and want of sympathy produced all the evils of cruelty and malignity. An intended reform produced injustice, litigation, misery, and discontent. The case is noticeable, for it is a type of a thousand subsequent English attempts to reform and improve Ireland." This description would apply, with hardly a word altered, to the wrong done by the Encumbered Estates Act in the reign of Queen Victoria. That memorable measure, as Mr. Gladstone said, was due not to the action of a party, but to the action of a Parliament. Sir Robert Peel was hardly less responsible for it than Lord John Russell. "We produced it," said Mr. Gladstone, "with a general, lazy, uninformed, and irreflective good intention of taking capital to Ireland. What did we do? We sold the improvements of the tenants" (House of Commons, April 16). It is the same story, from the first chapter to the last, in education, poor law, public works, relief Acts, even in coercion Acts—lazy, uninformed, and irreflective good intention. That is the argument from history. When we are asked what good law an Irish Parliament would make that could not equally well be made by the Parliament at Westminster, this is the answer. It is not the will, it is the intelligence, that is wanting. We all know what the past has been. Why should the future be different?

"It is an inherent condition of human affairs," said Mill in a book which, in spite of some chimeras, is a wholesome corrective of the teaching of our new jurists, "that no intention, however sincere, of protecting the interests of others can make it safe or salutary to tie up their own hands. Still more obviously true is it, that by their own hands only can any positive and durable improvement of their circumstances in life be worked out" (*Repres. Government*, p. 57). It is these wise lessons from human experience to which the advocate of Home Rule appeals, and not the wild doctrine that any body of persons claiming to be united by a sense of nationality possesses *an inherent and divine right* to be treated as an independent community. It is quite true that circumstances sometimes justify a temporary dictatorship. In that there is nothing at variance with Liberalism. But the Parliamentary dictatorship in Ireland has lasted a great deal too long to be called temporary, and its stupid shambling operations are finally and decisively condemned by their consequences. That is a straightforward utilitarian argument, and has nothing whatever to do with inherent and divine rights, or any other form of political moonshine.

There are some who believe that an honest centralized administration of impartial officials, and not Local Self-Government, would best meet the real wants of the people. In other words, everything is to be for the people, nothing by the people—which has not hitherto been a Liberal principle. Something, however, may be said for this view, provided that the source of the authority of such an administration be acceptable. Austrian administration in Lombardy was good rather than bad, yet it was hated and resisted because it was Austrian and not Italian. No rational person can hold for an instant that the source of a scheme of government is immaterial to its prosperity. More than that, when people look for success in the government of Ireland to "honest centralized administration," we cannot but wonder what fault they find with the administration of Ireland to-day in respect of its honesty or its centralization. What administration ever carried either honesty or centralization to a higher pitch than the Irish administration of Mr. Forster? What could be less successful? Those who have been most directly concerned in the government of Ireland, whether English or Irish, even while alive to the perils of any other principle, habitually talk of centralization as the curse of the system. Here, again, why should we expect success in the future from a principle that has so failed in the past?

Again, how are we to get a strong centralized administration in the face of a powerful and hostile parliamentary representation? It is very easy to talk of the benefits that might have been conferred on Ireland by such humanity and justice as was practised by Turgot in his administration of the Generality of Limoges. But Turgot was not confronted by eighty-six Limousin members of an active sovereign body, all interested in making his work difficult, and trusted by a large proportion of the people of the province with that as their express commission. It is possible to have an honest centralized administration of great strength and activity in India, but there is no Parliament in India. If India, or any province of it, ever gets representative government and our parliamentary system, from that hour, if there be any considerable section of Indian feeling averse from European rule, the present administrative system will be paralyzed, as the preliminary to being revolutionized. It is conceivable, if any one chooses to think so, that a body of impartial officials could manage the national business in Ireland much better without the guidance of public opinion and common sentiment than with it. But if you intend to govern the country as you think best—and that is the plain and practical English of centralized administration—why ask the country to send a hundred men to the great tribunal of supervision to inform you how it would like to be governed? The Executive cannot set them aside as if they were a hundred dummies; in refusing to be guided, it cannot escape being harassed, by them. You may amend procedure, but that is no answer, unless you amend the Irish members out of voice and vote. They will still count. You cannot gag and muzzle them effectually, and if you could, they would still be there, and their presence would still make itself incessantly felt. Partly from a natural desire to lessen the common difficulties of government, and partly from a consciousness, due to the prevailing state of the modern political atmosphere, that there is something wrong in this total alienation of an Executive from the possessors of parliamentary power, the officials will incessantly be tempted to make tacks out of their own course; and thus they lose the coherency and continuity of absolutism without gaining the pliant strength of popular government. This is not a presumption of what would be likely to happen, but an account of what does happen, and what justified Mr. Disraeli in adding a weak Executive to the alien Church and the absentee aristocracy, as the three great curses of Ireland. Nothing has occurred since 1844 to render the Executive stronger, but much to the contrary. There is, and there can be, no weaker or less effective Government in the world than a highly centralized system working alongside of a bitterly inimical popular representation. I say nothing of the effect of the fluctuations of English parties on Irish administration. I say nothing of the tendency in an Irish government, awkwardly alternating with that to which I have just adverted, to look over the heads of the people of Ireland, and to consider mainly what will be thought by the ignorant public in England. But these sources of incessant perturbation must not be left out. The fault of Irish centralization is not that it is strong, but that it is weak. Weak it must remain until Parliament either approves of the permanent suspension of the Irish writs, or else devises constitutional means for making Irish administration responsible to Irish representatives.

If experience is decisive against the policy of the past, experience too, all over the modern world, indicates the better direction for the future. I will not use my too scanty space in repeating any of the great wise commonplaces in praise of self-government. Here they are superfluous. In the case of Ireland they have all been abundantly admitted in a long series of measures, from Catholic Emancipation down to Lord O'Hagan's Jury Law and the Franchise and Redistribution Acts of a couple of years ago. The principle of self-government has been accepted, ratified, and extended in a hundred ways. It is only a question of the form that self-government shall take. Against the form proposed by the late Ministry a case is built up that rests on a series of prophetic assumptions. These assumptions, from the nature of the case, can only be met by a counter-statement of fair and reasonable probabilities. Let us enumerate some of them.

1. It is inferred that, because the Irish leaders have used violent language and resorted to objectionable expedients against England during the last six years, they would continue in the same frame of mind after the reasons for it had disappeared. In other words, because they have been the enemies of a Government which refused to listen to a constitutional demand, therefore they would continue to be its enemies after the demand had been listened to. On this reasoning, the effect is to last indefinitely and perpetually, notwithstanding the cessation of the cause. Our position is that all the reasonable probabilities of human conduct point the other way. The surest way of justifying violent language and fostering treasonable designs, is to refuse to listen to the constitutional demand.

2. The Irish, we are told, hate the English with an irreconcilable hatred, and would unquestionably use any Constitution as an instrument for satisfying their master passion. Irrational hatred, they say, can be treated by rational men with composure. The Czechs of Bohemia are said to be irreconcilable, yet the South Germans bear with their hatred; and if we cannot cure we might endure the antipathy of Ireland. Now, as for the illustration, I may remark that the hatred of the Czechs would be much too formidable for German composure, if the Czechs did not happen to possess a provincial charter and a special constitution of their own. If the Irish had the same, their national dislike—so far as it exists—might be expected to become as bearable as the Germans have found the feeling of the Czechs. But how deep does Irish dislike go? Is it directed against Englishmen, or against an English official system? The answers of every impartial observer to the whole group of such questions as these favour the conclusion that the imputed hatred of England in Ireland has been enormously exaggerated and overcoloured by Ascendency

politicians for good reasons of their own; that with the great majority of Irishmen it has no deep roots; that it is not one of those passionate international animosities that blind men to their own interests, or lead them to sacrifice themselves for the sake of injuring their foe; and, finally, that it would not survive the amendment of the system that has given it birth.

3. It is assumed that there is a universal desire for Separation. That there is a strong sentiment of nationality we of course admit; it is part of the case, and not the worst part. But the sentiment of nationality is a totally different thing from a desire for Separation. Scotland might teach our pseudo-Unionists so much as that. Nowhere in the world is the sentiment of nationality stronger, yet there is not a whisper of Separation. That there is a section of Irishmen who desire Separation is notorious, but everything that has happened since the Government of Ireland Bill was introduced, including the remarkable declarations of Mr. Parnell in accepting the Bill (June 7), and including the proceedings at Chicago, shows that the separatist section is a very small one either in Ireland or in America, and that it has become sensibly smaller since, and in consequence of, the proposed concession of a limited statutory constitution. The Irish are quite shrewd enough to know that Separation, if it were attainable—and they are well aware that it is not—would do no good to their markets; and to that knowledge, as well as to many other internal considerations, we may confidently look for the victory of strong centripetal over very weak centrifugal tendencies. Even if we suppose these centrifugal tendencies to be stronger than I would allow them to be, how shall we best resist them—by strengthening the hands and using the services of the party which, though nationalist, is also constitutional; or by driving that party also, in despair of a constitutional solution, to swell the ranks of Extremists and Irreconcilables?

4. Whatever may be the ill-feeling towards England, it is at least undeniable that there are bitter internal animosities in Ireland, and a political constitution, our opponents argue, can neither assuage religious bigotry nor remove agrarian discontent.

It is true, no doubt, that the old feud between Protestant and Catholic might, perhaps, not instantly die down to the last smouldering embers of it all over Ireland. But we may remark that there is no perceptible bad blood between Protestant and Catholic, outside of one notorious corner. Second, the real bitterness of the feud arose from the fact that Protestantism was associated with an exclusive and hostile ascendency, which would now be brought to an end. Whatever feeling about what is called Ulster exists in the rest of Ireland, arises not from the fact that there are Protestants in Ulster, but that the Protestants are anti-National. Third, the Catholics would no longer be one compact body for persecuting, obscurantist, or any other evil purposes; the abatement of the national struggle would allow the Catholics to fall into the two natural divisions of Clerical and Liberal. What we may be quite sure of is that the feud will never die so long as sectarian pretensions are taken as good reasons for continuing bad government.

It is true, again, that a constitution would not necessarily remove agrarian discontent. But it is just as true that you will never remove agrarian discontent without a constitution. Mr. Dicey, on consideration, will easily see why. Here we come to an illustration, and a very impressive illustration it is, of the impotence of England to do for Ireland the good which Ireland might do for herself. Nobody just now is likely to forget the barbarous condition of the broad fringe of wretchedness on the west coast of Ireland. Of this Lord Dufferin truly said in 1880 that no legislation could touch it, that no alteration in the land laws could effectually ameliorate it, and that it must continue until the world's end unless something be contrived totally to change the conditions of existence in that desolate region. Parliament lavishly pours water into the sieve in the shape of Relief Acts. Even in my own short tenure of office I was responsible for one of these terribly wasteful and profoundly unsatisfactory measures. Instead of relief, what a statesman must seek is prevention of this great evil and strong root of evil; and prevention means a large, though it cannot be a very swift, displacement of the population. But among the many experts with whom I have discussed this dolorous and perplexing subject, I never found one of either political party who did not agree that a removal of the surplus population was only practicable if carried out by an Irish authority, backed by the solid weight of Irish opinion. Any exertion of compulsory power by a British Minister would raise the whole country-side in squalid insurrection, government would become impossible, and the work of transplantation would end in ghastly failure. It is misleading and untrue, then, to say that there is no possible relation between self-government and agrarian discontent, misery, and backwardness; and when Mr. Dicey and others tell us that the British Parliament is able to do all good things for Ireland, I would respectfully ask them how a British Parliament is to deal with the Congested Districts.

Nearly as much may be said of the prevention of the mischievous practice of Subdivision. Some contend that the old disposition to subdivide is dying out; others, however, assure us that it is making its appearance even among the excellent class who purchased their holdings under the Church Act. That Act did not prohibit subdivision, but it is prohibited in the Act of 1881. Still the prohibition can only be made effective, if operations take place on anything like a great scale, on condition that representative, authorities resident on the spot have the power of enforcing it, and have an interest in enforcing it. Some of the pseudo-Unionists are even against any extension of local self-government, and if it be unaccompanied by the creation of a central native authority they are right. What such people fail to see is that, in resisting political reconstruction, they are at the same time resisting the only available remedies for some of the worst of agrarian maladies.

The ruinous interplay between agrarian and political forces, each using the other for ends of its own, will never cease so long as the political demand is in every form resisted. That, we are told, is all the fault of the politicians. Be it so; then the Government must either suppress the politicians outright, or else it must interest them in getting the terms of its land settlement accepted and respected. Home Rule on our scheme was, among other things, part of an arrangement for "settling the agrarian feud." It was a means of interposing between the Irish tenant and the British State an authority interested enough and strong enough to cause the bargain to be kept. It is said that the Irish authority would have had neither interest nor strength enough to resist the forces making for repudiation. Would those forces be any less irresistible if the whole body of the Irish peasantry stood, as Land Purchase *minus* Self-Government makes them to stand, directly face to face with the British State? This is a question that our opponents cannot evade, any more than they can evade that other question, which lies unnoticed at the back of all solutions of the problem by way of peasant ownership—Whether it is possible to imagine the land of Ireland handed over to Irishmen, and yet the government of Ireland kept exclusively and directly by Englishmen? Such a divorce is conceivable under a rule like that of the British in India: with popular institutions it is inconceivable and impossible.

5. It is argued that Home Rule on Mr. Gladstone's plan would not work, because it follows in some respects the colonial system, whereas the conditions at the root of the success of the system in the Colonies do not exist in Ireland. They are distant, Ireland is near; they are prosperous, Ireland is poor; they are proud of the connection with England, Ireland resents it. But the question is not whether the conditions are identical with those of any colony; it is enough if in themselves they seem to promise a certain basis for government. It might justly be contended that proximity is a more favourable condition than distance; without it there could not be that close and constant intercommunication which binds the material interests of Ireland to those of Great Britain, and so provides the surest guarantee for union. If Ireland were suddenly to find herself as far off as Canada, then indeed one might be very sorry to answer for the Union. Again, though Ireland has to bear her share of the prevailing depression in the chief branch of her production, it is a great mistake to suppose that outside of the margin of chronic wretchedness in the west and south-west, the condition not only of the manufacturing industries of the north, but of the agricultural industry in the richer parts of the middle and south, is so desperately unprosperous as to endanger a political constitution. Under our stupidily [Transcriber: sic] centralized system, Irishmen have no doubt acquired the enervating trick of attributing every misfortune, great or small, public or private, to the Government. When they learn the lessons of responsibility, they will unlearn this fatal habit, and not before.

I do not see, therefore, that the differences in condition between Ireland and the Colonies make against Home Rule. What I do see is ample material out of which would arise a strong and predominant party of order. The bulk of the nation are sons and daughters of a Church which has been hostile to revolution in every country but Ireland, and which would be hostile to it there from the day that the cause of revolution ceased to be the cause of self-government. If the peasantry were made to realize that at last the land settlement, wisely and equitably made, was what it must inexorably remain, and what no politicians could help them to alter, they would be as conservative as the peasantry under a similar condition in every other spot on the surface of the globe. There is no reason to expect that the manufacturers, merchants, and shopkeepers of Ireland would be less willing or less able to play an active and useful part in the affairs of their country than the same classes in England or Scotland. It will be said that this is mere optimist prophesying. But why is that to be flung aside under the odd name of sentimentalism, while pessimist prophesying is to be taken for gospel?

The only danger is lest we should allot new responsibilities to Irishmen with a too grudging and restrictive hand. For true responsibility there must be real power. It is easy to say that this power would be misused, and that the conditions both of Irish society and of the proposed Constitution must prevent it from being used for good. It is easy to say that separation would be a better end. Life is too short to discuss that. Separation is not the alternative either to Home Rule or to the *status quo*. If the people of Ireland are not to be trusted with real power over their own affairs, it would be a hundred times more just to England, and more merciful to Ireland, to take away from her that semblance of free government which torments and paralyzes one country, while it robs the other of national self-respect and of all the strongest motives and best opportunities of self-help. The *status quo* is drawing very near to its inevitable end. The two courses then open will be Home Rule on the one hand, and some shy bungling underhand imitation of a Crown Colony on the other. We shall have either to listen to the Irish representatives or to suppress them. Unless we have lost all nerve and all political faculty we shall, before many months are over, face these alternatives. Liberals are for the first; Tories at present incline to the second. It requires very moderate instinct for the forces at work in modern politics to foresee the path along which we shall move, in the interests alike of relief to Great Britain and of a sounder national life for Ireland. The only real question is not Whether we are to grant Home Rule, but How.

Glossary

à fortiori: in Latin, "to strength"; with convincing force

Q.E.D.... Q.E.F.: *quod erat demonstrandum*, or "that which was to be shown," versus *quod erat faciendum* or "that which was to be done"; borrowed from Euclid, the ancient Greek mathematician, Morley is alluding to the difference between planning to demonstrate the utility of an idea, as opposed to its already having been implemented and proven

Sir Robert Peel ...Lord John Russell: the Conservative prime minister during the Irish Famine, followed by the Whig prime minister during the Famine; Morley's point here is that all parties have failed to bring about successful reform in Ireland

Turgot ...Limousin: a reference to the famous proto-capitalist French minister on finance, Anne-Robert-Jacques Turgot, and his administration of the province of Limousin in the 1770s; Turgot's innovative taxation policy and enlightened administration is thought by many to have been intelligent enough to have held off the French Revolution, had it been implemented by the French monarchy over the entire country—here, Morley is using Turgot's example as a parallel to that conceived of for Ireland

Tories: a euphemism for Conservatives

Document Analysis

Professor Albert Venn Dicey taught constitutional law at Oxford, as a confirmed liberal in the mold of the famous libertarian philosopher John Stuart Mill. His nationalist and constitutional impulses overrode his politics, however, when it came to Ireland. His work *An Introduction to the Study of the Law of the Constitution* (1885) was cited often by politicians in debate over the Home Rule Bill in 1885 and 1886. Dicey believed that "no person is above the law and it is law that rules all"; on the other hand, he did not seem to believe that laws could be changed if they were considered unjust by the majority of a population. To Dicey, ending the Act of Union or altering it in any way was caving in to the public demands of a noisy minority of the Irish people, and thus unconstitutional. It was to this argument that Morley addressed his articles.

Morley opens by comparing the condition of Ireland to that of a sick patient who will surely die if no treatment is administered, but for whom a treatment is rejected because it might cause him pain. Essentially, he believed that the idea of trying Home Rule for Ireland was better than simple leaving the situation on the island in a lawless and violent state. "Are the conditions of the connection between England and Ireland, as laid down in the Act of Union, incapable of improvement? Is the present working of these conditions more prosperous and hopeful, or happier for Irish order and for English institutions, than any practicable proposal that it is within the compass of statesmanship to devise, and of civic sense to accept and to work? That is the question." Morley saw the idea of establishing Home Rule as an alternative that was within the reasonable boundaries of constitutional government, and that Dicey's idea of it as a fundamental and possibly fatal alteration of the constitution as a reactionary conservative response to the problem—all constitutions needed amending to stay healthy. The most recent example he alludes to is the extension of voting privileges to more than half of the adult male population of Britain in 1884 and 1885, and he expects more to come.

Dicey argued that the alteration of the constitution of Britain to provide Home Rule for the Irish people would "depriv[e] parliamentary institutions of their elasticity and strength, ...weaken[ ] the Executive at home, and lessen[ ] the power of the country to resist foreign attack." In Morley's opinion all of these problems already existed due to the troubles in Ireland, and only "considerations of political expediency as tested by practical experience" were worthy of solving those problems. In other words, Home Rule was an effort to solve the problem; however vehement Dicey's arguments against the idea, he had nothing to replace it with, and any ideas towards reform that he did support had been tried and failed.

Here, Morley makes an allusion to Ireland as a corporation—none of the reforms taken to make the corporation profitable and healthy had been made by the "Irish shareholders" themselves, meaning "the men who knew most about Ireland. The vice of the connection between the two countries has been the stupidity of governing a country without regard to the interests or customs, the peculiar objects and peculiar experiences, of the great majority of the people who live in it." He refers to James I's seventeenth century plantation policy, designed to settle Protestants in Ireland and convert the Catholic populace, as producing, in Dicey's own words, "'all the evils of cruelty and malignity'," To Morley, British reforms designed to alleviate the poverty of and prejudice against the Catholic Irish population have never worked in Ireland. Another example is the Encumbered Estates Act, a policy by which landed estates in deep debt during the famine of the 1840s could be sold to new owners, after which the previous owner's debts would be dropped. The idea of the government was to get new landlords to buy cheap land and employ more Irish tenant farmers; instead, most new landlords bought their new farms and evicted the old tenants in favor of higher rents or new land uses, making the conditions of the famine even worse. Good intentions were not enough to improve Ireland, obviously, so perhaps the Irish could be given the opportunity to improve themselves, through their own home parliament.

Morley was an adherent of liberal philosophy as much as he was a member of the Liberal Party—meaning, he was the sort of ideologue that influenced his party's members and policies because he knew what he was talking about philosophically as well as practically. Here, he refers to John Stuart Mill's *Considerations on Representative Government* (1861), referring to Mill's belief that the only "'safe and salutary'" means of effecting improvement for people is to allow them to do the work themselves. To Morley, this was the principle behind the effort to try Home Rule, and that the fears of future Irish independence were an irrelevancy; he says that any argument Dicey might make about the Irish naturally pursuing their own nationalist interests are "political moonshine."

On the other hand, he compares rule in the name of the Irish by English administrators to that of Austrian rule over the Italian province of Lombardy in the pre-independence era in Italian history. He notes that the Italians hated Austrian rule, not because it was inefficient or bad, but because it was Austrian. Herein lay the problem in Ireland, that no matter what reforms the British government might enact, it was not Irish, and therefore unacceptable. He notes that the Irish administration." of his Liberal predecessor as Chief Secretary, Sir William Forster, was "honest centralized administration." Yet Forster was roundly harassed by the Irish populace at Parnell's instigation and ended up calling for the passage of a Coercion Act, by which Parnell was thrown in prison for a short time before the Irish Parliamentary Party's alliance with the Liberals. He also compares Forster's difficulties with that of the famous French economist Turgot in France, who was turned out of office by the monarchy and still never had to face the equivalent of the Irish Parliamentary Party, "eighty-six ...members of an active sovereign body, all interested in making his work difficult, and trusted by a large proportion of the people of the province with that as their express commission." It is interesting that Morley goes on to compare the governance of Ireland to that of India, which would be "revolutionized" by a similar pursuit of Home Rule—twenty years later, he would begin that exact same process by supporting the so-called Morley-Minto Reforms.

Morley addresses what he considered to be the contradiction of having 100 members of the House of Commons being elected from Ireland yet having in place a government that refused to listen to them in the matter of their own governance. This was, in his view, a recipe for harassment. He asserts that "the three great curses of Ireland" were the Chief Secretary's position which he himself had occupied—a position created by the Conservative government of Sir Robert Peel and Benjamin Disraeli four decades earlier—the Anglican Church of Ireland, and the landlords who refused to live on the island where they made their profits. As it stood, the governance of Ireland was that of "a highly centralized system working alongside of a bitterly inimical popular representation"—an autocratic administration asserting its will over a people that hated it, and it would only change by "making Irish administration responsible to Irish representatives."

In the past, Morley asserts, the idea of self-government for Ireland had worked. Here he references a series of acts passed by British government that he curiously did not consider reforms, such as allowing Catholics to vote (none of whom were Irish, since they did not meet the property requirement), allowing the Irish to sit on juries, and extending the vote to a larger proportion of the electorate in 1884 (even though most Irish *still* did not meet the property requirement to vote—Morley had not done his homework in choosing these examples).

More usefully, he addresses the "prophetic assumptions" of those opposed to Home Rule, in five counter-statements. He dismisses the idea that the Irish leadership's violent rhetoric precludes the idea of their cooperation with Home Rule, because Home Rule will meet their demands. He compares Irish hatred for the English to the hatred of Czechs for their Austrian rulers in the Austro-Hungarian Empire, noting on the one hand that the Austro-Hungarian Empire survived anyway and that any hatred imputed to the Irish for the English was likely exaggerated by the Protestants in Ireland for their own benefit. He denies any overwhelming desire on the part of the Irish for complete separation from the United Kingdom, using Scotland as an example of a country with intense national pride that had no desire to end their union with England. He also praises Parnell for supporting the Liberals even after the Home Rule Bill (the Government of Ireland Bill) failed, and notes that Parnell's agents even suppressed efforts to support and fund terrorism by the Clan na Gael, an Irish

American fraternal society that met in Chicago in 1887 to discuss their response to the failure of the bill.

Morley's longest response to the naysayers on Home Rule addresses the notion that Irish self-government will still not "assuage religious bigotry nor remove agrarian discontent." He admits that this was true in Ulster ("one notorious corner"), but certainly less so in the rest of Ireland. Home Rule would end the Protestant Ascendancy and divide Catholics between those who considered Home Rule an answer to their problems and the minority—he assumed, probably correctly—who would see their religiously-inspired hatreds as more important than self-government. As for agrarian discontent, the turnover of land from landlord to peasant could not be solved right away with self-government, but the incompetence of British rule was proof that it would not be solved by the Parliament in London either. Lord Dufferin, a Protestant Irish diplomat and landlord in the west, had argued that western Ireland's land problems could not be solved simply by giving land from the aristocracy to the peasantry, without addressing the poverty endemic to the region. Morley agreed—though his solution seemed more draconian: to remove "surplus population" from the region, preferably by Irishmen running an Irish government run out of Dublin. Compounding the problem of poverty was "subdivision," the practice of willing one's tenant holdings to all of their children, thus splitting up already small plots of land that peasants merely leased from an aristocrat into even smaller and usually unprofitable farms. Even the selling of the lands of the Anglican Church of Ireland had not prevented this well-meaning but economically disastrous family practice. The Land Act of 1881 had made subdivision illegal, but, Morley argues, only officials on the scene could enforce it effectively. Ultimately, Morley believed it was "[im]possible to imagine the land of Ireland handed over to Irishmen, and yet the government of Ireland kept exclusively and directly by Englishmen."

Finally, Morley compares the potential of Home Rule in Ireland to that of "responsible government"—self-government—as practiced in "the Colonies," meaning the white settlement colonies of Canada, Australia, New Zealand, Newfoundland and Cape Colony in South Africa. The opponents to Home Rule did not believe self-government could work in Ireland like it did in, say, Canada—"They are distant, Ireland is near; they are prosperous, Ireland is poor; they are proud of the connection with England, Ireland resents it." Morley argues that each of these conditions actually made Home Rule likelier to work than fail. Ireland's proximity meant problems of communication and support were easier to repair; that Ireland's industrial might in the north and its agricultural wealth in the middle and south would grow with Home Rule; and that Home Rule would remove the English as an excuse for Irish problems, as an Irish-elected Home Rule government would be in charge of solving them. Catholicism and its hierarchical organization made Irishmen more likely to follow the rules of a popular government. Land settlements, whether successful or not, would no longer be blamed on a far-off Parliament in London. Elite Irish would become as supportive of the United Kingdom as their counterparts in England and Scotland. In the end, the only real obstacle to the success of Home Rule was the willingness of the British government to grant it in full. Should it not be granted, the alternative would be revolution and independence—therefore, "The only real question is not Whether we are to grant Home Rule, but How."

Essential Themes

Morley would go on after this speech to return to the Cabinet in 1892 as Chief Secretary for Ireland with the Liberals. His government tried another Home Rule Bill in 1892. Public and parliamentary opinion by then had swung closer to a truer consideration of the idea. Parnell had been discredited and removed as leader of the Irish Parliamentary Party, and Gladstone was in his eighties, an aging political warrior eliciting sympathy as he sought a last major legislative victory in favor of the security of the United Kingdom. The bill managed to pass the House of Commons, but it failed in the Conservative dominated House of Lords. Still, the tide against Home Rule had clearly turned, and violence in Ireland went down precipitously in the 1890s and 1900s. The target of Morley's articles,

A.V. Dicey, wrote three more books in opposition to Home Rule on constitutional grounds, and became increasingly disillusioned as public opinion and legal momentum swung against his arguments.

In the meantime, the Conservatives tried to ameliorate the situation in Ireland through land acts designed to get land into the hands of the peasantry. In 1887, the same year as Morley's speech, the Irish Land Act saw the government purchase bankrupt estates and sell them to tenants instead of new landlords. In 1906, the Wyndham Land Act lent money to tenants at practically nonexistent interest rates to buy out their landlords using the same money that would have gone into rents. Within ten years, 75% of the land in Ireland changed hands and the power of Protestant landlords over Catholic tenants was broken.

In the end, however, as Morley suspected, reform was a poor substitute for self-rule. Just as in the rest of Europe, Irish nationalism grew inexorably at the turn of the twentieth century as the Gaelic language was revived, Irish American money flowed into protest causes, a literary revival swept Dublin and London and the rise of socialism pitted Ireland's poor against its wealthy Protestant landlords and English industrialists. By 1913, another Liberal government floated a third Home Rule Bill through Parliament, and this time, new constitutional rules kept it from being blocked in the House of Lords.

As it turned out, though, Morley's dismissal of Ulster as a major obstacle to Home Rule was mistaken. Protestants all over Ireland, led by those in Ulster, bought guns in preparation for a civil war over Home Rule—or Catholic "Rome Rule," as they called it—and disaster was only averted temporarily by the coming of the First World War in 1914. Intellectual and socialist rebels held a rebellion at Easter 1916 that made Dublin a war zone; by the end of the war in Europe, those who had survived that rebellion declared their independence from the United Kingdom, launching another civil war in the United Kingdom that lasted into 1921. Ireland became mostly independent in 1922, with the United Kingdom retaining control—and thus, the same troubles Morley outlined—in Northern Ireland to the current day. Dicey was aghast with the birth of the Irish Free State; he died soon after its declaration in 1922. Morley himself professed that he was pleased to see Irish independence and died a year later in 1923.

—*David Simonelli, PhD*

Bibliography and Additional Reading

Jackson, Alvin. *Home Rule: An Irish History, 1800–2000.* New York: Oxford UP, 2003.

Johnson, Patrick. *Morley of Blackburn: A Literary and Political Biography of John Morley.* Lanham, MD: Fairleigh Dickinson UP, 2012.

Morton, Grenfell. *Home Rule and the Irish Question.* New York: Routledge, 2016.

O'Day, Alan. *Irish Home Rule, 1867–1921.* New York: Manchester UP, 1998.

Proclamation of the Provisional Government of the Irish Republic

Date: April 24, 1916
Authors: Patrick Pearse and Thomas MacDonagh
Genre: political declaration

Summary Overview

On the Monday after Easter, April 24, 1916, civilian soldiers seized the General Post Office in Dublin and proclaimed themselves to be the vanguard of a coming Irish rebellion against the British Empire. After making the Post Office their headquarters, one of their leaders, Patrick Pearse, stood on the stairs leading into the front door at noon to proclaim Ireland's independence from the British Empire. The Republic of Ireland today marks this moment as its birthdate, a moment of heroism in Irish history. The heroes of the Easter Rebellion, however, expected to be martyrs, to give their lives as a "blood sacrifice" to the cause of their nation's independence. Despite their correct assumption that they would all fail and die – or perhaps because of it – they launched Ireland on the path to rebellion against the British Empire that would finally end in the island's freedom.

Defining Moment

The rebels of Easter 1916 were the product of the long-term enmity between Britain and Ireland. The status of Ireland and its relationship to the United Kingdom was poorly defined – at different times in history, the English considered Ireland an occupied European Catholic nation, a sullen and often rebellious colony, or an integral part of the United Kingdom. Often, the island was all three at once. Meanwhile, as a whole, the Irish considered the English to be hated occupiers who treated the Irish as uncivilized inferiors.

In the early twentieth century, several historical events came together to establish a real breaking point for this contentious relationship. Irish nationalists had long proposed the idea of Home Rule, a form of self-government for Ireland under the British crown. Home Rule would reestablish an Irish parliament, government, and state that was subject to the English crown and its diplomatic and defense interests but otherwise independent. Most Irish, both Catholic and Protestant, supported the idea, but in the predominantly Protestant northern province of Ulster, the idea of Home Rule was considered a step toward the violent oblivion of Irish Protestants, and they opposed it implacably. Meanwhile, other Irishmen rediscovered their own sense of nationalism in other ways – through the rebirth of the Gaelic language, the rediscovery of traditional Irish sports like hurling and Gaelic football, and in the establishment of a powerful Irish literary tradition in the figures of Oscar Wilde, George Bernard Shaw, William Butler Yeats, and Sean O'Casey. All of these organizations helped found a political and economic union referred to by its founder, Arthur Griffith, as Sinn Fein, or "Ourselves Alone," in 1908. The growth of a distinct Irish culture is central to understanding the authors and the intentions of the 1916 Proclamation, since so many of them were involved in these groups in one way or another.

In 1912, a Home Rule bill finally passed in the British House of Commons, to be implemented in September 1914. Almost immediately, Protestants in Ireland opposed to Home Rule, especially in Ulster, began to prepare for armed resistance. They formed a paramilitary organization, the Ulster Volunteers, who imported guns illegally and drilled in preparation for civil war once Home Rule was implemented. In opposition, Irish nationalists – most but not all Catholic – founded their own paramilitary group, the Irish Vol-

The Easter Proclamation of 1916. Photo via Wikimedia Commons. [Public domain.]

unteers. The Irish Volunteers' early members included Eoin Mac Neill, founder of the Gaelic League; Patrick Pearse, promoter of the Gaelic language at his school, St. Enda's, in Dublin; Thomas MacDonagh, another poet and teacher at St. Enda's and founder of the Irish Theater; and Joseph Mary Plunkett, also a poet and playwright, and editor of the *Irish Review*, an important literary magazine that connected the Irish nationalist community. The Irish Volunteers also staged a spectacular gun smuggling operation in July 1914, and Ireland seemed on the verge of civil war just two months before Home Rule would be implemented.

Then, to the surprise of all concerned in Britain and Ireland, focus swung away from events in Ireland: the Great War broke out on the Continent. Britain joined the side of France and Russia in early August 1914, and all sides agreed that they would lay down their arms and that Home Rule would be shelved until the end of the war, with some kind of special arrangements to be made for the concerns of the Ulster Unionists. Two hundred thousand Irishmen, Protestant and Catholic, joined the war effort, including all the Ulster Volunteers and 170,000 of the Irish Volunteers, the vast majority, who renamed themselves the National Volunteers. About 13,500 Irish Volunteers refused to join the war to fight on the side of the British. They kept the name Irish Volunteers, and formed a Central Executive in Dublin, led by Mac Neill, its members also including Pearse, MacDonagh, and Plunkett.

It was in light of this historical background that the 1916 Easter Rising was organized. The Central Executive of the Irish Volunteers believed that there could be no better time to bring about Ireland's full independence than in the middle of a war involving Britain, when British troops would be otherwise occupied. They combined forces with a socialist paramilitary group, the Irish Citizens Army, led by one James Connolly and the future playwright Sean O'Casey. They also secured the aid of Sir Roger Casement, a prominent British diplomat and an Anglo-Irish sympathizer who made liaison with Germany to get a boatload of weapons shipped to the Irish coast. Casement also worked to secure a contingent of Irish POWs in Germany to form a brigade. Idealists all, the poets and playwrights in Dublin and the diplomat in Germany hoped that 1) an organized uprising with German support would excite the wider Irish populace into a general revolt, 2) Ireland would thereby force its independence in the middle of the war, and 3) the new republic would even secure for itself a place at the peace conference when the war ended.

All of this proved illusory, as was usual in Irish history. Casement could barely convince fifty of 2,000 POWs to join his brigade; the rest despised him as a traitor. The German government agreed to ship the guns, but lost interest in fomenting rebellion, since it seemed clear that the Irish population was uninterested, if not hostile. The ship carrying the guns never met its contact on the Irish shore and was scuttled before the British navy captured it; Casement was brought to Ireland on a German U-boat and arrested just hours after he reached land. It was not even Easter Sunday, and the plot had fallen apart. But people like Patrick Pearse, the most vocally supportive of the revolutionaries, were determined to go forward with the uprising anyway, because only "blood sacrifice" could rid Ireland of its servitude to the British crown and dependence on English culture. The Easter rebels determined that the blood sacrifice would be their own, for their nation's good.

Author Biography

The author of the 1916 Proclamation of the Provisional Government of the Irish Republic was Patrick Pearse. While Thomas MacDonagh is thought to have contributed to the wording, Pearse was the acknowledged author and perhaps the most romantic of any of the rebels. Born in Dublin in 1879, he was an early exponent of Irish cultural nationalism, university educated, and regularly published as a nationalist poet in both English and Gaelic. He later founded St. Enda's School, specifically to promote the cultural values he espoused. He was considered an extremist by many of his colleagues; the nominal leader of the Gaelic League and the Irish Volunteers, Eoin Mac Neill, even pulled his children out of St. Enda's because he feared the violent rhetoric of revolt that Pearse espoused. Fifteen of Pearse's teenaged pupils actually joined the Easter Rising, inspired by their teacher.

Pearse had few illusions about the success of the Rising. Yet his poetic nature and that of his colleagues allowed them to believe that it would have an almost mystical effect on the Irish people. "Bloodshed is a cleansing and sanctifying thing, and the nation which regards it as the final horror has lost its manhood," he wrote. Pearse believed his death and that of the other people occupying the General Post Office would be a victory because it would galvanize the Irish people into fighting for their freedom. It was certainly no mistake, then, that the 1916 Rising and its proclamation of a new Irish Republic was to take place over the Easter week – Pearse and the other rebels thought of themselves as almost Christ-like in their willingness to sacrifice themselves in service to the greater good of the Irish people.

Historical Document

Proclamation of the Provisional Government of the Irish Republic

The Provisional Government of the Irish Republic to the People of Ireland

IRISHMEN AND IRISHWOMEN: In the name of God and of the dead generations from which she receives her old tradition of nationhood, Ireland, through us, summons her children to her flag and strikes for her freedom.

Having organised and trained her manhood through her secret revolutionary organisation, the Irish Republican Brotherhood, and through her open military organisations, the Irish Volunteers and the Irish Citizen Army, having patiently perfected her discipline, having resolutely waited for the right moment to reveal itself, she now seizes that moment, and supported by her exiled children in America and by gallant allies in Europe, but relying in the first on her own strength, she strikes in full confidence of victory.

We declare the right of the people of Ireland to the ownership of Ireland and to the unfettered control of Irish destinies, to be sovereign and indefeasible. The long usurpation of that right by a foreign people and government has not extinguished the right, nor can it ever be extinguished except by the destruction of the Irish people.

In every generation the Irish people have asserted their right to national freedom and sovereignty; six times during the past three hundred years they have asserted it in arms. Standing on that fundamental right and again asserting it in arms in the face of the world, we hereby proclaim the Irish Republic as a Sovereign Independent State, and we pledge our lives and the lives of our comrades in arms to the cause of its freedom, of its welfare, and of its exaltation among the nations.

The Irish Republic is entitled to, and hereby claims, the allegiance of every Irishman and Irishwoman. The Republic guarantees religious and civil liberty, equal rights and equal opportunities to all its citizens, and declares its resolve to pursue the happiness and prosperity of the whole nation and of all its parts, cherishing all of the children of the nation equally, and oblivious of the differences carefully fostered by an alien Government, which have divided a minority from the majority in the past.

Until our arms have brought the opportune moment for the establishment of a permanent National Government, representative of the whole people of Ireland and elected by the suffrages of all her men and women, the Provisional Government, hereby constituted, will administer the civil and military affairs of the Republic in trust for the people.

We place the cause of the Irish Republic under the protection of the Most High God, Whose blessing we invoke upon our arms, and we pray that no one who serves that cause will dishonour it by cowardice, inhumanity, or rapine. In this supreme hour the Irish nation must, by its valour and discipline, and by the readiness of its children to sacrifice themselves for the common good, prove itself worthy of the august destiny to which it is called.

Signed on behalf of the Provisional Government:

THOMAS J. CLARKE
SEAN Mac DIARMADA
THOMAS MacDONAGH
P. H. PEARSE
EAMONN CEANNT
JAMES CONNOLLY
JOSEPH PLUNKETT

Document Themes and Analysis

The rebels chose the General Post Office in Dublin from which to make their stand because it was the most imposing British government building in Dublin besides Dublin Castle, where the British authorities sat, and the castle was considered too well-defended. Other strategic points were taken throughout the city over the course of the next twenty-four hours, all surrounding Dublin Castle. Upon seizing the Post Office, a flag with the Irish tricolor was raised over the building, and Patrick Pearse walked outside to read his proclamation to a confused group of passersby. It was titled "Poblacht na hEireann," or Republic of Ireland; most people who read it in Ireland would not know what the title meant in 1916, as they did not understand Gaelic. Pearse opened by calling on the Irish public, its "children," to take up arms in the name of the "dead generations" that had established Ireland as a nation. He then named all of the revolt's supporters and actors—the IRB, the Irish Volunteers, the Irish Citizens' Army, American supporters, and "gallant allies in Europe"—the Germans—who by that time had already failed the rising. Critical was one organization not named by Pearse: Sinn Fein, led by Arthur Griffith. Griffith had offered his support and been turned away, the rebels knowing of his opposition to the use of violence. Yet, throughout the country, it was assumed immediately, based on Griffith's support of independence and his rhetoric, that Sinn Fein must be involved; the rising was quickly and incorrectly termed "the Sinn Fein Rebellion."

Pearse then asserted the right of Irishmen to "ownership" of their island and their destinies, declaring that the Irish people would sooner disappear than submit that right to the British occupiers. He hearkened back to previous rebellions as proof, and declared Ireland's independence, to which he pledged the lives of all the rebels. He called on all Irishmen and Irishwomen – showing a striking equality and lack of chauvinism for the time – to join the rebellion, and promised that everyone would be treated equally, meaning Protestants. Pearse chalked up the hatreds between Protestants and Catholics to the deliberate policies of the British government, which was an exceptionally biased reading of the history of the same six rebellions he had appealed to in Ireland's past – in all of them, Protestants had been slaughtered indiscriminately by Catholics.

Pearse reaffirmed the provisional nature of the republic as constituted in the officers of the Rising, and then called upon God to protect the cause and keep it from devolving into the usual horrors of war, "cowardice, inhumanity, or rapine." He noted that the Irish nation had to be "worthy of the august destiny to which it is called," and read off the names of the signatories. Then he turned and walked back into the building.

The rebels hoped that the people of Ireland would read copies of the proclamation and join in the Rising. Yet, while the rebels did not fully expect this to happen, they may well have been surprised at the actual reaction—the Irish populace rejected them, considering them traitors of the worst sort at a time when the United Kingdom they were a part of was at war. When the insurgents laid down their arms a week later on April 30 and walked out of the General Post Office, they were spat upon and jeered at by surrounding crowds as British soldiers escorted them to jail.

British forces under Sir John Maxwell arrested 3,400 people, twice the number of actual participants in the Rising. Under the rules of martial law, which had been declared by the Lord Lieutenant of Ireland, Maxwell convened military courts martial as if they took place on the battlefield in France. This meant that there would be no jury and no defense witnesses. Close to 200 civilians were tried and ninety of them received death sentences. The leaders of the Rising, as expected, received the opportunity to give their "blood sacrifice," all of them being executed by firing squad over ten days in May. They received no funerals; their bodies were covered in quicklime as if they were corpses left to rot after a battle. Roger Casement—a Protestant with a better social pedigree—was executed months later in Pentonville Prison in London, after a formal trial for treason.

During his court martial, Pearse spoke, saying "You cannot conquer Ireland. You cannot extinguish the Irish passion for freedom. If our deed has not been sufficient to win freedom, then our children will win it by a better deed." He was right. If the insurgents had been considered fools and traitors during the

1916 Rising, they became martyrs immediately after they had died. The summary nature of the executions and the speed with which they took place after the Rising turned Irish public opinion decidedly in favor of the Rising.

Despite the fact that Sinn Fein had nothing to do with the Rising, it was still associated as the organization behind it. Scores of politically minded people flocked to join Sinn Fein and formed a political party out of it. In December 1918, the British coalition government held a general election, largely to cement its status as the group assigned to broker the peace agreement with Germany. The election ended up solidifying Sinn Fein's hold on the Irish public's political aspirations. It was the first in Britain's history to be conducted on the basis of universal adult male suffrage; the result was Sinn Fein collecting 73 out of 108 Irish seats in Parliament, swamping the old Home Rule Irish Parliamentary Party and the Ulster Unionists. Promptly, the elected Sinn Fein MPs refused to accept their seats in London, instead staying home in Dublin to form their own Dáil Eireann, an Irish parliament, just as Arthur Griffith had always wanted.

What Griffith had hoped for, however, was that the separation of governments could be concluded peacefully. Such was not to be the case; more as Pearse and his colleagues had expected, the independence of Ireland had to be obtained through the shedding of blood. The Irish War of Independence began in January 1919, the Irish Volunteers having renamed themselves the Irish Republican Army in October 1917, and they fought under the leadership of Michael Collins. Two years later, a truce was signed and the Irish nation was divided in peace negotiations between north and south. By the end of 1922, Collins and Griffith were also dead, De Valera was the new president of the Irish Free State, and the promises of the 1916 Proclamation were achieved. It would take another year of civil war to force acceptance of the geographic and religiously based split on the Irish population; the 1916 rebels' prediction of "blood sacrifice" came true with a vengeance.

—David Simonelli, PhD

Bibliography and Additional Reading

Coogan, Tim Pat. *Ireland in the 20th Century*. New York: Palgrave Macmillan, 2006.

McGarry, Fearghal. *The Rising—Ireland: Easter 1916*. New York: Oxford UP, 2010.

"1916: The 1916 Rising—Personalities and Perspectives." The National Library of Ireland. www.nli.ie/1916.

"The 1916 Rising". Department of the Taoiseach, Government of Ireland. www.taoiseach.gov.ie/eng/Historical_Information/State_Commemorations/The_1916_Rising.html.

"Wars & Conflict: 1916 Easter Rising." BBC History. www.bbc.co.uk/history/british/easterrising.

Wills, Clair. *Dublin 1916: The Siege of the GPO*. London: Profile Books, 2009.

The Russian Revolution

The Russian Revolution of 1917 overthrew the imperial government of Czar Nicholas II (of the long-ruling House of Romanov) and brought to power the Bolsheviks, or the more radical wing of the Russian Social-Democratic Workers' Party led by Vladimir Lenin. The Bolsheviks' consolidation of power after the revolution came to be seen as one of the clearest examples of totalitarianism in the modern era.

An early revolt in 1905 following the disastrous Russo-Japanese War of that year was crushed by the czar, aided by violent antirevolutionary groups, which also launched pogroms against Jews. Large-scale workers' strikes, however, led by the Mensheviks (rivals of the Bolsheviks), succeeded in winning significant concessions, including a new constitution and the creation of a parliament (Duma). Even so, the czar remained the central authority figure, and he failed to implement some of the reforms he had promised.

During World War I, the corruption and incompetence of Nicholas' regime was further exposed, and discontent increased in all classes of society. When food riots broke out, many soldiers refused to put them down. In March 1917 (February in the Old Style calendar), insurgents, aided by elements of the army, took Petrograd (St. Petersburg) and Moscow, and forced Nicholas to abdicate. A new provisional government was set up, and other workers' soviets (councils) were established in major cities and towns under the name of the Socialist Revolutionary Party. As Bolsheviks, Mensheviks, and other factions jockeyed for power, the government was repeatedly reorganized. By September, the Bolsheviks under Lenin had begun to gain the largest share of support among the soviets, the soldiers, and workers and peasants generally. (Lenin had proclaimed, "All power to the soviets," and "All land to the peasants.") On November 6 (October 24, Old Style), Bolsheviks stormed the Winter Palace and took over the government (the "October Revolution"). At the next All-Russian Congress of Soviets, the Mensheviks and delegates of the Socialist Revolutionary Party walked out as the Bolsheviks took control.

Russian participation in the war was ended, and private and church lands started being handed over to local soviets. A ruthless police force, the Cheka, began rounding up and eliminating members of the opposition. Meanwhile, a civil war erupted between Bolshevik (Red) and anti-Bolshevik (White) forces that lasted until 1920, resulting in great devastation, especially in southern Russia and Ukraine. Once again the Bolsheviks came out as the victors, White Russian forces having suffered from a lack of coordination and other factors. Two years later the Soviet Union officially came into being.

What Is to Be Done?

Date: 1902
Author: Vladimir Lenin
Genre: political tract

Summary Overview

Vladimir Ilyich Lenin, the architect of the 1917 Bolshevik Revolution in Russia and one of the chief founders of the Soviet Union, penned the political pamphlet *What Is to Be Done?* more than a decade before the start of the Russian revolution. Lenin's real surname was Ulyanov (sometimes spelled Ulianov). He began writing *What Is to Be Done?* in 1901, and it was published in 1902 under the name "N. Lenin." Although it is only a single document in the large corpus of Lenin's writings, it is often considered his most important. This is because it appears to provide a blueprint for the final form of the Bolshevik Party and therefore also for the revolutionary regime the party established after seizing power in Russia on November 7–8, 1917 (October 25–26, according to the Russian calendar still in use at that time). In *What Is to Be Done?* Lenin focuses on questions of political agitation and proper revolutionary organization. In particular, he rejects open mass membership in the Russian Social Democratic Labor Party (RSDLP), also called the Russian Social Democratic Workers Party. The RSDLP had been founded in Minsk in 1898 to unite the movement for "social democracy" which at the time was represented by various Russian revolutionary Socialist organizations. Instead, he emphasizes the need for a highly organized, "centralized" "secret" and "conspiratorial" party composed of "professional revolutionaries" who would direct to a successful conclusion the much larger workers' movement in Russia.

Defining Moment

Despite his view that social democrats must propagandize as widely as possible, Lenin wrote *What Is to Be Done?* with a narrow audience in mind. It was aimed first and foremost at certain Socialists and pro-worker groups then active in Russia or as émigrés (some of whom are explicitly named in the excerpts presented here). It was intended to convince as many of these people as possible of the correctness of Lenin's ideas—and of the wrongheadedness of alternatives—specifically on questions of party organization and activity in Russia at that time. More broadly, but certainly secondarily, it was written for the wider international Socialist movement of the day. The pamphlet was, of course, read somewhat beyond these circles as well, in-

Vladimir Lenin, 1920. Photo via Wikimedia Commons. [Public domain.]

cluding by the czarist authorities. Lenin had only recently adopted his famous pseudonym at this point, and his identity was not well known.

The pamphlet's real rise to fame came after 1917, once Lenin had established himself as the founder of a new and hugely controversial state. Whereas in the Soviet Union the *whole body* of Lenin's work quickly became a kind of secular scripture (especially after his death in 1924), in the West only *What Is to Be Done?* began to attract particular attention. Beginning in the late 1920s, Stalin, Lenin's successor, took the Soviet Union off in bold and terrible new directions. His first Five-Year Plan (1928–1932) forced breakneck industrialization on the country, and agriculture was brutally collectivized with disastrous results. At the same time, Lenin's works became increasingly available in translation abroad. Of all his writings, *What Is to Be Done?* seemed to offer Western observers the clearest insights into the roots and real nature of the Soviet system that Lenin had created and Stalin later dominated. This opinion, although not unchallenged, is still largely accepted today.

Author Biography

Like many champions of the working poor, Lenin was not of them. He was born into a prosperous family in Simbirsk (known as Ulyanovsk from 1924 to 1991) on the Volga River. His father was an inspector of schools and a ranking noble. Lenin was of mixed ancestry, including Russian, Swedish, German, Jewish, Kalmyk, and Mordvinian. Like most Russians, he was raised in the Orthodox Christian tradition. He was baptized as a sixteen-year-old in 1886. Lenin's "baptism" into the world of radical politics came the following year, when his older brother, Alexander, was arrested and executed for involvement in a plot to assassinate Alexander III, a very repressive czar. Lenin's sister was also implicated and sentenced to house arrest. Lenin soon enrolled in Kazan University but was subsequently expelled for his radical ideals. He studied independently for a time, focusing on Marxism, law, history, and languages, and he later enrolled in the University of Saint Petersburg, from which he graduated with a law degree in 1892.

After a short legal career, Lenin, already a convinced Marxist, turned increasingly to revolutionary propaganda and organization. He was arrested in late 1895 and sent to Siberia, where he shared company with other exiled Marxists, including Nadezhda Konstantinovna Krupskaya, who became his wife in 1898. Lenin's first major publication, *The Development of Capitalism in Russia*, appeared in 1899. This began a prolific writing career. After his release in 1900, Lenin traveled widely in Western Europe. He came into contact with most of the leading left-wing thinkers and activists of the day, joined the RSDLP, and cofounded its official paper, *Iskra* ("The Spark"). It was at this time that Lenin began to regularly use his pseudonym—which means "man from the Lena river"—instead of his real name. (The Lena River actually is thousands of miles east of Lenin's birthplace.) Lenin's ideas on capitalism, revolution, and Communism had already begun to develop beyond their Marxist origins into a somewhat altered theory known subsequently as Marxism-Leninism (or just Leninism). Some of its most characteristic innovations, which focused on questions of organization, can be seen in *What Is to Be Done?*

Historical Document

What Is to Be Done?

II: The Spontaneity of the Masses and the Consciousness of Social Democracy

...The [main] strength of the current movement [for worker liberation] is the awakening of the masses (primarily the industrial proletariat), while its [main] weakness is the insufficiency of consciousness and initiative among revolutionary leaders....The relationship between consciousness and spontaneity is of enormous general interest and must be treated in detail....

The Beginning of the Spontaneous Upsurge

We noted in the previous chapter the [great] *general* interest shown by educated Russian youth in the theory of Marxism during the mid-1890s. At around the same time, the labor strikes that followed the famous Saint Petersburg industrial war of 1896 showed a similar general character. Their spread across all of Russia clearly testifies to the depth of the newly awakened popular movement, and if we are speaking of a "spontaneous element" then, of course, it is precisely this strike movement that must be recognized above all as spontaneous. But there are different levels of spontaneity. There were strikes in Russia during the seventies and sixties...accompanied by the "spontaneous" destruction of machinery and so on. Compared with these "riots" the strikes of the nineties could even be called "conscious"—so significant was the progress the workers' movement had made during that time. This shows that the "spontaneous element" is, in essence, nothing other than consciousness in *embryonic form*. Even primitive riots represent a certain degree of awakening of consciousness: the workers were beginning to lose their age-old faith in the permanence of the system of their oppression, and [they] began...I shan't say to understand, but to feel the need for collective resistance, and decisively broke from slavish submission toward the bosses. But this was still more a case of despair and revenge than of [genuine class] *struggle*. The strikes of the 1890s show us much more significant flashes of consciousness: specific demands were voiced; advance thought was given to picking the best moment [to act]; there was discussion of well-known events and examples from other places. If the riots [of the 1860s–1870s] were simply uprisings of oppressed people, then the systematic strikes [of the 1890s] represented class struggle in embryo, but only in embryo. In and of themselves these strikes were [only] trade unionist struggles, and not yet social democratic struggles; they marked the awakening of antagonism between the workers and owners, but the workers did not have—indeed they could not have—[true] consciousness of the irreconcilable opposition of their interests to the current political and social structure; in other words, [they did not have] social democratic consciousness. In this sense, the strikes of the 1890s, regardless of the great progress made in comparison with the "riots" [of the 1860s–1870s], remained purely an expression of spontaneity.

We have said there *could not have been* social democratic consciousness among the workers. It could be brought [to them] only from outside. The history of all countries demonstrates that exclusively by its own efforts the working class is capable only of working out trade union consciousness—that is, the conviction that it is necessary to combine into unions [in order to] carry on a struggle with the owners, win from the authorities passage of this or that vital law, and so on. The teachings of socialism grew out of philosophical, historical, and economic theories worked out by educated representatives of the propertied classes, [that is, by] intellectuals. The founders of modern scientific socialism, Marx and Engels, themselves belonged—by their social status—to the bourgeois intelligentsia. In just the same way, here in Russia the theoretical teachings of social democracy also arose as a natural and inevitable result of the development of thought among the revolutionary socialist intelligentsia—that is, completely independently of the spontaneous growth of the workers' movement.

Bowing Down to Spontaneity: *Rabochaia mysl'*

...There can be no talk of an independent ideology worked out by the working masses themselves within the process of their own movement. There are only two choices: bourgeois ideology or socialist ideology. There is no middle path (for humankind has not worked out any 'third' ideology; moreover, in a society torn by class conflict there cannot be any kind of ideology that is non-class or above-class). Thus, *any* belittlement of socialist ideology, *any deviation* from it at all strengthens bourgeois ideology. People talk about spontaneity. But the *spontaneous* development of the workers' movement leads precisely toward its subordination to bourgeois ideology...for the spontaneous workers' movement is trade unionism...and trade unionism means the ideological enslavement of the workers to the bourgeoisie. Therefore, our task, the task of social democracy, is to *battle spontaneity*, to *divert* the workers' movement away from these spontaneous trade unionist strivings that lead it under the wing of the bourgeoisie, and to [instead] attract [the workers' movement] under the wing of revolutionary social democracy....

But why—the reader asks—does the spontaneous movement, a movement along the line of least resistance, lead in fact to domination by bourgeois ideology? For the simple reason that bourgeois ideology...is much older than socialist ideology, because [therefore] it has been worked out from all angles, because it has at its disposal *immeasurably* greater resources for its dissemination. The younger the socialist movement is in any given country, the more energetically must the struggle be waged against all attempts to strengthen non-socialist ideology, the more necessary does it become to warn the workers against the bad counsel of those whose cry out against "the exaggerations of the conscious element."

III: Trade Unionist and Social Democratic Politics

...We have already demonstrated how the "economists" while they do not completely reject "politics" instead simply and consistently stray away from a social democratic conception of politics into a trade-unionist one....

Political Agitation and Its Narrowing by the Economists

...Social democracy leads the working class struggle not just for improvement of the conditions under which [the workers] sell their labor, but also for the destruction of the social conditions that force the have-nots to sell themselves to the rich. Social democracy conceives of the working class not just in terms of its relationship to a given group of entrepreneurs, but in its relationship to all classes of modern society and to the government—and as an organized political force. Thus, social democrats must not limit themselves only to the economic struggle; and they must not allow themselves to be dragged into an almost exclusive focus on exposing economic [exploitation of the workers]. We must actively take up the political education of the working class and the development of its political awareness....

The question arises, what should the political education [of the masses] consist of? Is it enough to limit ourselves to propagandizing the idea of the hostility of the working class to the autocracy? Of course not. It is not sufficient merely to *explain* the political oppression of the workers (just as it is not sufficient merely to explain to the workers the irreconcilable nature of their interests and those of the owners). It is necessary [also] to carry out agitation in connection with every concrete example of [the workers'] oppression (just as we have begun to do with regard to concrete examples of economic oppression). Since *this* oppression [political rather than economic] falls upon the greatest diversity of social classes, and since it is apparent in the most varied areas of life and activity—professional, civic, private, family, religious, scientific, and so on—is it not evident that *we shall not be carrying out our mission* to develop the political consciousness of the workers if we do not *take upon ourselves* the organization of [efforts to] *expose all aspects of the political* [oppressiveness] of the autocracy? After all, in order to carry out agitation in response to concrete examples of oppression, it is necessary to [clearly] expose these examples (just as it was necessary to expose factory abuses in order to carry on economic agitation)....

The Working Class as the Vanguard Fighter for Democracy

...Class political consciousness may be brought to the workers *only from outside*—that is, from outside the economic struggle, outside the sphere of relations between workers and owners. The only place from which this knowledge can come is from the sphere of relations of *all* classes and [social] layers to the state and government, [from] the nexus of interrelations among *all* classes. Therefore, when one is asked what is to be done in order to bring political knowledge to the workers, the answer cannot be...[simply] "Go among the workers." To bring political knowledge *to the workers* the social democrats must *go among all classes of the population*, must send detachments...to all *sides*....

IV: The Amateurishness of the Economists and the Organization of Revolutionaries

Organization of Workers and Organization of Revolutionaries

A social democrat who understands the political struggle as simply an "economic struggle with the owners and the government" will, naturally enough, conceive of the "organization of revolutionaries" as—more or less—an "organization of workers." And this is what actually happens, so that when speaking about [questions of] organization we are literally speaking different languages. In fact, I can recall a conversation with a reasonably consistent Economist whom I had not known previously. We were talking about a pamphlet entitled "Who Will Carry Out the Political Revolution? [*Kto sovershit politicheskuiu revoliutsiiu?*]." We quickly agreed that the pamphlet's main deficiency was that it ignored the question of organization. It seemed that we were firmly of one mind, but as the conversation progressed it became clear that we were talking about different things entirely. [The Economist started] accusing me of ignoring strike funds, mutual aid societies, and the like, but I had in mind the organization of revolutionaries—[which is] absolutely necessary for "accomplishing" the political revolution. And as soon as our differences became apparent I don't think there was a single thing at all about which I was in agreement with this "economist."

What was the source of our disagreement? It was precisely this: regardless of whether we are talking about organizational issues or political ones, the "economists" are always slipping away from social democracy and into trade unionism. The political struggle of social democracy is much broader and more complex than the economic struggle that pits the workers against their bosses and the authorities. In just the same way (indeed, because of this), the organization of the revolutionary Social Democratic Party must also be of a *different sort* than the organization of workers. First of all, the workers must be organized by trade; second, their organizations must be as broad as possible; third, they must be as un-conspiratorial as possible (I am speaking here and elsewhere, of course, only about autocratic Russia). In contrast, the organization of revolutionaries must encompass first and foremost people who are revolutionary activists by trade (which is why I speak of an organization of *revolutionaries*, meaning revolutionary social democrats). Given that all members of the organization will share this general characteristic, *we must completely erase all distinction among them as to which is a worker and which an intellectual*, not to mention distinctions of trade among them. This organization definitely must not be very broad, and it must be as secret as possible....

In countries with political freedom, the distinction between a trade organization and a political one is perfectly clear, as is the distinction between trade unionism and social democracy. Of course, the relationship of the latter to the former will inevitably take different forms in different countries, depending on [relevant] historical, legal, and other conditions. They might be more or less close or complex....But in free countries there is never any conversation about them being basically the same thing. However, in Russia the oppressiveness of the autocracy immediately wipes out all distinctions between social democratic organization and labor unions, because any and all labor unions and any and all [organized] circles are forbidden, for the primary manifestation and weapon of the workers' economic struggle—the strike—is a criminal (and sometimes even a political) act! Thus, our circumstances, on the one hand, very much "push" those workers leading the economic struggle into political issues while, on the other hand, they "push" social democrats to mix trade unionism with social democratism....

The moral to be drawn here is simple: if we start by firmly establishing a strong organization of revolutionaries, then we can guarantee the stability of the movement overall and bring to fruition the goals both of social democracy and of the trade union movement. But if we start with a broader worker movement, one that is supposedly more "accessible" to the masses (but, in fact, just more accessible to the gendarmes, thereby making revolutionaries more accessible to the police), then we shall realize neither of these goals...and, because of the fragmented nature [of our movement] we will only be giving the masses over to trade unions of the Zubatov and Ozerov type....

...I affirm: 1) That no revolutionary organization can be durable without a stable organization of leaders to preserve continuity; 2) That the greater the number of the masses who are attracted in spontaneous fashion to the struggle—who form the basis of the movement and who participate in it—then the more urgent does the need become for such an organization and the more solid must such an organization be (for it also becomes easier for the demagogues to attract the undeveloped stratum of the masses); 3) That such an organization must consist chiefly of persons engaged in revolutionary activity as their profession; 4) That in an autocratic country, the more we *narrow* the membership of such an organization to the participation only of persons for whom revolutionary activity is their profession and who have received professional training in the art of struggle against the political police, then the harder will it be [for the authorities] "to fish out" such an organization; and 5) The *broader* will the roster become of persons both from the working class and other social classes who are participating in the movement and actively working for it.

...If we rely on a broad organization we shall never be able to achieve the necessary level of conspiratorial work; and without this one cannot even talk about waging a solid and continuous struggle against the government. But the concentration of all conspiratorial functions in the hands of the smallest possible number of professional revolutionaries does not at all mean that these few will "think for everyone" or that the crowd will not take part in *the movement*. Quite the opposite, the crowd will itself produce these professional revolutionaries—and in ever-increasing numbers—because the crowd will realize that it is not sufficient to simply have a few students or working men—veterans of the economic struggle—come together in a "committee"; [they will understand instead] that it takes years to turn oneself into a professional revolutionary; and so the crowd will start to think not only of amateurish methods, but of this kind of training instead. The centralization of the conspiratorial functions *of the organization* does not at all mean the centralization of all functions *of the movement*. The active participation by the very widest number of the masses in illegal literature will not diminish, but will *increase* tenfold because a dozen or so professional revolutionaries will centralize the conspiratorial functions of this enterprise. Only in this way shall we get to a point where the reading of illegal literature, contributing to it, and even distributing it *will all cease to be conspiratorial work*, for the police will soon realize the absurdity and the impossibility of pursuing through legal and administrative channels every publication of which there will be thousands of copies. And this concerns not only the press, but every function of the movement, even demonstrations....The centralization of the conspiratorial functions of the organization of revolutionaries will not weaken but will enrich the breadth and content of the activity of a whole mass of other organizations that are geared toward the general public and are therefore much less formalized and less conspiratorial: including workers' trade unions, workers' circles for self-education and the reading of illegal literature, socialist circles, and also democratic circles in *all* other strata of the population, and so on. These kinds of circles, unions, and organizations are necessary everywhere and in the *absolute greatest* numbers, with the greatest diversity of functions; but it would be absurd and dangerous to *mingle* them with the organizations of revolutionaries, to destroy the barrier between them, to extinguish in the [minds of] the masses their already incredibly faint awareness that in order to "serve" the mass movement we need people who specially and wholly devote themselves to social democratic activity—and that to make a professional revolutionary of oneself takes patience and persistence.

Yes, this awareness is indeed incredibly faint. Our primary sin in terms of organization is that *with our amateurishness we have denigrated the prestige of the revolutionary* in [Russia]. Limp and shaky on questions of theory; with a narrow viewpoint; reliant on the spontaneity of the masses to justify his own apathy; more resembling a trade-union secretary than a tribune of the people; incapable of putting forward a broad and bold plan, one that would earn the respect even of our opponents; inexperienced and clumsy in practicing his trade—the struggle with the political police: Excuse me! Such a person is not a revolutionary, but just some kind of miserable amateur.

Nobody [within our movement] should take offense at my sharp comments, for when I speak of a lack of preparedness, I speak most of all about myself. I worked in a circle that undertook very broad, all-encompassing tasks—and all us, the members of this circle, suffered to the point of illness because we knew we were showing ourselves to be amateurs at that very historical moment when it could have been said—to adapt a well-known saying: give us an organization of revolutionaries and we will turn Russia upside down! And the more I have since thought about the burning shame I felt at that time, the angrier I have become with these pseudo social democrats who by their teachings bring disgrace to the rank of the revolutionary, who do not understand that our task is not to help lower the revolutionary to the rank of an amateur but to *elevate* the amateurs to [the rank of] revolutionaries....

"Conspiratorial" Organization and "Democratism"

...The objection will be raised that such a powerful and strictly secret organization, one that concentrates in its hands all the threads of conspiratorial activity, one that is highly centralized...may too easily throw itself into a premature attack, may carelessly push the movement [to act] before [the necessary wider levels of] political discontent [have been reached], before the ferment and anger of the working class [has matured]. We reply: abstractly speaking, it cannot be denied, of course, that a militant organization *could* throw itself into an ill-conceived battle that *could* end in a defeat—one that might have been avoided in different circumstances. But we cannot limit ourselves to abstract reasoning when looking at this issue. It is possible, speaking abstractly, for any battle at all to end in defeat, and there is no way to *reduce* this possibility except through organized preparation for battle. If we [avoid abstractions and] deal instead with the concrete realities of the current Russian situation, then one has to come to the more optimistic conclusion that a solid revolutionary organization is absolutely indispensable [both] for giving stability to the movement and to *prevent* it from carrying out ill-conceived attacks. Precisely now, when there is no such organization, and when the revolutionary movement is growing rapidly and spontaneously *we already see* two opposite extremes (which, not surprisingly, "meet"). [These are] the completely ill-founded "economism" with its doctrine of moderation; and the equally ill-founded "excitative terror" which strives "to create artificially the symptoms of the end-stages of a [revolution] that is currently developing and becoming stronger, [but which is still] nearer its beginnings than its end" ([Vera Zasulich] in "Zaria")....*Already there exist* social democrats who fail to resist these extremes. This is hardly surprising, because—among other reasons—the "economic struggle against the owners and the government" will *never* be enough for a revolutionary, and opposite extremes will always appear here and there. Only a centralized and militant organization—one that persistently follows social democratic policies and satisfies, so to speak, all revolutionary instincts and strivings—is capable of protecting the movement from wrong-headed attacks and also of preparing an attack that promises success.

We face yet another criticism—that our views on organization contradict "the democratic principle."...Let us look more closely at this "principle" put forward by the "economists." Everyone will agree, no doubt, that "the principle of broad democracy" requires the two following conditions: first, complete openness, and, second, that all [offices and] functions be decided by election. Without openness it would be silly to talk about democracy at all, and we mean openness that is not limited just to the members of the organization. We call the organization of the German Social Democratic Party democratic because everything in it is done openly, even the sessions of the Party Congress. But no one will call an organization democratic when it is [necessarily] sealed off from all non-members by a cloak of secrecy. So let us ask—what sense is there in promoting the "principle of broad democracy" when the basic condition underlying this principle [that of openness] *is impossible* for a secret organization *to fulfill?* The "principle of broad [democracy]" thus turns out to be simply a resonant but empty phrase....

Things are no better when we look at the second condition of democratism—elections. In countries with political freedom this condition makes perfect sense. "Everyone who accepts the principles of the Party program and supports the Party as best he can is considered a member" says the first paragraph of the organizational by-laws of the German Social Democratic Party. And since the whole political arena is open for all to see—just like the stage before a theater audience—so can everyone see how someone accepts, rejects, supports, or opposes [a given position]. All such things are well-known to all and sundry simply by reading the papers or by [attending] popular assemblies. Everyone knows that a given political figure started out from such-and-such a position, went through whatever changes, responded in this way or that to a difficult situation, and distinguishes himself by this or that set of qualities. And so it is only natural that *all* members of the Party may make an informed choice and elect or not elect a particular person to a particular post. [Similarly, the fact that] anyone...can oversee every step taken by a Party member...creates a self-mechanism akin to that which in biology is called "survival of the fittest." The "natural selection" provided by complete openness, the electoral process, and general public oversight guarantees that every activist finds his appropriate place in the end, gets the most suitable role based on his strengths and abilities, suffers all the consequences of his own mistakes, and demonstrates publicly his ability to realize these mistakes and to correct them in the future.

Now try putting this picture into the frame of our [Russian] autocracy! Is it conceivable that [here] everyone "who accepts the principles of the Party program and supports the Party as best he can" could remain informed about every step taken by a revolutionary conspirator? That they could all elect this or that revolutionary—when the revolutionary is *obliged* in the interests of work to hide his very identity from 90 percent of the people? Think for just a moment...and you will see that "broad democratism" of Party organization in the darkness of the autocracy, under the "[artificial] selection" of the gendarmes is nothing other than an *empty and dangerous toy*. I say "empty" because, in fact, no revolutionary organization of any sort has ever put this *broad* democratism into practice [under the conditions of autocracy] and never could, no matter how much it wished to. I say "dangerous" because any attempt to put "broad democratism" into practice would only help the police to expose [us]; would prolong indefinitely the current amateurishness [of the movement]; would distract...[revolutionary activists] from the serious, urgent work involved in transforming themselves into professional revolutionaries and [would burden them instead] with the "paperwork" involved in setting up elections. This "game of democratism" can develop only abroad—among people who are unable to find themselves real and vital work, in [their] various little groups.

...The single serious organizational principle for activists in our movement must be the strictest [level of] conspiracy, the strictest selection of members, [and] the preparation of professional revolutionaries. Once these qualities are achieved then we are assured of something greater than "democratism"—namely: complete comradely confidence among revolutionaries. And this is even more absolutely necessary among us [than in other countries] for in Russia there can be no question at all of replacing this [loyalty] with any general public oversight. But it would be a great mistake to assume that the impossibility of actual "democratic" oversight thereby renders the members of revolutionary organization beyond any accountability at all ....[On the contrary, these revolutionaries will] feel their *responsibility* vividly, knowing by their own experience that an organization of genuine revolutionaries will stop at nothing to rid itself of a substandard member. Moreover, there is a well-developed and time-honored system of thinking among Russian (and international) revolutionary circles that mercilessly punishes any and all slacking-off from the responsibilities of comradeship (indeed, "democratism"—real, not toy democratism—is a constituent part of this larger system of comradeship). Take all of this under consideration, and you will understand that all these conversations and resolutions about our [supposed] "anti-democratic tendencies" reek with the musty odor of outsiders playing at being generals.

Local and All-Russian Work

...There is one more question that is frequently raised and deserves examining in detail. This concerns the relationship between local and all-Russian work. Some have voiced a worry that the formation of a centralized organization might shift the center of gravity towards all-Russian work in general, and away from local control; [and they worry] that this may threaten, in turn, to undermine the [the movement's] connection with the mass of workers and generally weaken the solidity of local agitation. We answer that our movement has suffered in recent years precisely because of the fact that local activists are totally swamped by local work and that it is therefore necessary to shift the center of gravity towards all-Russian work. Such a shift will not weaken but will strengthen our ties with [the working mass] as well as the stability of local agitation.

Glossary

Saint Petersburg industrial war of 1896: Lenin's name for a textile workers' strike that lasted more than three weeks and was suppressed by the government of Czar Nicholas II

Vera Zasulich: Russian revolutionary (1849–1919), who contributed to the publication "Zaria" (sunrise, or morning star; sometimes Mother Russia)

Document Analysis

The full Russian version of *What Is to Be Done?* runs to about 150 pages arranged in five sections, all of which treat in one way or another the question of how best to organize for a successful Socialist revolution in Russia (as opposed to in other countries). It was written in dialog with other Socialist pamphleteers of the time—that is, with other would-be leaders or spokespersons for working-class movements, both Russian and foreign. Writing in a fairly polemical style, and often naming names, Lenin takes his opponents to task for one or another fault in their basic approach and lays out what he believes is the one proper path forward. The excerpts presented here represent the heart of Lenin's arguments and are drawn from sections 2–4. Sections 1 and 5 deal, respectively, with trends in Marxist criticism and ideas for establishing an all-Russian political newspaper.

"The Spontaneity of the Masses and the Consciousness of Social Democracy" proposes and analyzes a critical distinction between two aspects of the overall struggle for worker liberation: "spontaneity" and "consciousness." Scholars have debated how best to translate and understand these and other key Russian terms—and by extension how best to understand Lenin himself. In general as well as in the context of Lenin's analysis, "spontaneity" connotes actions carried out without forethought or planning—emotional responses, gut reactions, and the like. They are often exhibited by crowds or unorganized groups. The reactions of masses of workers to everyday problems and oppressions are often spontaneous, as in a demonstration, riot, or act of sabotage carried out by workers against their employers and under the influence of anger and raised emotions. "Consciousness" on the other hand, connotes clarity and purposiveness, and it is accompanied and informed by a proper understanding of the whole structure of forces and circumstances at play. "Conscious" actions are carefully planned and done with a specific, achievable end result in mind. Lenin's twin goals in *What Is to Be Done?* are to define the two tendencies in all their details, varieties, and ramifications, and then to promote the idea that only through conscious action and proper organization could the goal of worker liberation be achieved. Spontaneity is presented more negatively. At times it is an indispensable but volatile force—something that, when properly controlled and directed, can achieve important results. More often, Lenin views spontaneity as a blind alley and critical weakness in the movement.

In "The Beginning of the Spontaneous Upsurge," Lenin begins with a few examples of "spontaneity" and "consciousness." He notes that workers' own actions are usually spontaneous, but at the same time he suggests that spontaneous actions can develop eventually into at least the "embryo" of conscious ones. Thus, workers might be expected eventually to achieve a level of consciousness themselves. However, Lenin also seems to reject this thought, stating instead that workers' actions ultimately remain spontaneous. For example, in the last paragraph of this section, Lenin asserts that true social democratic consciousness can be brought to the workers only "from outside"—that is, from dedicated revolutionary intellectuals—and that it can never develop out of workers' own experiences. This ambiguity in Lenin's thinking provides material for those who see him as an elitist and would-be tyrant as well as for those who see him instead as genuine supporter of the interests of the working masses.

In this same section, Lenin makes the first of numerous contrasts between "trade unionist struggles" and "social democratic" ones. Shortly thereafter, he compares "trade union consciousness" with "social democratic consciousness." In each case, social democratic consciousness is presented as the higher form. Roughly speaking, trade union consciousness corresponds to spontaneous movements. Trade union consciousness focuses on the (spontaneous) short-term economic concerns of workers, such as pay and working conditions. The ultimate purpose of trade unions is to negotiate with—and within—the capitalist system, not to overthrow it. Trade union goals are thus inherently nonrevolutionary. They are also economic, not political. It was Lenin's conviction as a Marxist that true worker liberation required not only the economic adjustments that workers wanted (such as pay raises or shorter hours) but also a worldwide political revolution that would usher in a total transformation of the economic system by abolishing private ownership of the means of production.

Since Lenin viewed most workers as "capable only of working out trade union consciousness" he identified a compelling need for the input of revolutionary intellectuals. Around 1900 these men and women had typically come *not* from the working class but, like Lenin, from the property-owning class (the bourgeoisie). Lenin calls these revolutionary intellectuals the "social democrats" and he sees them as the only bearers of true political consciousness. Without them, the workers remain stuck forever either at trade union consciousness or mere "embryonic" forms of social democratic class consciousness. With them, however, real change is possible, even inevitable. The question remains, however, what is to be the form and organization of the merging of these two elements? Should the revolutionary social democrats lead the workers? Or was this to be a more equal partnership? What would the roles of each be? Lenin returns to these questions throughout *What Is to Be Done?*

Rabochaia mysl', translated as The Workers' Thought, was the name of a radical newspaper of the time, and Lenin critiques its stance in this subsection. Lenin again shoots down any questions about the workers' developing an "independent ideology" for their own liberation. There are, he asserts, only two possible ideologies: bourgeois and Socialist. The first leads to oppression of the workers, the second to their liberation. Any effort by the workers to find their own "middle path" simply plays into the hands of autocracy and the employers. Statements like these have convinced many observers that from the start Lenin was completely dismissive of the workers and ready to use them as a means to his ends; that he was at heart undemocratic, paternalistic, and even dictatorial—characteristics that would later describe the Soviet regime.

Lenin defends himself from these charges at several points. In a lengthy footnote to this section (not reproduced), he argues that the workers *can and will* play a vital role in their liberation, but not *as* workers. Rather, he places his hopes on individual members of the working class who—through experience, hard work, and persistent study—will gain a sufficient level of education and themselves become revolutionary intellectuals and true social democrats. He cites as examples the French Socialist Pierre-Joseph Proudhon (a former print worker) and the German Socialist Wilhelm Weitling (a former tailor). Lenin returns to this theme later in the excerpts provided here.

In the section titled "Trade Unionist and Social Democratic Politics," Lenin again contrasts the two aspects of the workers' struggle. By "economists" Lenin does not mean what is now commonly understood by the term but rather a group of moderate Marxists, including Russian social democrats then living in exile in Europe. The term *economists* derives from the group's preference for focusing on precisely those same worker economic demands and concerns that Lenin criticizes as "spontaneous." Unlike Lenin, the "economists" believed that spontaneous worker action could grow into a genuine revolutionary movement that would sweep away the Russian autocracy and usher in a period of liberal bourgeois capitalism that would itself eventually sow the seeds of Socialist revolution. In comparison with Lenin, the economists generally took a longer-term view of the revolutionary movement and placed greater emphasis on following and supporting, rather than controlling and leading, the spontaneous actions of the workers. Lenin too, like any Marxist, accepted that the coming of Socialism would have to be preceded by a period of capitalism. But to a greater degree than many of his contemporaries, he maintained that capitalism had already taken hold in Russia, and he had already argued that point in detail in *The Development of Capitalism in Russia*.

In the subsection, Political Agitation and Its Narrowing by the Economists, Lenin continues to distinguish between social democracy as he understands it and economism. Economism has a "narrow" viewpoint focused on workers' day-to-day economic struggles, while social democracy assumes a broader and more commanding perspective. Social democracy takes into account the full range and structure of class relations, and it emphasizes the importance of the political struggle against the Russian autocracy. Lenin urges social democrats not to lapse into economism. He calls for specific forms of propaganda and education aimed at opening workers' eyes to the larger issues and ideas of social democracy.

By calling the working class the "vanguard" Lenin emphasizes the critical role the workers themselves will play in their own liberation. But then he restates that the workers cannot develop "class political consciousness" by themselves or from within the sphere of their own economic interests and struggles. They must see their struggle in the much larger context of class relations; that is, from the viewpoint of intellectual Marxists or social democrats.

In the critically important subsection, Organization of Workers and Organization of Revolutionaries, Lenin further pursues his division of revolutionary activity into two camps: the conscious "political struggle of social democracy" versus the spontaneous and trade unionist "economic struggle that pits the workers against their bosses and the authorities." Thereafter, he arrives at the heart of his argument, or at least the part that has attracted the greatest attention. This is the question of how best to *organize* revolutionary activity.

Lenin makes two points. First, he argues that both camps have an important role to play, although he clearly considers the "political struggle of social democracy" to be the primary one. Second, he argues that because the roles are *different*, each must be *differently organized*. Workers' organizations should be "by trade" "broad" and "un-conspiratorial" meaning that they should operate openly. But the organization of revolutionaries, he asserts, must be very different. It must "not be very broad" and it should be "as secret as possible." The organization must comprise "first and foremost people who are revolutionary activists by trade"—that is, persons engaged full-time in revolution. Later in the same section and then repeatedly throughout much of the document, Lenin refers to these persons as "professional revolutionaries." This term has become almost iconic in the literature about Lenin and *What Is to Be Done?*

"Professional revolutionaries" as Lenin explains, are more than mere full-time activists. They are also revolutionary intellectuals; they are men and women from any background, including the working masses, who have by experience and study made themselves experts in class theory and Socialist literature. Some scholars have argued that the word and concept of a "professional" does not translate perfectly from Russian to English and that this should be noted particularly in regard to Lenin's famous phrase. In English, the word generally refers to persons engaged in certain fields of work, such as law, medicine, or higher education. In Russian, it can sometimes be used more broadly in the sense of a trade or skill. An alternative translation, "revolutionary by trade" has recently been offered.

For critics of Lenin and of the Soviet system more generally, the seeds of future tyranny may be found exactly here in Lenin's organizational blueprint for a small, compact, secretive party of "professional revolutionaries"—a party that is closed off to the broad mass of workers and certain of its own status as the correct and politically conscious leader of a wider spontaneous movement. Add to this Lenin's conviction that the spontaneous workers' movement, if left to its own devices, would head into defeat and disaster. In light of Lenin's biases, many of his critics have identified in *What Is to Be Done?* a formula destined to eventuate in a highly undemocratic system of leaders (the Bolsheviks) and followers (the workers).

Lenin does not see it this way, however. Much of the rest of *What Is to Be Done?* counters arguments of this sort, which had been leveled at him already from various quarters. In this section he takes on some of these criticisms. In the paragraph beginning "in countries with political freedom" Lenin argues that while an open party organization might be appropriate in other places, in the autocratic Russia of 1902 it is not. Openness would simply make it easier for the police to infiltrate and break up social democratic circles, dooming the movement to failure. Moreover, unlike the situation in western Europe, in Russia most public expressions of the workers' spontaneous and economic struggles (such as strikes and demonstrations) were illegal, as was also true for "conscious" political revolutionary activity. Thus, the two struggles tended to be easily confused with each other. Lenin maintains they need to be kept separate, both conceptually and organizationally. Leadership by conscious and conspiratorial social democrats is also necessary to thwart the drift into spontaneity, which Lenin asserts would "only be giving the masses over to trade unions of the Zubatov and Ozerov type."

After restating his convictions about party organization in five short statements of principle, Lenin attends to another criticism: that his plan to concentrate "all conspiratorial functions in the hands of the smallest possible number of professional revolutionaries" will mean that "these few 'will think for everyone'" and take over the entire movement. Lenin counters that without a stable and professional organization to guide it, the movement will inevitably fail. Moreover, the masses will, in fact, participate more, not less, because the "professional revolutionary" will provide a kind of highly respected role model that ever-increasing numbers of ordinary workers will emulate. He continues, however, to speak of the need for a barrier between the mass movement and the organization of professional social democrats.

Lenin rejects two further criticisms. The first is that the organization he envisions—one that is "powerful and strictly secret" and "concentrates in its hands all the threads of conspiratorial activity" and "is highly centralized"—may ruin the revolution by acting before the masses of workers are sufficiently ready to back them up. The danger, he says, is the reverse. By acting without proper organizational leadership, the working masses themselves risk a devastating loss. He condemns the economists again and also "excitative" terrorists—groups who resort to spontaneous acts of violence and terror intended to bring about revolution before the objective conditions for it were ready.

Lenin then returns to charges that he is being antidemocratic. He expands on his ideas about the unsuitability of open and democratic practices in the context of the autocratic political climate of czarist Russia. How, he asks, can social democrats talk and vote openly, even among themselves, when everything they do is illegal and they must hide their very identities from the czarist authorities?

In the subsection concerning Local and All-Russian Work, Lenin deflects the concern that centralization of social democratic organization will undermine local control and activity and thus place excessive power in the hands of professional revolutionaries. He answers that centralization will instead free up local activists for more productive work and improve the effectiveness of local agitation.

Essential Themes

What Is to Be Done? appeared at a critical moment in the history of the Russian labor movement as well as in the history of the RSDLP. In the very early 1900s the conditions for social revolution in Russia were developing rapidly. Industrialization, although it was still nascent, had expanded significantly, especially under the influence of the Russian minister of finance, Count Sergey Yulyevich Witte, who had pursued a major expansion of railroads and other industries. Foreign investment capital had begun to pour into the country. The number of industrial workers, or urban proletarians, in Russia had reached two to three million (out of a total population of about 160 million). Most of these workers were concentrated in the few large cities, including Moscow and Saint Petersburg, where conditions were particularly oppressive and exploitative. Worker unrest festered, and workers began to organize. The government responded only with minor concessions, such as an 1897 law that established a maximum 11 1/2-hour workday in larger factories. Meanwhile, worker discontent and demands continued to rise.

Beginning in the 1880s, a growing number of Russian intellectuals had begun to look at these developments through the lens of Marxist philosophy, which initially had been expounded abroad. The explosive pamphlet The Communist Manifesto, by the German thinkers Karl Marx and Friedrich Engels, had been published in 1848. Marxism—soon dubbed "scientific Socialism"—viewed all history as a struggle between economic classes, primarily between those who owned the means of production and those who did not. Developed further in Marx's other writings, the theory offered a grand analysis of industrial capitalism and predicted its inevitable demise at the hands of class-conscious proletarians who would destroy the very foundation of the system that oppressed them.

Convinced that the march of history was on their side, Lenin and other members of the RSDLP sought to introduce into the broad workers' movement the concepts and ideals of Marxism, but they did not all agree on the appropriate methods for doing so. By far the largest and leading Socialist party in Europe at the time was the German Social Democratic Party, which in most respects provided a model for the much smaller Russian group. Matters were complicated, however, by the differences between the German and Russian political environments. German intellectual Socialists benefited from relatively advanced political freedoms that allowed the Social Democratic Party to participate openly in the political process. German industrial workers could legally unionize, demonstrate, and read and share ideas without necessarily bringing on government reprisal.

None of this was true in autocratic czarist Russia when Lenin wrote *What Is to Be Done?* All political power emanated from the czar. At least prior to 1905, Russia had neither a parliament nor a constitution. Political parties were illegal, and their members faced harassment and arrest at every turn; moreover, the legal system did not recognize basic civil rights. Workers could not legally organize, demonstrate, or strike. Between 1898 and 1903, Russia experimented briefly with so-called "police unions" which were groups of workers authorized by the state and under police control. The intent behind allowing these unions was to undermine or control working-class movements rather than to achieve significant change, however. To Lenin, all of these circumstances meant that social democracy would have to work very differently in Russia than elsewhere. In particular, it would have to be differently organized, which is the main theme of *What Is to Be Done?*

The title of Lenin's work is borrowed from the identically titled 1863 novel by Nikolay Gavrilovich Chernyshevsky. A leading radical thinker in his own right, Chernyshevsky wrote in the immediate aftermath of the epochal 1861 emancipation of Russia's serfs by Czar Alexander II. This event—and the difficulties and discontent it engendered among the newly liberated peasants—provided the context within which a generation of pre-Marxist Russian radicals wrote and worked. Chernyshevsky was one of the founders of an unsuccessful Russian revolutionary movement known as Populism or Narodism, which advocated agitation among the peasants in order to weld them into a revolutionary force for the overthrow of the czarist regime and its replacement with a decentralized system based on peasant communes. The movement largely burned out in the summer of 1874. Although Lenin later criticized Narodism as utopian and unachievable, he was greatly impressed with Chernyshevsky's depiction of the revolutionary hero as a practical and utterly dedicated individual who through immense personal effort could affect the course of history.

The ideas put forth in *What Is to Be Done?* split the RSDLP into two factions (effectively in 1903 and finally and officially in 1912). Those who rejected Lenin's ideas—preferring instead a broader and more open movement and a more orthodox interpretation of Marxism—became known as Mensheviks ("minoritarians"), while Lenin's supporters became the Bolsheviks ("majoritarians"). *What Is To Be Done?* also helped shape the subsequent form and function of the Bolshevik Party itself, thus laying at least some of the groundwork for the Bolshevik seizure of power in 1917.

Beyond this effect, however, historians are not of one mind when assessing the document's overall importance and impact. While many argue that it remains the single clearest expression of Lenin's basic political ideology and also serves as a key for understanding the eventual Soviet system he founded, others have pointed out that Lenin himself rarely, if ever, referred back to this work after about 1907; that his thought underwent significant modifications thereafter; that many aspects of subsequent Bolshevik Party practice and organization are not covered here; and that the pamphlet in general should be seen as a specific response to particular debates and circumstances current only in 1901–1902 and not as a timeless and essential statement of Bolshevik ideology.

—Brian Bonhomme, PhD

Bibliography and Additional Reading

Haimson, Leopold H. The Russian Marxists and the Origins of Bolshevism. Cambridge, Mass.: Harvard UP, 1955.

———. "Russian Workers' Political and Social Identities: The Role of Social Representations in the

Interaction between Members of the Labor Movement and the Social Democratic Intelligentsia." In Workers and Intelligentsia in Late Imperial Russia: Realities, Representations, Reflections, ed. Reginald Zelnik. Berkeley: University of California Press, 1999.

Harding, Neil. Lenin's Political Thought: Theory and Practice in the Democratic Revolution. London: Macmillan, 1977.

Lih, Lars T. Lenin Rediscovered: What Is to Be Done? in Context. Boston: Brill Academic Publishers, 2005.

"Marxism and Workers' Organisation: Writings of Marxists on Trade Unions, the General Strike, Soviets and Working Class Organisation." Marxists Internet Archive Website. marxists.org/subject/workers/index.htm.

Mayer, Robert. "Lenin and the Concept of the Professional Revolutionary." History of Political Thought 14, no. 2 (1993): 249–263.

Service, Robert. Lenin: A Biography. Cambridge, Mass.: Harvard UP, 2000.

Schapiro, Leonard. "Lenin's Intellectual Formation and the Russian Revolutionary Background." In his Russian Studies. New York: Viking, 1987.

"Vladimir Lenin Works Index." Lenin Internet Archive Web site. marxists.org/archive/lenin/works/index.htm.

Vladimir Lenin on the Tasks of the Soviet Government

Date: October 25 (November 7), 1917
Author: V. I. Lenin
Genre: newspaper report; speech

Summary Overview

At the start of the twentieth century, Russia was the largest country in the world, one of the richest in resources, and yet socially and technically backward. It was a monarchy with social conditions echoing those of the Middle Ages. Economically, Russia was an agricultural country with relatively backward methods of production. Industry started to grow in the second half of the nineteenth century, mostly in the European part of Russia; with it, a working class began to emerge, albeit small, not well organized, and not very powerful.

In 1904 Russia was engaged in a war against Japan. Although more powerful and having greater resources, Russia lost the war, an outcome that resulted in domestic crisis and eventually in a revolution during the years 1905–07. One of the leading forces of the 1905 revolution was the Bolshevik party, which in 1903 grew out of the Russian Social-Democratic Workers' Party. Bolsheviks prompted and coordinated many of the workers' protests. In October 1905 the tsar issued a manifesto promising to establish a Duma (parliament) and issue a constitution. A general strike and a December 1905 uprising in Moscow were suppressed by force. A period of pseudo-constitutionalism followed, with the Bolsheviks boycotting elections and discounting parliament.

The beginning of the twentieth century in Europe witnessed the forming of two large political-military blocs. In the years 1891–93 Russia had entered an alliance with France, and in August 1907 with Great Britain, thus completing the forming of the Triple Entente (Russia, France, Great Britain). In the summer of 1914, the Triple Entente entered war against Germany and Austria-Hungary. In the first year of war, Russia managed to gain some territory in Austro-Hungarian Galicia, losing some in northern Poland. From 1915 Russia kept on retreating and loosing significant territory. By 1917, Russia was rocked by a revolution aimed at its tsarist government and its failed policies, both foreign and domestic. Vladimir Lenin, who came to head the Bolsheviks (and eventually the communist government), was a key figure on the revolutionary stage.

Defining Moment

Three years of withering war, difficult working and living conditions, and great losses—both in men and materiel—resulted in growing frustration and unhappiness in the country. By the beginning of 1917, there were growing protests, demonstrations, and strikes by workers, particularly in Saint Petersburg, Moscow, and a few other cities with industry. In February, the Tsarist government was overthrown by a coalition of workers and soldiers. The Duma, formally dissolved by the Tsar, called to order a provisional government under Prince Lvov (Georgy Yevgenyevich), while workers created an alternative Provisional Executive Committee of the Soviet of Workers Deputies. Tsar Nicholas II was dethroned and arrested.

The provisional government tried to control the political situation, continue the war against Germany, and oversee the country. In opposition, the Petrograd Soviet of Workers' and Soldiers' Deputies contested the government's prerogatives, held considerable influence over the army, and wanted to exit the war and concentrate the nation's activities on domestic issues and building the economy. Despite having considerable backing from the common people, the Soviet could not successfully challenge the position of the social-democratic government. This changed, however, with the return of Vladimir Lenin in April 1917.

Since 1904, Lenin had been in exile. He returned to Russia likely with permission from and the financial aid of German authorities, who welcomed any internal chaos that might be created as a way to further weaken of Russia, allowing Germany thereby to focus its military efforts on Russia's allies: France and Great Britain. Lenin's arrival turned into a triumphant scene in Saint Petersburg, and his so-called "April Theses" became the program of the Petersburg Soviet and ordinary people. Lenin argued that the February Revolution was only the first stage of change. He called for a further revolution, which would lead toward full victory over capitalists and the bourgeoisie ("middle class"), leading eventually to a socialist-communist economy and improved social conditions.

In spite of increased backing for the Bolsheviks, their coup of July 1917 failed and the government under Alexander Kerensky managed to control the immediate situation, even issuing an arrest warrant for Lenin—who had to flee to Finland. Yet, the provisional government of Kerensky had no tools to stabilize the political, economic, and social crises in the long run.

The next attempt to overthrow the government was launched under the control of the Petrograd Soviet of Workers' and Soldiers' Deputies, under Lenin's authority, and took place on October 24-25 (November 6-7, new style), 1917. The Bolsheviks managed to inspire large groups of soldiers and started taking control over strategic points in Saint Petersburg. By the second day they called on the government, gathered in the Winter Palace, to surrender and give up all control to the Bolsheviks. It was on this day (Oct. 25), in the evening, that Lenin addressed the victorious Petrograd Soviet of Workers' and Soldiers' Deputies, making an enthusiastic appeal to continue the revolution.

Author Biography

Vladimir I. Lenin (born V.I. Uljanov, 1870-1924) was a Russian lawyer by training, a publicist, communist activist, creator of the Bolshevik party, and organizer of the October Revolution. In the years 1893-95 he was active in various Marxist underground organizations. Arrested in 1895, he later (1900) emigrated

Bolshevik political cartoon poster from 1920, showing Lenin sweeping away monarchs, clergy, and capitalists. By Viktor Deni (1893-1946). Image via Wikimedia Commons. [Public domain.]

from Russia to Switzerland, also spending time in Germany and England. His political writings and ideology led, in 1903, to the breaking up of the Russian Social-Democratic Workers' Party and the creation of the Bolshevik party. The latter was to be a new type of party: ideologically coherent, composed of revolutionary activists, and designed to produce professional politicians under a strict hierarchical structure.

Upon his return to Saint Petersburg in 1905, Lenin became a key leader in the 1905-07 revolution, after which he emigrated again (France, Switzerland, Austro-Hungarian Galicia). He was abroad when World War I erupted, as well as during the ensuing February Revolution of 1917. In April 1917 he returned to Russia, published his "April Theses," and undertook to change the social-democratic revolution into a socialist. In June he led an unsuccessful coup attempt, after which he was forced to disappear under threat of arrest. Once again he went abroad and found shelter in nearby Finland, just across the border from Saint Petersburg. At the end of October 1917 he led a military coup, which this time proved successful, overthrowing the (provisional) government headed by Alexander Kerensky. The Petrograd Soviet of Soldiers' and Workers' Deputies announced itself as in charge of the government.

Historical Document

On the Tasks of the Soviet Government

Comrades, the workers' and peasants' revolution, about the necessity of which the Bolsheviks have always spoken, has been accomplished.

What is the significance of this workers' and peasants' revolution? Its significance is, first of all, that we shall have a Soviet government, our own organ of power, in which the bourgeoisie will have no share whatsoever. The oppressed masses will themselves create a power. The old state apparatus will be shattered to its foundations and a new administrative apparatus set up in the form of the Soviet organizations.

From now on, a new phase in the history of Russia begins, and this, the third Russian revolution, should in the end lead to the victory of socialism.

One of our urgent tasks is to put an immediate end to the war. It is clear to everybody that in order to end this war, which is closely bound up with the present capitalist system, capital itself must be fought.

We shall be helped in this by the world working-class movement, which is already beginning to develop in Italy, Britain and Germany.

The proposal we make to international democracy for a just and immediate peace will everywhere awaken an ardent response among the international proletarian masses. All the secret treaties must be immediately published in order to strengthen the confidence of the proletariat.

Within Russia a huge section of the peasantry has said that they have played long enough with the capitalists, and will now march with the workers. A single decree putting an end to landed proprietorship will win us the confidence of the peasants. The peasants will understand that the salvation of the peasantry lies only in an alliance with the workers. We shall institute genuine workers' control over production.

We have now learned to make a concerted effort. The revolution that has just been accomplished is evidence of this. We possess the strength of mass organization, which will overcome everything and lead the proletariat to the world revolution.

We must now set about building a proletarian socialist state in Russia.

Long live the world socialist revolution! (Stormy applause.)

Translated by Yuri Sdobnikov and George Hanna.

Glossary

Bolshevik: member of one faction of the Russian Social-Democratic Workers' Party under the leadership of V.I. Lenin; the group split from the main party during the party's second congress in 1903. bourgeoisie: in social theory, a social bloc made up of the middle class; it is mainly a concept advanced by Karl Marx (1818-1883), who argued that the bourgeoisie revolutionized industry and modernized society but later exploited workers (the proletariat), thus pushing them toward revolution.

soviet: a council; in Russia these were political and governing bodies formed during the revolution, usually representing workers and soldiers (also, later, peasants) and fulfilling various governing tasks.

proletariat (proletarian masses): the lower classes in society; in Marx's and Lenin's theory, the proletariat is made up mainly of wage workers in industry.

Document Themes and Analysis

This document is a printed version, published in the newspaper *Izvestia,* of a short speech delivered by V.I. Lenin to the Petrograd Soviet of Workers' and Soldiers' Deputies on October 25, 1917 (or November 7, 1917 according to the calendar used today). It is possible that the text of this press account is not identical to the words spoken by Lenin himself, but there is no more accurate or reliable record from which to draw. In any case, Lenin begins by stating that the revolution in Russia has been accomplished and, in effect, the country will now be under the control of Soviet workers and soldiers, with no input from the bourgeoisie. All organizations will be destroyed and replaced by Soviet ones. Referring to the third revolution, Lenin likely counts the first two as being the unsuccessful revolution of 1905 and the bourgeois revolution of February 1917. This latest one, of October, is then the third and final one and will result in a socialist/communist state.

In order to achieve that grand goal, notes Lenin, there is an immediate need to end the existing world war, since is the outcome of the activities of capitalist society. The end of the war should be accomplished, he says, through the input of the Italian, British, and German working classes. Any peace talks and treaties should be transparent and made known publically in order to win the trust of the workers.

In Russia, where the working class is weak, Lenin points to the need to form an alliance with the huge numbers of peasants, who, so far, have backed capitalists but can be and must be educated to serve hand in hand with Bolsheviks. This will be accomplished through land reform and the securing of peasant ownership of the land. The workers will take control of all production in Russia. Industry needs to be nationalized. Thus will a method to build a proletarian socialist state in Russia be put in place, according to Lenin. It is only through the hindsight of history that today we can understand how difficult was the task facing the new nation and how violently that task was carried out by Bolshevik leaders—Lenin, Stalin, and many others—in the years and decades to come.

—*Jakub Basista, PhD, DLitt*

Bibliography and Additional Reading

Miéville, China. *October: The Story of the Russian Revolution.* London; Brooklyn, NY: Verso, 2017.

Sebestyen, Victor; *Lenin: The Man, the Dictator, and the Master of Terror.* New York: Pantheon, 2017.

Victor G. "On Lenin's Address to Petrograd Soviet," *Workers Vanguard* No. 861, 6 January 2005, www.icl-fi.org/english/wv/861/letter-lenin.html .

■ Soviets in Action

Date: 1918
Author: John Reed
Genre: article

Summary Overview

Czarist Russia had been on the tipping point of revolution several times during the end of the nineteenth and the beginning of the twentieth centuries, but in 1917 the scales finally did tip. There were two revolutions in 1917. The first, the February Revolution, removed Czar Nicholas II from power and abolished the traditional monarchy of the Russian government. The second, the October Revolution, brought the Bolsheviks to power when they overturned the provisional revolutionary government. This was the first major step in the transformation of a long-standing monarchical empire into what soon would become the Union of Soviet Socialist Republics (USSR).

John Reed's piece "Soviets in Action," from the American socialist magazine The Liberator (edited by Max Eastman), highlights how the movement toward the revolution was pressed by the Russian workers and peasants, fulfilling the Communist goal of having workers own the means of production rather than being separated from their own labor and earnings. It is both descriptive and laudatory, as is befitting for a writer who believed in the cause.

Defining Moment

For centuries, Russia had been expanding its territory into Asia. In 1904 it came into conflict with Japan, leading to the Russo-Japanese war. The Russians were not only defeated but embarrassed on the world stage for falling victim to such a small adversary. Moreover, the Russian people had suffered greatly while the government waged war, producing distrust and unrest. In the aftermath of the conflict, Czar Nicholas II, of the long-standing Romanov dynasty, attempted to implement some minor reforms, but dissatisfaction with his rule remained. In 1914, despite the fact that the country was is in no shape to fight another war, Russia was drawn into World War I when Germany invaded France, a Russian ally at the time. The Russians mobilized with surprising speed and were able to force the Germans to take units away from the French front; their actions may have helped keep Germany from winning the war within a few

John Reed, c. 1915. Photo via Wikimedia Commons. [Public domain.]

After the capture of the Winter Palace. Petrograd. 26 October 1917. Photo by P. Novitsky

months. After that initial success, however, Russia experienced great losses on the battlefield and severe hardships at home. By 1917, unrest and protests had become widespread.

These disturbances were not initially considered to be of a revolutionary nature. Protests and strikes demanding higher wages and better treatment had been occurring on and off for many years. Now there were "bread protests" too, over the lack of food. In the capital of Petrograd (St. Petersburg), in February 1917, some 30 percent of all workers were involved in strikes. People decried the autocracy of the czar and directed their ire toward him and the elite.

On the third day of the strike, the character of the protests changed. Their purpose became more general, and their activities became more aggressive. Police stations were raided and the police were disarmed. The military governor of Petrograd attempted to repress the strike by force using both police and some cadets from the Imperial Guard regiments. The strikers were not overcome, however; in fact, the show of force seemed only to strengthen their revolutionary resolve. Imperial Guard regiments were reported to have defected and joined the protestors.

Although the city was in turmoil, the monarchy remained in place and forces were available to oppose the emerging revolution—or so it seemed. Military officials and council members surrounding the czar repeatedly urged him to agree to the reforms demanded by the revolutionary groups; yet Nicholas refused. There was general agreement among the revolutionary forces that the autocracy needed to be overthrown, but the more conservative members of these groups still hoped to preserve the monarchy itself, including the Romanov dynasty. Ultimately, however, Nicholas came to recognize that the will to remove him was overwhelming; he abdicated in favor of his brother Michael, who refused the crown. The monarchy was now officially over, and the new Provisional Government began its work, headed by the moderate Alexander Kerensky. The revolution proceeded to its next phase.

Author Biography

John Reed was an American journalist with communist leanings who supported the Russian revolutionaries; in 1919, he helped to found a short-lived Communist political party in the United States. He participated in workers' strikes and demonstrations, and was jailed more than once for his activities, which seemed to further radicalize his inclinations toward workers' rights. In 1917, when the United States entered the First World War, Reed spoke out strongly against the decision. He believed that the war was mostly about economic rivalry and did not represent the great fight against tyranny that many claimed for it. Reed's antiwar statements, in what by then had become a fervently prowar country, left his career in tatters. He was present in Russia during the October Revolution, which brought the Bolsheviks to power. He strongly supported the Bolshevik concepts of government by the people and joined causes in Russia where he could offer his help.

When Reed returned to the United States in 1919, he continued to speak in support of the Russian Revo-

EXTREMISTS' RISE TO POWER IN RUSSIA

From Outset of Revolution They Have Thwarted Efforts of Moderate Governments.

SAPPED KERENSKY'S RULE

Supported Premier Only When the Korniloff Movement Filled Them with Apprehension.

The New York Times headline from 9 November, 1917. Photo via Wikimedia Commons. [Public domain.]

lution. He published his best known work, *Ten Days That Shook the World,* about the October Revolution, that same year. He also participated in ever more aggressive actions, and was repeatedly fined and jailed as a result. Ultimately, he was indicted for sedition and fled to Russia with a forged passport. There, his feelings about the revolution appeared to have cooled, as the Russian authorities began to argue that they needed to work within established systems to maintain control. Reed died in 1920 after contracting spotted typhus and was given a hero's funeral in Russia.

Historical Document

John Reed: "Soviets in Action"

1918

Through all the chorus of abuse and misrepresentation directed against the Russian Soviets by the capitalist press there runs a voice shrill with a sort of panic, which cries: "There is no government in Russia! There is no organisation among the Russian workers! It will not work! It will not work!"

There is method in the slander.

As all real socialists know, and as we who have seen the Russian Revolution can testify, there is today in Moscow and throughout all the cities and towns of the Russian land a highly complex political structure, which is upheld by the vast majority of the people and which is functioning as well as any new-born popular government ever functioned. Also the workers of Russia have fashioned from their necessities and the demands of life an economic organisation which is evolving into a true industrial democracy.

The Soviet state is based upon the Soviets—or Councils—of Workers, and Peasants' Soviets. These Councils—institutions so characteristic of the Russian Revolution—originated in 1905, when, during the first general strike of the workers, Petrograd factories and labour organisations sent delegates to a Central Committee. This Strike Committee was named Council of Workers' Deputies. It called the second general strike of the fall of 1905, sent out organisers all over Russia, and for a short time was recognised by the Imperial Government as the authorised spokesman of the revolutionary Russian working class.

Upon the failure of the 1905 Revolution, the members of the Council either fled or were sent to Siberia. But so astoundingly effective as a political organ was this type of union that all revolutionary parties included a Council of Workers' Deputies in their plans for the next uprising.

In March 1917, when, in the face of all Russia rearing like a sea, the Tsar abdicated and Grand Duke Michael declined the throne, and the reluctant Duma was forced to assume the reins of government, the Council of Workers' Deputies sprang fully-fledged into being. In a few days it was enlarged to include delegates of the Army, and called the Council of Workers' and Soldiers' Deputies. Except for Kerensky the Duma Committee was composed of bourgeois, and had no connection with the revolutionary masses whatever. Fighting had to be done, order had to be restored, the front guarded. The Duma members had no way of executing these duties; they were obliged to appeal to the representatives of the workers and soldiers—in other words, the Council. The Council took charge of the work of Revolution, of co-ordinating the activities of the people, preserving order. Moreover, it assumed the task of assuring the Revolution against its betrayal by the bourgeoisie.

From the moment when the Duma was forced to appeal to the Council, two governments existed in Russia and these two governments struggled for the mastery until November 1917, when the Soviets, with the Bolsheviks in control, overthrew the coalition government.

There were, as I have said, Soviets of both Workers' and of Soldiers' Deputies. Somewhat later there came into being Soviets of Peasants' Deputies. In most cities the Workers' and Soldiers' Soviets met together; they also held their All-Russian Congress jointly. The Peasants' Soviets, however, were held aloof by the reactionary elements in control, and did not join with the workers and soldiers until the November revolution and the establishment of the Soviet Government.

The Soviet is based directly upon the workers in the factories and the peasants in the field. At first the delegates of Workers', Soldiers' and Peasants' Soviets were elected according to rules which varied with the needs and population of various localities. In some villages the peasants chose one delegate for each fifty voters. Soldiers in garrison were given a certain number of delegates for each regiment, regardless of its strength; the army in the field, however, had a different method of electing their Soviets. As for the workers in the great cities, they soon found out that their Soviets became unwieldy unless the delegates were limited to one for each five hundred. In the same way, the first two All-Russian Congresses of Soviets were roughly based upon one delegate for each twenty five thousand voters, but in fact the delegates represented constituencies of various sizes.

Until February 1918 anybody could vote for delegates to the Soviets. *Even had the bourgeoisie organised and demanded representation in the Soviets, they would have been given it.* For example, during the regime of the Provisional Government there was bourgeois representation in the Petrograd Soviet—a delegate of the Union of Professional Men which comprised doctors, lawyers, teachers, etc.

Last March, the constitution of the Soviets was worked out in detail and applied universally. It restricted the franchise to: citizens of the Russian Socialist Republic of both sexes who shall have completed their eighteenth year by the day of election; all who have acquired the means of living through labour that is productive and useful to society and who are members of labour unions. Excluded from the right to vote were: employers of labour for profit; persons who lived on unearned increment; merchants and agents of private business; employers of religious communities; former members of the police and gendarmerie; the former ruling dynasty; the mentally deficient; the deaf and dumb; and those who had been punished for *selfish and dishonourable misdemeanours.*

As far as the peasants are concerned, each hundred peasants in the villages elect one representative to the Volost, or Township, Soviet. These Volost Soviets send delegates to the Uyezd, or County, Soviets, which in turn send delegates to the Oblast, or Provincial, Soviet, to which also are elected delegates from the Workers' Soviets in the cities.

The Petrograd Soviet of Workers' and Soldiers' Deputies, which was in operation when I was in Russia, may serve as an example of how the urban units of government function under the socialist state. It consisted of about 1200 deputies, and in normal circumstances held a plenary session every two weeks. In the meantime, it elected a Central Executive Committee of 110 members, based upon party proportionality, and this Central Executive Committee *added to itself by invitation* delegates from the central committees of all the political parties, from the central committees of the professional unions, the factory shop committees, and other democratic organisations.

Besides the big City Soviet, there were also the Rayori, or Ward, Soviets. These were made up of the deputies elected from each ward to the City Soviet, and administered their part of the city. Naturally, in some wards there were no factories, and therefore normally no representation of the ward either in the City Soviet or in Ward Soviets of their own. But the Soviet system is extremely flexible, and if the cooks and waiters, or the street sweepers, or the courtyard servants, or the cab drivers of that ward organised and demanded representation, they were allowed delegates.

Elections of delegates are based on proportional representation, which means that the political parties are represented in exact proportion to the number of voters in the whole city. And it is *political parties and programmes* which are voted for—not candidates. The candidates are designated by the central committees of the political parties, which can replace them by other party members. Also the delegates are not elected for any particular term, but are subject to recall *at any time*.

No political body more sensitive and responsive to the popular will was ever invented. And this was necessary, for in time of revolution the popular will changes with great rapidity. For example, during the first week of December 1917, there were parades and demonstrations in favour of a Constituent Assembly -that is to say, against the Soviet power. One of these parades was fired on by some irresponsible Red Guards, and several people killed. The reaction to this stupid violence was immediate. *Within twelve hours the complexion of the Petrograd Soviet changed*. More than a dozen Bolshevik deputies were withdrawn, and replaced by Mensheviki. And it was three weeks before public sentiment subsided—before the Mensheviki were retired one by one and the Bolsheviki sent back.

At least twice a year delegates are elected from all over Russia to the All-Russian Congress of Soviets. Theoretically these delegates are chosen by direct popular election: from the provinces, one for each hundred and twenty five thousand voters—from the cities, one for each twenty five thousand; in practice, however, they are usually chosen by the provincial and the urban Soviets. An extraordinary session of the Congress can be called at any time upon the initiative of the All-Russian Central Executive Committee, or upon the demand of Soviets representing one third of the working population of Russia.

This body, consisting of about two thousand delegates, meets in the capital in the form of a great *Soviet*, and settles upon the essentials of national policy. It elects a Central Executive Committee, like the Central Committee of the Petrograd Soviet, which invites delegates from the central committees of all democratic organisations.

This augmented Central Executive Committee of the Russian Soviets is the *parliament* of the Russian Republic. It consists of about three hundred and fifty persons. Between All-Russian Congresses it is the supreme authority; it must not act outside the lines laid down by the last Congress, and is strictly responsible in all its acts to the next Congress. For example, the Central Executive Committee can, and did, order that the peace treaty with Germany be signed, but it could not make this treaty binding on Russia. Only the All Russian Congress has power to ratify the treaty.

The Central Executive Committee elects from its midst eleven Commissars, to be chairmen of committees in charge of the different branches of government, in place of ministers. These Commissars can be recalled *at any time*. They are strictly responsible to the Central Executive Committee. The Commissars elect a chairman. Ever since the Soviet Government has been formed, this chairman—or Premier—has been Nicolai Lenin. If his leadership were unsatisfactory, Lenin could be recalled at any moment by the delegation of the masses of the Russian people, or in a few weeks' time directly by the Russian people themselves.

The chief function of the Soviets is the defence and consolidation of the Revolution. They express the political will of the masses, not only in the All Russian Congresses, for the whole country, but also in their own localities, where their authority is practically supreme. This decentralisation exists because the local Soviets create the central government, and not the central government the local Soviets. In spite of local autonomy, however, the decrees of the Central Executive Committee, and the orders of the Commissars, are valid throughout all the country, because under the Soviet Republic there are no sectional or private interests to serve, and the cause of the Revolution is everywhere the same.

Ill-informed observers, mostly from the middle class intelligentsia, are fond of remarking that they are in favour of the Soviets, but against the Bolsheviks. This is an absurdity. The Soviets are the most perfect organs of working class representation, it is true, but they are also the weapons of proletarian dictatorship, to which all anti-Bolshevik parties are bitterly opposed. So the measure of the adherence of the people to the policy of proletarian dictatorship is not only measured by the membership of the Bolshevik Party—or, as it is now called, the Communist Party—but also by the growth and activity of local Soviets all over Russia.

The most striking example of this is among the peasants, who did not take the leadership of the revolution, and whose primitive and almost exclusive interest in it was the confiscation of the great estates. The Soviets of Peasants' Deputies at first had practically no other function except the solution of the land question. It was the failure of the land solution under the coalition government which turned the attention of the great mass of peasants to the social reasons behind this failure—that, coupled with the ceaseless propaganda of the left wing of the Socialist Revolutionary Party, and of the Bolsheviki, and the return to the villages of the revolutionary soldiers.

The traditional party of the peasants is the Socialist Revolutionary Party. The great inert mass of peasants whose only interest was in their land, and who had neither fighting stamina nor political initiative, at first refused to have anything to do with the Soviets. Those peasants, however, who did participate in the Soviets soon awoke to the idea of the proletarian dictatorship. And they almost invariably joined the Left Socialist Revolutionary Party, and became fighting partisans of the Soviet government.

In the Commissariat of Agriculture in Petrograd hangs a map of Russia, sprinkled with red-headed pins. Each of these red-headed pins represents a Soviet of Peasants' Deputies. When I first saw the map, hanging in the old headquarters of the Peasants' Soviets at 6 Fontanka, the red points were sprinkled sparsely over the vast country, nor did the numbers grow. For the first eight months of the revolution there were *volosts, uyezds*, whole provinces in fact where only one or two large towns would show a Peasants' Soviet, and perhaps a scattering of villages. After the November Revolution, however, you could see all Russia redder under your eyes, as village after village, county after county, province after province, awoke and formed its Peasant Council.

At the time of the Bolshevik insurrection a Constituent Assembly with an anti-Soviet majority could be elected; one month later it would have been impossible. I saw three All-Russian Peasants Conventions in Petrograd. The delegates arrived—the vast majority of them Right Socialist Revolutionaries They met in session—and very stormy sessions they always were—under the presidency of conservatives of the type of Avksentiev and Peshekhanov. In a few days they would move to the left and be dominated by pseudo-radicals like Tchernov. A few days later the majority would become very radical, and Maria Spiridonova would be elected chairman. Then the conservative minority would split off and set up a rump convention, which in a few days dwindled to nothing. And the main body would send delegates to join the Soviets at Smolny. This happened every time.

I shall never forget the Peasants' Conference which took place towards the end of November, and how Tchernov fought for control and lost it, and that wonderful procession of grizzled proletarians of the soil who marched to Smolny through the snowy streets, singing, their blood-red banners floating in the bitter wind. It was dark night. On the steps of Smolny hundreds of working men were waiting to receive their peasant brothers, and in the dim light the two masses moving one down and the other up, rushed together and embraced, and wept, and cheered.

The Soviets can pass decrees effecting fundamental economic changes, but these must be carried out by the local popular organisations themselves. The confiscation and distribution of the land, for example, were left to the Peasants' Land Committees. These Land Committees were elected by the peasants at the suggestion of Prince Lvov, first premier of the Provisional Government Some settlement of the land question was inevitable, by which the great estates should be broken up and distributed among the peasants. Prince Lvov asked the peasants to elect Land Committees, which should not only determine their own agricultural needs, but should also survey and make a valuation of the landed estates. But when these Land Committees attempted to function, the landlords had them arrested.

When the Soviets seized the power, its first action was to promulgate the Decree of the Land. This Land Decree was not a Bolshevik project at all, but the programme of the Right (or moderate) Socialist Revolutionary Party, drawn up on the basis of several hundred peasant memorials. It abolished forever private title to land or to natural resources in Russia, and gave over to the Land Committees the task of apportioning the land among the peasants, until the Constituent Assembly should finally settle the question. After the dissolution of the Constitution Assembly, the Decree was made final.

Outside of these few general propositions, and a section providing for the emigration of surplus population in congested neighbourhoods, the details of confiscation and distribution were left entirely to the local Land Committee. Kalagayev, the first Commissar of Agriculture, drew up an elaborate set of rules to guide the peasants in their action. But Lenin, in a speech before the Central Executive Committee, persuaded the government to leave the peasants to manage the matter in a revolutionary way, merely advising the poor peasants to combine against the rich peasants. ("Let ten poor peasants oppose every rich peasant," said Lenin.)

Of course no peasant could own his land, but still, he could take what land was due him and treat it as his private property. But the policy of the government, acting through the local Land Committee, is to discourage this tendency. Peasants who wish to become private landlords may do so, but they are not assisted by the government On the other hand, peasants who farm co-operatively are given credit, seed, implements and modern technical training.

Attached to the Land Committees are agricultural and forestry experts. In order to co-ordinate the practices of the local Committees a central body is elected from them, known as the Main Land Committee, which sits in the capital, in close touch with the Commissariat of Agriculture.

When the March Revolution broke, the owners and administrators of many industrial plants either left or were driven out by the workers. In the government factories, where labour had long been at the mercy of irresponsible bureaucrats appointed by the Tsar, this was particularly the case.

Without superintendents, foremen, and in many cases engineers and bookkeepers, the workers found themselves faced with the alternative of keeping the works going or of starving. A committee was elected, one delegate from each "shop" or department; this committee attempted to run the factory. Of course, at first this plan seemed hopeless. The functions of the different departments could be co-ordinated in this way, but the lack of technical training on the part of the workers produced some grotesque results.

Finally there was a committee meeting at one of the factories, where a workman rose and said: "Comrades, why do we worry? The question of technical experts is not a difficult one. Remember *the boss* wasn't a technical expert; *the boss* didn't know engineering or chemistry or bookkeeping. All he did was to own. When he wanted technical help, he *hired* men to do it for him. Well, now we are the boss. Let's *hire* engineers, bookkeepers, and so forth—to work for us!

In the government factories the problem was comparatively simple, since the Revolution automatically removed the "boss," and never really substituted another. But when the Factory Shop Committees spread to the privately-owned works, they were viciously fought by factory owners, most of whom were making contracts with the unions.

In the private factories, too, the shop committees were the product of necessity. After the first three months of the Revolution, during which the middle class and the proletarian organisations worked together in utopian harmony, the industrial capitalists began to be afraid of the growing power and ambition of the workers' organizations—just as the country landowners feared the Land Committee, and the officers the soldiers' committees and Soviets. Along about the first part of June began the more or less conscious campaign of the entire bourgeoisie to halt the Revolution, and break down the democratic organisations. Beginning with the Factory Shop Committees, the industrial owners planned to make a clean sweep of everything, including the Soviets. The army was disorganised, supplies and munitions and food diverted from it, and actual positions betrayed to the Germans—like Riga; in the country the peasants were persuaded to hoard their grain, and provoked to disorders, which gave the excuse to the Cossacks to "restore peace"; and in industry, more important than all, the machinery and operation of the factories themselves were sabotaged, transportation was still further wrecked, and the coal mines, metal mines and sources of raw materials damaged as much as possible. Every effort was made to shut down the factories and starve the workers back into submission to the old industrial regime.

This the workers were forced to resist. The Factory Shop Committee sprang up and took charge. At first, of course, Russian workers made ludicrous mistakes, as all the world has been told again and again. They demanded impossible wages—they attempted to run complicated scientific manufacturing processes without proper experience; in some cases, even, they asked the boss to return at his own terms. But *such cases are the great minority. In the majority of plants the workers were resourceful enough to be able to conduct the industry without bosses.*

The owners attempted to falsify the books, to conceal orders; the Factory Shop Committee was forced to find out ways to control the books. The owners tried to strip the works—so the committee had to rule that nothing should go in or out of the plant without permission. When the factory was going to close down for lack of fuel, raw material, or orders, the Factory Shop Committee had to send men half across Russia to the mines, or down into the Caucasus for oil, to Crimea for cotton; and agents had to be sent out by the workers to sell the product. In the breakdown of the railroads, committee agents had to make agreements with the Railwaymen's Union for transportation of freight. To guard against strike-breakers, the committee had to take over the function of hiring and discharging workers.

Thus the Factory Shop Committee was the creation of Russian anarchy, forced by necessity to learn how to manage industry, so that when the time came the Russian workers could take over actual control with little friction.

As an instance of how the masses worked together, there is the matter of two hundred thousand *poods* of coal, which was taken from the bunkers of the Baltic battle fleet in December, and turned over by the sailors' committees to keep the factories of Petrograd running during the coal famine.

Obukhov Works was a steel plant manufacturing supplies for the Navy. The chairman of the Obukhov committee was a Russian–American, Petrovsky by name, well known here as an anarchist. One day the foreman of the torpedo department told Petrovsky that the department would have to close down owing to the impossibility of procuring certain small tubes used in the manufacture of torpedoes. The tubes were manufactured by a factory across the river, whose product was contracted for three months ahead. The closing down of the torpedo department meant that four hundred men would be out of work.

"I'll get the tubes," said Petrovsky. He went direct to the tube factory, where, instead of calling upon the manager, he sought the chairman of the local Factory Shop Committee. "Comrade," he said, "if we don't get tubes in two days, our torpedo department will have to close down, and four hundred of the boys will be out of a job."

The chairman called for his factory's books, and discovered that some thousands of the tubes were contracted for by three private plants in the vicinity. He and Petrovsky thereupon visited these three plants, and called on the Factory Shop Committee chairmen. At two of the factories it was discovered that the tubes were not immediately needed; and next day the tubes were delivered to the Obukhov Works, and the torpedo department didn't shut down.

In Novgorod was a textile mill. At the outbreak of the revolution the owner said to himself. "Here's trouble coming. We won't be able to make any profits while this revolution is on. Let's shut down the works until the thing blows over." So he shut down the works, and he and the office force, the chemists, engineers and manager, took the train for Petrograd. The next morning the workers opened the mill.

Now these workers were perhaps a little more ignorant than most workers. They knew nothing of the technical processes of manufacture, of bookkeeping or management, or selling. They elected a Factory Shop Committee, and finding a certain amount of fuel and raw materials in stock, set to work to manufacturing cotton cloth.

Not knowing what was done with cotton cloth when manufactured, they first helped themselves to enough for their families. Next, some of the looms being out of order, they sent a delegate to a nearby machine-shop saying that they would give cotton cloth in exchange for mechanical assistance. This done, they made a deal with the local city co-operative, to supply cloth in exchange for food. They even extended the principle of barter so far as to exchange bolts of cloth for fuel with the coal miners of Kharkov, and with the Railwaymen's Union for transportation.

But finally they glutted the local market with cotton cloth, and then they ran up against a demand which cloth could not satisfy—rent. This was in the days of the Provisional Government when there were still landlords. Rent had to be satisfied with money. So they loaded a train with cloth and sent it, in charge of a committeeman, to Moscow. The committeeman left his train at the station, and went down the street. He came to a tailor shop and asked if the tailor needed cloth.

"How much?" asked the tailor.

"A train-load," answered the committeeman.

"What does it cost?"

"I don't know. What do you usually pay for cloth?"

The tailor got his cloth for a song, and the committeeman, who had never seen so much money at one time, went back to Novgorod highly elated.

So it was that all over Russia the workers were getting the necessary education in the fundamentals of industrial production, *and even distribution*, so that when the November Revolution came they could take their places in the machinery of workers' control.

It was in June 1917 that the first meeting of delegates from the shop committees was held. At this time the committees had hardly spread outside of Petrograd. It was a remarkable gathering, composed of delegates of the actual rank and file, most of them Bolsheviks, many of them Anarcho-Syndicalists; and its character was that of protest against the tactics of the trade unions. In the political world the Bolsheviks were reiterating that no socialist had any right to participate in a coalition government with the bourgeoisie. The meeting of shop committee delegates put itself on record as taking the same attitude toward industry. In other words, the employing class and the workers have no interests in common; no class conscious worker can be a member of an arbitration or conciliation board except to acquaint the employers with the demands of the workers. No contracts between employers and the workers. Industrial production must be absolutely controlled by the workers.

At first the unions fought bitterly against the Factory Shop Committees. But the shop committees, who were in a position to clutch the command of industry at its heart, easily extended and consolidated their power. Many workmen could not see the necessity of joining a union; but all of them saw the necessity of participating in the elections of the shop committee, which controlled their immediate jobs. On the other hand, the shop committees recognised the value of the unions; no new worker was employed unless he could show a union card; it was the shop committees which applied locally the regulations of the different unions. At the present time the unions and the Factory Shop Committees work in perfect harmony, each in its place.

Private ownership of industry in Russia is not yet abolished. In many factories the owner still holds title, and is allowed a certain limited profit on his investment, on condition that he works for the success and increase of scope of the enterprise; but control is taken away from him. Those industries whose owners attempt to lock out their workers, or who, by fraud or force, try to hinder the operations of the plant, are immediately confiscated by the workers. Conditions, hours and wages in all industries, private or government-owned, are uniform.

The reason for this survival of semi-capitalism, in a proletarian state, lies in the backwardness of Russia's economic life, the surrounding highly-organised capitalist states, and the necessity for *industrial production* in Russia *immediately*, to combat the pressure of foreign industry.

The agency by which the state controls industry, both labour and production, is called the Council of Workers' Control. This central body, sitting in the capital, is composed of delegates elected from local Councils of Workers' Control, which are made up of members of Factory Shop Committees, Professional Union officials, and technical engineers and experts. A central executive committee manages the affairs of each locality, composed of common workmen, but the majority is composed of *workmen from other districts*, so that its rulings shall be unprejudiced by sectional interests. The local councils recommend to the All-Russian Council the confiscation of plants, report on the needs in fuel, raw materials, transportation and labour in their districts, and assist the workmen in learning to manage the various industries. The All-Russian Council has power to confiscate plants and to equalise the economic resources of the different localities.

If it had not been for democratic organisations which existed already before the revolution, there is little doubt that the Russian revolution would have been starved to its knees long before this time. The ordinary commercial machinery of distribution had been completely smashed. Only the consumers' co-operative societies managed to feed the people, and their system has since been adopted by the municipalities, and even by the government. Before the revolution there were more than twelve million members of the co-operative societies of Russia. It is a very natural way for Russians to combine, because of its resemblance to the primitive co-operation of Russian village life for centuries. In the Putilov factory, where more than 40,000 workers are employed, the co-operative society fed, housed and *even clothed* more than 100,000 people—sending all the way to England for clothing.

It is this quality in the Russians that is forgotten by people who think that Russia can have no government, because there is no central force; and whose mental picture of Russia is a servile committee in Moscow, bossed by Lenin and Trotsky, and maintained by Red Guard mercenaries. Quite the contrary is true. The organisations which I have described are reproduced in almost every community in Russia. And if any considerable part of Russia were seriously opposed to the Soviet government, the Soviets could not last an hour.

[Source: John Reed. "Soviets in Action." *The Liberator*. 1918.]

Document Themes and Analysis

In his "Soviets in Action," John Reed's delight in the new opportunities offered by the different soviets (i.e., elected governing councils) and the way they created possibilities for representation and organization for the ordinary citizens of Russia is evident. He goes into detail regarding the way the soviets are organized and how they function, highlighting how any group that wants to create a soviet could do so. His focus on organization is key because the original Bolshevik premise was entirely novel: a government designed for the people and providing all to the people. At the time, some critics claimed that whole soviet concept was impossible in practice, because there was centralized authority. Reed aimed to show that the government was fully organized, but organized on a different basis than any previously known.

The central characteristic of a communist government, at least in this early instance, is the notion that the workers must govern themselves rather than being led by elites who do not understand or care about their daily situation. The deprivations caused by the Russo-Japanese War and World War I had led to a sense among the common folk that top officials in the country did not have their best interests at heart. A more adept monarch than Alexander II might have been able to make peace with the revolutionaries and steer his country toward less radical change, but the Russian czar in 1917 was not that person. In consequence, he was overthrown.

The initial impulse of the Russian Revolution was to upend the way the system of government operated, above all the question of who was in charge. The Provisional Government under Kerensky relied on a parliament (duma) as well as workers' councils and land owners for input. The more radical Bolsheviks sought more fundamental change in the form of proletarian rule and the elimination of private ownership—in other words, a communist state. Kerensky's government lasted only six months before it was swept away in a second popular uprising, under Vladimir I. Lenin, that would change the course of world history.

Although John Reed was a strong supporter of the revolution when he wrote "Soviets in Action," soon after his larger work, *Ten Days That Shook the World*, came out, he began to cool on Bolshevism, as the government under Lenin fell back on methods of state-sanctioned repression and violence to secure order and control. The Soviet government soon took on authoritarian qualities that any previous czar would have been familiar with. Under Lenin's successor, Josef Stalin, the idea that workers' soviets were key to running the government was, at best, a façade, for under Stalin's dictatorship, the degree of centralized, authoritarian control would reach new heights.

—Michael Shally-Jensen, PhD

Bibliography and Additional Reading

Miéville, China. *October: The Story of the Russian Revolution*. New York: Verso, 2017.

Rabinowitch, Alexander. *The Bolsheviks Come to Power: The Revolution of 1917 in Petrograd*. Chicago: Haymarket Books, 2017.

Reed, John. *Ten Days That Shook the World*. New York: New York: Penguin Classics, 2007.